D1552680

OXFORD HISTORICAL MONOGRAPHS

EDITORS

THE TOWNSHENDS
AND THEIR WORLD:
GENTRY, LAW, AND
LAND IN NORFOLK

c.1450–1551

C. E. MORETON

CLARENDON PRESS · OXFORD
1992

Oxford University Press, Walton Street, Oxford OX2 6DP

Oxford New York Toronto
Delhi Bombay Calcutta Madras Karachi
Petaling Jaya Singapore Hong Kong Tokyo
Nairobi Dar es Salaam Cape Town
Melbourne Auckland

and associated companies in
Berlin Ibadan

Oxford is a trade mark of Oxford University Press

Published in the United States
by Oxford University Press, New York

British Library Cataloguing in Publication Data
Data available

Library of Congress Cataloging in Publication Data
Moreton, C. E.
The Townshends and their world : gentry, law, and land in Norfolk
c. 1450–1551 / C. E. Moreton.
p.   cm.—(Oxford historical monographs)
Includes bibliographical references and index.
1. Norfolk (England)—History.   2. Townshend, Roger, Sir, d. 1493—Family.
3. Land use, Rural—England—Norfolk—History—16th century.   4. Land tenure—
Law and legislation—England—Norfolk.   5. Gentry—England—Norfolk—History—
16th century.   6. Landowners—England—Norfolk—Biography.   7. Townshend family.
I. Title.   II. Series.
DA670.N6M67   1992
942.6'1043'0922—dc20   91-45280
ISBN 0-19-820299-7

Typeset by Colset Private Limited
Printed and bound in
Great Britain by Bookcraft Ltd,
Midsomer Norton, Bath

In memory of
Millicent Bennett

ACKNOWLEDGEMENTS

I have incurred more than a few debts whilst working on the Townshends. First and foremost, I am deeply grateful to the present head of the family, the seventh Marquess Townshend, for making my study of them possible by permitting me to consult his family's private papers. Secondly, I must thank Cliff Davies for his kind help and advice, both as the supervisor of my doctoral thesis on the Townshends and as the sub-editor of this book. Moreover, I must acknowledge the advice and encouragement of the following: Jennifer Bennett, Bruce Campbell, Steve Gunn, Christopher Haigh, Helga Hammerstein, Gerald Harriss, David Ibbetson, Maurice Keen, Diarmaid MacCulloch, Malcolm Parkes, Simon Payling, Colin Richmond, Ian Robinson, Diana Spelman, Roger Virgoe, and Susan Vokes. It goes without saying that any errors are mine alone. Last, but by no means least, many thanks are due to Paul Rutledge and the other helpful staff at the Norfolk Record Office in Norwich; to Jane Kilvert, Lord Townshend's secretary; to Anne Gelling at the Oxford University Press; and to the Reed family who so generously provided me with board and lodging whilst I was working at Raynham Hall.

CONTENTS

LIST OF MAPS

LIST OF FIGURES

LIST OF TABLES

ABBREVIATIONS

AHR	*Agricultural History Review*
APC	*Acts of the Privy Council*, ed. J. R. Dasent, 32 vols. (London, 1890–1907)
BIHR	*Bulletin of the Institute of Historical Research*
B-L	Bradfer-Lawrence Collection, Norfolk Record Office, Norwich
BL	British Library
Blomefield	F. Blomefield, *Topographical History of Norfolk*, 2nd edn., 11 vols. (London, 1805–10)
Bulwer	*The Visitation of Norfolk in the Year 1563*, ed. G. H. Dashwood *et al.*, 2 vols., Norfolk and Norwich Archaeol. Soc. (1878–95), ii, ed. W. E. G. L. Bulwer
CAD	*A Descriptive Catalogue of Ancient Deeds in the Public Record Office*, 6 vols. (PRO texts and calendars; London, 1890–1915)
CCR	*Calendar of the Close Rolls Preserved in the Public Record Office* (PRO texts and calendars; London, 1896–)
CFR	*Calendar of the Fine Rolls Preserved in the Public Record Office* (PRO texts and calendars; London, 1911–)
CIPM, Henry VII	*Calendar of Inquisitions Post Mortem Henry VII*, 3 vols. (London, 1898–1956)
CPR	*Calendar of the Patent Rolls Preserved in the Public Record Office* (PRO texts and calendars; London, 1891–)
Complete Peerage	G. E. Cockayne (ed.), *Complete Peerage of England, Scotland, Ireland and the United Kingdom*, new edn. by V. Gibbs *et al.*, 13 vols. (London, 1910–59)
DNB	*Dictionary of National Biography*
Dashwood	*The Visitation of Norfolk in the Year 1563*, ed. G. H. Dashwood *et al.*, 2 vols., Norfolk and Norwich Archaeol. Soc. (1878–95), i.
EHR	*English Historical Review*
EcHR	*Economic History Review*
HP	S. T. Bindoff (ed.), *The History of Parliament, 1509–1558*, 3 vols. (London, 1982)
LI *Admissions*	*The Records of the Honourable Society of Lincoln's Inn, Admissions*, i, ed. W. P. Baildon (London, 1896)

LI *Black Books*	*The Records of the Honourable Society of Lincoln's Inn. The Black Books*, i, ed. R.D. Walker (London, 1897)
LQR	*Law Quarterly Review*
LSE	London School of Economics
LP	*Letters and Papers, Foreign and Domestic, of the Reign of Henry VIII*, ed. J.S. Brewer, J. Gairdner, and R.H. Brodie, 22 vols. in 35 (London, 1862–1932)
NA	*Norfolk Archaeology*
NRO	Norfolk Record Office, Norwich
OED	*Oxford English Dictionary*
PL	*Paston Letters and Papers of the Fifteenth Century*, ed. N. Davis, 2 vols. (Oxford, 1971–6)
PP	*Past and Present*
PRO	Public Record Office, Chancery Lane, London
RP	*Rotuli Parliamentorum*, ed. J. Strachey *et al.*, 6 vols. (London, 1767–77)
Statutes of the Realm	*Statutes of the Realm*, ed. A. Luders *et al.*, 11 vols. (London, 1810–28)
TRHS	*Transactions of the Royal Historical Society*
VCH	*The Victoria History of the Counties of England*
Visitations	*The Visitacion of Norfolk . . .*, ed. W. Rye, Harleian Soc., 32 (1891)
Wedgwood	J.C. Wedgwood, *History of Parliament, Biographies of the Members of the Commons House, 1439–1509* (London, 1936)

NOTE ON MANUSCRIPT SOURCES:
THE TOWNSHEND PAPERS

As a collection, the deeds and personal and estate papers of the Townshend family, the main source material for this book, have endured their fair share of vicissitudes. However, the bulk of the material concerning my period, the later fifteenth and the first half of the sixteenth centuries, is still in the family's possession at Raynham Hall in Norfolk, where I have been privileged to consult it. I nevertheless had also to study material, originally from Raynham, at the British Library, the Norfolk Record Office at Norwich, and the London School of Economics during my researches. The Introduction to *The Papers of Nathaniel Bacon of Stiffkey*, ed. A. Hassell Smith *et al.*, 2 vols., Norfolk Rec. Soc., 46, 49 (1979–83), vol. i, pp. xviii-xxxvii, provides a useful history of the Raynham archive, but the main points should be recapitulated here.

For many years the family papers dating back to the medieval period, which had accumulated in the muniment room at Raynham Hall, together with those of the Bacons and other families united to the Townshends by marriage, remained untouched. In the late eighteenth and early nineteenth centuries, however, they came to the notice of enthusiastic antiquaries. Later, various local historians were permitted to borrow parts of the collection, not all of which found their way back to Raynham. Some of this material, for example, passed through several hands before being acquired by the British Library.

The greatest damage was done at two large auctions in 1911 and 1924 when thousands of Raynham manuscripts were sold, some ending up in distant parts of the world. Many, however, did not go abroad and the Norfolk Record Office has become the repository for most of the Townshend and Bacon papers acquired by private collectors in this country. It has been my second major source of Townshend material, though the smaller collection in the British Library has also proved immensely useful.

The material I consulted at Raynham Hall had hitherto been hardly touched by historians and is organized in a very rudimentary fashion;

some of it has remained completely unsorted. I have therefore had to use my own system when citing source material from Raynham Hall:

'R', followed by a number, identifies one of the drawers of documents in the library; 'R(Attic)' refers to a document in the attic. Anything in inverted commas following these locational references is a reference to the labelling on the particular envelope, bundle, or packet, or, in the case of the attic, box, in which the document (deed, roll, or other) is to be found.

Thus, 'R27, "RAYNHAM—HEN IV–HEN VI", deed of 25 Jan. 1417', refers to a deed of that date contained in a packet or envelope labelled 'RAYNHAM—HEN IV–HEN VI' from library drawer number 27; and 'R(Attic), "*Norfolk manorial*—Raynham Haviles", 1485/6–1508/9 Raynham accounts' refers to a roll of Raynham accounts to be found in the attic in the box labelled '*Norfolk manorial*—Raynham Haviles'.

The following footnote references are used for frequently cited MSS from the Raynham archive:

(1) 'R31, RT II estate book': a paper booklet, containing valors and general estate notes for the first half of the sixteenth century, which belonged to Sir Roger Townshend II;

(2) 'R33, RT II receipt book': a paper booklet of Roger II's receipts for 1499/1500, with a note of leases granted between midsummer 1501 and midsummer 1502;

(3) 'R49, Townshend cartulary': a booklet containing copies of deeds and agreements, mainly second half of the fifteenth century;

(4) 'R55, RT II valors': a booklet of estate valors and receipts for 1507/8 which belonged to Roger II;

(5) 'R57, RT II "declaration" ': a booklet, bearing the date 24 Feb. 1551, listing and valuing Roger II's landed property;

(6) 'R58, RT I memo-book': a personal memorandum book of the early 1490s which belonged to Sir Roger Townshend I (written in his own hand);

(7) 'R58, RT II memo-book': a personal memorandum book of the early 1500s which belonged to Roger II (in his own hand);

(8) 'R58, Raynham account roll': a large set of fifteenth-century (1472/3–82/3) Raynham bailiffs', receivers', household stewards', and other officers' accounts, bound together in one roll.

INTRODUCTION

The Townshends of East Raynham in north-west Norfolk, a family which survives to this day, enjoy a distinguished record. Since the reign of Charles II they have been peers of the realm, but the Townshends of the eighteenth century, especially 'Turnip Townshend' the agricultural improver, are probably the most famous.[1] The subjects of this book are, however, those less well-known Townshends who founded the family's fortunes.

Before the mid-fifteenth century the Townshends were obscure yeomen farmers, yet one hundred years later they were among the leading gentry of their county. The men behind this sudden rise were two successive heads of the family. The first, the lawyer Sir Roger Townshend (c. 1435–93), attended Lincoln's Inn, enjoyed a successful career, and died a judge of the Common Pleas after investing much of his substantial earnings in land. He was followed by his son, another Sir Roger (1478–1551), who enlarged and consolidated the estate his father had created in their native Norfolk. During the troubled years of the Reformation this second Roger Townshend proved himself a loyal servant of the Tudor government in the same county, where he was one of the busiest justices of the peace.

Why do these early Townshends warrant our attention? There is nothing new in writing about the English gentry, whether of the Middle Ages or later, for they are very much in vogue. The typical approach is to examine them on a regional or county basis, and this owes much to one of the great historiographical controversies of this century, the Tawney–Trevor–Roper debate on the fortunes of the late

---

[1] *Complete Peerage*, vol. xii, pt. i, pp. 804–5. Other 18th-cent. Townshends included Charles Townshend, the prominent politician, and George, first Marquess Townshend, who took command of the British troops attacking Quebec after the death of General Wolfe; see L. B. Namier and J. Brooke (eds.), *The History of Parliament, 1754–1790*, 3 vols. (London, 1964), iii. 539–48; *Complete Peerage*, vol. xii, pt. i, pp. 808–9.

Tudor and early Stuart gentry.[2] Exhilarating though the debate was,
its sweeping generalizations ultimately made it futile and others were
stimulated to seek the truth by studying the gentry at a local level.[3]

Historians working on earlier periods have also adopted the local
study. Until the middle of this century, when K. B. McFarlane introduced a fresh perspective with his pioneering work on the nobility,[4]
later medieval history was largely history in the mode of William
Stubbs. It was concerned with parliament and the central institutions
of royal authority, and it failed to acknowledge the role in government
of the upper classes, upon whom the king depended to control the
localities. However, much of McFarlane's work was on the aristocracy and this encouraged later generations of scholars to investigate
the gentry. They, like their counterparts among the seventeenth-
century specialists, have usually worked at a regional or county level
and their work has proved extremely valuable.[5] Even if we still await
a full-scale study on later medieval East Anglia, Virgoe and others
have published several important articles,[6] and the sixteenth century

---

[2] R. H. Tawney, 'The Rise of the Gentry 1558–1640', *EcHR* 11 (1941), 1–38;
L. Stone, 'The Anatomy of the Elizabethan Aristocracy', *EcHR* 18 (1948), 1–53; H. R.
Trevor-Roper, 'The Elizabethan Aristocracy: An Anatomy Re-anatomised', *EcHR*
2nd ser. 3 (1951), 279–98; id., *The Gentry 1540–1640, EcHR* supplement 1 (1953).
[3] e.g. T. G. Barnes, *Somerset 1625–1640: A County's Government During the 'Personal
Rule'* (London, 1961); A. Everitt, *The Community of Kent and the Great Rebellion 1640–1660*
(Leicester, 1966); J. S. Morrill, *Cheshire 1630–1660: County Government and Society during
the English Revolution* (Oxford, 1974); A. Fletcher, *A County Community in Peace and War:
Sussex 1600–1660* (London, 1975).
[4] Esp. *The Nobility of Later Medieval England* (Oxford, 1973) and *England in the Fifteenth
Century* (London, 1981).
[5] e.g. N. Saul, *Knights and Esquires: The Gloucestershire Gentry in the Fourteenth Century*
(Oxford, 1981); S. M. Wright, *The Derbyshire Gentry in the Fifteenth Century*, Derbyshire
Rec. Soc., 8 (1983); S. J. Payling, 'Political Society in Lancastrian Nottinghamshire',
D.Phil. thesis (Oxford, 1987).
[6] R. Virgoe, 'Three Suffolk Parliamentary Elections of the Mid-Fifteenth Century',
BIHR 39 (1966), 185–96; id., 'The Murder of James Andrew: Suffolk Faction in
the 1430s', *Proceedings of the Suffolk Institute of Archaeology*, 34 (1980), 263–8; id., 'The
Recovery of the Howards in East Anglia, 1485–1529', in E. W. Ives, J. J. Scarisbrick,
and R. J. Knecht (edd.), *Wealth and Power in Tudor England* (London, 1978), 1–20; id.,
'The Crown, Magnates and Local Government in East Anglia', in J. R. L. Highfield
and R. Jeffs (edd.), *The Crown and Local Communities in England and France in the Fifteenth
Century* (Gloucester, 1981), 72–87; M. Sayer, 'Norfolk Involvement in Dynastic Con-
flict, 1469–71 and 1483–1487', *NA* 36 (1977), 305–26; A. R. Smith, 'Litigation and
Politics: Sir John Fastolf's Defence of his English Property', in A. J. Pollard (ed.), *Pro-
perty and Politics, Essays in Later Medieval English History* (Gloucester, 1984), 59–75; R. H.
Britnell, 'The Pastons and their Norfolk', *AHR* 36 (1988), 132–44.

is well served by MacCulloch on Tudor Suffolk and Hassell Smith on the gentry of Elizabethan Norfolk.[7]

This book on the Townshends is in part intended to contribute to the history of later medieval and early modern Norfolk, but it is not a county study. The county approach has served us well, but research on the gentry which avoids it is valuable because it redresses a balance. County studies quite properly focus on county or regional institutions and administrative proceedings, but they may lead us to assume that these were always the central concerns of all the gentry: in fact only about one-third of the gentry usually took part in local government.[8] They also tend to read as compilations of self-contained chapters rather than unified wholes. In a family-based study, on the other hand, the family can link seemingly disparate themes and provide an overall unity.

Research on individual gentlemen or families of the late Middle Ages and early sixteenth century is often difficult and sometimes impossible. This arises from a paucity of source material wide-ranging enough to allow detailed work on that scale, a problem which left Colin Richmond, the author of *John Hopton: A Fifteenth-Century Suffolk Gentleman*,[9] with more imponderables than he would have liked. Richmond attempted simply to achieve 'the real particularity of one gentleman at one place at one time', rather than to ask general questions about the gentry and their society.[10] But such a narrow aim brought with it severe limitations because, with Hopton, he was hampered by lack of evidence and forced into sheer speculation.[11] Nevertheless, his was a brave attempt and it rescued the gentry from the local administrative context in which they are usually set.

One solution where source material for a single individual or family is scanty is to investigate more than one family, as ably demonstrated by Saul in the context of fourteenth-century Sussex and Finch in the context of Tudor and early-Stuart Northamptonshire.[12] Another is to

<hr/>

[7] D. N. J. MacCulloch, *Suffolk and the Tudors* (Oxford, 1986); A. Hassell Smith, *County and Court: Government and Politics in Norfolk, 1558–1603* (Oxford, 1974).

[8] J. Cornwall, 'The Early Tudor Gentry', *EcHR* 2nd ser. 17 (1964–5), 471.

[9] Cambridge, 1981.

[10] Ibid., pp. xvi–xvii.

[11] Cf. the trenchant comments of C. Carpenter, 'Fifteenth Century Biographies', *Historical Journal*, 25 (1982), 730.

[12] N. Saul, *Scenes from Provincial Life: Knightly Families in Sussex, 1280–1400* (Oxford, 1986); M. E. Finch, *Five Northamptonshire Families, 1540–1640*, Northamptonshire Rec. Soc., 19 (1956).

combine an individual with a theme like the law, as has Ives with the
fifteenth-century lawyer Thomas Kebell.[13] Through Kebell, Ives
manages to combine a technical and often difficult subject with the
concerns and approaches of social history.

I have been most fortunate because the surviving Townshend
papers are comparatively intact and abundant; and this by itself justi-
fies a study of the Townshends. Narrowness is, of course, an inherent
danger and I have sought to avoid this by making the Townshends my
central but not my exclusive concern. This book is therefore about the
Townshends and their world rather than the Townshends alone.

---

[13] E. W. Ives, *The Common Lawyers of Pre-Reformation England: Thomas Kebell: A Case Study* (Cambridge, 1983).

1

THE FAMILY

(1) ORIGINS

Until the later fifteenth century the Townshends were unknown as
gentry, although Townshends had lived in their part of north-west
Norfolk since the mid-fourteenth century and perhaps earlier.[1] The
first Townshend known as a 'gentleman' was a self-made man, the
prominent lawyer Sir Roger Townshend I (d. 1493). Before his
lifetime the history of the family is clouded in obscurity and downright
invention. This was partly the fault of the Townshends themselves
because, in common with other families, they fabricated a pedigree
during the heraldic visitations of the second half of the sixteenth
century in order to disguise their true origins.[2] A fictitious family
tree, sometimes including Norman ancestry, was perpetuated by
successive generations of gullible antiquarians and local historians.[3]

The earliest identifiable Townshend is Roger Townshend of South
Raynham. Although he was the first of a series of Roger Townshends,
there is so little to say about him that he is not distinguished here as
Roger I (see family tree, Fig. 1.1). We know, however, that he was
a prosperous free tenant by the 1390s.[4] He apparently married an
Eleanor, but a deed of 1406 shows that at that date he had a wife
named Matilda.[5] There is little more to add. In about 1418 his house
was broken into and he had a horse stolen.[6] Generally he led life at
a village level. Generally, because in 1413 he led a group of tenants
from South Raynham who petitioned the chancellor; the result of a

---

[1] e.g. NRO, B–L I a (volume of deeds for the Raynham parishes, 13th–17th cents.);
dated and undated deeds in R10 and R57.
[2] W. Rye, *A History of Norfolk* (London, 1885), 29–31.
[3] BL, Harl. MS 4,756; A. Collins, *Peerage of England*, rev. edn., 9 vols. (London,
1812), ii. 454–60; Blomefield, vii. 130–1; Dashwood, 306.
[4] e.g. R27, R33, R(Attic): 'Scales' and 'Ingoldisthorpe's' manor court rolls.
[5] J. Durham, *The Townshends of Raynham* (Cambridge, 1922), 3; R27, 'RAYNHAM–
HEN IV–HEN VI', deed of 21 Apr. 1406.
[6] R57, 1413–17 Raynham and Helhoughton leet roll, m. 5.

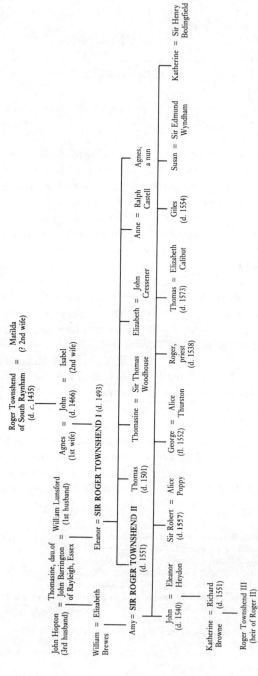

Fig. 1.1. Townshend Family Tree

local dispute over common grazing rights.[7] The individualism and assertiveness of the East Anglian peasant cannot be overlooked in a region where the manorial system was comparatively weak.[8] Ten years later he must have felt the onset of old age, because he conveyed to his son John and John's trustees all his lands, tenements, pastures, and sheep-folds, reserving himself an interest in a few acres and an annuity of £4. 6s. 8d. for the rest of his life.[9] Roger and his wife were buried in the parish church of South Raynham, an indication that he had local status.[10] He probably died not long after mid-1435 when he made John an unconditional grant of all his personal property.[11]

(2) JOHN TOWNSHEND

John Townshend was unjustly described by the Tudor antiquary John Leland as a 'meane man of substance'.[12] A wealthy yeoman, he was never accorded the style of 'gentleman', he died in 1466 owning two manors and other lands in the Raynham neighbourhood worth about £40 per annum.[13] During his last, bedridden days he was daily attended by no less than a doctor of theology,[14] and his will is impressive. For the good of his soul he founded a chantry, to run for twenty years, and he left money to no less than eleven local churches, including gifts of £20 and £10 respectively to the parishes of East and South Raynham. To his wife, Isabel, he left £40 in cash and a life annuity of £4, along with crops, livestock, and household 'stuff'.[15]

[7] PRO, C1/5/55.

[8] D. C. Douglas, *The Social Structure of Medieval East Anglia* (Oxford, 1927), 205–18.

[9] R27, 'RAYNHAM—HEN IV–HEN VI', indenture of 30 Nov. 1428 (counterpart in R35, 'South Raynham deeds 1409–78').

[10] Burial place named in John's will (NRO, NCC 45–6 Jekkys). Not everyone was buried inside their parish church, so even in death the medieval sense of hierarchy was preserved: cf. P. W. Fleming, 'Charity, Faith and the Gentry of Kent 1422–1529', in Pollard (ed.), *Property and Politics*, 50.

[11] R35, 'South Raynham deeds 1409–78', deed of 4 June 1435.

[12] *The Itinerary of John Leland*, ed. L. Toulmin Smith, 5 vols. (London, 1906–10), ii. 12.

[13] 'Yeoman' in a Chancery suit of the early 1460s (PRO, C1/28/77); will of 16 Feb. 1466: proved 4 Jan. 1467 (NRO, NCC 45–6 Jekkys); writ of *diem clausit extremum*, 11 July 1466 (*CFR* (1461–71), 176); R58, RT I memo-book, fo. 10ᵛ.

[14] NRO, NCC 45–6 Jekkys; Denys Holkham, Cambridge graduate and local friar from the Carmelite house at Burnham Norton: A. B. Emden, *Biographical Register of the University of Cambridge to 1500* (Cambridge, 1963), i. 311.

[15] NRO, NCC 45–6 Jekkys.

His will shows that he ran to at least four servants. Whether the three men and the woman named included everyone he then employed is unclear. During the mid-fifteenth century he also had one or more shepherds.[16] His sheep pasture perhaps provided the basis for part, if not most, of his prosperity, but he had other commercial interests. In the early 1440s, for instance, he and Henry Thursby, the Lynn merchant, bought tithe grain from Coxford Priory, a local religious house.[17]

John was a man of local standing because he acted as a trustee for the magnate who dominated west Norfolk, Thomas, Lord Scales; not only for that lord's Norfolk estates but also for those elsewhere in East Anglia.[18] His own choice of trustees indicates that he was a member of the affinities of both Scales and his son-in-law and successor, Anthony Woodville.[19] From these lords he farmed the manor of 'Scales' in South Raynham, of which he was a tenant, for £16 per annum between the mid-1440s and early 1460s.[20]

He also farmed a manor in Tittleshall during the 1440s from Coxford Priory.[21] His dealings with the priory pose intriguing but unanswerable questions, for there is a considerable gap in its history between the late-thirteenth and the late-fifteenth centuries.[22] At some stage before Michaelmas 1444 the bishop of Norwich commissioned John, Robert Appulby,[23] and John Gygges of Wighton to administer the goods and income of the priory. By virtue of this commission, John, in association with the prior, John Dereham,[24] accounted, presumably to the bishop, for the house's income and expenditure during the mid-1440s.[25] The most likely explanation is that the prior and his

[16] R57, 1430–61 'Scales' manor court and leet roll, m. 10; R32, 1434–56 'Ingoldisthorpe's' manor court and leet roll, m. 14d.
[17] R(Attic), 'Coxford Priory', 1444/5 priory account roll.
[18] PRO, C1/28/77.
[19] See Ch. 2, 1 below.
[20] NRO, Townshend 36 MS 1,455 1 B1, mm. 10–12.
[21] R(Attic), 'Coxford Priory', 1446/7 priory account roll.
[22] H. W. Saunders, 'A History of Coxford Priory', *NA* 17 (1910), 322.
[23] Canon and civil lawyer, former diplomat, and collector of benefices in Norfolk and elsewhere: A. B. Emden, *Biographical Register of the University of Oxford to AD 1500*, 3 vols. (Oxford, 1957–9), i. 41.
[24] Prior from 1438 to 1449: Saunders, 'Coxford Priory', 354.
[25] R(Attic), 'Coxford Priory', priory account rolls for 1444/5 and 1445/6 refer to the commission. Another in the same box for 1446/7 shows that it had ended by Michaelmas 1446. These accounts must have found their way into the Raynham archive after the earl of Arundel sold the former priory to the Townshends at the end of the 16th cent.: Saunders, 'Coxford Priory', 329.

brethren had been mismanaging their house, since the payment of its debts features prominently in these accounts. John himself was one of its creditors.[26] Why he should have been appointed to this commission is a mystery. He must have been a man of some education, if of a practical kind.[27]

Nothing is known of Isabel, his second wife. It is unlikely that she was the mother of Roger, his eldest surviving son.[28] His first wife, Agnes, was the daughter of William Gygges of Wighton and conceivably the sister of the above-mentioned John Gygges. She must have married John shortly before the beginning of 1471.[29] Despite speculation, it cannot be proved that John had other children besides Roger and a daughter.[30]

Joan, his daughter, married during his lifetime.[31] Her husband was John Blakeney, esquire. Originally from Honingham in Norfolk, Blakeney was a startling match for a yeoman's daughter. He was the son of a chief justice of the Common Pleas for Ireland and a crown servant. Under Henry VI he was both a clerk of the signet and an usher of the chamber, and a man of considerable influence.[32] A member of at least three parliaments in the late 1440s, he was a knight of the shire for Norfolk in 1447. He survived the change of dynasty and was still a 'king's servant' and a clerk of the signet in 1466.[33] He died in 1471.[34] Relations between the Townshends and the Blakeneys were close. Both Blakeney and his second son,

---

[26] In 1444/5 over £73 of the priory's expenses of some £176 went on debt repayment. In 1445/6 the respective figures were £69 and £195. During 1444/5 John was paid £28. 11s. 9d., the last repayment of a larger sum which the priory owed him.

[27] He owned at least one book, a psalter: R58, RT I memo-book, fo. 7ᵛ.

[28] Referred to in the mid-1470s as the widow of Roger's father rather than as Roger's mother; still alive in 1493: R58, Raynham account roll, m. 8; R58, RT I memo-book, fo. 12ᵛ.

[29] R27, 'RAYNHAM—HEN IV–HEN VI', deed of 25 Jan. 1417; R32, 'Deeds Raynham 1401–1419', deed of 26 Jan. 1417.

[30] W. Rye, *Norfolk Families*, 2 vols. (Norwich, 1913), ii. 924. This is not unlikely: e.g. who is the 'Mr Tounshend of Pykenham' to whom Roger I sent grain in the early 1480s?: R(Attic), '*Norfolk manorial*—Raynham Haviles', 1485/6–1508/9 Raynham accounts, m. 1.

[31] NRO, NCC 45–6 Jekkys.

[32] Wedgwood, 81–2; A. J. Otway-Ruthven, *The King's Secretary and the Signet Office in the Fifteenth Century* (Cambridge, 1939), 158; D. A. L. Morgan, 'The House of Policy: The Political Role of the Late Plantagenet Household, 1422–1485', in D. Starkey (ed.), *The English Court from the Wars of the Roses to the Civil War* (London, 1987), 48; *RP*, v. 216.

[33] Wedgwood, 81–2; *CPR* (1461-7), 448.

[34] PRO, PROB11/6, fo. 22. Despite the date, there is no evidence that he died from anything but natural causes. Joan died in 1503 (NRO, NCC 315–17 Popy).

Thomas, were trustees for Roger I, and in the early sixteenth century
Thomas provided for Roger II to succeed to the Blakeney manor at
Honingham if the Blakeney male line became extinct.[35] Possibly
John Townshend's associations with the affinity of Thomas, Lord
Scales, a political ally of the duke of Suffolk and a supporter of the
Lancastrian crown, helped to bring about the Blakeney–Townshend
alliance.[36]

Joan's marriage underlines the mystery of John Townshend's
position; evidently a substantial and able man of business, yet always
a 'yeoman'. 'Yeoman' is of course an extremely imprecise designa-
tion. Possibly John preferred to build up the family fortunes with an
eye to the future; what William Fuller was later to call a 'gentleman
in ore'.[37]

(3) ROGER TOWNSHEND I

(i) Career

The Townshend family became accepted as gentry under Roger
Townshend I, the son and heir of John Townshend, because of
his legal career. Such a career was a common method of social
advancement in Norfolk, a county with an early reputation for
litigiousness.[38] In the mid-fifteenth century attempts were made to
limit the number of common attorneys who swarmed over Norfolk
and Suffolk.[39] The Townshends were just one of several prominent
Norfolk gentry families which rose through the law during the late
Middle Ages.[40]

Roger entered Lincoln's Inn before 8 September 1454.[41] His
choice of inn was probably not arbitrary, since it had strong East
Anglian connections.[42] The new entrant had to find a mainpernor

---

[35] Blomefield, ii. 448.   [36] Smith, 'Litigation and Politics', 69.

[37] Quoted by M. L. Campbell, *The English Yeoman under Elizabeth and the Early Stuarts*,
2nd edn. (London, 1960), 33. See W. G. Hoskins, *The Age of Plunder* (London, 1976),
56, for the yeoman class.

[38] *The Chronicle of Jocelin of Brakelond*, ed. H. E. Butler (London, 1949), 12.

[39] *RP*, v. 326–7.

[40] Others included the Cleres, Heydons, Hobarts, Pastons, and Wyndhams.

[41] LI *Admissions*, 12.

[42] Of 100 Norfolk lawyers from the Middle Ages to 1830, 43 attended Lincoln's
Inn, 25 Gray's Inn, 22 the Inner Temple, and 10 the Middle Temple: B. Cozens-
Hardy, 'Norfolk Lawyers', *NA* 33 (1965), 268.

(surety) to pay his bills in case he should default in the future, and a Norfolk man was most likely to find a sponsor from his own part of the country.[43] Roger's sponsor is unfortunately unknown. A fifteenth-century legal training could begin at the age of 15, but Roger must have reached his majority by the time he entered his inn.[44] This places his date of birth somewhere between 1430 and 1435. He presumably attended a grammar school in Norfolk and possibly an inn of Chancery.

In 1477, some twenty-four years after joining Lincoln's Inn, he was selected to become a serjeant at law.[45] A principle of promotion by seniority linked to one's date of entry operated within the inns, but in practice those who began a private legal career while still a student and who had the ability necessary for high office rose to the top of the profession.[46] Roger possessed the requisite ability, and by 1460 he was a governor or senior fellow of his inn, a position he held regularly until called to the coif. The first signs of his practising the law are in 1463 when he and another lawyer were paid £40 by the Exchequer for their services in a case in which two Italian merchants stood charged with the murder of a royal servant.[47] He was also a law reporter, a function he continued to perform as a judge.[48]

As a serjeant at law he was committed to a judicial future and immediately liable for service on the assize commissions. Assize work limited the opportunity for private 'winnings' but, in the event, he did not become an assize justice until the Lent vacation of 1482 when he was appointed to the northern circuit.[49] He had, therefore, several years to devote to self-enrichment,[50] but his freedom was probably curtailed before this appointment since he became a king's serjeant in 1481.[51] He nevertheless valued his royal retainer because he petitioned for its renewal a day after Richard III assumed the throne.[52]

---

[43] Ives, *Kebell*, 36.

[44] Ibid., 36. Over three years earlier he was a trustee in a land conveyance: R58, 'Raynham Deeds 1426–1480', deed of 17 Jan. 1451.

[45] Ordered to take up office on 9 June 1478 by letters close of the previous October: *CCR* (1476–85), no. 177.

[46] Ives, *Kebell*, 47.

[47] PRO, E403/828; *CCR* (1461–8), 183.

[48] A. W. B. Simpson, 'The Source and Function of the Later Year Books', *LQR* 87 (1971), 114–15.

[49] Ives, *Kebell*, 75.

[50] *CPR* (1476–85), 556, 568, 578–80.

[51] On 25 May: ibid., 270.

[52] PRO, SC8/185/9237.

He remained on the northern circuit for five years before joining the more lucrative and less arduous home circuit, despite his promotion in the interim as a judge of the Common Pleas in September 1485, the month following the Battle of Bosworth, and his knighthood in mid-1486.[53] He may have served for so long in the north because no vacancy arose on another circuit when he had the chance to fill it. Only after the death of John Sulyard, JKB, did he move to the home circuit.[54] Other considerations might also have played a part. In a later period it was not uncommon for a puisne judge to remain on the same circuit for several years, even after seniority entitled him to a more attractive one, perhaps because long familiarity with the officials and local magnates of a particular area conveyed considerable administrative advantages.[55] Roger's familiarity with the north must explain why he continued to serve on commissions there after he joined the home circuit.[56]

Some notes he made while on the home circuit during the summer of 1492 survive in a personal notebook.[57] In these he refers to Guildford, Horsham, Sevenoaks, Dartford, and Chelmsford as being among the assize towns at which he and his associate sat.[58] Unfortunately, it is impossible to reconstruct their exact route because he does not mention any venues in Hertfordshire, one of the counties of the circuit, and because itinerary arrangements remained flexible until the later seventeenth century.[59] Horsham was a particularly eventful venue because here his horse died and he had to buy another from the vicar of the town. He noted two of the cases they heard at Horsham: one of these happened to involve Thomasine Hopton,

[53] Ives, *Kebell*, 68–9; *CPR* (1485–94), 18; W. A. Shaw, *The Knights of England*, 2 vols. (London, 1906), ii. 23. Judges were knighted almost as a matter of course in this period. For example, only three of the eighteen judges besides Roger I who rode the assize circuits between 1483 and 1513—John Kingsmill, JCP, William Fairfax, JCP, and William Grevill, JCP—were never knighted. Like Roger, four of the eighteen, Guy Fairfax, JKB, William Hussey, CJKB, William Hody, B.Exch., and Thomas Frowyk, JCP, were knighted shortly after joining the bench: Ives, *Kebell*, 68–73, 461; and relevant entries in: E. Foss, *Biographical Dictionary of the Judges of England* (London, 1870); *DNB*; Wedgwood; *LP*; Shaw, *Knights*.

[54] Ives, *Kebell*, 68–9; *CPR* (1485–94), 236; *CIPM, Henry VII*, vol. i, no. 439.

[55] J. S. Cockburn, *A History of English Assizes 1558–1714* (Cambridge, 1972), 57.

[56] *CPR* (1485–94), 285, 484, 495, 506–8.

[57] R58, RT I memo-book, fo. 2ᵛ.

[58] Sir Thomas Bryan, CJ, was the other appointee for the home circuit for this round of assizes: Ives, *Kebell*, 68. It is possible, however, that Roger could have been riding alone because he does not mention him: cf. Cockburn, *Assizes*, 24.

[59] Cockburn, *Assizes*, 19, 28–9.

Roger's mother-in-law, but, with commendable impartiality, it was referred to arbitration. At Dartford they secured, 'with much labour', an indictment for the murder of three boys from the presenting jurors. Roger's notes also show that justices on circuit lodged with the sheriff or local notables as they did in the later sixteenth century.[60] In Essex he spent two nights with the king's servant, Sir Thomas Montgomery, and in Kent he stayed a night with Robert Rede, serjeant at law.[61]

It is unclear why Roger made these notes, but he may well have simply been recording events that interested him and struck him as deserving of record: elsewhere in the same notebook he noted the fate of the unfortunate rector of Cley in north Norfolk, killed by lightning on 11 August 1492.[62] The educated layman of the late fifteenth century did not necessarily use his literacy for practical purposes only.

Roger's ability ensured him a busy career. Besides his work on the assizes and at Westminster, he attended the peers as a law officer in six parliaments between 1483 and 1491.[63] He was also appointed to numerous commissions in his native Norfolk and elsewhere. From 1466, when he first joined the Norfolk bench, he served on every known magistrates' panel before his death on 9 November 1493, and must have been one of the busiest justices in the county.[64] He was also frequently appointed to various *ad hoc* commissions.[65] Membership of a commission did not necessitate constant attendance by every member, but the burden on Roger was greater than most because lawyers were naturally the best-qualified to attend to its business.

The favour shown to him by the new dynasty should cause no surprise, although he had served the Yorkist kings. His career as a justice of the peace in Norfolk, like those of most other lawyers from the county, was not affected by dynastic change.[66] Prominent

---

[60] Ibid., 9.

[61] R58, RT I memo-book, fo. 2ᵛ. Montgomery: Sayer, 'Norfolk Involvement', 306–7; *The Coronation of Richard III: The Extant Documents*, ed. A. F. Sutton and P. W. Hammond (Gloucester, 1983), 375. Rede: Ives, *Kebell*, 474–5.

[62] R58, RT I, memo-book, fo. 2ᵛ.

[63] Wedgwood, 864. In 1488 he was a trier of Gascon petitions: *RP*, vi. 410.

[64] *CPR* (1461–7), 568; (1467–77), 622; (1476–85), 566; (1485–94), 494; PRO, PROB11/10, fos. 11–12; *CIPM, Henry VII*, vol. i, nos. 1,028, 1,136, 1,143. See Ch. 2, 3 below, for his attendance at the quarter sessions.

[65] *CPR, passim.*

[66] Sayer, 'Norfolk Involvement', 311–12. The evidence for the Norfolk peace commissions of the second half of the 15th cent. suggests that the extent to which John Heydon compromised himself through his factional attachments was exceptional (*CPR*,

lawyers usually survived political crises. Those who came to grief
were those who 'abandoned the safety of self-effacing obedience' and
entered the world of politics.[67] Roger was a conformist who eschewed
partisanship and accepted each upheaval in the political world as it
came. He is an excellent example of a lawyer who advanced himself
by securing powerful patrons and clients whilst at the same time
skilfully avoiding the consequences of any misfortune they might have
met. During Edward IV's reign he acquired the most powerful
patronage of all, royal patronage, and this more than anything else
must have helped his career to flourish. For, by the mid-1470s at the
latest, he was retained by the queen, receiving 4 marks per annum for
his legal services.[68] His work for Elizabeth Woodville paid dividends,
since it attracted the attention of another important client, Thomas
Grey, marquis of Dorset, her son by her first marriage. Grey granted
him an annual fee in the same period and a few years later leased
out to him the manor of 'Pekhalle' in Tittleshall, a township near
Raynham.[69] Roger's son, Roger II, seems to have inherited the Grey
retainer; Grey's heir was paying him 2 marks per annum in the early
years of Henry VIII's reign.[70]

Anthony Woodville, the queen's brother, most probably introduced her to Roger's services since John Townshend had served both
Woodville and his father-in-law, Thomas, Lord Scales, and the
Townshends came from a region where the Scales–Woodville influence was particularly strong.[71] Other lawyers of Roger's period
similarly benefited themselves through the nexus of a local magnate.
Thomas Kebell, for example, had the good fortune to come from a
part of Leicestershire dominated by William, Lord Hastings, and
was thereby able to attract the attention of a lord who became one of
his most important clients.[72]

The Woodville connection obviously served Roger well but it did

---

passim), though Thomas Jenny's service to the Howards might have prevented
his reappointment to the bench when Henry VII took power: *Pl.,* no. 802; *CPR*
(1476–85), 566; (1485–94), 494.

[67] Ives, *Kebell*, 234.

[68] R58, Raynham account roll, loose membrane and mm. 6, 16 (1474/5, 1475/6,
1476/7 receivers' accounts). The queen was granted various Duchy of Lancaster lands
in Norfolk in 1467 and so became an immediate landed presence in the Townshends'
part of the county: *RP*, v. 628.

[69] R58, Raynham account roll, m. 16 (1476/7 receiver's account: 23s. 4d. delivered
as part payment of his fee from Grey), m. 21 (1480/1 Raynham bailiff's account).

[70] R31, RT II estate book, fos. 5ʳ, 13ᵛ.

[71] See Ch. 2, 1 below.   [72] Ives, *Kebell*, 94.

not hamper him when their enemy, Richard, duke of Gloucester, seized the throne, just as the work he had earlier performed for Elizabeth de Vere, the widow of the twelfth earl of Oxford, did not damn him in Gloucester's eyes. He had been a 'working feoffee'—a position often occupied by lawyers and clerics—for the countess, and as such he and others had attempted to resist the forced surrender of her property to the duke in the early 1470s.[73] Indeed, during Richard III's reign he farmed two previously confiscated De Vere manors in Norfolk, Toftrees and Shereford, from the crown,[74] and helped to investigate the treasons of William Colyngbourne, the composer of a derogatory rhyme about the king and his henchmen. He also acted as a trustee for one of those henchmen, William Catesby, a lawyer of the period who did become involved in politics, and in 1485 he was one of those in Norfolk from whom Richard III felt he could secure a loan.[75] Unlike Catesby, however, Roger flourished under Henry VII. If he did have political opinions he appears to have kept them to himself. Probably he would have agreed with the sentiments expressed in a speech which Sir Thomas More imagined John Morton, bishop of Ely, making in 1483:

[I]f the worlde woold haue gone as I would haue wished, king Henryes son had had the crown & not king Edward [IV]. But after that god had ordered hym to lese it and kinge Edwarde to reigne, I was neuer soo mad that I would . . . striue against the quicke. . . . I purpose not to spurne against a prick, nor labor to set vp that god pulleth down.[76]

The Wheel of Fortune, a popular metaphor in the Middle Ages, was most apposite for Roger's times.[77]

Roger had other noble clients. One of his earliest was John Mowbray, duke of Norfolk. Although he acted as a trustee for the duke, it appears that money-lending was the most important service

---

[73] R38, loose deed of 24 July 1472; *CPR* (1476–85), 434; *PL*, no. 845; *Calendars of the Proceedings in Chancery in the Reign of Queen Elizabeth*, ed. J. Bailey, 3 vols. (London, 1827–32), vol. i, pp. xc–xci; M. A. Hicks, 'The Last Days of Elizabeth Countess of Oxford', *EHR* 103 (1988), 76–95.

[74] R58, Raynham account roll, mm. 21, 25, 26; R(Attic), *'Norfolk manorial* T–W and mixed', 1484/5 Toftrees and Shereford accounts.

[75] *CPR* (1476–85), 319–20; Wedgwood, 884; *CCR* (1476–84), no. 1338; *VCH, Worcs.*, iii. 320; *British Library Harleian Manuscript 433*, ed. R. Horrox and P. W. Hammond, 4 vols., Richard III Society (1979–83), iii. 130. He was asked for £100.

[76] *The Complete Works of St Thomas More*, ii, ed. R. S. Sylvester (Yale, 1963), 92.

[77] See H. R. Patch, *The Goddess Fortuna in Mediaeval Literature* (Cambridge, Mass., 1927), esp. 147–77.

he offered. Mowbray's financial circumstances were unfavourable during the 1460s. In 1464 he owed his kinsman John Howard over £546 and in 1467 he borrowed £100 at interest from Roger. Roger probably provided legal counsel to Howard himself since the latter twice paid him a fee in 1466.[78] It is hardly a coincidence that Roger sat for Bramber, the Sussex pocket borough of the dukes of Norfolk, in the parliament of 1467-8.[79] It is not so clear how he came to represent the Wiltshire borough of Calne in 1472-5.[80] Calne was owned by the Zouches of Haryngworth, but John, Lord Zouche, was a minor at the time. Possibly Zouche's stepfather, Sir Gilbert Debenham, the royal retainer from East Anglia, helped to secure this seat for a compliant lawyer.[81] But if by this stage Roger was already serving the queen he would in any case have been viewed as a suitable candidate by the crown. Edward IV seems to have made serious efforts to obtain a docile Commons for this parliament, as it included 'an unusually high proportion of royal servants'.[82] Other nobles for whom Roger worked were Henry Stafford, duke of Buckingham— who was paying him £2 per annum for acting as his attorney in the central lawcourts at Westminster by 1475[83]—and Sir John Bourchier, a cadet member of a powerful family during Edward IV's reign.[84]

Less distinguished clients included the Yorkist courtier, Sir Richard Crofte,[85] the priory of Christ Church, Canterbury,[86] the Pastons of Norfolk, and a Suffolk gentry family, the Hoptons of Blythburgh. His work for the Hoptons, who were his in-laws, shows how multifarious the duties of a lawyer could be, for he was their steward, councillor, and trustee as well as a general legal adviser.[87]

---

[78] *Manners and Household Expenses of England in the Thirteenth and Fifteenth Centuries*, ed. T. H. Turner, Roxburghe Club, 57 (1841), 462, 467, 581, 328, 380.

[79] PRO, C219/17/1/105; Wedgwood, 864; A. Crawford, 'The Career of John Howard, Duke of Norfolk, 1420-85', M. Phil. thesis (London, 1975), 89; *HP*, i. 201.

[80] PRO, C219/17/2/135; Wedgwood, 864.

[81] J. C. Wedgwood, *History of Parliament, Register of the Ministers and Members of Both Houses, 1439-1509* (London, 1938), 704; *Complete Peerage*, xii. pt. ii, 945-6; Wedgwood, 265-6.

[82] C. Ross, *Edward IV* (London, 1974), 214, 344-5.

[83] C. Rawcliffe, *The Staffords, Earls of Stafford and Dukes of Buckingham, 1394-1521* (Cambridge, 1978), 227.

[84] *CPR* (1494-1509), 40.

[85] *CPR* (1549-51), 176-7; Wedgwood, 237-8.

[86] *Christ Church Letters*, ed. J. B. Sheppard, Camden Soc., NS 19 (1877), 31.

[87] Ibid., 160; Richmond, *John Hopton*, 126-7; *CCR* (1476-85), no. 492; *CIPM, Henry VII*, vol. ii, no. 200; *CPR* (1476-85), 142-3.

Although Sir John Paston once addressed Roger as 'hys best betrustyd frende', his relations with the Pastons were not always easy.[88] There is no doubt that they depended heavily on him for advice, not least in connection with the disputed Fastolf inheritance. In mid-1465 he and the Pastons' servant Richard Calle were present in Chancery while it investigated the conflicting claims to Fastolf's former property.[89] A decade later he and John Morton—then master of the Rolls—were asked to remind William Waynflete, bishop of Winchester, to speak on the Pastons' behalf to the duke and duchess of Norfolk about Caister.[90] Not long before, Waynflete himself had challenged the family's title to Saxthorpe. In 1470 William Gurney twice entered the manor to hold courts and collect rents on the bishop's behalf, but on the second occasion he was persuaded to desist until he had met Sir John Paston in London. The younger John Paston suggested that if Sir John himself were unable to meet Gurney in person he should 'let Townysend tak a wey wyth hym'.[91] Presumably Roger stood a fair chance of reaching an accommodation with the latter since Gurney was a fellow lawyer and a friend.[92]

William Paston, another lawyer, also respected Roger's abilities and once admonished his nephew Sir John to 'Take auyse off Townysend'.[93] Later, however, Sir John feared he would lose Roger's services because William was slow to pay him 100 marks which the Pastons owed.[94] Perhaps a clash of personalities was inevitable between two hard-headed lawyers, not least because Roger profited from the Pastons' monetary troubles. The penurious Sir John mortgaged two Norfolk manors to him to raise money and lost one of them as a result.[95] It was probably one of these transactions which so distressed Margaret Paston, the younger John reporting to his brother that their mother 'wepyth and takyth on meruaylously' and was determined to 'puruey for hyr lond þat ye shall non selle of it, for she thynkys ye wold and it cam to yowr hand'. Margaret herself had nevertheless also made use of Roger's services as a money-lender in order to buy wine.[96] But by the late 1470s Sir John's requests for loans had begun to grate, perhaps because Roger came to doubt his

---

[88] *PL*, no. 247.

[89] *PL*, no. 740.

[90] *PL*, no. 292. Previously Roger I advised the family after the duke had seized the castle: ibid., nos. 342–3; *The Paston Letters*, ed. J. Gairdner, repr. of 1904 edn. (Gloucester, 1986), no. 768.

[91] *PL*, nos. 338, 340.   [92] See (iii) below.   [93] *PL*, no. 92.

[94] *PL*, no. 271.   [95] See Ch. 3, 1(iii), Ch. 4, 1 below.   [96] *PL*, no. 212.

credit-worthiness. Again short of money, Paston tried without success in October 1479 to borrow more from him. He subsequently informed his mother that Roger had 'foodyd me forthe euyre synys'.[97]

On one occasion Roger acted for the Pastons as an arbitrator in a minor legal dispute.[98] Arbitration was a routine part of a lawyer's work, and his mother-in-law's case of 1492 demonstrates how it could supplement the common law.[99] He himself was an arbitrator in at least two other disputes. With William Hussey, then king's attorney, and John Sulyard he made an award in 1478 between the Daniel and Berney families concerning the ownership of two Norfolk manors.[100] A decade later he and Hussey arbitrated in a property dispute between Walter Hungerford and Edward, Lord Hastings.[101] Arbitrators acceptable to both parties were, of course, necessary for the process to work. An attempt to settle a quarrel between a local landowner and the prior of West Acre in 1492 broke down because Roger was rejected as an impartial referee by the former. This may have been connected with the fact that the dispute occurred on Roger's Raynham doorstep.[102]

It is often impossible to write biographies in the modern sense of medieval people because the personalities of most are unknown, but something of Roger I's character filters through to us.[103] The diary-like entries in his notebook provide some human touches. In it he not only recorded the death of his horse while on circuit and the fate of the rector of Cley, but also how he himself fell and hurt his foot a few months later and was unable to attend mass for several days afterwards.[104] Perhaps he attended daily; his will, with its grand religious bequests, suggests a conventional piety typical of the old-established religion which his son was to help destroy,[105] but it is also in keeping with the character of the hard-headed man we know he was. He

[97] i.e., 'put me off ever since': *PL*, no. 315.
[98] *PL*, no. 247.
[99] See 3(i) above. For arbitration and the law, see Ch. 3 below.
[100] *CCR* (1476–85), no. 274; manors at West Tofts and Bradeston.
[101] *CCR* (1485–1500), no. 407.
[102] R58, RT I memo-book, fo. 3ʳ.
[103] Cf. Carpenter, 'Fifteenth Century Biographies', 729–34.
[104] R58, RT I memo-book, fos. 2ᵛ, 5ʳ.
[105] PRO, PROB11/10, fos. 11–12. See Richmond, *John Hopton*, 248, for useful comments on this document. One should not doubt the piety of 15th cent. gentlemen, the majority of whom took their religion very seriously. On the day he died Sir John Heveningham heard three masses and was about to 'sey a lytell devocion' in his garden when he suddenly collapsed: Fleming, 'Charity', 41–2; *PL*, no. 26.

requested a chantry to function for eighty years on behalf of his soul while, for its immediate safety, he expected one thousand masses to be sung within a week.[106] He was not an uncultured man. As a senior fellow he had been in charge of the library at Lincoln's Inn,[107] and when he died he owned at least thirty-four books, a good collection by lay standards, although one not out of the ordinary for one of his background and education.[108] He certainly laid no claim to scholastic prowess, because he once asserted in the Common Pleas that he was 'not a good sophister'.[109] He is best thought of as a very competent lawyer—not afraid to speak his mind—with a drive which could sometimes border on the ruthless, as Sir John Paston discovered to his cost: 'iff I had passyd my daye [for repaying a loan], it had ben harde to have trustyd to hys [Roger's] cortesye, jn so moche I fynde hym also ryght loose in the tonge.'[110] A man who would 'have the vttremest off hys bargayn', Roger expected to take something out of life in return for what his considerable energies had put in.[111]

(ii) Family

Lawyers were in a good position to know of available brides.[112] Roger married Eleanor Lunsford, the stepdaughter of his client, John

---

[106] As his executrix, his wife Eleanor paid £14. 5s. for 778 masses to be sung at London, Norwich, and Lynn after his death: BL, Add. MS 41,305, fo. 5ʳ. It is interesting to find a blank after *probatum* in the prerogative court of Canterbury's copy of the will. Ecclesiastical courts would normally approve a will if the statement of the testator's intention was found to be satisfactory and the conditions in which the will was made corresponded with the formal requirements for validity: M. Sheehan, *The Will in Medieval England* (Toronto, 1963), 205. Did Eleanor back down at the last moment because she felt that in practical terms the will as it stood could not be implemented? Did testators who made especially extravagant religious requests seriously expect them to be carried out to the very last letter? (Cf. Richmond, *John Hopton*, 248).

[107] In 1475 the treasurer of the inn ordered the governors to pay Roger 30s. for the library (LI *Black Books*, 59). This library must have been one of the earliest in the inns of court. It has indeed been argued that libraries were probably unnecessary in the inns until after the introduction of printing: J. Conway Davies (ed.), *Catalogue of Manuscripts in the Library of the Honourable Society of the Inner Temple*, 3 vols. (Oxford, 1972), i. 3–4. It is difficult to know what to make of Dugdale's claim that the library at Lincoln's Inn was not furnished with books until the beginning of the 17th cent.: ibid., 4.

[108] C. E. Moreton, 'The "Library" of a Late Fifteenth-Century Lawyer', *The Library*, 6th ser. 13 (1991), 338–46.

[109] *The Reports of Sir John Spelman*, ed. J. H. Baker, 2 vols., Selden Soc., 103–4 (1977–8), ii. 125. Erasmus once remarked that the 'study of English law is as far removed as can be from true learning': R. W. Chambers, *Thomas More* (London, 1938), 85. But this is unfair; see E. W. Ives, 'The Common Lawyers', in C. H. Clough (ed.), *Profession, Vocation and Culture in Later Medieval England* (Liverpool, 1982), 181–217.

[110] *PL*, no. 286.   [111] Ibid.   [112] Ives, *Kebell*, 370.

Hopton of Blythburgh, Suffolk.[113] On 5 December 1467 he agreed
terms with Thomasine Hopton, Eleanor's mother.[114] Roger was a
hard bargainer and obtained more from Thomasine than she was
willing to tell her husband. As far as Hopton knew, Eleanor's
marriage portion was to be 400 marks, but Thomasine promised
Roger another 50 marks which 'John her husband schal not kow
[know] of.' He was also to be kept ignorant of the full extent of two
other promises: 'to make the chaumber of the seid Roger worth an C
marcs', and to provide Eleanor with an extensive wardrobe. Hopton
did agree, however, to bear the marriage-costs, and that after the
deaths of himself and Thomasine the couple were to have the reversion
of lands worth 20 marks per annum. For his part Roger agreed to
provide his bride with a jointure of lands to the value of 40 marks, and
a life interest after he died in such lands which he bought with her
marriage portion. He was, in the event, to award her with such an
interest in almost the whole of his estate after his death; perhaps a
proof of affection.[115] Roger enjoyed a close relationship with the
Hoptons for the rest of his life. Townshend and Hopton properties
coincided at Wissett in Suffolk, making frequent contact inevitable,
and Thomasine continued to retain him as a councillor after her
husband's death.[116] He was clearly the Hoptons' good friend and not
simply an in-law and employee. Shortly after John Hopton died in
1478, he and Eleanor went to stay with the widowed Thomasine,
perhaps for as long as three months, at Yoxford, her manor in
Suffolk.[117]

Roger had at least two sons and four daughters by Eleanor.[118]
Roger II, born in about 1478 at Whissonsett, was ultimately the only
surviving son.[119] Still a minor at his father's death, the younger

---

[113] Daughter of William Lunsford of Battle, Sussex. Her mother, Thomasine, was
Hopton's second wife: pedigree in Richmond, *John Hopton*, 100–1.

[114] R49, Townshend cartulary, fo. 32 (copy of marriage agreement). They had
married by 22 Apr. 1468: ibid., fos. 26ᵛ–27ᵛ, 29.

[115] *CIPM, Henry VII*, vol. i, nos. 1,028, 1,136, 1,143. The main exception was
lands near Lynn worth over £14 p.a. which he set aside to support a chantry.

[116] Richmond, *John Hopton*, 126–7.

[117] R58, Raynham account roll, m. 19d.

[118] A late 15th-cent. child's brass in East Raynham church (George, son of Roger
Townshend, esq.) suggests he had another, short-lived, son.

[119] Birth noted in margin of the family's 1477/8 sheep accounts. They ran from
Michaelmas to Michaelmas: R50, 1477/8 sheep accounts, fo. 13ᵛ. Roger II was 16
when the inquisitions post mortem for his father were held in the second half of 1494:
CIPM, Henry VII, vol. i, nos. 1,028, 1,136, 1,143.

Roger was contracted at an early age to Amy, one of the daughters and co-heirs of William Brewes.[120] She was quite a match for the Townshends, for she brought with her a significant estate and her grandfather, Sir Thomas Brewes of Fressingfield, Suffolk, had been an important figure in East Anglia.[121] Sir Thomas's earlier associations with Roger I probably derived from a common friendship with the Hopton family. Amy's mother was one of John Hopton's daughters and, like Roger, Brewes was a Hopton trustee.[122]

Thomas, Roger I's younger son, was intended to succeed to the Townshends' lands outside Norfolk, but he survived his father by only a few years. Admitted to Lincoln's Inn on 20 October 1499, he was still alive a year later when his elder brother paid a fee to the pensioner of the inn on his behalf. But by the following February Thomas had died, because Roger II paid 10 shillings for a trental (a set of thirty masses) for him.[123]

Thomasine, the eldest of Roger I's children, married during his lifetime.[124] Her husband was Thomas, the eldest son of Sir Edward Woodhouse of Kimberley. This match, another prominent one for the Townshends, probably occurred shortly before 12 September 1488, when Roger settled on the couple the reversion of three manors in Litcham which he had bought from Sir Edward a decade earlier.[125]

Roger left £200 each in his will for the marriages of two of his other daughters, Elizabeth and Anne.[126] Shortly before he died, he was negotiating a match with Alexander Cressener, the grandfather of Elizabeth's future husband John Cressener. The families were already connected, because John's widowed mother Anne had by then married Eleanor Townshend's nephew, Edward Knyvet.[127] The Cresseners, whose estates lay in south-west Suffolk and Essex, were, like the Breweses and Woodhouses, leading East Anglian gentry. They had a distinguished pedigree, because Alexander's mother was

---

[120] By Oct. 1490: ibid., no. 648.

[121] Wedgwood, 108–9; Sayer, 'Norfolk Involvement', 323 n.; *Manners and Household Expenses*, 398–400.

[122] *CIPM, Henry VII*, vol. i, no. 648; vol. ii, no. 200; *CCR* (1476–85), no. 492.

[123] *CIPM, Henry VII*, vol. i, nos. 1,028, 1,136; LI *Admissions*, 29; R58, RT II memo-book, fos. 6ᵛ, 9ᵛ.

[124] PRO, PROB11/10, fo. 11.

[125] R49, Townshend cartulary, fos. 41ᵛ–42ʳ; R58, RT I memo-book, fo. 7ʳ; *CCR* (1468–76), no. 1,485; (1476–85), no. 154; PRO, CP25/1/170/193, no. 67.

[126] PRO, PROB11/10, fo. 11.

[127] R58, RT I memo-book, fo. 2ᵛ.

an aunt of Edward IV.[128] Anne Townshend married Ralph, the eldest son of Leonard Castell of Raveningham. Like Elizabeth, she married after her father's death.[129] Howard followers by the early sixteenth century, the Castells were a lesser family than the Cresseners but of a relatively ancient lineage. In Norfolk they owned manors at Raveningham, Bedingham, and Horningtoft. The Townshends were their tenants at Horningtoft, a parish a few miles south-east of Raynham. Outside the county they had interests in Lincolnshire and Suffolk.[130] Perhaps rather a feckless character (his mother-in-law doubted his 'wysdom and sadnes'), Ralph had a son by Anne but predeceased his father, Leonard, who died in 1511.[131]

Agnes, Roger I's remaining daughter, became a nun at the Benedictine abbey at Barking before the end of the fifteenth century.[132] Roger quite conceivably performed legal work for this Essex house, because he stayed two nights there in August 1492 after finishing his summer assize circuit.[133] As Agnes had no dependants he left her no more than a life annuity of £2 in his will.[134] Barking was one of the last abbeys to be suppressed and Agnes remained there until its dissolution. She died shortly afterwards in the Townshend household at East Raynham.[135]

The marriages of Roger I's children firmly established the Townshends as members of the Norfolk gentry. They are a sign of their local standing and demonstrate the close-knit, interrelated, and local nature of gentry society. Roger I looked for suitable alliances in his home territory, although his career gave him wider horizons than many gentry possessed.

---

[128] *CIPM, Henry VII*, vol. ii, nos. 21, 84; *Complete Peerage*, xi. 543.

[129] PRO, PROB11/10, fo. 11.

[130] R60, loose bill of 11 Feb. 1513 mentioning Thomas, Lord Howard, an executor of Leonard Castell; *CPR* (1499–1509), 520; G. A. Carthew, *The Hundred of Launditch and Deanery of Brisley in the County of Norfolk*, 3 vols. (Norwich, 1877–9), i. 182, 184; NRO, B–L VI a (xi); *LP*, vol. i, pt. i, no. 20 (p. 269).

[131] R(Attic), 'Townshend family before 1552', fragmentary copy of Eleanor Townshend's will; Carthew, *Launditch*, i. 184.

[132] Roger II visited his sister at Barking in early 1500: R58, RT II memo-book, fo. 10^r.

[133] R58, RT I memo-book, fo. 2^v.

[134] PRO, PROB11/10, fo. 11; R12, 'HELHOUGHTON Temp. HEN VIII', deed of 10 Feb. 1538 ensuring its continued payment.

[135] *VCH, Essex*, ii. 120; D. Knowles and R. N. Hadcock, *Medieval Religious Houses, England and Wales*, 2nd edn. (London, 1971), 256; *LP*, vol. xv. 547; PRO, C142/96/32.

(iii) Associates

'If friendship is to be found anywhere, it is to be found surely in the choice of a man's feoffees.'[136] The general lack of evidence of a personal nature for the late Middle Ages (the Paston Letters are a rarity) makes this a useful maxim. Roger I made numerous acquaintances during his lifetime but, unless they became his trustees, it is questionable whether they were particularly close associates, let alone friends. Through his career he knew some of the most eminent lawyers of his day, like James Hobart and Sir William Hussey, but where did professional associations end and, if at all, personal friendships begin? It would not have been surprising if Morgan Kidwelly and John Fisher, with whom he rode the northern assize circuit for several years, became friends, but we cannot prove this.[137] In fact, the only leading legal contemporary with whom Roger was indisputedly on good terms was the Suffolk man, John Sulyard, a fellow student at Lincoln's Inn, who was created a serjeant at law with him in the same ceremony. A cousin of Eleanor Townshend, Sulyard hunted with Roger and John Hopton, and was several times appointed by Roger as a trustee.[138]

In the case of Sulyard family, rather than professional, ties might have been more important. Many of Roger's trustees were men connected by blood or marriage, like his brother-in-law John Blakeney and his son-in-law Thomas Woodhouse.[139] His marriage broadened his circle of acquaintances and thus his trustees. Among his wife's family these included her nephew, Edward Knyvet of Rayleigh, Essex, her brother-in-law, William Tendering of Harkstead and Holbrook, Suffolk, and her half-brother, Nicholas Sidney.[140] Family

---

[136] Saul, *Provincial Life*, 62.

[137] Ives, *Kebell*, 69.

[138] Wedgwood, 827–8; *CCR* (1476–85), no. 177; Richmond, *John Hopton*, 241; R49, Townshend cartulary, fos. 28ᵛ–29ʳ, 31ʳ, 40ᵛ–41ᵛ; R18, 'N & S CREAKE, Temp. EDW. IV (1471–1481)', deeds of 20 Nov. 1473 and 11 July 1475; R28, 'RAYNHAM EDW. IV to HENRY VII', deed of 7 May 1480.

[139] Blakeney: R33, 'Raynhams, deeds 13th cent. and 1353, 1420–1486/7', deed of 22 Apr. 1468. Woodhouse: R49, Townshend cartulary, fo. 40ʳ⁻ᵛ; R32, 'Deeds, Raynhams 1447–1490', deed of 4 Feb. 1490; R19, 'N & S CREAKE Temp. HEN VII', deed of 18 Sept. 1492.

[140] Knyvet: R49, Townshend cartulary, fos. 9ʳ⁻ᵛ, 40ʳ⁻ᵛ; R32, 'Deeds, Raynhams 1447–1490', deed of 4 Feb. 1490; Richmond, *John Hopton*, 49, 124 n., 125–6. Tendering: PRO, CP25/1/6/82, no. 31; R49, Townshend cartulary, fos. 43ʳ–44ʳ; Richmond, *John Hopton*, 129–30; Wedgwood, 844. Sidney: R49, Townshend cartulary, fos. 9, 43ʳ–44ʳ; Richmond, *John Hopton*, 101–2.

connections also played their part in his friendships with other gentry. Sir William Calthorpe, an associate of the Hoptons, and Roger acted for each other in property conveyances as early as the mid-1460s. Nevertheless, as a neighbouring landowner—he resided at Burnham Thorpe, a few miles north of Raynham—Calthorpe was bound to come into contact with the Townshends.[141]

Roger possibly first met Sir Robert Wingfield, the royal retainer for whom he was a trustee in the 1470s, through their common service to the Mowbray dukes of Norfolk. He performed legal work for the Wingfields and, in a will dated 1479, Sir Robert's wife Anne named him among the friends to whom she awarded a powerful say in the settlement of her lands after her death.[142]

The Brandons were related to both the Sidneys and Wingfields. They prospered by serving the Mowbrays and, above all, by supporting Henry Tudor. When Roger chose Robert Brandon, the uncle of the future duke of Suffolk, as a trustee in November 1485 he must have appreciated their links with the new king.[143] Robert Clere, another East Anglian, also entered Tudor service. He married a daughter of Sir William Hopton and was prominent in Townshend affairs after Roger I's death, first as one of Eleanor Townshend's trustees and then as her executor. He was subsequently a trustee for Roger II.[144] Roger I had been a leading feoffee and legal adviser of Clere's mother.[145]

Clere trained as a lawyer but does not appear to have acted for Roger I as a trustee.[146] Roger no doubt picked those lawyers who were his trustees primarily for their legal expertise but, as the example of John Sulyard shows, one cannot say that none was on friendly terms with him. He must have liked John Pigeon, an obscure Norwich attorney employed by the Townshends, because he

[141] Ibid., 253; R29, 'HORNINGTOFT Temp. Edw. IV', deed of 30 Dec. 1465; *CIPM, Henry VII*, vol. i, nos. 975–6; vol. iii, no. 457; Wedgwood, 108, 149–50.

[142] Ibid., 956–7; R49, Townshend cartulary, fos. 40ᵛ–41ᵛ; R18, 'N & S CREAKE, Temp. EDW. IV (1471–1481)', deeds of 20 Nov. 1473 and 11 July 1475; PRO, CP25/1/170/193, no. 63; *CCR* (1476–85), no. 479.

[143] R49, Townshend cartulary, fo. 43ʳ–44ʳ; S.J. Gunn, *Charles Brandon, Duke of Suffolk, c. 1484–1545* (Oxford, 1988), 2.

[144] Wedgwood, 90; R49, Townshend cartulary, fo. 9ʳ⁻ᵛ; will of Eleanor, see n. 131 above; BL, Add. MS 41,139, fo. 6ᵛ.

[145] *CPR* (1476–85), 96; NRO, NCC 131–5 Wolman.

[146] Wedgwood, 190; LI *Black Books*, 49.

bequeathed him 20 shillings.[147] He also knew Henry Spelman well. They worked together as lawyers and Henry was a legal adviser of the Wingfields and the Cleres.[148] Another trustee, John Fincham, a long-serving Norfolk justice of the peace, had also been a feoffee of John Townshend.[149] William Gurney of Thurston, Sir William Calthorpe's son-in-law, must have been a friend. Possibly a contemporary at Lincoln's Inn, he acted with Roger as a Hopton trustee and was one of the men whom Roger appointed most frequently for the same capacity.[150]

Master William Pickenham was easily the most distinguished of the other men who were most often Roger's trustees; the rest were servants and estate officials. Pickenham, a relative of Eleanor Townshend, had considerable influence in East Anglia. An ecclesiastical lawyer, he was archdeacon of Suffolk and served Thomas Bourchier, archbishop of Canterbury, and other members of that family. His Yorkist connections were probably all that stood between him and a bishopric after 1485.[151]

The servants and estate officials who Roger I most often appointed his trustees were William Wayte of Tittleshall, the Townshends' scribe; William Fuller of Walsingham, their estate receiver for much of the 1470s; the clerk Edmund Herberd, their long-serving household steward;[152] and Thomas Gygges. The Gyggeses were lesser gentry from north-west Norfolk and, if the maiden name of Roger's mother is anything to go by, were in some way related to the Townshends.[153]

---

[147] R12, 'HELHOUGHTON Temp. HEN. VII', deed of 10 Mar. 1487; R32, 'Deeds, Raynhams 1447–1490', deed of 4 Feb. 1490; R19, 'N & S CREAKE Temp. HEN. VII', deed of 18 Sept. 1492; Spelman's *Reports*, i. 209, 66; PRO, CP40/938, rot. 408; PRO, PROB11/10, fo. 11.

[148] PRO, CP25/1/224/120, no. 24; R49, Townshend cartulary, fos. 40ᵛ–41ᵛ; R18, 'N & S CREAKE, Temp. EDW. IV (1471–1481)', deeds of 20 Nov. 1473 and 11 July 1475; *Select Cases in the Council of Henry VII*, ed. C. G. Bayne and W. H. Dunham, Selden Soc., 75 (1958), 66; *CPR, passim; CCR* (1476–85), nos. 479, 603; NRO, NCC 131–5 Wolman.

[149] R33, 'Raynhams, deeds 13th cent. and 1353, 1420–1486/7', deed of 22 Apr. 1468; R18, 'N & S CREAKE, Temp. EDW. IV (1471–1481)', deeds of 20 Nov. 1473 and 11 July 1475; *CPR, passim*; R49, Townshend cartulary, fos. 21ᵛ–22ᵛ.

[150] Raynham deeds too numerous to cite; Richmond, *John Hopton*, 253 n.; LI *Admissions*, 12; *CCR* (1476–85), no. 492.

[151] Numerous Raynham deeds; Richmond, *John Hopton*, 153, 215–16.

[152] Numerous Raynham deeds. Wayte: R50, 1477/8 sheep accounts, fo. 19ᵛ; Fuller: R58, Raynham account roll, mm. 1, 16; Herberd: R58, Raynham account roll, mm. 8, 10, 17, 20; NRO, NCC 388–9 Ryxe.

[153] See section 2 above.

It is difficult to identify particular members of this family because it was a large one and they tended to share the same Christian names. A Thomas Gygges became a Townshend bailiff in 1477,[154] and their employees of the late fifteenth and early sixteenth centuries usually included a Gygges. It is unlikely that this was always the same man, but during Roger I's lifetime 'Thomas Gygges' was probably more often than not Thomas Gygges the lawyer.[155] His family were, at any rate, the Townshends' friends. John Gygges of Burnham, one of Roger's trustees in the past, appointed him the supervisor of his will in 1476 and, in turn, Roger bequeathed to John's heir the not-insubstantial sum of £5.[156] Friendships with families of a lower social status suggest that gentle society in the late Middle Ages was a good deal less stratified and more fluid than appearances might suggest. In the fourteenth century the rich and well-connected Sussex knight, Sir William de Etchingham, hunted with his tenants and immediate neighbours among the lesser gentry. Richmond's John Hopton provides a fifteenth-century parallel.[157]

By all accounts, Roger I had a restricted circle of friends who, if not lesser men or others from his immediate neighbourhood, were usually connected by family ties.[158] Even his trustees for Sharpenhoe, the manor he bought in Bedfordshire, were from these two groups and not gentry of that shire.[159] The later medieval lawyer was by no means immune from the intensely provincial nature of English life. Roger's legal career acquainted him with other lawyers and with the gentry and aristocracy in Norfolk and elsewhere, but these were often professional relationships.[160] The Pastons, for example, were hardly

[154] R13, 1477/8 Helhoughton account roll; R58, Raynham account roll, m. 18.
[155] LI, *Admissions*, 18; *CPR* (1485–94), 494; (1494–1509), 652. He died in 1497: PRO, PROB11/11, fo. 112A.
[156] R33, 'Raynhams, deeds 13th cent. and 1353, 1420–1486/7', deed of 22 Apr. 1468; R49, Townshend cartulary, fos. 28ᵛ–29ʳ, 30; *CAD*, vol. iv, no. A.8,471; PRO, PROB11/10, fo. 11.
[157] Saul, *Provincial Life*, 63–6; Richmond, *John Hopton*, 166. See also my 'A Social Gulf? The Upper and Lesser Gentry of Late Medieval England', *The Journal of Medieval History*, 17 (1991), 255–62.
[158] Cf. the similarly narrow circles of trustees of the 15th-cent. Derbyshire gentry: Wright, *Derbyshire Gentry*, 53.
[159] PRO, CP25/1/6/82, no. 31.
[160] Ives, *Kebell*, 335–6. For the narrow range of Roger I's trustees see App. 1, below. Hassell Smith's pioneering work on a part of north Norfolk in the late 16th cent. reveals that a substantial gentleman like Nathaniel Bacon of Stiffkey had practically no social contact with other leading gentry in the county outside his own family, and that

close friends and they never served him as trustees. What is most striking, however, is the absence of the nobility among his trustees. His services to the great were reciprocated in cash rather than 'good lordship', although his Commons seat of 1467/8 was probably the exception to this rule.[161]

(4) ROGER TOWNSHEND II

(i) Career

Since he was born by 1478, Roger II was about 18 years old when he entered Lincoln's Inn on 10 July 1496.[162] Although it is not much to go on, we can gain a glimpse of his life as a law student from a memorandum book which he kept while he studied at the inn.[163] Among his expenses were small sums he disbursed for 'boat hire', and he must have regularly travelled across or along the river.[164] It is impossible to know whether these trips were for business or pleasure, but he certainly had time to enjoy himself. He always went out drinking on Fridays, and not infrequently on other days as well, a practice from which he did not abstain during Lent.[165] Nevertheless he probably worked conscientiously enough, for he owned several legal textbooks, some of which he lent out to his fellow students.[166] We also know that he bought books, because in early 1500 he recorded paying 2s. 8d. for a printed book *des arbriggementes*.[167] Unfortunately, the memorandum book tells us very little about life within the inn itself. Roger probably shared a chamber there with another student, as he refers to his 'bedfellawe'. He also attended commons for which he paid a fee to the steward of the inn. On another occasion he contributed to a 'reader's supper'.[168]

The reader was an established member of the inn elected to deliver

his most regular social contacts were with the lesser gentry and upper yeomanry within his immediate locality: 'Studying a Small Community in North Norfolk', seminar paper delivered at Oxford in Oct. 1988.
[161] Cf. the similar situation in Derbyshire: Wright, *Derbyshire Gentry*, 54–5.
[162] LI *Admissions*, 28; LI *Black Books*, 128, 146.   [163] R58, RT II memo-book.
[164] Ibid., fos. 8ᵛ, 9ᵛ.   [165] Ibid., fos. 8 ff.   [166] Ibid., fo. 3ᵛ.
[167] A book of abridgements; probably a collection of abridged statutes: ibid., fo. 9ᵛ.
[168] R58, RT II memo-book, fos. 8ʳ, 1ʳ, 2ᵛ, 4ᵛ, 8ᵛ.

a 'reading' or course of lectures to the students. Those chosen to read had reached an important landmark in their legal career. Having given their first reading they could be admitted to the bench, the governing body of the society, and it was from among the benchers of the inns of court that men were selected to fill the country's top legal posts.[169] The extant records of Lincoln's Inn show that Roger II never gave a reading and did not become a bencher.[170] Perhaps this was a matter of deliberate choice on his part since, as an established gentleman, he was not required to make his own way in the world to the same extent as his father. In any case, failure to attain a place on the ruling body of an inn of court did not preclude a successful career on a lower rung of the professional ladder. It was as a *legisperitus* that Roger persuaded the Norwich magistrates in the summer of 1509 to refer a case of riot to the next assizes.[171] A few years later a Norfolk priory granted him a rent-free lease of lands in Raynham in return for his past and future legal counsel.[172] In 1519 he was appointed one of the attorneys of Norwich Priory during one of its many disputes with the city's authorities.[173] Since 1504 he had regularly been appointed to gaol-delivery commissions and in the early 1540s served on several commissions of oyer et terminer for Norfolk and other eastern counties.[174] By 1525 he received over £18 annually in fees from two peers, a Cambridge college, and several religious institutions, although some of these were for offices like estate stewardships which were not strictly legal.[175] His expertise was respected by Thomas Howard, the third duke of Norfolk, who summoned him and other lawyers with a seat on the Norfolk bench when he needed advice on county affairs.[176] Roger's legal abilities must also have helped him to

---

[169] E. W. Ives, 'Promotion in the Legal Profession of Yorkist and Early Tudor England', *LQR* 75 (1959), 349.

[170] LI *Black Books*.

[171] *Records of the City of Norwich*, ed. W. Hudson and J. C. Tingey, 2 vols. (Norwich, 1906–10), i. 307.

[172] R60, 'Raynham Deeds, 1413–1546', indenture of 17 Feb. 1514 between him and the prior of Hempton.

[173] *CAD*, vol. v, no. A12,527.

[174] *CPR* and *LP*, *passim*.

[175] All these offices and retainers appear to have been confined to Norfolk. Peers: earl of Arundel and Henry, Lord Morley; priories: Norwich, Walsingham, West Acre, Binham, Lynn, Flitcham, Pentney, Coxford, and Horsham St Faith. He was also steward for the Norfolk properties of Christ's College, Cambridge, and a college of priests at Pontefract, Yorkshire: R31, RT II estate book, fo. 39ᵛ. For the latter see *VCH, Yorks.*, iii. 318–19.

[176] PRO, SP1/106/83 (*LP*, vol. xi, no. 470).

become a royal councillor, because by 1526 he was a member of the Council Learned in the Law. A few years later he sat as a councillor in the Court of Requests.[177] He nevertheless found his true *métier* in administering Norfolk, a task for which he was on one occasion commended to the king himself by Thomas Cromwell.[178] His career was, in short, primarily that of a valued royal agent in his county.

Roger II had a long life; he died in his early seventies on 25 November 1551, having outlived both his eldest son and his grandson.[179] His longevity suggests he usually enjoyed good health, though by the late 1540s he was affected by illness and had delegated much of the day-to-day running of his estate to his son Thomas.[180] He was still a minor when Roger I died, but the crown's rights of wardship, if it chose to exercise them, extended only to his person. He was already married and Roger I had been careful to place all his land in trust.[181] Whether he ever did become a royal ward is unknown. In any event, his mother, with her life interest in most of the estate, ran the family's affairs until her death on 5 September 1499.[182]

Not all of Roger's early career was spent at Lincoln's Inn since he spent a part of it in the royal household. He joined the funeral procession of Henry VII as an esquire of the body,[183] and presumably it was at court that he met Edmund Dudley. In December 1508 he agreed that John, his eldest son, should marry Helena Ashburnham, one of Dudley's nieces, and Dudley subsequently paid over a substantial part of Helena's marriage portion to him. As a result, Henry VIII made certain unknown demands of him after Dudley's fall, though, fortunately for Roger, these were waived in 1512.[184]

By 1533 Roger was a knight of the body, but the extent to which

---

[177] PRO, SP1/59/77 (*LP*, vol. iv, pt. iii, app. 67); BL, Lansdowne 12 (57), fo. 125[r].

[178] PRO, SP1/84/70 (*LP*, vol. vii, no. 694).

[179] His heir was his great-grandson, another Roger: PRO, C142/96/32.

[180] PRO, C1/1277/50; LSE, R (SR) 1,032, 88,918; R33, 'Raynhams, deeds 1515-93', deed of 18 Oct. 1550. He had dental problems, however, as a young man: R58, RT II memo-book, fo. 8[v].

[181] *CIPM, Henry VII*, vol. i, nos. 1,028, 1,136, 1,143. It seems to have been accepted at this date that even if a tenant-in-chief had alienated all his lands to trustees and had then declared his will (as had Roger I), the crown retained its right of wardship of the body and marriage of the heir: J. M. W. Bean, *The Decline of English Feudalism, 1215-1540* (Manchester, 1968), 251.

[182] *CIPM, Henry VII*, vol. ii, no. 493. Roger II gained control of his inheritance the following Michaelmas: R58, RT II memo-book, fo. 1[r].

[183] *LP*, vol. i, pt. i, no. 20.

[184] Ibid., no. 1,123. By early 1509 Roger had received £100 from Dudley, an instalment of £266. 13*s*. 4*d*. which was owed: R31, RT II estate book, fo. 5[r].

he had attended court during the interim is unclear.[185] It was perhaps as a courtier that he stood surety for George Neville, Lord Burgavenny, in 1522.[186] His court career must have had a bearing on the appointments of his son Robert as Queen Jane Seymour's attorney and his son Roger as a royal chaplain in the 1530s, and it seems to have had some influence on his choice of associates, but his attendance there was not continuous.[187] He always remained on its fringes, for he never achieved access to the privy chamber. He was a crown servant but certainly never an intimate.

His administrative career began in February 1501 when he joined the Norfolk bench. He remained a justice of the peace until he became sheriff of Norfolk and Suffolk in November 1511. He was then absent from all the known peace commissions until that enrolled on 23 February 1524.[188] Two years of this absence are accounted for by his time as sheriff—he held the office again in 1518/19 and in 1526—because sheriffs were excluded from the bench.[189] He does not appear to have left the country during this period: although he provided men for the fleet he cannot, as claimed, have served in person in the campaigns of 1512 or 1513. He was, in any case, sheriff during the first campaign.[190] He seems to have been a justice of the peace again by 1521, though there are no surviving enrolments for the Norfolk bench between 1515 and 1524.[191] At the very least we are left with a gap of about five years when he was apparently absent from the bench. It is impossible to prove that this was connected with a pardon he obtained in July 1514.[192] If he had incurred disgrace it was insufficient to prevent either his appointment as a subsidy commissioner or to a gaol-delivery panel during these unexplained years.[193]

---

[185] BL, Royal MS 7 F. XIV. 100, fo. 129. This list of household officers is misdated by *LP*, vol. ii, pt. i, no. 2,735.

[186] *LP*, vol. iii, pt. ii, no. 2,712.

[187] *LP*, vol. xvii, no. 220 (87); vol. xii, pt. ii, no. 617.

[188] MacCulloch, *Suffolk*, app. II; PRO, *Lists and Indexes*, ix. 88.

[189] Ibid., *Proceedings Before the Justices of the Peace in the Fourteenth and Fifteenth Centuries*, ed. B. H. Putnam (London, 1938), p. lxxxi.

[190] He supplied twelve men in 1512 and thirty in 1513: PRO, E36/2/4; PRO, E101/62/17. The claim, made in *HP*, iii. 470, reads too much from *LP* entries (vol. i, pt. i, nos. 1,453, 1,661) which do not in fact prove that he served in person, only that he supplied men. My thanks are due to Dr S. Gunn for his helpful comments on this problem.

[191] PRO, SP1/22/202–3 (*LP*, vol. iii, pt. i, no. 1,356); PRO, SP1/233/56 (*LP*, Addenda, pt. i, no. 319); MacCulloch, *Suffolk*, app. II.

[192] PRO, C67/62/1.

[193] *HP*, iii. 470; *LP*, vol. ii, pt. ii, no. 2,554.

From 1524 onwards, however, Sir Roger Townshend (as he now was) served continuously on the bench until his death.[194] The circumstances of his knighthood are unknown. He was distrained several times during the first decade of the sixteenth century but had refused the honour, which he finally received in late 1520 or early 1521.[195] Keeping the king solvent was one of his most important duties in the early 1520s. The government evidently trusted him since he was selected to administer in Norfolk Wolsey's 'general proscription' of 1522/3.[196] Shortly afterwards he and other commissioners assessed the local populace for the subsidy granted to the king in 1523.[197] He was again a subsidy commissioner, and a collector of benevolences, later in life.[198] He also served on other commissions: it is no surprise that he was often a commissioner of sewers, for some of his lands lay near the fens. On two occasions he wrote a joint letter—with the duke of Suffolk in 1528 and the duke of Norfolk in 1538—to express concern about sea-flooding in the fens, potentially serious because of the threat to crops.[199]

He had become linked with the Howards some considerable time before 1538, quite possibly as one of their legal advisers. As early as 1509 they sent him gifts of venison from their deer park at Framlingham and in 1512 Nicholas Appleyard, the earl of Surrey's servant, made him one of his trustees, along with Surrey himself and several other Howards and Howard men.[200] Among his own trustees in the same period were Sir Edward and Edmund Howard.[201] He

---

[194] MacCulloch, *Suffolk*, app. II.

[195] PRO, E198/4/38; E198/4/19; E198/4/20; E198/4/26. Still an esquire on 20 Nov. 1520 but a knight by 31 May 1521: R38, loose deed; R50, 'Cawston'.

[196] *LP*, vol. iv, pt. i, no. 214; R50, a booklet of Roger II's containing loan assessments for Lynn and nine hundreds in west Norfolk, a hitherto undiscovered source for the loan (see App. 2, below). The commissioners for the loan were chosen carefully by the government: J. J. Goring, 'The General Proscription of 1522', *EHR* 86 (1971), 685; *The County Community Under Henry VIII*, ed. J. Cornwall, Rutland Rec. Soc., 1 (1980), 3.

[197] PRO, E179/150/207; E179/151/325; E179/150/221; E179/150/251; E179/150/253.

[198] PRO, subsidy rolls (E179) for Norfolk; *LP*, vol. xx, pt. i, no. 623 (viii); vol. xxi, pt. i, no. 970 (32).

[199] *LP*, vol. iv, pt. ii, no. 3,883; vol. xiii, pt. i, no. 690.

[200] BL, Add. MS 27,451, fos. 13, 19; City of London Record Office, Hustings Roll 231, no. 21. I am grateful to Susan Vokes for these references.

[201] R19, 'N & S CREAKE Temp. HEN. VIII', deed of 20 Mar. 1512; R28, 'RAYNHAM HENRY VIII-PHILIP & MARY', deeds of 12 Aug. 1512 and 12 Mar. 1514; R36, 'Stibbard deeds 1512-1601', deed of 14 Sept. 1512.

also farmed the Howard manor and sheep pasture at North Creake and associated with prominent Howard retainers like Sir Philip Tilney during the first quarter of the sixteenth century.[202] But these useful connections did not bind him irrevocably to the family, for he acted against the ducal interest in Suffolk as a government administrator in 1517.[203]

As a leading magistrate of his shire, he inevitably took part in administering the changes brought about at the Reformation. He and his son Robert were appointed commissioners of first fruits and tenths in 1535 and so helped to produce the survey known as the 'Valor Ecclesiasticus'.[204] Later in the same year he was ordered to arrest the prior of Blackfriars, Norwich, who had preached an ambiguous Easter sermon about the king's ecclesiastical supremacy.[205] He also helped to suppress the lesser monasteries of Norfolk and Suffolk. The suppression began in late September 1536 but was interrupted on 6 October when the government, confronted with the Pilgrimage of Grace, ordered the commissioners to suspend their work for fear of provoking more opposition elsewhere.[206] When the rebellions broke out the duke of Norfolk ordered Roger and several other gentlemen to stay in the county to ensure its security, although originally he had been commanded to attend the king with fifty men. He guarded Kenninghall with Thomas Howard and Robert Holdich, the duke's steward, and several hundred 'tall fellows'.[207]

Urged on by the duke of Norfolk, the government permitted Roger and his fellow commissioners for the suppression to recommence work the following January.[208] This was both premature and unwise because the Reformation had begun to meet considerable opposition in parts of the county, opposition which challenges assumptions that traditional Catholicism had little part to play in the Norfolk unrest of this period.[209] The most serious signs of unrest occurred in the spring

[202] PRO, WARD7/6/68 (Tilney a Townshend trustee); PRO, PROB11/25, fo. 32 (Roger II appointed overseer of Tilney's will).
[203] See Ch. 2, 1 below.
[204] *LP*, vol. viii, no. 149; *Valor Ecclesiasticus*, ed. J. Caley and J. Hunter, 6 vols. (London, 1810-34), vol. iii, pp. i-ii, 369, 494.
[205] PRO, SP1/84/70 (*LP*, vol. vii, no. 694); *LP*, vol. viii, no. 67.
[206] PRO, SP5/2/247-58 (*LP*, vol. xii, pt. i, no. 455); *LP*, vol. xi, nos. 261, 774; vol. xii, pt. i, no. 231.
[207] *LP*, vol. xi, nos. 580, 659.
[208] *LP*, vol. xii, pt. ii, no. 32; PRO, SP5/2/257-9 (*LP*, vol. xii, pt. i, no. 455).
[209] e.g. M. H. and R. Dodds, *The Pilgrimage of Grace, 1536-1537, and the Exeter Conspiracy, 1538*, 2 vols. (Cambridge, 1915), i. 177; MacCulloch, *Suffolk*, 299.

of 1537 at Walsingham, the famous pilgrimage centre. Here two local yeomen employed as lay choristers by Walsingham Priory, Ralph Rogerson and George Guisborough, began recruiting followers for a revolt. By playing an important part in forestalling them, Roger II helped to prevent a major East Anglian uprising a decade before Ket's Rebellion (Elton has described what is now known as the Walsingham Conspiracy as the 'most serious plot hatched anywhere south of the Trent' during the troubled 1530s)[210] and performed his greatest service to the Tudor dynasty.[211]

The Walsingham men already had bitter agrarian grievances against the gentry, and these combined potently with their opposition to the Dissolution which precipitated their attempted revolt. In Norfolk, particularly in the west of the county, the gentry monopolized large-scale sheep-farming. This need not have created social tensions, had not the substantial sheep-farmers abused their privileges (in the west these were bound up with the local foldcourse custom), overrode tenants' customary rights, and threatened their livelihoods. Significantly, the Walsingham men complained that the 'gentylmen of the countrys [sic] have don them greett wrongs and taken awaye theyr lyvyngs'.[212]

It is not surprising that their grievances gave rise to a bitter anti-gentry animus, nor that they expressed a desire to 'put don the gentilmen',[213] but, already inspired by the Pilgrimage of Grace,[214] they were provoked into action by the suppression of the lesser monasteries. Although Walsingham Priory itself was in fact one of the greater religious houses and therefore not liable for suppression at this time, the would-be rebels preferred to believe a rumour to the contrary.[215] As for the secular clergy among them or among their active sympathizers, they were undoubtedly motivated by wild rumours concerning the fate of parochial religion which abounded in

---

[210] G. R. Elton, *Policy and Police: The Enforcement of the Reformation in the Age of Thomas Cromwell* (Cambridge, 1972), 144.

[211] I deal with the affair more fully in my 'The Walsingham Conspiracy of 1537', *Historical Research*, 63 (1990), 29–43.

[212] PRO, SP1/119/34 (*LP*, vol. xii, pt. i, no. 1,056).

[213] PRO, SP1/119/35 (*LP*, vol. xii, pt. i, no. 1,056).

[214] A rebel bill circulated Walsingham and other Norfolk towns at the time of the Pilgrimage, and the Walsingham men were said to have planned to march north to help the defeated northern rebels: *LP*, vol. xi, no. 1,260; Dodds, *Pilgrimage of Grace*, i. 327–8; PRO, SP1/119/36 (*LP*, vol. xii, pt. i, no. 1,056).

[215] PRO, SP1/119/37 (*LP*, vol. xii, pt. i, no. 1,056 (2)).

Norfolk as well as other parts of the country.[216]

The Walsingham conspirators planned to raise the countryside by firing the coastal beacons and taking over the administration of the local musters. After assembling they intended to seize control of strategically important bridges on the London road and the town of Lynn, the gateway to the north and west, and to march into Suffolk to rally the populace. The gentry were to be captured and their property taken; those who resisted would be killed. They did not see themselves as rebels against the Crown: they were acting for the 'commonwealth' by raising a company that would bring their grievances to the attention of the king.[217]

Over twenty men, predominantly yeomen and husbandmen, but also several clergy, including the subprior of Walsingham, Nicholas Mileham, were finally involved in planning the rebellion, but they were betrayed at the end of April 1537 by one of those they tried to recruit, a servant of Sir John Heydon, before they could put their plan into effect. Heydon contacted Roger II and they began immediately to make arrests, Cromwell dispatching his agent Richard Southwell from London to assist them. By the middle of May they and other magistrates had rounded up most of the ringleaders and imprisoned them in Norwich Castle.[218] At the end of the month the leading conspirators were executed in batches, eleven men in all, at Norwich, Yarmouth, Walsingham, and Lynn. In the aftermath of the executions various people unwise enough to utter words of sympathy for the dead men were dealt with, and further investigations revealed the names of several men not hitherto suspected of involvement in the affair. They were promptly arrested.[219]

Roger II continued to enforce the Reformation for the rest of his life. A year after the Walsingham affair the duke of Norfolk commended him to Cromwell for apprehending a former friar who denied the royal supremacy.[220] In 1546 he arrested a shoemaker who broke

---

[216] *LP*, vol. viii, no. 518; vol. xii, pt. i, no. 1,316.

[217] PRO, SP1/119/36-7 (*LP*, vol. xii, pt. i, no. 1,056); PRO, KB9/538/8.

[218] PRO, SP1/119/30, 29 (*LP*, vol. xii, pt. i, nos. 1,045(2), 1,045); PRO, SP1/119/33-8 (*LP*, vol. xii, pt. i, no. 1,056); PRO, SP1/119/51 (*LP*, vol. xii, pt. i, no. 1,063); PRO, SP1/120/24 (*LP*, vol. xii, pt. i, no. 1,171); PRO, KB9/538/4-8; PRO, SP1/120/224-7 (*LP*, vol. xii, pt. i, no. 1,300).

[219] PRO, SP1/120/224-7 (*LP*, vol. xii, pt. i, no. 1,300); PRO, SP1/120/230 (*LP*, vol. xii, pt. i, no. 1,300); PRO, KB9/538/8; PRO, SP1/121/70-2; SP1/121/85-9 (*LP*, vol. xii, pt. ii, no. 56; vol. xii, pt. ii, no. 68).

[220] BL, Cleo., E IV, fo. 102 (*Original Letters Illustrative of English History*, ed. H. Ellis, 3 series, 11 vols. (London, 1824-46), 1st ser. ii. 85-9).

a recent act restricting the reading of the scriptures in the vernacular and which forbade women and the lower orders reading the Bible.[221] He also served on both the Henrician and the Edwardian chantry commissions and took the opportunity to buy from the Crown the yearly rent of a chantry which his father had founded.[222]

His own religious attitudes are unclear. It is most unlikely that he participated in the Dissolution as a convinced reformer although he benefited materially from it.[223] In his younger days he seems to have been pious in a conventional manner, since he commonly inscribed 'IHS' or 'Maria' at the top of many of the pages of his notebooks, and, ironically, made oblations to the shrine at Walsingham.[224] On the eve of the Reformation he was steward of at least four local priories, including Walsingham, yet he was active in the Dissolution.[225] His clerical son, another Roger, associated with some of the most prominent reformers of the day, and at least two of the local clergy with whom he himself was on friendly terms in his later years, the rectors of East Raynham and Shereford, David Moresby and Humphrey Wilson, appear to have inclined towards reform.[226] Roger II's will might be described as 'Protestant', because he sought no masses or saintly intercessions.[227] On the other hand, he associated with the 'conservative' Howards for much of his life, believed as a commissioner for the suppression that Pentney Priory deserved sparing, and sympathized with Princess Mary to the extent of sending her a gift of forty sheep in 1548 while she was at Kenninghall.[228] He himself was probably not quite sure of what he believed in an atmosphere of

[221] *Records of the City of Norwich*, ii. 172; *Statutes of the Realm*, iii. 894–7 (34 & 35 Hen. VIII, c. 1).
[222] *LP*, vol. xxi, pt. i, no. 30; *CPR* (1548–9), 136.
[223] See Ch. 4, 1 and App. 6 below.
[224] e.g. NRO, Townshend 193 MS 1,612 1 C7; R22, 1498/9–1508/9 manorial account roll ('Easthall' in Stanhoe).
[225] *Valor Ecclesiasticus*, iii. 388, 391, 393, 395.
[226] Moresby, rector of East Raynham by 1533 (R60, 1533 East Raynham rectory court roll) was a frequent trustee and witnessed Roger's will: PRO, C142/96/32; NRO, NCC 31 Lyncolne. Wilson, rector of Shereford by 1547, Roger's estate auditor by 1549, was, like Moresby, one of his trustees: G. Baskerville, 'Married Clergy and Pensioned Religious in Norwich Diocese, 1555', *EHR* 48 (1933), 51; NRO, Townshend 163 MS 1,582 1 D4, fo. 42ʳ; PRO, C142/96/32. Both men were deprived in 1555 for being married priests: Baskerville, 'Married Clergy', 51.
[227] NRO, NCC 31 Lyncolne.
[228] M. D. Knowles, *The Religious Orders in England*, 3 vols. (Cambridge, 1948–59), iii. 481–2; LSE, R(SR) 1,032, 88,918 (1544/5–1547/8 Townshend sheep accounts), fos. 27ʳ, 28ʳ, 32ᵛ.

sometimes rapid and no-doubt bewildering change. The reminiscences of a minister of the established church from Elizabethan Yorkshire, Michael Sherbrock, may enable us to understand the likely position of Roger and many like him as far as the Reformation was concerned. Sherbrock wrote that he once questioned his father's motives for helping to pillage a local abbey after the Dissolution. His father replied that he had not been opposed to the old religion, but that he took part in the assault against it so that he might share some of the spoils which others would have taken if he had not.[229] In other words, he did not challenge what he saw as a *fait accompli*. In a similar fashion Roger accepted each new religious development as it came; such conformity fits what we know of him as an administrator.

Roger must be regarded as a conformist as a knight of the shire for Norfolk in the Reformation Parliament of 1529–36, and he sent gifts of wildfowl to Thomas Cromwell while it sat.[230] He later represented his county in the parliaments of 1536 and 1542.[231] Conformist though he may have been, he was not a nonentity as a member of the Commons house. The common council of the City of London would otherwise hardly have solicited his support for a bill to cleanse the Fleet ditch in January 1542, just after the first session of his last parliament had opened.[232]

He had sufficient resources to secure his own election to parliament by 1529, but as a trusted royal servant[233] he could also have counted on the support of the government and the duke of Norfolk. His Howard ties were, if anything, stronger in the second half of Henry VIII's reign; MacCulloch calls him a Howard 'henchman'.[234] He was in the duke's party which attended Anne of Cleves on her way to London in 1539, and by 1546 his grandson Richard (by then his heir-apparent) resided at Kenninghall as a member of the ducal household.[235]

---

[229] J.J. Scarisbrick, *The Reformation and the English People* (Oxford, 1984), 70.

[230] *HP*, iii. 470–1; NRO, B–L VII b(3), fo. 42[r].

[231] *HP*, iii. 470–1.

[232] City of London Record Office, rep. 10, fo. 242[v]. They also sought the support of three other lawyers: John Caryll, Richard Catlyn, and Sir Richard Pollard, the first and last of whom were distinguished crown servants: *HP*, i. 590, 593–4; iii. 122–3. The bill was read once (in the Lords) but got no further: H. Miller, 'London and Parliament in the Reign of Henry VIII', *BIHR* 35 (1962), 145.

[233] Still a councillor in 1538: *LP*, vol. xiii, pt. ii, no. 34.

[234] D.N.J. MacCulloch, 'Kett's Rebellion in Context', *PP* 84 (1979), 54.

[235] *LP*, vol. xiv, pt. ii, no. 572; PRO, E179/151/333.

He nevertheless escaped the consequences of the duke of Norfolk's disgrace in 1546/7 by the simple, if cynical, expedient of taking part in the destruction of his son, the earl of Surrey, once the factional infighting at court had made inevitable the Howards' downfall. One of the commissioners appointed to inquire into the trespasses the earl had supposedly committed in Norfolk, he helped summon the jury which indicted him at Norwich.[236] Other Howard men behaved in a similar fashion. Sir Richard Southwell took part in the denunciations at court and Sir Edmund Knyvet, the duke's nephew, testified against Surrey. The petty jury at the trial contained several erstwhile Howard followers.[237] If Roger's main concern was to earn the confidence of the new Edwardian regime he succeeded, because he retained his place on the bench and remained a royal councillor.[238] He was not, however, usually involved in the manœuvrings of the great; combating the seditions of lesser men occupied far more of his time.

From the government's point of view he and his fellows generally performed with commendable efficiency, but Ket's Rebellion caught them out while they were divided among themselves. Roger was no less guilty than many others in taking part in the squabbles of Edwardian Norfolk, and he continued a quarrel with Nicholas Le Strange after the rising was crushed.[239] Most of the gentry were powerless to act effectively against the rebels, although in his case he had the excuse of old age and sickness.[240] As Ket approached Norwich the city sent messages to Raynham and to Sir William Paston at Oxnead seeking help. Paston sent two cannon to aid its defence, but there is no record of how Roger responded.[241] He had in any case too many problems of his own, because he was certainly affected by the rebellion. Ket exercised his greatest influence over a fifteen-to-twenty-mile radius around Norwich and trouble occurred on three of the Townshends' most easterly manors.[242] At Guist and Scarning several of Roger's tenants joined the rebels but events at Heydon were far more serious. There the whole parish rose up, seized the banner from the parish church, and marched to join the rebels on

[236] *LP*, vol. xxi, pt. ii, no. 697.

[237] S. E. Lehmberg, *The Later Parliaments of Henry VIII 1536–1547* (Cambridge, 1977), 233–4; *LP*, vol. xxi, pt. ii, no. 697.

[238] MacCulloch, *Suffolk*, app. II; *CPR* (1548–9), 309.

[239] PRO, SP10/8/60.

[240] He was ill in mid-1549: PRO, C1/1277/50.

[241] F. W. Russell, *Kett's Rebellion in Norfolk* (London, 1859), 32, 76.

[242] S. K. Land, *Kett's Rebellion* (Ipswich, 1977), 100.

Mousehold Heath.[243] Inside Norwich itself the house of his son
Robert was broken into and looted.[244] Although the camp at
Mousehold became the focus of attention, rebels were active in the
west of the county. A camp in north-west Norfolk appears to have
been set up at Downham Market after an initial attempt to establish
one at Castle Rising failed.[245] A list of men pardoned in 1550 for
their part in the rising shows that several came from the Burnham
parishes a few miles north of East Raynham. A couple of others came
from Great Massingham and Houghton near Harpeley just to the
west of Raynham, and a third from Great Ryburgh immediately to
the east. Another rebel, a husbandman, came from Tittleshall, right
on Roger's doorstep.[246] Not surprisingly he felt insecure at Raynham
and sought the sanctuary of King's Lynn.[247]

Roger won no glory during the rebellion but lost no credit with the
central government. The rebellions of 1549 were used to justify
Somerset's overthrow, and the new regime kept confidence in men
like him, perhaps partly because they realized that the gentry across
the country had usually disliked the Protector's social and agrarian
reforms.[248] A few months before his death it appointed Roger one of
its joint-lieutenants for Norfolk, a fitting conclusion to the career of
one of the county's most dedicated administrators.[249]

(ii) Family

Roger II had at least six sons and two daughters by his wife Amy.
Like him she enjoyed a long life, predeceasing him by only four
months.[250] Compared with her formidable mother-in-law, Amy
seems a colourless figure, but it would be unwise to assume a lack of
character from a lack of evidence. Nearly as little is known of their
eldest son, John. Born during the 1490s, he was still a minor when he
married Eleanor, the daughter of Sir John Heydon, in late 1511 or
early 1512. As part of the marriage contract Roger agreed to settle

[243] NRO, Townshend 159 MS 1,578 1 D4, fos. 20, 28, 38ᵛ.
[244] PRO, CP40/1152, rot. 111.
[245] MacCulloch, 'Kett's Rebellion', 40.
[246] *CPR* (1549–51), 328–9.
[247] NRO, Townshend 163 MS 1,582 1 D4, fo. 24ʳ.
[248] B. L. Beer, *Rebellion and Riot* (Kent, Ohio, 1982), 128, 178, 211–12; M. L. Bush,
The Government Policy of Protector Somerset (London, 1975), 98–9.
[249] *APC*, iii. 376.
[250] On 25 July 1551: PRO, C142/96/37, C142/98/70.

three manors on the couple. John thereby became a landowner worth £40 per annum.[251] In 1522 the earl of Surrey retained him to serve in France, so presumably he took part in the earl's pointless *chevauchée* of that year.[252] He settled on the family's manor at Brampton in Suffolk where he died on 4 August 1540. He lived to see Richard, the eldest of his three sons, marry Katherine, the daughter and heir of the prominent Essex lawyer Humphrey Browne, a match which enhanced further the Townshends' legal connections.[253] Richard must have served Princess Mary after the fall of the duke of Norfolk, because he died at Kenninghall in July 1551, the victim of a 'dangerous sickness', a few months before his grandfather.[254]

The marriages of Roger II's daughters, like that of his eldest son, reflected his local standing. Susan, the elder, married Edmund, the eldest son of Sir Thomas Wyndham of Felbrigg, Tudor courtier and naval commander, during the first decade of the sixteenth century.[255] This alliance, which cost Roger 500 marks, was a valuable one because Thomas was able to recover the extensive Norfolk estates which his father, Sir John Wyndham, forfeited as a traitor in 1502.[256] But the Wyndhams were made to pay financially for Sir John's treason; at the end of his life Thomas calculated that he had handed over to the Crown 2,850 marks to redeem the family property.[257] Roger was one of several peers and gentlemen who stood surety for him on various occasions.[258]

Katherine, Roger's younger daughter, was married to Henry, the

[251] BL, Add. MS 41,139, fos. 10ᵛ–11ʳ; R(Attic), 'MARRIAGE SETTLEMENTS, PAPERS, etc.', indenture of 31 Oct. 1511; PRO, E179/150/259; App. 7 below.

[252] PRO, SP1/28/248–9. I am obliged to Susan Vokes for this reference.

[253] PRO, E150/641/41; Dashwood, 307; R(Attic), 'MARRIAGE SETTLEMENTS, PAPERS, etc', indenture of 3 July 1537.

[254] PRO, C142/96/32; NRO, NCC 30 Lyncolne, will of 20 July 1551, proved 9 May 1552. He was dead when Roger II made his will on 31 July: NRO, NCC 31 Lyncolne.

[255] NRO, WKC 3/5, 399 × 4 (indenture of 1542). This deed shows the marriage was agreed when Thomas Wyndham was still an esquire; he was knighted in 1512: *LP*, vol. i, pt. i, nos. 833 (58), 1,471; Rye, *Norfolk Families*, 1,039. They probably married before 1507, during Edmund's minority, because Roger had a share in the Wyndham manors of Wicklewood and Crownthorpe, later part of Susan's jointure, by the beginning of that year: R55, RT II valors, fo. 5ʳ. For Thomas Wyndham, see *DNB* under the entry for Thomas Wyndham, his son by a second wife.

[256] H. A. Wyndham, *A Family History, 1410–1688: The Wyndhams of Norfolk and Somerset*, (London, 1939), 42–3; *Statutes of the Realm*, iii. 61–4.

[257] *Testamenta Vetusta*, ed. N. H. Nicolas, 2 vols. (London, 1826), ii. 587.

[258] e.g. BL, Add. MS 21,480, fo. 46; PRO, E36/214/384, 468.

eldest son and heir of Sir Edmund Bedingfield of Oxborough, by
1535.[259] This was a natural match because the Townshends and
Bedingfields, two of the county's leading families,[260] had long been
on good terms. Sir Edmund's father had been a Townshend trustee,
as were both Sir Edmund and his elder brother Sir Thomas
Bedingfield.[261] In his will dated 1549 Sir Edmund left Roger, his
'good brother and friend', all his goods and chattels not otherwise
assigned. Roger in turn appointed Henry the supervisor of his
will.[262]

Of all his children, Roger's second son Robert enjoyed the most
prominent career. He entered Lincoln's Inn and joined his father on
the Norfolk bench in 1526.[263] He was already an important lawyer
when he was retained (the exact date is unknown) by Queen Jane
Seymour.[264] In June 1540 he was created a serjeant at law and
shortly afterwards became recorder of Lynn.[265] His career culmi-
nated in May 1545 when he was made a justice of Cheshire, Flint,
Denbigh, and Montgomery and knighted.[266] Before he became a
judge Robert was primarily a valued local agent of the Crown in
Norfolk like his father, though he seems to have joined the royal army
which invaded France in 1544.[267] In the 1520s he assisted the
county's subsidy commissioners, and later, as a magistrate, he helped
to administer the Reformation and crush sedition.[268] The duke of
Norfolk once commended his usefulness to Cromwell: 'Would that the
king had three or four such as Master Townshend in every shire!'[269]
The evidence relating to his private legal practice suggests that, like

[259] *HP*, i. 408.

[260] In the early 1520s the Bedingfields held at least £400-worth of lands: PRO,
E179/150/251.

[261] e.g. R49, Townshend cartulary, fos. 43–4; R19, 'N & S CREAKE Temp. HEN. VIII'
and R36, 'Stibbard deeds 1512–1601', 2 deeds of 1512; R28, 'RAYNHAM HENRY VIII–
PHILIP & MARY', 2 deeds of 1514; PRO, C142/96/32. Sir Edmund succeeded his
brother in Mar. 1538: PRO, C142/61/5, 9.

[262] PRO, PROB11/36, fos. 142–3; NRO, NCC 31 Lyncolne. Edmund in fact
outlived Roger, dying in 1553.

[263] LI, *Admissions*, 36 (adm. 4 May 1515); *LP*, vol. iv, pt. i, no. 2,002.

[264] Grant of 19 Mar. 1542 referring to Robert as 'late attorney' of the late Queen
Jane: *LP*, vol. xvii, no. 220 (87).

[265] LI *Black Books*, 256; H. Le Strange, *Norfolk Official Lists* (Norwich, 1890), 200.

[266] *LP*, vol. xx, pt.-i, nos. 836, 846 (67, 80, 81); Shaw, *Knights*, ii. 57.

[267] *LP*, vol. xix, pt. i, no. 274.

[268] PRO, E179/150/221, 251; *LP*, vol. viii, no. 149; PRO, SP1/106/183 (*LP*,
vol. xi, no. 470); *LP*, vol. xiii, pt. ii, no. 554; *Original Letters*, 3rd ser. iii. 162 (*LP*,
vol. xv, no. 86).

[269] *LP*, vol. xiii, pt. ii, no. 554.

Roger I, he benefited from the misfortunes of the impecunious. He was probably the 'Master Townshend' who acted as an adviser to the bankrupt heir of William Ellis, baron of the Exchequer, in 1534.[270] In the same period he acquired an interest in the estate of Arthur Uvedale of Wickham, a profligate gentleman with lands in southern England.[271]

Robert married Alice, widow of William Curson, and daughter and co-heir of Robert Poppy of Twyford, an obscure Norfolk gentleman, shortly after entering Lincoln's Inn.[272] It was a successful marriage which produced six sons.[273] He died in February 1557 at Ludlow, where he had acquired a lease of the former Austin priory.[274] His father left him only a small portion of the family estate which, because of Roger's longevity, he scarcely had the opportunity to enjoy.[275] Robert's career was therefore mainly that of a self-made man.

George, Roger's third son, married another Alice, the grand-daughter of Sir John Thurston, a London goldsmith with East Anglian connections, in 1536 after obtaining a dispensation for a marriage without preliminary banns.[276] George entered Lincoln's Inn in 1528 and was called to the bar in 1534 but, unlike Robert, he did not advance very far as a lawyer.[277] He misbehaved on several occasions during his time there and was almost expelled for his most serious misdemeanour. This was when he and other students broke into the pantry during a learning vacation in 1530, spilling and

---

[270] *LP*, vol. vi, no. 1,481.

[271] *LP*, vol. xx, pt. ii, no. 1,815; PRO, C1/1078/41; G. L. Gower, 'Notices of the Family of Uvedale', *Surrey Archaeol. Collections*, 3 (1865), 110–11.

[272] PRO, C142/108/69 refers to a no-longer-extant marriage indenture of 1 Oct. 1516.

[273] Spelman's *Reports*, ii. 396. They also had six daughters.

[274] PRO, C142/108/69; PRO, E150/873/4.

[275] See App. 7 below.

[276] Durham, *Townshends*, 26, states that George married Alice, a daughter of Thurston, in 1516, but the latter had no daughter bearing that name. The only possible candidate is Alice, daughter of his son and heir Richard Thurston, a London broiderer. George and Alice received their dispensation in Feb. 1536, and in the same year Roger II settled two of his manors on the couple: PRO, PROB11/20, fos. 181–3, 183ᵛ–185ᵛ; PROB11/21, fo. 6; *Faculty Office Registers, 1534–1549*, ed. D. S. Chambers (Oxford, 1966), 41; PRO, WARD 7/6/68; App. 7 below. George's reasons for acquiring the dispensation must remain a subject of speculation. Banns allowed any possible objections to a marriage to be made in good time and helped ensure that individuals married according to the wishes of friends and parents: R. A. Houlbrooke, *The English Family, 1450–1700* (London, 1984), 86. Perhaps the imminent prospect of a bastard child meant that they were in a hurry to marry.

[277] LI *Admissions*, 44; LI *Black Books*, 239.

spoiling the wine stored there which no doubt they had intended to steal. The governors thereupon insisted that each member of the inn should reveal under oath what they knew of the crime. George was one of several who refused to take the oath, despite being threatened with expulsion. Fortunately, two former members of Lincoln's Inn, the king's serjeants Robert Norwich and Thomas Willoughby, interceded on behalf of the culprits, and George was allowed to pay a fine of 5 marks instead.[278] George never attained any distinction but he took a minor part in county affairs, witnessing the suppression of West Acre Priory in 1538 and participating in the Norfolk shire election of 1547.[279]

The next son, another Roger, entered the Church. He was a typical ecclesiastical careerist who used his canon-law training as a stepping-stone to preferment. Already a Cambridge graduate when instituted to the family livings at Heydon and Salle in 1523, he obtained his doctorate in canon law and was admitted to Doctors' Commons, the society of advocates, ten years later.[280] Cranmer noticed that he was a man of ability and sought his attendance a few months after he became a doctor. Associated with the archbishop in investigating a case of alleged heresy in 1535, he was appointed a royal chaplain in 1537.[281]

He had other official duties, because in the last few years of his life he worked in the Faculty Office. This department, established by the Dispensations Act of 1533 (25 Henry VIII, c. 21), was under the dual control of the archbishop of Canterbury and the Chancery, and replaced the Roman Curia in its role of granting various dispensations and licences to both clergy and laity. In the case of the laity the most important dispensations from the canon law related to marriage, and it was from the Faculty Office that George Townshend acquired his licence to marry without banns.[282] But once the Dissolution had

---

[278] Ibid., 228–9. George did not lack friends, because the fine was reduced to 20s. after further intercessions, this time from William Sulyard.

[279] *LP*, vol. xiii, pt. i, no. 85; PRO, C219/19/64.

[280] *Grace Book B*, ed. M. Bateson, 2 vols. (Cambridge, 1903–5), vol. ii. 87, 94 (adm. BA 14 Dec. 1520); Blomefield, vi. 249, viii. 274; C. H. and T. Cooper, *Athenae Cantabrigiensis*, 3 vols. (Cambridge, 1858–1913), i. 531–2. Also rector of North Creake by 1535 and Lydd, Kent, by his death: *Valor Ecclesiasticus*, iii. 372; PRO, PROB11/27, fos. 169ᵛ–170).

[281] *LP*, vol. vi, no. 681; vol. viii, no. 1,063; vol. xii, pt. ii, no. 617.

[282] PRO, PROB11/27, fos. 169ᵛ–70; *Statutes of the Realm*, iii. 672–3; *Faculty Office Registers*, pp. xi ff., 41.

begun Roger was kept busy sealing and dispatching a 'great number of capacities' permitting former inmates of suppressed religious houses to acquire secular benefices or to leave religion altogether.[283]

Little is known about the early working of the Faculty Office, but it is almost certain that by 1536 Roger headed the department as 'master of the faculties'.[284] It is perhaps significant that the earliest recorded appointment as master in Cranmer's register is that of Dr Nicholas Wotton in October 1538, the month in which Roger died.[285] Roger may well, in fact, have been the original appointee to the post when the office was established, rather than Edmund Bonner, later bishop of London, as is traditionally thought.[286]

Roger himself benefited from the dispensations system. Already a non-resident pluralist,[287] in August 1537 he paid a fee of £20 to the Faculty Office to have licence to acquire another benefice, provided that his total annual income from his benefices did not exceed £300 as a result.[288] His presence in the Faculty Office, like his royal chaplaincy and his brother Robert's service to Jane Seymour, is most significant as another indication of his family's good standing with those at the centre of power. Thomas Cromwell exerted his influence and authority over the faculty administration from its beginning and would surely have approved Roger's appointment.[289]

Roger progressed further in his career in January 1538 when he was collated to a prebend of the cathedral church of Salisbury, and in September he became chancellor of the diocese. Since he died the following month, however, he scarcely had time to exercise the latter office.[290] The bishop of Salisbury at the time was the reformer, Nicholas Shaxton. He and Roger were on close enough terms for Shaxton to risk royal displeasure on his behalf. In 1538 the king censured the bishop for granting him an advowson intended for a

[283] PRO, PROB11/27, fo. 170.
[284] *Faculty Office Registers*, p. xxv.
[285] Ibid. Wotton was appointed on 16 Oct. Roger's will is dated 7 Oct. It was proved on 28 Oct. but he was dead by the 18th: PRO, PROB11/27, fo. 170; J. M. Horn, *Fasti Ecclesiae Anglicanae, 1300–1541*, iii (London, 1962), 19.
[286] *Faculty Office Registers*, p. xxv.
[287] By 1535 he held in Norfolk the rectory of North Creake as well as those at Heydon and Salle, and he subsequently became rector of Lydd, Kent: *Valor Ecclesiasticus*, iii. 356, 361, 372; PRO, PROB11/27, fos. 169ᵛ–170.
[288] *Faculty Office Registers*, 105. For his dispensation George paid the comparatively paltry 10s., the normal fee for a marriage without banns: ibid., 41 and *passim*.
[289] Ibid., pp. xxii–xxiii.
[290] *Fasti Ecclesiae Anglicanae*, 74, 19.

royal nominee. The royal will appears to have prevailed and Roger
was obliged to surrender his grant, although Shaxton protested that
it was wrong to take back what had been given, particularly where a
friend like Dr Townshend was concerned.[291]

Shaxton's religious views were unwelcome to most of the populace
of the city of Salisbury, and it is possible that Roger was appointed
chancellor to assist in the work of reform.[292] Their friendship probably dated from Cambridge when it is likely that Roger associated
with members of the university's reforming circle. Cranmer's
patronage is not the only indication of Roger's reforming sympathies.
The opening lines of his will do not call upon the invocations of the
saints, and in it he stated his belief in justification by faith, as well as
ordering a 'hole bible in englishe' to be placed in each of his parish
churches, an attempt to put into practice one of Cromwell's second
set of Injunctions. It also shows that he bought books from the
Dutch Protestant bookseller, Reyner Wolf.[293] A fellow canon lawyer,
Thomas Thirlby, was a witness to this will. Despite his later record
as a Marian bishop, Thirlby was at this stage in his career also
patronized by Cranmer.[294]

Of all his children, Roger II was perhaps closest to his fifth son,
Thomas, his estate 'supervisor' in his later years. Fatherly affection
may explain why he set aside a greater part of his estate for Thomas
than for his other younger sons.[295] Thomas became an administrator
of some expertise, because he was associated with his nephew, Osbert
Monford, as a purveyor of grain and other foodstuffs for the royal
armies and garrisons in France during the mid-sixteenth century.[296]
He married Elizabeth, daughter of John Calibut of Castle Acre, in
1538/9, and died in 1573.[297]

---

[291] *LP*, vol. xiii, pt. ii, nos. 214, 283.

[292] *DNB* (s.v. Shaxton); Elton, *Policy and Police*, 100–7.

[293] PRO, PROB11/27, fos. 169ᵛ–70. For Wolf see *DNB*, s.v.; A. Pettegree, *Foreign
Protestant Communities in Sixteenth-Century London* (Oxford, 1986), 93–4.

[294] For Thirlby see T. F. Shirley, *Thomas Thirlby, Tudor Bishop* (London, 1964).

[295] Thomas was left lands worth some £60 p.a. His elder brothers, Robert and
George, received about £28- and £43-worth respectively (see App. 7).

[296] *LP*, vol. xx, pt. ii, no. 936; *APC*, ii. 200, 263, iv. 415. Monford married a
daughter of Thomas's elder brother John (Dashwood, 307). For Monford as a purveyor
see R. Tittler and S. Battely, 'The Local Community and the Crown in 1553: The
Accession of Mary Tudor Revisited', *BIHR* 57 (1984), 134–5.

[297] PRO, E150/663/7. Thomas supposedly had an earlier wife, Anne, daughter of
'Richard Southwell of Horsham St Faith'. If this is correct, she would have had to have
been the daughter of Sir Richard Southwell (d. 1564), who obtained Horsham Priory

Giles, the youngest son of Roger and Amy, never married. He entered Lincoln's Inn in 1528, the same year as George, and was useful enough as a lawyer to be appointed to the Norfolk bench in 1542. He was dead by 4 May 1554.[298]

Although Roger II was careful not to make excessive provision for his younger sons from his estate,[299] several of the cadet branches of the family which they founded did remarkably well. Thomas Townshend of Bracon Ash, the eldest son of Robert Townshend (Roger II's second son), was a considerable Norfolk gentleman who, in 1578, entertained Queen Elizabeth in 'a house of some pretensions'.[300] Sir Henry Townshend of Cound, Shropshire (d. 1621), a younger brother of this Thomas, was an administrator of some importance in the Welsh marches and north Wales and the father of Hayward Townshend, the famous Elizabethan parliamentary journalist.[301] The heir of George Townshend (Roger II's third son), John Townshend, married the daughter of Richard Catlyn, a successful Norfolk lawyer, while John's daughter and heiress married a claimant to the earldom of Westmorland.[302] The Townshends show that the younger scions of a gentry house did not inevitably sink below the status enjoyed by their forebears and members of the main line of the family.

(iii) Associates

Roger II's associates included some of the leading East Anglian gentry of the day. Among his feoffees were Sir John Shelton and Sir William Paston, and he performed the same role for Sir Richard Southwell.[303] Other trustees included several prominent East Anglian lawyers

---

from the crown after the Dissolution: Durham, *Townshends*, 27; T. H. Swales, 'The Redistribution of the Monastic Lands in Norfolk at the Dissolution', *NA* 34 (1966), 22.

[298] LI *Admissions*, 44; *LP*, vol. xvii, no. 362 (60); probate copy of will, dated 15 Apr. 1552, proved 4 May 1554 (NRO, B-L VII b(1)).

[299] See App. 7 below.

[300] Durham, *Townshends*, 19.

[301] P. W. Hasler (ed.), *The History of Parliament, 1558–1603*, 3 vols. (London, 1981), iii. 516.

[302] Durham, *Townshends*, 26; *HP*, i. 593–4; *History of Parliament, 1558–1603*, iii. 516.

[303] Shelton: e.g. R50, loose deed of 16 Sept. 1512; PRO, E326/7261; R38, indenture of 18 July 1537 (Townshend-Browne marriage settlement). Paston: e.g. NRO, BRA 926/18 (372 × 8); PRO, E326/7261; R12, 'HELHOUGHTON Temp. HEN. VIII', deed of 19 Mar. 1525; PRO, CP25/2/29/188, no. 21. Southwell: PRO, CP25/2/29/145, no. 31.

(some undoubtedly friends as well as legal advisers),[304] and Howard retainers like Sir Philip Tilney, Nicholas Appleyard, Edward White, and Robert Holdich.[305]

But family ties were important to Roger, and gentlemen like Amy's nephew Anthony Hansard and families like the Bedingfields, Blakeneys, Cresseners, Castells, Wyndhams, and Woodhouses also provided him with suitable trustees. Sir Thomas Woodhouse in particular was almost an automatic choice.[306] As a young man Roger appears to have been particularly close to his brother-in-law, although Woodhouse was many years his senior.[307] Earlier, when a dispute between the Townshends and Sir Thomas Hansard went to arbitration, Woodhouse had represented Roger who was still a minor.[308]

Because he was a member of the early Tudor court, Woodhouse was probably able to help Roger enter the royal household.[309] There are signs that Roger's time at court influenced his choice of trustees in the early sixteenth century. When he made a number of important settlements in 1512 and 1514, perhaps because military service seemed possible, he selected, among others, courtiers like Sir Edward and Edmund Howard, Sir William Sidney, Giles Alington, Anthony Wingfield, John Vere (later fifteenth earl of Oxford), and Charles Brandon, the future duke of Suffolk.[310] Although these men were

---

[304] e.g. William Coningsby, Christopher Heydon, Miles Hobart, Christopher Jenney, Francis Monford, and William Wotton (numerous deeds in Raynham archives). Wotton (d. 1528), a baron of the Exchequer, commended his wife and children to the care of Roger, one of his executors: PRO, PROB11/22, fos. 313–14.

[305] Tilney: PRO, C1/96/32. Appleyard: deeds of 1512 and 1514 in R19, 'N & S CREAKE Temp. HEN. VIII', R36, 'Stibbard deeds 1512–1601', and R28, 'RAYNHAM HENRY VIII–PHILIP & MARY'. White: R(Attic), 'Deeds—Stanhoe & Barwick', deed of 20 June 1525. Holdich: R38, loose deed of 20 Nov. 1520; R12, 'HELHOUGHTON Temp. HEN VIII', deed of 19 Mar. 1525.

[306] Numerous Raynham deeds.

[307] e.g. BL, Add. MS 41,139, fos. 7ᵛ, 20ʳ (bought a horse on Woodhouse's behalf, lent him money, and bought grain with him); BL, Add. MS 21,480, fo. 84ʳ; PRO, E36/214/434 (stood surety for Woodhouse when he was in bond to the king, 1505); NRO, B–L II e, 1501/2–1517/18 Townshend sheep accounts, fo. 134ʳ (gift of sheep). Woodhouse was escheator of Norfolk and Suffolk as early as 1479/80: CFR (1471–85), no. 526; CPR (1476–85), 215.

[308] BL, Add. MS 41,305, fo. 28ʳ; Ch. 3, 1(v) below.

[309] Knight of the Bath, marriage of Prince Arthur, 1501; household knight, funeral of Henry VII: Shaw, *Knights*, i. 147; *LP*, vol. i, pt. i, no. 20 (p. 17); cf. E. W. Ives, 'Court and County Palatine in the Reign of Henry VIII: The Career of William Brereton of Malpas', *Transactions of the Historic Society of Lancashire and Cheshire*, 123 (1972), 1–38.

[310] R28, 'RAYNHAM HENRY VIII–PHILIP & MARY', deeds of 1512 and 1514; R36, 'Stibbard deeds 1512–1601', deed of 1512; R58, 'Raynham Deeds 1492–1527', deed of 1514.

obviously chosen for their connections, he was on good terms with Brandon and his family. Before Brandon became an important royal favourite, he, like Roger, was merely one of ninety-three esquires of the body at the end of Henry VII's reign.[311] They were, therefore, equals when they stood surety for Sir Robert Brandon, Charles's uncle, in 1508.[312] But Roger was left behind on the fringes of the royal court when Charles became a royal intimate. As far as courtiers were concerned, Roger was perhaps closer to Sir Robert Drury, an East Anglian like Brandon.[313] Roger's court and council service apparently had little bearing on his choice of associates later in life. Sir Henry Wyatt was perhaps one of the few exceptions to this rule, though it should be noted that he too had lands in East Anglia.[314] But one should beware of making artificial distinctions, since in any case many of the East Anglian gentry had court links.

Among the East Anglian gentry in general one finds several of Roger's friends. Relations between the Townshends and the Le Stranges had deteriorated by Edward VI's reign, but earlier they were good. Roger was a friend of Robert and John Le Strange, contemporaries of his at Lincoln's Inn, and an executor of their elder brother Sir Roger.[315] The Townshends and various relatives were often guests of Sir Thomas Le Strange, Robert's son, at Hunstanton.[316] Another guest was Sir Edward Knyvet. Knyvet, who died in 1528, had been a contemporary of Roger's at court and made him the supervisor of his will.[317] The 1541 will of William Yelverton of Rougham reveals another friend and trustee. In earlier years Roger had farmed the Yelverton manor at Bayfield and been their household guest.[318]

[311] Gunn, *Brandon*, 39.
[312] *LP*, vol. i, pt. i, no. 447. Roger stood surety for Sir Robert on later occasions.
[313] Acted as a trustee and stood surety for him: *CCR* (1500–9), nos. 911, 990; BL, Add. MS 21,480, fo. 47ᵛ; PRO, E36/214/386. For Drury, see *HP*, ii. 57–8.
[314] A trustee for Wyatt, 1533: *CAD*, vol. iii, no. D.1,165. For Wyatt see *DNB*, s.v. Sir Thomas Wyatt; PRO, SP1/59/77 (*LP*, vol. iv, pt. iii, app. 67).
[315] PRO, SP10/8/60; LI *Black Books*, *passim*; R49, Townshend cartulary, fos. 35ᵛ–36ᵛ and PRO, C142/96/32 (Le Stranges as Roger's trustees); PRO, CP25/2/28/188, no. 25, Carthew, *Launditch*, i. 211–12, PRO, PROB11/17, fos. 165–6 (Roger as a Le Strange trustee); PRO, PROB11/15, fos. 13–15.
[316] *LP*, vol. iv, pt. ii, no. 3,005; 'Extracts from the Household and Privy Purse Expenditure of Le Strange of Hunstanton, 1519–78', ed. D. Gurney, *Archaeologia*, 25 (1834), *passim*. Sir Thomas played cards with Robert, Roger II's son: ibid., 473.
[317] Ibid., 484; *LP*, vol. iv, pt. ii, no. 3,005; vol. i, pt. i, no. 82; vol. iii, pt. i, no. 703; NRO, NCC 22–5 Attmere.
[318] *Testamenta Vetusta*, ii. 716; PRO, C142/96/32; PRO, CP25/2/28/188, no. 10; PRO, E326/7261; PRO, CP25/2/29/190, no. 21; I. S. Leadam, 'The Inquisition of

The will of Thomas Gygges of Burnham, who died in 1506, shows that, like his father, Roger II also had less-exalted friends. Thomas ordered his heir John to be placed in Roger's care if his mother also died during his minority.[319] Some thirty years later John appointed Roger as a trustee for the marriage settlement of his daughter and heir-apparent, Susan Gygges.[320] Other friends of lesser status included various family servants and estate officials. As a young man Roger enjoyed a drink in the company of his bailiff, Thomas Faukener. At the end of his life he regarded his servant and family legal attorney, Robert Coke, as his friend. So did his son Giles, who left Coke a gold ring and a sum of money in his will.[321] William Salmon, a Townshend trustee for thirty years, must also have been close to his master.[322] A prosperous local yeoman from Walsingham, this estate official commended his wife to the care of Roger, his 'especiall good master', in a will of 1545.[323] Roger was likewise bound to other servants, just as his contemporary, Sir William Paston, was to his.[324] Paston generously bequeathed to three of his employees a life interest in one of his manors.[325] In the previous century Roger I had also been a good master. Before his chaplain, Robert Dapelyn, died, he advised him to augment a chantry which the latter had earlier founded. When he drew up his will, Dapelyn appointed his employer as one of his testamentary supervisors and directed the priest serving the chantry to include Roger in his

---

1517. Inclosures and Evictions II', *TRHS* NS 7 (1893), 164; NRO, B–L II e, 1501/2–1517/18 Townshend sheep accounts, fos. 157^r, 161^v.

[319] NRO, NCC 348–9 Ryxe. Roger was also made an executor and was to have the Gygges manor at Burnham if all Thomas's heirs died.

[320] *CAD*, vol. v, no. A.13,542.

[321] Faukener: R58, RT II memo-book, fo. 12^v. Coke: NRO, Townshend 159 MS 1,578 1 D4, fo. 51^r; PRO, CP40/1123, rot. 131; 1136, rot. 312; 1139, rot. 404; 1140, rot. 417; 1143, rot. 112; 1145, rot. 515, 633; 1147A, rot. 111; 1152, rot. 111; NRO, NCC 31 Lyncolne; NRO, B–L VII(b) 1. Coke, the father of the great Sir Edward, was of the minor gentry. His father-in-law, William Knyghtley, had earlier been the Townshends' attorney. In 1534/5 Roger II paid William 47*s*. 6*d*. for his services: E. A. Habon, *Edward Coke* (Cleveland, Ohio, 1949), 13–14; PRO, CP40/1048A, rot. 522; 1051, rot. 121; PRO, KB27/1045, rot. 60d; NRO, B–L VII b(3), fo. 17^r.

[322] Numerous Raynham deeds.

[323] NRO, NCC 236–8 Deynes.

[324] e.g. he was an executor of Thomas Shorte, his Helhoughton bailiff and trustee of the early 16th cent.: NRO, NCC 170–2 Spurlinge; R13, 1484/5–1507/8 and 1508/9–1546/7 Helhoughton account rolls; PRO, CP25/28/188, no. 10; PRO, C142/96/32.

[325] PRO, PROB11/37, fos. 111–17.

prayers.[326] But perhaps these are all instances of paternalism rather than straightforward friendship. Traditional concepts held that the good lord should care for his tenant as a father would his children, and the Townshends fulfilled that role for these men.[327] The Norfolk gentry as a whole, however, were not always considered good masters, and the Townshends sometimes clashed with their tenants.[328] Ket and his followers associated their grievances with the misdeeds of their social superiors, and called upon the gentry to exercise their 'paternalistic responsibilities'.[329]

During Roger II's lifetime the Townshends were of the county élite and, because he attended Lincoln's Inn, the royal court, and the council chamber, his horizons were hardly restricted; but, like his father, he had a narrow circle of friends and associates.[330] Even the household men he chose as trustees in the early sixteenth century were East Anglian.[331] His was not, however, an exceptional case. His friend Sir Thomas Le Strange was scarcely a backwoods gentleman, but the Le Strange household books illustrate a world peopled mainly by Sir Thomas's fellow East Anglians and kin.[332] Historiographical controversy about the provincialism or otherwise of the English gentry has bedevilled seventeenth-century studies.[333] It is clear, nevertheless, that most of the seventeenth-century gentleman's social relationships were formed within his locality.[334] The fifteenth and sixteenth centuries were no different. The Townshends and others knew the outside world, but their kin and friendship networks show that they limited their contact with it.[335]

---

[326] Blomefield, iv. 205; NRO, NCC 259 A. Caston (will of 23 Nov. 1485; proved 7 Sept. 1487).

[327] Beer, *Rebellion and Riot*, 70-1.   [328] See Ch. 3, 2 and Ch. 5, 4 below.

[329] MacCulloch, 'Kett's Rebellion', 47-7; id., *Suffolk*, 305-6; R. B. Manning, 'Violence and Social Conflict in Mid-Tudor Rebellions', *Journal of British Studies*, 16 (1977), 39.

[330] See App. 1 below for his trustees.

[331] e.g. Giles Alington, John Audeley, Thomas Bedingfield, Charles Brandon, John Heveningham, Arthur Hopton, Edmund and Edward Howard, William Sidney, John Vere, Anthony Wingfield: R28, 'RAYNHAM HENRY VIII-PHILIP AND MARY', deed of 12 Aug. 1512.

[332] 'Extracts', *passim*. His wife Anne was an aunt of Queen Catherine Parr and Roger, one of his younger sons, was a royal ambassador: ibid.: 419, 548.

[333] C. Holmes, 'The County Community in Stuart Historiography', *Journal of British Studies*, 19 (1980), 54-73.

[334] e.g. A. Everitt, 'The County Community', in E. W. Ives (ed.), *The English Revolution 1600-1660* (London, 1968), 49, 54; Fletcher, *A County Community*, 44, 53.

[335] Cf. C. Given-Wilson, *The English Nobility in the Late Middle Ages: The Fourteenth-Century Political Community* (London, 1987), 83.

2

THE TOWNSHENDS AND THEIR COUNTY

INTRODUCTION

Despite their contacts with the outside world and their landholdings in other counties, the Townshends were, above all else, Norfolk men. As such, they provide a good medium for discussing the Norfolk gentry and local government in the later fifteenth and first half of the sixteenth centuries.

The Crown depended on the gentry in the localities for most of the day-to-day running of the shires. But what of the Norfolk gentry when Roger I and his son were active in local government? The relatively complete returns for the 1524/5 subsidy offer us a useful picture at a point roughly in the middle of this period, and provide a sample of 179 gentlemen, about a third of whom were of the rank of esquire or above, who resided in Norfolk at the time.[1] This shows a correlation

---

[1] See App. 3 below. This figure, based on the returns for each of the four years of the subsidy, can only represent a minimum since some of the rolls are badly worn or damaged; but it compares favourably with Virgoe's calculation that in 1481 Norfolk had at least 120 gentlemen—again a minimum figure: R. Virgoe, 'The Benevolence of 1481', *EHR* 104 (1989), 42. My basic criterion for inclusion in this sample is the title 'gentleman', although I have also taken into account those not distinguished in the returns as such but who were certainly gentry. They may have escaped having their style attributed to them through scribal error or, more likely, because they concealed their status. Social status as well as apparent wealth must have been used as guides for making assessments by the subsidy commissioners (cf. ibid., 42). Others have used economic criteria for determining who were gentry, e.g. Cornwall, 'Tudor Gentry', 456–71; id., *Wealth and Society in Early Sixteenth Century England* (London, 1988), but these are not entirely satisfactory. Wealth did not necessarily create a gentleman or an esquire. John Townshend died in 1466 possessed of land worth about £40 p.a., in theory the minimum amount of land necessary for a knight. He was never, however, a gentleman although many less substantial men, some of minuscule landed means (see App. 3), were. The parvenu Henry Fermor was only a 'gentleman' during the 1520s, despite being a sizeable landowner and one of the wealthiest men in Norfolk: PRO, E179/150/207, 259, 221, 251. The point is that contemporaries knew who were 'gentlemen' and who were not. Recognition of gentility was essentially a social process: D. A. L. Morgan, 'The Individual Style of the English Gentleman', in M. Jones (ed.), *Gentry and Lesser Nobility in Late Medieval England* (Gloucester, 1986), 18.

between landed wealth and status, for the landholdings of those of the rank of esquire and above were far greater than those of the 'mere gentleman'. It also shows that these men were not evenly distributed about the county and were most heavily concentrated in the eastern half, particularly the north-east, of Norfolk, which in general population terms was the most settled area.[2] This was the richest part of the county; here the soil was especially fertile, land-values were high, riverine and coastal communications were good, and economic development and farming methods advanced.[3]

However, many of these men formed what is for us an anonymous subclass because only a minority actively participated in local government. There was, therefore, another correlation, that between status and office-holding. The majority of the known resident knights and esquires, for example, became justices of the peace, whilst the 'mere gentlemen' who attained a place on the bench were a minority; a more realistic aspiration for them was the humbler office of escheator.[4] But rank was not the sole criterion for membership of the bench; the location of a gentleman's residence in the county might also be important.[5] During the first half of the sixteenth century the Norfolk justices were fairly evenly spread about the county although most concentrated in its populous eastern and north-eastern parts.

The rule of Norfolk was not, however, the exclusive concern of the gentry owing to the presence in the region of one or more great magnates. These noblemen cannot be ignored, so the following discussion begins with a review of their effect on local society, as well as the relationship the Townshends had with some of them, before moving on to the parliamentary representation of the shire, the magistrates' bench, and the part that Roger II and his fellow gentry played in controlling the county in the troubled mid-Tudor period.

(1) THE MAGNATE

Many parts of the country during our period were dominated by one or more great magnates. The magnate's power depended ultimately

---

[2] See App. 3 below.
[3] B. M. S. Campbell, 'Agricultural Progress in Medieval England: Some Evidence from Eastern Norfolk', *EcHR* 2nd ser. 36 (1983), 26–46.
[4] See App. 3 below.
[5] M. L. Zell, 'Early Tudor Justices of the Peace at Work', *Archaeologia Cantiana*, 93 (1977), 131–2.

upon the possession of great estates and an affinity or following centred on those estates.[6] The fashion for county studies with their
emphasis on the gentry has perhaps helped to obscure the importance
of the nobleman in local affairs, but they remained a fact of life during
the lifetimes of the Townshends.[7] The Crown itself acknowledged
their importance, and Edward IV pursued a policy of ruling through
his nobility. During the 1460s he attempted to create and delimit areas
of territorial influence for his trusted followers among the great.[8]
Where these men were promoted favourites, great estates had to be
created for them. Lord Hastings was rewarded with enormous grants
in the Midlands and Lord Herbert received grants similar in scale in
south Wales to ensure his role as the king's 'master lock' in the
region.[9] The Crown still depended on the nobility for general supervision of their localities in the sixteenth century, increasingly so as
successive governments attempted to impose different versions of
religious uniformity and to cope with growing social problems.[10]
In Edward VI's reign Lord Seymour of Sudeley could 'loke upon a
Charte of England . . . and declare how strong he was . . . and what
Shire and Places were for hym', whilst in that of Elizabeth the fourth
duke of Norfolk was a 'prince' in his county.[11]

When Roger I began his career the regional power-balance in East
Anglia had swung in favour of Thomas Howard's fifteenth-century
predecessors, the Mowbrays.[12] The disputes between competing
lords and respective bands of followers which had plagued Norfolk
during the middle of the century had largely disappeared, but disorder
was still a problem. The dukes of Norfolk and Suffolk now eschewed
direct competition with each other but continued to pursue their
territorial ambitions, in which the gentry, either as followers or
victims, could not always remain uninvolved.[13] Such was ducal
unreliability that Edward IV promoted Mowbray's relative John

[6] C. Carpenter, 'The Beauchamp Affinity: A Study of Bastard Feudalism at Work',
EHR 95 (1980), 515–16.

[7] G. W. Bernard, *The Power of The Early Tudor Nobility* (Brighton, 1985), 3.

[8] Ross, *Edward IV*, 334.

[9] J. R. Lander, *Government and Community: England 1450–1509* (London, 1980), 228.

[10] Bernard, *Power*, 207.

[11] J. P. Cooper, *Land, Men and Beliefs* (Oxford, 1983), 87; Hassell Smith, *County and
Court*, 24. It is worth pointing out that the third duke of Norfolk was also *potens Princeps*:
e.g. PRO, E150/642/8.

[12] Virgoe, 'Three Suffolk Parliamentary Elections', 192.

[13] Sayer, 'Norfolk Involvement', 30.

Howard as an important regional influence in his own right and a surer representative of Yorkist interests.[14] Norfolk was far less disturbed during Henry VII's reign because East Anglia was dominated by a single magnate, the earl of Oxford. Oxford, a mainstay of the Tudor crown, exercised his regional supremacy in a positive fashion, rallying the gentry to support the king in times of crisis and preventing their quarrels from getting out of control.[15] The disgraced Howards recovered considerable regional influence before Oxford died in 1513, but the second duke of Norfolk never achieved the same monopoly of power.[16] For more than twenty years he and his successor faced a challenge in Charles Brandon, promoted duke of Suffolk in 1514. Until his removal to Lincolnshire in 1538 Brandon was always an obstacle to Howard supremacy in East Anglia, although he was never able to construct an effective affinity nor to compete with the Howards on an equal footing in Norfolk. His regional presence probably encouraged the Howards increasingly to confine their interests to Norfolk. The third duke of Norfolk acquired a large amount of monastic property in the county, particularly in the west, with the result that he became a more immediate presence than hitherto for gentry like the Townshends who were from that part of the county.[17]

The lords with the most immediate influence during the lifetime of Roger I's father John, and for much of his own, were Thomas, Lord Scales, and his son-in-law and successor Anthony Woodville. The Scales lordship in Norfolk, centred on Middleton, was mainly situated in the west of the county and included a manor at Raynham.[18] Both lords took an interest in local affairs. Woodville was perhaps the most powerful magnate active in Norfolk shortly before his death.[19] Middleton Castle was the focus of the Scales affinity. Those who lived under the shadow of a baronial castle were those most likely to be

[14] Crawford, thesis, 90A. Edward could also look to the queen's Duchy of Lancaster interests in Norfolk as an instrument of royal authority: R. Horrox, *Richard III: A Study of Service* (Cambridge, 1989), 80.
[15] Virgoe, 'Recovery', 9.
[16] Ibid., 19.
[17] MacCulloch, *Suffolk*, 58–60, 65–6; Gunn, *Brandon*, 39–54, 78–81, 123–30, 224–5; Virgoe, 'Recovery', 19–20; Swales, 'Redistribution', 21.
[18] *CIPM, Henry VII*, vol. i, no. 35.
[19] *PL*, nos. 449, 561, 563, 472, 478, 483, 495, 592–7; *The Paston Letters*, nos. 162, 210; E. W. Ives, 'Andrew Dymmock and the Papers of Antony Woodville, Earl Rivers, 1482–3', *BIHR* 41 (1968), 222–3; R. Virgoe, 'An Election Dispute of 1483', *Historical Research*, 60 (1987), 37–8.

members of a lord's retinue, and so it was with John Townshend.[20] Not surprisingly, his membership of the Scales affinity meant that his trustees were predominantly Scales men. Roger Sambroke, for example, was keeper of the Scales household; the lawyer John Fincham was Woodville's receiver; John Yates of Norwich was a Scales trustee.[21]

The lesser man like John was the most likely to remain within the pull of a single magnate's territorial orbit. Paradoxically, those who are usually considered the typical members of an affinity, the gentry, could be the least attached to it. Possessing greater social status and means and, consequently, wider horizons than the more humble retainer, they were less dependent and more likely to seek good lordship elsewhere or to have several patrons. Roger I's rise into the gentry and his legal career broke his family's association with a single lord. In any case, he was later to have differences of opinion with Woodville.[22] His Mowbray connections in the late 1460s are the first indications of a wider pursuit of patronage. His services on behalf of the second duke of Buckingham and the countess of Oxford show that an able lawyer was too useful to be the exclusive monopoly of a single lord.[23]

Lawyers in particular, but in many cases the gentry in general, could not afford to become too closely attached to any one lord, in case their master should come to grief. Roger I's career as a justice of the peace and local commissioner, unlike those of other Mowbray men, was not interrupted by the Readeption of Henry VI during which the Mowbrays' influence declined.[24] The most dramatic evidence of the limitations of his Mowbray loyalties came in the aftermath of the ducal siege of Caister Castle in 1469, when he was prepared to give the Pastons professional advice after Mowbray had had the younger John Paston and two family servants indicted.[25]

The Townshends do not appear to have had any direct links with the thirteenth earl of Oxford, although Roger I had served his mother and despite the fact that the earl's influence in the county was

---

[20] Saul, *Knights and Esquires*, 73.

[21] Sambroke: R(Attic), '*Norfolk manorial* T–W and mixed', 1448/9 roll of collectors' and farmers' accounts for several Scales manors; Fincham: Ives, 'Andrew Dymmock', 219 n.; Yates: R11, 'HELHOUGHTON Temp. HEN. VI (1441–1460)', deed of 10 Oct. 1456.

[22] See Ch. 3, 1(ii) below.

[23] See Ch. 1, 3(i) above.

[24] Sayer, 'Norfolk Involvement', 311–13.

[25] *PL*, nos. 342–3; *The Paston Letters*, no. 768.

strongest in the west.[26] Roger II was, however, on good terms with Sir Robert Drury, one of Oxford's leading councillors, and among the earl's followers were other close Townshend associates and trustees.[27] Perhaps we should, therefore, regard their contact with the earl as being by proxy.

The Townshends' ties with the Howards in the sixteenth century were far stronger than those which linked Roger I to the Mowbrays but, like his father, Roger II and other gentry were prepared to act against the ducal interest. In 1517 Wolsey became concerned about the injustices committed by Howard officials at Bungay, part of the ducal liberty in Suffolk, and he sent Roger and Sir Thomas Wyndham, an associate and relative of the duke, to investigate. Their subsequent written report to the cardinal adopted a distinctly unfriendly tone towards Howard and accused him of hampering their enquiries by detailing his servants to keep an eye on them.[28]

Ruthless self-interest was a trait which the Townshends shared with other Howard retainers. During the mid-fifteenth century the then duke of Norfolk's affinity was eroded because he was unable to exercise enough power on behalf of his followers.[29] As we have seen, when Howard fell in the mid-sixteenth century, his affinity quickly collapsed because Roger II and his fellow gentry were quick to disown their former connections. Ruthless perhaps, but he and other prominent Howard men preserved their places on the bench and their local standing.[30]

The Townshends' dealings with the great illustrate that 'bastard feudalism' was still very much alive in the sixteenth century. But they illustrate also the limitations of the bastard-feudal relationship as observed by McFarlane in the context of the later Middle Ages.[31] Roger I's associations with the aristocracy show that the rising gentleman could use, just as much as he could serve, the bastard-feudal connection. It is no coincidence that he acquired powerful

[26] *RP*, vi. 282, 473-4; *CIPM, Henry VII*, vol. i, no. 33; *PL*, nos. 401, 854.

[27] *CCR* (1500-9), nos. 911, 990; BL, Add. MS 21,480, fo. 47^v; list of followers named in the earl's will: 'The Last Testament and Inventory of John de Veer, Thirteenth Earl of Oxford', ed. W. H. St John Hope, *Archaeologia*, 66 (1914), 318-19.

[28] PRO, STAC2/34/29. I am grateful to Dr D. MacCulloch for this reference.

[29] Virgoe, 'Murder of James Andrew', 266.

[30] See Ch. 1, 4(i) above.

[31] K. B. McFarlane, 'The Wars of the Roses', in id., *England*, 248-54. More recently Carpenter has argued for the stability of the bastard-feudal relationship: 'Beauchamp Affinity', 518-19.

patrons when his career was on the verge of taking him into the highest
ranks of his profession. His son became far more firmly attached to
a magnate but, until the events of 1546–7, it was in the interests of a
Norfolk gentleman to be linked to the Howards. No one could be more
aware of this than the duke of Suffolk, who had failed to construct an
effective East Anglian affinity. Dependent on relatives and outsiders
like Sir William Pennington for a following, he could do little when
Pennington was murdered by Howard followers in 1532.[32]

Howard was brought down by factional politics at the centre of
power. Sixty years earlier Lord Hastings had suffered a similar fate,
and his retainers also accommodated themselves with a new regime
remarkably quickly.[33] Roger II's volte-face in 1546 shows that little
had changed. Like their fifteenth-century predecessors, sixteenth-
century gentlemen were quick to look to themselves when their lord
began to totter. This helps to explain an apparent paradox: the ease
with which the great magnate could fall.

(2) PARLIAMENT

Magnate influence in Norfolk is also apparent in the parliamentary
context, where the great lords made attempts to influence shire elections. Nevertheless, McFarlane has argued that they did not 'control'
the suffrage of fifteenth-century Norfolk, and that the gentry themselves could have a considerable say in elections, illustrating his point
by citing gentry opposition to John Howard, the duke of Norfolk's
prospective candidate as knight of the shire in 1455.[34] There are also
signs that the gentry acted for themselves in the sixteenth century: in
the 1539 election Sir Edmund Knyvet, with the support of some of his
fellows, presented himself as an alternative candidate to Richard
Southwell.[35]

McFarlane's argument is a valid one, but external influences were
none the less a factor in both fifteenth- and sixteenth-century elections. After all, it should not be forgotten that Howard was in fact

---

[32] Gunn, *Brandon*, 125; *HP*, iii. 353; *LP*, vol. v, no. 1,139.
[33] *The Stonor Letters and Papers, 1290–1483*, ed. C. L. Kingsford, Camden Soc., 3rd
ser. 29–30 (1919), ii. 161.
[34] 'Parliament and Bastard Feudalism', in id., *England*, 4–11; *PL*, no. 527.
[35] *HP*, ii. 483.

elected in 1455.[36] As for the 1539 episode, it was Southwell, the nominee of the government, and not Knyvet, who was returned.[37]

Although not directly relevant to Norfolk, since he sat for boroughs outside the county, Roger I's parliamentary career bears all the hallmarks of external patronage.[38] But was Roger II, who did represent the shire (in 1529-36, 1536, and 1542), merely a nominee on the occasions that he was elected a knight of the shire, as the *History of Parliament* suggests,[39] and if so, had he been nominated merely to serve Howard interests?

In the period immediately before Roger I began his parliamentary career, the mid-fifteenth century, the Crown was especially weak and magnate influence over the shire representation of Norfolk and Suffolk was at its greatest.[40] For England generally, Ross argued that Edward IV made sustained efforts to pack the Commons with household men.[41] For Norfolk in particular it is striking that, from Edward's reign to that of Henry VII, the majority of the knights of the shire had household connections, if not at the time of their election then at least subsequently during their careers. These connections were more significant than magnate patronage. When the magnates used their influence, therefore, it tended to be on behalf of candidates acceptable to the Crown.

The names of twelve men who served as knights of the shire for Norfolk between 1461, when Roger I was beginning his career, and 1509, have survived.[42] At least ten of these were associated with the royal household at some stage during their careers; of these, seven were definitely household men when elected,[43] and the others— Robert Brandon, Philip Calthorpe, and Sir Robert Clere—were all

---

[36] Wedgwood, 473.

[37] Lehmberg, *Later Parliaments*, 43-4.

[38] See Ch. 1, 3(i) above.

[39] *HP*, iii. 470-1.

[40] Virgoe, 'Three Suffolk Elections', 185-96.

[41] Ross, *Edward IV*, 341-4.

[42] John Paston I (1461); John Berney (1461); William Knyvet (?1463, 1467, 1470); Sir John Paston II (1467); Sir Richard Harcourt (1472); Sir Robert Wingfield (1472); John Radcliffe (1478, Nov. 1483, 1484); Sir Thomas Howard (1478, Jan. 1483, ?Nov. 1483); Thomas Lovell (?1485); Sir Robert Brandon (1491); Philip Calthorpe (1491); Sir Robert Clere (1495). Lovell attended parliament in 1485 but may not have represented Norfolk: *HP*, ii. 548-9.

[43] John Paston I, Sir John Paston II, Harcourt, Howard, Wingfield, Radcliffe, Lovell: *PL*, note to no. 236, nos. 632, 634; Wedgwood, 419-20, 474, 956-7; Virgoe, 'Election Dispute', 33; *HP*, ii. 548-9.

household men by 1509. Brandon and Clere had had, moreover, household associations long before then.[44] The parliamentary representation of Norfolk in the later fifteenth century conforms with the pattern that Lehmberg identified for Henry VIII's reign. He pointed out that most English knights of the shire were courtiers as well as prominent men in their county; few men prominent in their shires but hardly known at court represented counties.[45] It is easy enough to find evidence that several of these fifteenth-century shire knights were connected with magnates: Wingfield and Harcourt were, for example, respectively clients of the dukes of Norfolk and Suffolk as well as their candidates for the 1472 election.[46] But by backing these men the dukes were at the same time complying with the royal desire for a tractable Commons to be elected. In the 1478 election the nobility were specifically directed to help secure the country-wide return of trustworthy men on the king's behalf.[47]

It is sometimes assumed that the dukes of Norfolk were 'preeminent' in Norfolk shire elections for much of the second quarter of the sixteenth century, since eleven of the shire knights elected between 1529 (the earliest date for the century for which the returns are known) and 1558 were related either to the Howards or their Boleyn relatives, or were in their service.[48] Five of the six known knights of Henry VIII's reign fit this pattern.[49] But more significant were their court and government connections. It is unnecessary to restate Roger II's here, and the court pedigree of Sir James Boleyn, his fellow knight in the Reformation Parliament, needs no emphasis.[50] As for the others, Sir Thomas Paston, a gentleman of the privy chamber, spent most of his comparatively short life at court;[51] Edmund Wyndham attended the duke of Richmond during the royal bastard's French sojourn of the early 1530s; and he and Richard Southwell, Cromwell's protégé,

---

[44] *LP*, vol. i, pt. i, no. 20 (pp. 14, 16–17). Brandon was a knight of the body by May 1500: *CCR* (1485–1500), no. 1,231. Clere was knighted at the creation of the duke of York in 1494 and attended the reception of Queen Catherine in 1501: ibid., no. 797; Shaw, *Knights*, i. 144; Wedgwood, 190.

[45] S. E. Lehmberg, *The Reformation Parliament, 1529–1536* (Cambridge, 1970), 18.

[46] *PL*, no. 354; Wedgwood, 419–20; Sayer, 'Norfolk Involvement', 308, 314.

[47] Ross, *Edward IV*, 344.

[48] *HP*, i. 148.

[49] Sir Roger Townshend II (1529, ?1536, 1542); Sir James Boleyn (1529); (Sir) Richard Southwell (1539, ?1542); Edmund Wyndham (1539); Sir Thomas Paston (1545). The sixth, Christopher Heydon (1545), had no obvious Howard links: *HP*, ii. 352–3.

[50] *HP*, i. 456.   [51] *HP*, iii. 68.

were the king's choice as knights of the shire in 1539.[52] Howard clients though they were, these men demonstrate the degree to which the duke himself was obliged to identify with the court. His successor was ruined because he made the fatal mistake of isolating himself from Elizabeth's court;[53] indeed, the court interests of the Howard following help to explain their readiness to take part in his downfall. For a Richard Southwell or Edmund Knyvet, those interests were too valuable to be sacrificed.

The duke did not 'control' Norfolk elections for the narrow purposes of family aggrandizement; rather, he used his influence to support the Crown's interest as his fifteenth-century predecessors appear to have done. His own interests were best served by supporting that interest. We know that he followed Cromwell's directions and promoted the Crown's candidates in 1536 and 1539: he was just one of several magnates with whom Cromwell worked for this purpose in Norfolk and elsewhere. In 1539 he acted in various shires to ensure that 'such shalbe chosen that I doubt not shall serue his highness according to his pleasyr'.[54] The 1545 elections demonstrate the limits to Howard's influence over county elections when he did try to act independently. By now the rising Seymour and Parr–Herbert factions had begun to monopolize Crown favour and his position at court was insecure. Both factions were well represented in the subsequent parliament, but few of Norfolk's supporters got into the Commons, and none of these was a shire knight, let alone a shire knight for Norfolk.[55] As for the county's boroughs, the duke's influence in this and most other elections is indiscernible. His pocket boroughs were in Sussex.[56] The Elizabethan period offers a parallel: the then duke of Norfolk exercised considerably more influence over the county's boroughs than his predecessor—they each usually elected at least one Howard nominee—but county elections were another matter. Ducal control is only clearly apparent in the 1566 by-election, when he secured the return of Clement Paston and Roger II's heir, Roger Townshend III, but even here it should be remarked that Paston, like Roger II, had had a career at court.[57]

[52] Ibid., 675–6; PRO, SP1/146/242, 274 (*LP*, vol. xiv, pt. i, nos. 672, 706).

[53] Hassell Smith, *County and Court*, 21–2.

[54] Lehmberg, *Later Parliaments*, 3, 4, 7, 43–4. Quoted by R. J. Swales, 'The Howard Interest in Sussex Elections', *Sussex Archaeological Collections*, 114 (1976), 52.

[55] Lehmberg, *Later Parliaments*, 211–13.

[56] *HP*, i. 149–54, 201–2, 204–5, 208–9; Swales, 'Howard Interest'.

[57] Hassell Smith, *County and Court*, 39; *History of Parliament 1558–1603*, iii. 185.

(3) THE BENCH

A seat in parliament was more than the average gentleman could aspire to. If he occupied a higher position on the social scale than the mere parish or lesser gentry, however, he had a greater chance of becoming a justice of the peace. Just as in the later sixteenth century, this office was not automatically available to established families during the lifetimes of the two Roger Townshends.[58] But between 1466 and 1551 the Townshends occupied a position on the bench almost without a break, and in 1542 Roger II and two of his sons, Robert and Giles, were appointed simultaneously.[59] Fathers and sons normally served consecutively, but the legal abilities of the younger Townshends earned them their places. More often than not during this period simultaneous service was due to the presence of one or more lawyers in the family concerned.[60] Interestingly, Roger III, who had a far less prominent career in local government than his great-grandfather, was never appointed a justice of the peace.[61] The magistrate's office was not a mere sinecure for the county's leading families.

The Townshends were working justices of the peace and mainstays of local government. The evidence for the attendance of Norfolk justices at the quarter sessions during the fifteenth century suggests that Roger I was the most active magistrate in the county after he joined the bench in 1466.[62] From December 1466 until September 1493, a few weeks before he died, he was present for about one-fifth of the time the justices were in session, though during the three years beginning in September 1478 he was present for nearly one-third of the time.[63] It is probably not surprising that he attended so assiduously during these three years: on attaining the coif in June 1478 he became the most senior lawyer in the county,[64] and he was free of

[58] MacCulloch, *Suffolk*, app. II. Cf. Hassell Smith, *County and Court*, 57–9, app. III.
[59] *LP*, vol. xvii, pt. i, no. 362 (66).
[60] An assertion based on MacCulloch, *Suffolk*, app. II.
[61] *History of Parliament, 1558–1603*, iii. 520.
[62] The sessions attendance figures for 15th-cent. Norfolk, based on payments made to JPs, have been worked out by Diana Spelman, to whom I am most grateful for permitting me to use her tables.
[63] Sept. 1478–Sept. 1479: 27 days out of a total of 105; Sept. 1479–Sept. 1480: 24 out of 80; Dec. 1480–Sept. 1481: 20 out of 67.
[64] Sir William Yelverton died in late 1477 or early 1478: E.C. Robbins, 'The Cursed Norfolk Justice', *NA* 26 (1938), 46–7, and the three other senior lawyers on the bench at this time—James Hobart, Henry Spelman, and John Fincham—were below the rank of serjeant at law.

assize work until 1482.[65]

The State Papers alone suggest that his son was also an active justice of the peace,[66] and this is confirmed by the evidence for the latter's attendance at the sessions. In the later years of Henry VIII's reign, for example, only Sir Richard Southwell—and he was *custos rotulorum*—was present more often than Roger II, although other lawyers like John Corbet regularly attended.[67]

The peace commissions to which Roger I, Roger II, and Robert Townshend were first appointed afford some useful insights into Norfolk county society and the changes which occurred within it during the late fifteenth and early sixteenth centuries.[68] The composition of Roger I's first peace commission indicates the considerable state of disorder that the county was in during the late 1460s. The government's concern with this problem explains why it appointed no less than ten lords (eight lay and two spiritual) in an attempt to bolster its authority.[69] A second noticeable element is a household one; in parallel with his policy towards parliament, the insecure Edward IV seems to have tried to exert Crown control by appointing his servants to the bench. John Howard and Robert Wingfield were, for example, both important royal retainers.[70] Also appointed were John Wykes (a household esquire, former master of the horse, usher of the chamber, and royal steward of Castle Rising), a man of no apparent Norfolk connections,[71] and John Twyer. Twyer became a Norfolk gentleman only through marriage and seems to have been another Yorkist court attachment.[72] During the first half, at least, of Edward IV's reign there was consistently an alien household presence on the bench; normally in the persons of Wykes and Twyer, but there were others.[73] In 1465, for instance, James Baskerville, a household

---

[65] Ives, *Kebell*, 75.

[66] See Ch. 1, 4(i) above and section 4 below.

[67] MacCulloch, *Suffolk*, app. II.

[68] Those enrolled on 24 July 1466, 18 February 1501, and 11 February 1526 respectively. Roger II was empanelled on 16 February 1501, but this commission mistakenly included the sheriff, Sir Robert Clere, and was superseded by a fresh panel enrolled two days later. The personnel named on 18 February were as before, except that John Le Strange replaced Clere: *CPR* (1494–1509), 652; PRO, *List and Indexes*, ix. 88.

[69] Dukes of Clarence, Norfolk, and Suffolk; earls of Warwick, Oxford, Northumberland (John Neville, Warwick's brother), and Essex; Lord Scales (Anthony Woodville); bishops of Norwich and Ely: *CPR* (1461–7), 568.

[70] Howard: Crawford, thesis, 6–7. Wingfield: Wedgwood, 956–7.

[71] *CPR* (1461–7), 23; *PL*, no. 664; BL, Harl. MS 642, fo. 179ᵛ; PRO, E101/412/2, fo. 36ᵛ; Morgan, 'Individual Style', 31–2.

[72] Sayer, 'Norfolk Involvement', 307, 322.

[73] *CPR*, *passim*.

retainer from the West Country, was appointed to his one-and-only Norfolk peace commission.[74] The sheriffs the king chose for Norfolk and Suffolk in his early years reflect a similar policy, for on several occasions outsiders like Sir Thomas Montgomery and Roger Ree were picked.[75] Apart from the professional lawyers like Roger I, necessary for the day-to-day work of any peace commission, few of the remaining members of the panel might be described as 'Norfolk gentry' rather than 'outsiders' or 'lawyers'.[76]

The bench at this date was, therefore, not synonymous with the Norfolk gentry nor even with the upper gentry: the (incomplete) list of Norfolk gentlemen distrained for knighthood in 1465 shows, for example, that several potential knights were not appointed to the 1466 commission.[77] The connections between the Crown and the county élite were much weaker than they were by the end of the century; hence the king frequently relied on the household to provide him with shire knights, justices of the peace, and sheriffs.

The situation had changed when Roger II became a justice of the peace for the first time. The link between the working membership of the royal administration and local government in Norfolk was stronger than it had ever been by 1501.[78] As in earlier years, a household element, together with others who had personally served the king, were justices of the peace, but the bench was far more synonymous with the county gentry than during the 1460s. Henry VII did not need to introduce non-Norfolk men from among his personal retainers, because of the stronger links between the county and the Crown: the bonds which bound justices of the peace like the three Lovells, Sir William Knyvet, James Hobart, Robert Southwell, and Sir William Boleyn to the Tudor dynasty were close.[79] These ties meant that Henry VII did not try to bolster the authority of Norfolk

---

[74] *CPR* (1461-7), 474; Wedgwood, 48.

[75] Sayer, 'Norfolk Involvement', 307. Sayer also labels Alexander Cressener an outsider but he was an East Anglian, if not from Norfolk.

[76] Roger I, Sir William Yelverton, John Fincham, Henry Spelman, William Paston, and William Lumnour. It seems likely that James Arblaster was also a lawyer: Hicks, 'Countess of Oxford', 85 n. John Paston should perhaps be included in this list because of his legal training.

[77] PRO, E198/4/37, m. 8.

[78] Virgoe, 'Crown, Magnates and Local Government', 81.

[79] Lovells: *HP*, ii. 548-9; Sayer, 'Norfolk Involvement', 320; *The Paston Letters*, no. 1,016, vi. 187; Shaw, *Knights*, ii. 29-30. Knyvet: *The Knyvett Letters, 1620-1644*, ed. B. Schofield, Norfolk Rec. Soc., 20 (1949), 16; Wedgwood, 520-1. Hobart: ibid., 458-9. Southwell: *HP*, iii. 352. Boleyn: *HP*, i. 456.

peace commissions with peers to the same extent as did Edward IV. Loyal gentry were far more useful than a gaggle of peers, most of whom would not have been active members. On Roger II's first commission there was effectively only one peer, the earl of Oxford,[80] who devoted much of his energies to regional affairs on behalf of the Crown, his presence complementing that of the justices with Crown attachments.[81]

The legal element in this commission was stronger than that of 1466—perhaps because the magistrate's work-load had increased and become more specialized[82]—as was the knightly element. The bench had become more important in county affairs and, as a consequence, was more attractive to the upper gentry. They were now usually represented on it—if they could produce a candidate of appropriate age and experience.[83] This meant that there was little room for those middle-ranking gentlemen who technically could support the estate of knighthood.[84] The bench gradually increased in size in later years, partly to accommodate those whose 'worship' would have suffered had they been excluded. The bench and the upper gentry could never become completely synonymous, but they had become much closer to being so by 1501 than they were in the 1460s.[85]

The bench to which Robert Townshend was appointed in 1526 included most of the greatest landowners in the county. As was the case in 1501, the links between many of its personnel and the court or government were close. In the 1520s, for example, Sir Philip Calthorpe was chamberlain of Princess Mary's household, and (like Roger II) Sir Robert Clere, Sir William Paston, Sir John Shelton, Sir Thomas Woodhouse, Sir Edmund Bedingfield, and Sir James Boleyn had court connections during their careers.[86] A definite

---

[80] The others were the infant Prince of Wales, and the earl of Suffolk who fled abroad in mid-1501: Lander, *Government and Community*, 347.

[81] Virgoe, 'Recovery', 9.

[82] Zell, 'Early Tudor Justices', 125; G. E. Mingay, *The Gentry: The Rise and Fall of a Ruling Class* (London, 1976), 126.

[83] MacCulloch, *Suffolk*, app. II.

[84] PRO, E198/4/19 (distraints of 1501).

[85] There survives a 17th-cent. copy of a list of Norfolk gentry dated 10 Henry VII (All Souls College, MS 155, fos. 365–6). This totals 105 men: of the eight knights, all were JPs for the county at some stage during their careers; of the fifty-one esquires, only thirteen were definitely Norfolk JPs; of the forty-six gentlemen listed, only four.

[86] Calthorpe: PRO, E179/69/9–10. Clere: Wedgwood, 190; *LP, passim*. Paston: ibid., *passim*; *DNB* (s.v. Sir William Paston). Shelton: Swales, 'Redistribution', 24; *LP, passim*. Woodhouse: ibid., *passim*. Bedingfield: PRO, E179/69/27. Boleyn: *HP*, i. 456.

corollary between social status and landed wealth and a place on the bench by this date is borne out by Appendices 4 and 5.

It is possible to explain why some of those who one might expect to have been empanelled were not. The commission was probably drawn up while Sir John Heydon was still sheriff and therefore ineligible for the bench, but not enrolled until after he had vacated the office.[87] Francis Lovell was away from the county because he was a member of Wolsey's household.[88] Why Sir Thomas Bedingfield was excluded is less clear, but his family was represented by his younger brother Sir Edmund, and he himself subsequently became a justice of the peace.[89] Sir Edward Knyvet was never a JP but there are no signs that he was out of favour. He had had a household career but seems to have opted out of the county's administrative affairs.[90] Henry Fermor obviously did not yet warrant a place on the bench, for he was a newcomer to Norfolk who had made his fortune as a London merchant.[91]

The wealthiest and most important and the lawyers dominated, as they did in 1501, so there is little room for the middle-ranking landowners in Appendix 4.[92] There is no evidence that Inglose, Berney, Jermy, Thursby, Gurney, or Carville were ever justices. Henry Hunston of Walpole served just once, in 1514.[93] It should be pointed out that Edmund Wyndham, Roger II's son-in-law, who occupies a lowly position on the table as a landowner but who was nevertheless a magistrate, was a greater man than these. He was the head of a family which was one of the county's most substantial, but during the 1520s his inheritance was burdened with the provisions his father had made for other members of it.[94] As for Sir James

---

[87] Appointed sheriff 10 Nov. 1524. His successor, Roger II, was appointed to the commission despite becoming sheriff on 27 Jan. 1526: PRO *List and Indexes*, ix. 88. This shows that a commission's personnel could be selected some time before it was enrolled.

[88] PRO, E179/69/10.

[89] A JP from 1531 until his death in March 1538: *LP, passim*.

[90] *LP, passim*. Known to have been on only two Norfolk commissions: array (1511) and that for the 1524/5 subsidy. He was exempted from the shrievalty in 1527: *LP*, vol. i, pt. i, no. 833 (58); vol. iii, pt. ii, p. 1,366; vol. iv, pt. ii, no. 3,213 (29).

[91] Hassell Smith, *County and Court*, 198; Swales, 'Redistribution', 25.

[92] See App. 5 below. Thomas Wingfield, presumably the cadet member of the family from Great Dunham (J. M. Wingfield, *Some Records of the Wingfield Family* (London, 1925), 36), might also have been a lawyer. It is otherwise difficult to explain why he was on the commission.

[93] *LP, passim*.

[94] *HP*, iii. 675–6.

Boleyn, he was not a man of great landed wealth at this date when compared with the excluded middle-ranking men, but his powerful connections made him a man of status and an obvious candidate for the bench.[95]

The 1524/5 subsidy assessments bear out the foremost gentry's dominance. Norfolk had nineteen knights in the mid-1520s, eighteen of whom resided in the county.[96] Only four of the nineteen were never magistrates, a far cry from the mid-1430s when half of the known Norfolk knights never became justices of the peace.[97] Three of the four, moreover, though resident in the county at the time, hardly qualified as members of the Norfolk gentry.[98] Neither did Sir Philip Tilney, the Suffolk knight on the 1526 commission, but he was related to the Howards, and no doubt the duke put in a word for his relative and for two other retainers, Robert Holdich and Edward White.[99] In fact, many of the commission had Howard associations. The duke of Suffolk had, in contrast, few such connections with the Norfolk justices, indicating his relatively weak position in the county. He probably helped to secure his cousin, Sir William Pennington, a place on the bench a few years later, but any advantage he thereby gained was soon offset by the latter's murder.[100]

The duke of Norfolk's associations with the personnel of the bench are another indication of how, during the late fifteenth and early sixteenth centuries, it had become an important institution as far as

[95] Assessed at a mere £40 in lands for the 1524/5 subsidy: PRO, E179/150/222.

[96] The non-resident, Sir Philip Calthorpe, was assessed at court: PRO, E179/69/3a, 3. The others: Sir John Audeley, Sir Thomas Bedingfield, Sir Edmund Bedingfield, Sir Thomas Blennerhasset, Sir James Boleyn, Sir Edward Boleyn, Sir Robert Brandon, Sir Robert Clere, Sir John Cressener, Sir John Heydon, Sir Christopher Heydon, Sir Edward Knyvet, Sir Thomas Lovell, Sir William Paston, Sir William Pennington, Sir John Shelton, Sir Roger Townshend II, and Sir Thomas Woodhouse.

[97] Virgoe, 'Crown, Magnates and Local Government', 79. The four were Blennerhasset, Cressener, Sir Edward Boleyn, and Knyvet.

[98] Blennerhasset also had lands in Suffolk and Essex and, as a Howard household officer, spent much time at their manor of Framlingham in Suffolk: *HP*, i. 443; *LP*, *passim*; PRO, C142/52/9, 49; *Suffolk in 1524: Being the Return for a Subsidy Granted in 1523*, ed. S. H. A. H[ervey], Suffolk Green Books, 10 (1910), 417. Cressener resided at Attleborough but his estates lay in Suffolk and Essex: PRO, E179/150/202, 251; *CIPM, Henry VII*, vol. ii, no. 21; PRO, C142/82/87. Sir Edward Boleyn was a cadet with little land of his own. His wife's Yorkshire estates and position at court meant that his main interests lay outside Norfolk: Blomefield, vi. 388; Leland's *Itinerary*, iv. 13.

[99] Tilney: MacCulloch, *Suffolk*, 56. Holdich: *LP*, vol. xi, no. 659; PRO, E179/151/313. White: MacCulloch, *Suffolk*, 64.

[100] *LP*, vol. v, no. 166 (12); Gunn, *Brandon*, 125.

general county affairs were concerned, one in which the local magnate was obliged to take an interest. Several of the Townshends' memorandum books from this period contain references to the quarter sessions and assizes as events for the conduct of private business and social intercourse, just as they were in the later sixteenth century.[101] These meetings, especially those at Norwich, brought the otherwise scattered gentry together as a group more often than did the less-frequent shire elections.[102] Roger II regularly travelled from Raynham to attend the sessions or the assizes at Norwich, Walsingham, Lynn, or Thetford, where, apart from participating in official business, he took the opportunity to collect rents and debts, to buy wine, and to arrange leases with his fellow gentry and others.[103] Sir Thomas Le Strange made similar journeys from Hunstanton in the extreme north-west of the county.[104] For the county's ruling classes the sessions and the assizes were also ideal venues for resolving disputes and discussing matters of general concern. The assize justices acted as an important link between the court and government and the counties, as did the court connections of many of the Norfolk gentry, although in Henry VIII's reign Thomas Cromwell was careful also to maintain direct contact with the gentry. The duke of Norfolk provided another link, and he often oversaw the activities of various commissions.[105]

(4) CONTROLLING THE COUNTY

It was important for the duke and gentry to co-operate because East Anglia, like other parts of the country, was much troubled by political, social, and religious discontents in the mid-Tudor period.[106] The

---

[101] R58, RT I memo-book, fos. 3ᵛ, 4ᵛ, 5ʳ; BL, Add. MS 41,139, fos. 1ᵛ, 7ʳ, 9ᵛ, 19ʳ; Cockburn, *Assizes, passim*. Cf. Hassell Smith, *County and Court, passim*.

[102] Though not always; Roger I recorded that no one turned up for the 1492 quarter sessions at Walsingham: R58, RT I memo-book, fo. 5ʳ.

[103] R33, RT II receipt book, fos. 3ʳ, 4ʳ, 11ʳ; NRO, Townshend 193 MS 1,612 1 C 7, fos. 10ʳ, 11ʳ; BL, Add. MS 41,139, fos. 7ʳ, 9ᵛ.

[104] 'Extracts', 419, 420, 435, 452, 466, 474, 500, 522, 541.

[105] Cockburn, *Assizes*, 3–10; *LP, passim*.

[106] M. E. James, 'Obedience and Dissent in Henrician England: The Lincolnshire Rebellion 1536', *PP* 48 (1970), 3–78; C. S. L. Davies, 'The Pilgrimage of Grace Reconsidered', in P. Slack (ed.), *Rebellion, Popular Protest and the Social Order in Early Modern England* (Cambridge, 1984), 16–38; Elton, 'Politics and the Pilgrimage of Grace', in id., *Studies in Tudor Politics and Government*, iii (Cambridge, 1983), 183–215; id., *Reform and Reformation* (London, 1977), 279–81.

Walsingham Conspiracy and Ket's Rebellion feature in the preceding chapter because they are an essential part of any discussion of Roger II's career. They were, however, just two particularly serious instances of unrest to affect Norfolk during his lifetime. He and his fellow magistrates were also kept busy combating other local stirs or signs of sedition.

The unrest came from the lower orders; there are hardly any signs of disaffection among the ruling classes of the region. Purely political sedition was rare, although in 1516 there were reports that four East Anglian merchants were communicating with Richard de la Pole, the Yorkist pretender.[107] The government took these threats seriously because of the region's proximity to the continent and because the old De la Pole estates were situated in East Anglia. In 1522 the council imprisoned a man from East Dereham after hearing reports that he had retained one hundred men to support a landing by De la Pole.[108]

During the same period the downfall of the duke of Buckingham caused a minor stir in the Townshends' part of Norfolk. In the summer of 1521 one Lewis ap Rese, alias Polen, deposed before Roger II that he had overheard John Stede of Warham utter seditious words a couple of weeks earlier to his servant John Fowler. Stede was supposed to have said that he would have been a different man had the duke of Buckingham lived for another three years because then the duke would have been king. A couple of days later Roger, with the assistance of John Shelton and Sir Edward Boleyn, examined Fowler. The servant would not support ap Rese's accusation and only agreed that his master regretted Buckingham's fate. Roger sent the details of ap Rese's deposition and Fowler's confession to Thomas Larke, Wolsey's servant, and asked how to proceed in the matter. At the same time he put in a good word for Stede, a gentleman worth £20 per annum in lands who was noted for his 'honest reputacon'.[109] Roger spoke from personal experience, since at the time Stede had land in Syderstone within one of his foldcourses and paid him rent.[110]

That autumn Stede and Fowler bound themselves to appear at a

[107] *LP*, vol. ii, pt. i, no. 1,510.

[108] Gunn, *Brandon*, 40.

[109] PRO, SP1/22/202-3 (*LP*, vol. iii, pt. i, no. 1,356); PRO, SP1/233/56 (*LP*, Addenda, no. 319). Stede also possessed some £80-£100 worth of goods at this date: PRO, E179/150/212, 257.

[110] R53, paper of 1522/3 calculating Stede's holding within Roger's pasture at Syderstone.

future date before the Star Chamber; the recognizance was cancelled the following July.[111] Stede seems to have escaped any serious penalties arising from the charges made against him; he cannot have been guilty of more than indiscretion prompted by a sense of personal grievance. Buckingham had owned property in Norfolk worth nearly £100 per annum and was the lord of several manors in the north of the county, including Warham.[112] Stede's alleged remark that he would have advanced in status had Buckingham become king suggests that he had been one of the duke's local retainers or estate officials, so that when the duke fell any hopes of future advancement in the service of a powerful master were dashed.

A similar episode occurred near the end of Roger's career. In September 1550 he and two other magistrates, the earl of Sussex and Sir William Fermor, discovered a seditious letter which implicated a man from Dereham named Goodrich in some kind of treasonous activity, and they sent it on to the Privy Council. They were, however, cautious about assuming that he was guilty, just as Roger had been in the case of John Stede nearly twenty years earlier, because in a covering letter they wrote that Goodrich had served the king well during Ket's Rebellion and had suffered at the hands of the rebels.[113] The privy councillors themselves felt that the circumstances in which the letter was discovered seemed suspicious and that an enemy may have intended to damage Goodrich.[114] Nevertheless, they ordered the justices to see whether they could find three Wisbech men also mentioned in the letter. Whether one accepts or not Elton's argument that despotic government and arbitrary measures were not the order of the day in Tudor England, care was taken to find the facts behind a case and the innocent did have a reasonable chance of reprieve.[115]

The outcome of the Goodrich affair is unknown; like the Stede case it probably turned out to be a minor matter. But these and similar episodes demonstrate that the local authorities were expected to report any possible instances of political dissension. Roger II was suitably diligent in this respect. On one occasion he sent Thomas Cromwell a

[111] *LP*, vol. iii, pt. ii, no. 2,145 (61).
[112] Rawcliffe, *Staffords*, 183; B.J. Harris, *Edward Stafford, Third Duke of Buckingham, 1478-1521* (Stanford, Calif., 1986), 237.
[113] *APC*, iii. 131-2. If Goodrich was the lawyer John Goodrich who had served on several commissions in the county, he was indeed a respectable man: *LP*, vol. xiii, pt. i, no. 646 (48); vol. xv, no. 942 (1); vol. xvii, no. 881 (31); vol. xx, pt. i, no. 622 (vi).
[114] Unfortunately, we are not told how the magistrates acquired the letter.
[115] Elton, *Policy and Police*, 327, 374-5.

deposition accusing a Norfolk man of demanding the minister's removal from office, and on another he informed the Privy Council of a rhyme against the king which was circulating the county.[116] Nothing was too trivial to investigate in an age of unrest, and mid-Tudor governments were realistic enough not to expect the political devotion of all the king's subjects. When Edward VI came to the throne the sheriffs and the trusted and most important gentry in each shire (in Norfolk the latter were Roger II, Sir William Paston, Sir John Heydon, and Sir Edmund Bedingfield) were ordered to watch the behaviour of their neighbours and to remain alert for 'seditious persons'.[117]

What I have termed purely political sedition may not have been the norm, but there was plenty of unrest in mid-Tudor Norfolk generated by the social, agrarian, and economic discontents of the lower orders. During the 1520s matters were aggravated by heavy taxation and a series of bad harvests at the end of the decade, both of which threatened the less well-off with considerable hardship.

To support an ambitious foreign policy, the king made unprecedented fiscal demands on his subjects. The loan of 1522—never repaid—mulcted the population on an unheard-of scale, and it was swiftly followed by the subsidy granted by parliament in 1523. The second instalment of this tax was due by 9 February 1525 but was nearly everywhere still being paid when Henry asked for an 'amicable grant'. This last innovation caused serious discontent in Suffolk. The opposition to it was possibly not provoked by absolute poverty but rather because it hit an already vulnerable cloth industry and came hard on the heels of other substantial levies.[118]

The authorities were obliged to tread warily. The duke of Norfolk negotiated with the Lavenham rebels because he was well aware that his men would be reluctant to attack their fellow commons.[119] As for Roger II's part of Norfolk, resentment against taxation had become evident by the summer of 1523 when he and two other magistrates examined several men from Gayton. It emerged that a husbandman,

---

[116] PRO, SP1/162/157 (*LP*, vol. xv, no. 1,029 (49)); *APC*, i. 41 (*LP*, vol. xvii, no. 881 (31)).

[117] *APC*, ii. 10–11.

[118] Goring, 'General Proscription'; G. W. Bernard, *War, Taxation and Rebellion in Early Tudor England: Henry VIII, Wolsey and the Amicable Grant of 1525* (Brighton, 1986), 117–24.

[119] Ibid., 81.

Peter Wilkinson, had declared that the people should depose the king rather than pay him any more taxes.[120]

Wilkinson had reacted to a rumour that soon even those worth £2 per annum or less would be required to hand over half of what they had. Given the demands the government was beginning to make, it is perhaps not surprising that he believed it. Rumours hostile to the king or the government were always treated seriously; they could upset the peace and the line between wild rumour and possible treason was tenuous.[121] Although the source of most rumours was almost impossible to track down, the government had unusual faith in its ability to get to the bottom of them. In 1538, for example, it was widely put about in East Anglia that the king planned to take all unmarked livestock into his own hands. On being chided by Cromwell for failing to deal with this story, the duke of Norfolk in turn scolded the gentry for their remissness in the matter. But all that emerged was a report of a mysterious gentleman who rode about in the guise of a royal commissioner informing the populace that he had been instructed to round up all unmarked beasts.[122]

The three bad harvest years of 1527–9 were ominous for the local authorities in East Anglia. With grain scarce prices rose to a dangerous level and there were cases of hoarding.[123] By Christmas 1527 such was the dearth of corn that the commons of Norwich were ready to rise, and soon afterwards there were disturbances in both the city and the county.[124] At the end of 1529 the duke of Suffolk helped the city oligarchy to crush another insurrection. In the previous year he had attended the Thetford assizes in person, a measure of the authorities' fear of popular unrest.[125]

These circumstances probably encouraged an attempt to hold an unlawful assembly in the Suffolk town of Bury St Edmunds in 1528. Sir Robert Drury detained three men at the local gaol, one of whom, a thatcher called John Davy, had tried to raise a company of several hundred 'good poor fellows', apparently with the intention of marching to place their grievances before the king. Drury subse-

---

[120] PRO, SP1/27/324–6 (*LP*, vol. iii, pt. ii, no. 3,082).

[121] Elton, *Policy and Police*, 46–7, 49–50.

[122] *LP*, vol. xiii, pt. ii, nos. 52, 57, 554.

[123] W.G. Hoskins, 'Harvest Fluctuations and English Economic History, 1480–1619', *AHR* 12 (1964), 31; J. Thirsk (ed.), *The Agrarian History of England and Wales*, iv (Cambridge, 1967), 817; *LP*, vol. v, no. 1650.

[124] Blomefield, iii. 198.

[125] Gunn, *Brandon*, 81.

quently sent them to London and they were interrogated in the Tower by Roger II, who was then in the capital serving as a member of the king's Council Learned in the Law, and two other members of the same body, Thomas Lucas and Roger Wigston.[126]

Drury, another lawyer, quite rightly believed that the men could not be put to death because they had committed no overt act of treason.[127] The government acted through the due processes of the law, even if these were sometimes used unfairly. The duke of Norfolk—certainly no lawyer—found such restrictions irksome, sometimes believing the death penalty to be the appropriate punishment for the seditious lower orders in situations where it was not legally applicable.[128]

There was no love lost between the lower orders and the authorities in mid-Tudor East Anglia, for much of the unrest was the occasion for the display of a bitter anti-gentry animus on the part of the former. At the root of much of it was the gentry's activities as engrossing sheep-farmers who eroded the precious tenurial and common rights of the lesser man.[129] The gentry were clearly regarded as the enemy in a series of disturbances. During the Pilgrimage of Grace, John Walter of Griston tried unsuccessfully to launch an anti-gentry rebellion in south-west Norfolk, 'for yt were a good turn yf ther were as many jantylman in Norff [*sic*] as ther be whyt bulls'. Among those he thought a desirable target was Roger II, one of the magistrates who brought him to justice when his seditious words were reported to the authorities a few years later.[130] The other would-be rebels who participated in the Walsingham Conspiracy also planned to 'put don the gentilmen'.[131] Across the county boundary at Bungay, part of the Howard liberty in north-east Suffolk, the inhabitants were well aware of the events at Walsingham. In May 1537 the duke of Suffolk apprehended one of them, Richard Bishop, who had hoped to raise a company of three hundred 'good fellows' to subdue the gentry. On informing Cromwell, the duke also reported that a play had been

---

[126] *LP*, vol. iv, pt. ii, nos. 4,012, 4,013; PRO, SP1/48/81 (*LP*, vol. iv, pt. ii, no. 4,309). For Lucas and Wigston see *HP*, ii. 553; iii. 611–13.

[127] *LP*, vol. iv, pt. ii, no. 4,012. Cf. Elton, *Policy and Police*, 80.

[128] *LP*, vol. iv, pt. ii, no. 4,014; PRO, SP1/106/183 (*LP*, vol. xi, no. 470). Cf. Elton, *Policy and Police*, 302.

[129] See Ch. 5, 4 below.

[130] PRO, SP1/160/157, 172 (*LP*, vol. xv, nos. 748, 755).

[131] Ch. 1, 4(i) above; PRO, SP1/119/35, 30 (*LP*, vol. xii, pt. i, nos. 1,056, 1,045 (2)).

performed there in which a man with the part of 'Husbandry' had augmented his part with many anti-gentry references which did not belong to the plot.[132] Back in Norfolk a popular rising was planned at Fincham in the south-west at the same time as, but seemingly independent of, the Walsingham Conspiracy. The instigator, a local husbandman, had planned to ring the bells of the parish church to raise the people 'for the comon welth'.[133] The first of the gentry to have suffered would have been the local squire, John Fincham.[134]

The gentry-hatred of this unrest in Norfolk had important consequences. In other parts of the country the gentry had become alienated from the court and government and joined the commons in rebellion.[135] In Norfolk the loyalty of many of the leading men of the shire was assured by their links with the court, but the threat from below gave them a further and pressing reason to remain amenable to the government. Later, during Ket's Rebellion, they hardly distinguished themselves, but their loyalty was to an unpopular government. Those who were afterwards accused of complicity with the uprising were the victims of private feuds.[136] With the revolt crushed, the main thought of many gentlemen was to seek revenge against the suppressed commons.[137] Serious social tensions survived 1549, for popular discontent was tangible enough to cause Roger II's nephew, Roger Woodhouse, to moat his house 'about double' for fear of the lower orders.[138] Before Princess Mary's successful coup of 1553, unrest and rebellion in Norfolk arose from inter-'class' divisions within the county rather than differences between the local élite and central government.

The government owed much to the Norfolk gentry for their loyalty

---

[132] *LP*, vol. xii, pt. i, no. 1,212.

[133] A similar plan was planned by the 1525 rebels at Lavenham as a warning against attack: MacCulloch, *Suffolk*, 292.

[134] PRO, SP1/121/173-6 (*LP*, vol. xii, pt. ii, no. 150).

[135] James, 'Obedience and Dissent', 3–78; Elton, 'Politics and the Pilgrimage of Grace', 183–215.

[136] MacCulloch makes much of accusations made against Sir Richard Southwell, suggesting he might have encouraged the rebels on behalf of the Lady Mary, the king's sister and political opponent of Somerset's government: D. N. J. MacCulloch, 'Kett's Rebellion in Context. A Rejoinder', *PP* 93 (1981), 171–3. But this is surely too ingenious. Would he, as a substantial sheep-farmer and a magistrate who played a major role in crushing the Walsingham Conspiracy, really have behaved in such a Machiavellian fashion? In any case, Southwell's accuser was his old enemy, Sir Edmund Knyvet.

[137] PRO, SP10/8/55(1).

[138] Beer, *Rebellion and Riot*, 203.

during the 1530s, since it is clear that the restless commons would have joined the northern rebels if they could. The Lincolnshire Rising and the Pilgrimage of Grace sent shock-waves through East Anglia and, even after they were finished as effective movements, continued to inspire the commons. Those Norfolk men who served in the royal forces sent against the Pilgrims in October 1536 brought back a rebel bill, probably Aske's second manifesto, to their own county before the end of the year, and copies soon circulated in various towns, including Norwich and Lynn.[139] Their commander, the duke of Norfolk, was obliged to admit that many of his troops considered the Pilgrims' cause 'good and godly'.[140] One of the men involved in the Fincham plot had served in Yorkshire as a soldier.[141] Shortly before Christmas 1536 a priest from Walsingham supposedly declared that, had Norfolk and Suffolk risen with Lincolnshire and the north, the rebels could have 'gone through the realm', and the Walsingham conspirators proposed to march north to help the northern men.[142] One of the main features of the above-mentioned plot of John Walter was for the commons to march to Lynn to lie in wait for those gentry returning home from the north, where they had served against the Pilgrims.[143] At Diss in February 1537 a fiddler had sung a song implying that England would have been made 'merry' if the duke of Suffolk had not remained loyal to the king when sent against the Lincolnshire rebels and had allowed them to join the Yorkshire men.[144]

In several instances the Norfolk commons sympathized as strongly as they did with the northern rebels because they were similarly fired by religious grievances.[145] Norfolk was one of England's most economically and culturally advanced counties, but the grip of

---

[139] *LP*, vol. xi, no. 1,260; Dodds, *Pilgrimage of Grace*, i. 327–8.

[140] D.M. Palliser, 'Popular Reactions to the Reformation During the Years of Uncertainty, 1530–70', in C. Haigh (ed.), *The English Reformation Revised* (Cambridge, 1987), 97.

[141] PRO, SP1/121/175 (*LP*, vol. xii, pt. ii, no. 150).

[142] PRO, SP1/121/31; SP1/119/30 (*LP*, vol. xii, pt. ii, no. 21; vol. xii, pt. i, no. 1,045(2)).

[143] Section 4 above; PRO, SP1/160/157 (*LP*, vol. xv, no. 748).

[144] *LP*, vol. xii, pt. i, no. 424.

[145] Moreton, 'Walsingham Conspiracy', 38–43. Some have even questioned the importance of religion in the Pilgrimage of Grace: e.g. A.G. Dickens, 'Secular and Religious Motivation in the Pilgrimage of Grace', in G.J. Cuming (ed.), *Studies in Church History*, iv (Leiden, 1967), 39–64. But see Davies, 'Pilgrimage of Grace', and id., 'Popular Religion and the Pilgrimage of Grace', in A. Fletcher and J. Stevenson (edd.), *Order and Disorder in Early Modern England* (Cambridge, 1985), 58–91.

traditional Catholicism there during Henry VIII's reign should not be underestimated. Too often it is assumed that religion had little part to play in the Norfolk unrest of this period.[146] Most of the county was still conservative in terms of religion in the late 1530s, when in practical terms the Reformation had barely begun at the parish level. Both clergy and laity adhered to the old ways, including the prior of Blackfriars, Norwich, whom Cromwell ordered Roger II to apprehend in mid-1535.[147] Three years later he helped to examine a former friar, Anthony Browne, whom he had arrested for denying the royal supremacy. Browne's fate was martyrdom, because he could not accept a temporal prince as head of the Church although he was prepared to deny the pope.[148] Others continued to believe in the pope and the doctrine of purgatory, or were suspected of doing so.[149]

In pre-Reformation days the bishop of Norwich, Richard Nix, complained of religious dissent but recognized at the same time that his diocese as a whole was not greatly 'infected' by heresy. The problem, where it existed, lay among the merchant community and those who dwelt by the sea.[150] After the Reformation had begun, a more immediate danger was those who adhered to the old ways. A few months before the Walsingham Conspiracy of 1537 was formed, a Buckenham man schemed to have Roger II and his fellow commissioners for the suppression murdered in their beds as they stayed overnight at the local priory.[151] The Walsingham Conspiracy is in one respect a classic example of agrarian unrest, but it was precipitated by opposition to the Dissolution of the monasteries.[152] Devotion to Our Lady of Walsingham in north-west Norfolk survived the destruction of the priory and its famous shrine, which the conspirators tried to defend. In January 1540 Roger II wrote to Cromwell about a woman from Wells whom he had set in the stocks for propagating a tale of a miracle effected by the image of Our Lady of Walsingham after it was carted off to London. Referring to the population of the area, he concluded that 'I cannot perceyve but the

---

[146] e.g. Dodds, *Pilgrimage of Grace*, ii. 177; Elton, *Policy and Police*, 150.

[147] PRO, SP1/84/70 (*LP*, vol. vii, no. 694).

[148] BL, Cleo., E IV, fo. 102 (*Original Letters*, 1st ser. ii. 85–9).

[149] *LP*, vol. xii, pt. ii, nos. 740, 864; *Proceedings and Ordinances of the Privy Council*, ed. N. H. Nicolas, 7 vols. (London, 1834–7), vii. 213–14.

[150] *LP*, vol. iv, pt. iii, no. 6,385.

[151] PRO, SP1/120/179–82 (*LP*, vol. xii, pt. ii, no. 1,268).

[152] Moreton, 'Walsingham Conspiracy', 38–43.

seyd Image is not yett out of sum of ther heddes'.[153] The already-mentioned unrest at Fincham was primarily an enterprise 'for the comon welth' against the gentry; yet one of those arrested, Harry Jervis, said that he wished the Yorkshire men had prospered so that the traditional holy days abolished in mid-1536 might have been restored.[154] Jervis was a husbandman who was bound to be affected by the abolition of the holy days, but this does not make his views any less 'religious'. Holy days and other rituals connected with the harvest year could not readily be relinquished because they were what religion was about at the parish level; it is wrong to try to distinguish between 'religious' and 'material' factors.[155] Defence of the old religion could provide a powerful ideological justification for unrest originally rooted in other causes, and become a major constituent of that unrest.

Times had changed by 1549: religious issues were no longer at the forefront and Ket's men did not try to defend the old religion. Those who gathered on Mousehold Heath held outdoor services using the new Prayer Book.[156] But by then the Reformation was not new and the destruction of the monasteries was a *fait accompli*. The rebels of the previous decade had reacted to an attack on an established religion rather than an already-changed one. Once the initial assault had been made, further attacks appeared less outrageous.

Despite the unrest stirred by devotion to the old religion in Henrician Norfolk, the local authorities had also to deal with those at the other end of the religious spectrum whose activities they regarded as seditious. For some the king's reforms did not go far enough. The continental reformer Philip Melanchthon put his pen to paper to protest against Henry's Six Articles of 1539, and at the end of 1540 the Privy Council was informed by the diocesan and civic authorities at Norwich that they had apprehended one Thomas Walpole for distributing printed copies of the diatribe. By the beginning of the new year the council had traced it back through several people to the London printer, Richard Grafton. Walpole himself had obtained it from two servants of Thomas Goodrich, the reforming bishop of Ely, and the authorities suspected Goodrich of having encouraged him.

[153] *Original Letters*, 3rd ser. iii. 162 (*LP*, vol. xv, no. 86).

[154] PRO, SP1/121/174–5 (*LP*, vol. xii, pt. ii, no. 150).

[155] C. Haigh, 'The Recent Historiography of the British Reformation', in id. (ed.), *Reformation Revised*, 25; Davies, 'Pilgrimage of Grace', 25.

[156] S. T. Bindoff, 'Ket's Rebellion', in J. Hurstfield (ed.), *The Tudors* (London, 1973), 83–4. But it might be argued that they used the Prayer Book to demonstrate their political loyalty to the king in whose name it was brought out.

They had also discovered that Walpole had a confederate in Norfolk, a physician from East Dereham. Roger II and the sheriff were immediately ordered to arrest the man and to send him with all speed to London where, among others, Walpole, one of the bishop's men, and Grafton were safely under lock and key.[157]

What happened next is unclear, but Grafton did not remain in disgrace for long.[158] Like the Walsingham affair, this episode demonstrates just how efficiently the government could work with the local authorities, as well as the potential effectiveness of the mid-Tudor justice of the peace. While he had been in power Thomas Cromwell had recognized that his hold over the localities depended on gentlemen like Roger II.[159] But his control over the Norfolk gentry was never in doubt; the county's magistrates constantly sought his advice on how they should proceed. Shortly after the Walsingham Conspiracy had been betrayed and events were moving fast, Roger and Richard Southwell were obliged to make decisions on the spot without referring to the minister; but they apologized for having to do so.[160]

The gentry did not behave so efficiently after the fall of the duke of Norfolk. Howard had played an important role in local government, and the Seymours and their allies made a costly mistake when they engineered his downfall in 1546/7. The gentry were incapable of preventing Ket's Rebellion because they lacked direction, and with the duke gone there was no one to curb the disputes which broke out among them. Not only did Roger II—in association with Sir Edmund Bedingfield—quarrel with Nicholas Le Strange; in September 1547 a dispute arose between Sir William Paston and Sir Thomas Woodhouse of Waxham concerning debts owed by the latter. Woodhouse later counter-attacked by accusing Paston of abusing tenants' rights.[161] Paston, a hard-headed if not ruthless landlord, also clashed with Sir John Clere. Clere's tenants at Winterton

---

[157] *LP*, vol. xvi, nos. 349, 351, 366, 420; *Proceedings . . . of the Privy Council*, vii. 107 (*LP*, vol. xvi, no. 424).

[158] Only shortly before his arrest Grafton, an enthusiastic reformer, had been licensed to print the authorized version of the Bible in English. He later received other royal commissions although he was arrested for a second time in 1543 after overstepping the mark again. He was the king's printer throughout Edward VI's reign. See *HP*, ii. 240.

[159] Elton, *Policy and Police*, 382.

[160] PRO, SP1/120/142 (*LP*, vol. xii, pt. i, no. 1,125).

[161] PRO, SP10/8/60; Beer, *Rebellion and Riot*, 91; BL, Add. MS 27, 447, fos. 78–91.

and Somerton complained about the activities of Paston and his bailiff there and sued Paston in the Court of Requests.[162] Moreover, after January 1547 the bench lost much of its former cohesiveness because of the addition of new men by Protector Somerset.[163] In these circumstances the gentry, many of whom were in any case alienated by the government's social policies, and so less inclined to co-operate with it, were in no position to combat effectively a serious rebellion.[164] A similar power-vacuum occurred after the fourth duke of Norfolk fell in 1572, when once again the gentry were unable to run affairs by themselves. After he was removed from the scene competition for power and precedence among the gentry of Elizabethan Norfolk immediately increased. They divided into opposing factions and often used their position on the bench or other local offices to pursue sometimes bitter disputes with each other.[165]

Despite the efforts of some of the lower orders, the magnates—particularly the duke of Norfolk—and the gentry were extremely successful in preventing an East Anglian revolt as serious as Ket's Rebellion before 1549. The 1525 stirs at Lavenham, the most serious outbreak of unrest in this period, were potentially very threatening, but judicial handling of the situation saved the day.[166] Vigilance was the authorities' most effective weapon, as Richard Bishop, the would-be rebel at Bungay in Suffolk, acknowledged when he complained that it was impossible for men to walk together without the local constables appearing to demand the content of their conversation. He also observed that the duke of Norfolk had deliberately left two of his men in the parish during the Pilgrimage of Grace to prevent a rising there.[167] The Walsingham conspirators were forced to adopt the subterfuge of meeting at a shooting match at nearby Binham because of the difficulty of assembling without arousing the suspicions of the magistrates.[168] The situation was best summed up by the duke of Norfolk in a couple of letters he wrote to Cromwell in September 1536. In the first he boasted that it was impossible for the commons in 'these parts' to assemble in any significant number without his arriving

---

[162] PRO, REQ2/14/171.
[163] MacCulloch, 'Kett's Rebellion', 54.
[164] Ibid., 54; Elton, *Policy and Police*, 135; Beer, *Rebellion and Riot*, 36–7, 211–13.
[165] Hassell Smith, *County and Court*, *passim*.
[166] Bernard, *War, Taxation and Rebellion*, 81.
[167] *LP*, vol. xii, pt. i, no. 1,212.
[168] PRO, SP1/120/142 (*LP*, vol. xii, pt. i, no. 1,125).

rapidly on the scene. A few days later he assured the minister that an insurrection 'wolbe more difficill to be done in this cuntre than in any shire in this realme; we be to many jantleman here to suffer any suche besynes'.[169] This is a significant remark, for it shows how closely Howard identified himself with the gentry who, on an earlier occasion, he referred to as 'my fellows'.[170]

It is worth asking why the lower orders in Roger I's Norfolk seem to have been quiescent when compared with their sixteenth-century successors. Fifteenth-century East Anglia was a disorderly region, in which 'gret riotts, extorcyons, oryble wrongis and hurts'[171] occurred, but it suffered from the disorder of the rulers rather than the ruled. There are no real signs that a popular revolt was likely: Friar Brackley's partisan claim that the depredations of Sir Thomas Tuddenham, John Heydon, and their associates in the early 1450s might provoke a popular rising can hardly be taken at face value.[172] Moreover, although Norwich was disturbed by riots in 1437 and 1443, these arose from an internal factional dispute among its oligarchy in the first instance, and from the city's feud with Norwich Priory in the second; they were not occasions of popular revolt.[173] Later, during the mid-1470s, the king attempted to tax the country more heavily than at any other time since the reign of Henry V to pay for his French campaign, and Margaret Paston complained that the 'Kyng goth so nere vs in þis cuntre, both to pooere and ryche, þat I wote not how we shall lyff'.[174] But we should take her claims with a pinch of salt. The country was being asked for a total in taxes more realistic than the inadequate sums the government usually managed to raise. Those who complained most, 'men of good substance' like the Pastons, rather than the commons, were the targets of Edward IV's benevolence of 1474–5.[175] As for the commons, they were

[169] *LP*, vol. xi, no. 434; PRO, SP1/106/183 (*LP*, vol. xi, no. 470). Cf. Lancashire where a crucial shortage of gentry had important consequences for that region's history and development: C. Haigh, *Reform and Resistance in Tudor Lancashire* (Cambridge, 1975), 106–7.

[170] *LP*, vol. xi, no. 434.

[171] *The Paston Letters*, no. 210.

[172] *PL*, no. 605.

[173] P. C. Maddern, 'Violence, Crime and Public Disorder in East Anglia, 1422–1442', D.Phil. thesis (Oxford, 1984), 159–209.

[174] Lander, *Government and Community*, 80–5, 97; Ross, *Edward IV*, 216–17; *PL*, no. 224.

[175] Ross, *Edward IV*, 217; Virgoe, 'Benevolence', 26.

cushioned in this period by low grain prices.[176] The few rebels that there were in Roger I's Norfolk were individual gentry, and there is no sign that their tenants among the lower orders followed them. In any case, they became rebels outside East Anglia. The East Anglian rebels of 1483—Sir William Knyvet, Thomas Lovell of Beachamwell, John Wingfield (the sheriff), Robert Brewes, and William and Thomas Brandon—joined the rising in other parts of the country.[177] Sir Gilbert Debenham, who rebelled against Henry VII and went over to Perkin Warbeck, did so in Ireland.[178]

Thorold Rogers's view of the late Middle Ages as a 'golden age' for the peasantry has stood the test of time. The lower orders in Henrician England had more reason to feel discontented than their predecessors, because conditions had become harsher. In the second quarter of the sixteenth-century England was still an under-populated country, but indications of a marked quickening in population-growth become evident. By the 1520s prices of foodstuffs had increased sharply, real wages had fallen by about one-third, and the struggle for land was growing in intensity.[179] It was easier for the landlord to behave in a fashion detrimental to the commons' interests, and some of them did so.

The great events of the late fifteenth century were the overthrow of kings and struggles between over-mighty subjects. Materially speaking, it did not much matter to most of the population of Norfolk in the fifteenth century—however politically aware they might have been—who ruled the country, but in the sixteenth the great events did affect the lesser man. The king's foreign wars and divorce prompted the government to make unprecedented fiscal demands on its people and to bring about a religious revolution. It is hardly surprising that some of the lower orders were provoked by these novelties.

---

[176] Thirsk, *Agrarian History*, 816.
[177] *RP*, vi. 244–51; Sayer, 'Norfolk Involvement', 317. This rising against Richard III was essentially one of the gentry of southern England: C. Ross, *Richard III* (London 1981), 104.
[178] Wedgwood, 266.
[179] J. Hatcher, *Plague, Population and the English Economy, 1348–1530* (London, 1977), 65; I. Blanchard, 'Population Change, Enclosure, and the Early Tudor Economy', *EcHR* 2nd ser. 23 (1970), 427, 434–5, 440–1.

(5) CONCLUSIONS

The infighting among the gentry which followed the fall of the
Howards in 1546 means that it is difficult to speak of a Norfolk 'county
community' at the time of Roger II's death, although it might be
argued that some sense of such a community existed in the mid-
fifteenth century. In 1455 John Howard was not acceptable to some
of the gentry as a candidate knight of the shire because he had 'no
lyvelode in the shire, nor conversement'.[180] But, on the other hand,
the Norfolk gentry showed no signs of the sense of community and
social cohesion supposedly possessed by the Cheshire gentry in the
early 1400s.[181] For much of the fifteenth century they appear more
divided than united, not least because some of them feuded as
members of opposing magnates' affinities.[182] MacCulloch has argued
that the misdoings of competing magnates in Norfolk drove the gentry
to react by viewing themselves as a county community.[183] But their
coming together in the face of common adversity hardly proves that
they formed themselves into such a community. The bitterly disputed
shire election of 1461 shows an absence of the consensus and community feeling amongst the county's élite which an occasion like it was
supposed to represent.[184] During the later fifteenth and the first half
of the sixteenth centuries, it was the dominance of relatively responsible great magnates in East Anglia, rather than the development of a
sense of county community among the gentry, that prevented gentry
disputes getting out of hand.

Norfolk was by no means exceptional in this respect. Historians have tended recently to react against the county-community
concept.[185] One of the strongest arguments against it is that of
topography. Many counties were not in fact coherent entities;
physical geography made fourteenth-century Sussex, for example, a
'county of communities', not a county community, whilst the
extremely localized nature of society in sixteenth-century Lancashire

[180] *PL*, no. 527.
[181] M. J. Bennett, 'A County Community: Social Cohesion Amongst the Cheshire
Gentry, 1400–1425', *Northern History*, 8 (1973), 24–44.
[182] Virgoe, 'James Andrew', 263–6; *PL*, passim.
[183] MacCulloch, *Suffolk*, 105–7.
[184] C. H. Williams, 'A Norfolk Parliamentary Election, 1461', *EHR* 40 (1925),
79–86; Crawford, thesis, 78–85.
[185] See the useful discussion in Given-Wilson, *English Nobility*, 77.

was reinforced by its geographical divisions.[186] Norfolk itself was a large county, with its fair share of variations in soil-types and thus agricultural occupations.[187] The gentleman with estates in the wood-pasture region of the south-east had more in common with his neighbour in north-east Suffolk than did a gentleman from the Breckland or the fens in the west. Geography helps to defeat MacCulloch's argument that a county community existed in Tudor Suffolk. He undermines his own hypothesis by discussing at some length the geographical, as well as the historical and administrative, divisions within the county.[188] The unity, good order, and sense of community which he claims for the Suffolk gentry in the second half of the sixteenth century, in sharp contrast to their unruly Norfolk fellows, is flatly contradicted by his description of the struggles between religious 'puritans' and 'conservatives' in the same period.[189]

The aftermath of Howard's fall shows not only a lack of gentry unity but also demonstrates the important effect he and other magnates had on East Anglian society during the Townshends' lifetimes. In the mid-fifteenth century the Crown sought household men to represent Norfolk in parliament and to sit on its bench because of the gangsterism of the great. Edward IV's successors continued this policy. The bench had become more synonymous with the Norfolk gentry, or rather the upper gentry, by the time Robert Townshend joined it, but by then many of the county's justices of the peace and members of parliament had court connections. Howard himself was very much a 'court' magnate; he acted in support of 'court' candidates in county elections and many of his most important gentry followers had strong ties with the court and central government, ties which were encouraged by the threat of revolt from below in Henry VIII's reign.

The turbulent Norfolk of the Townshends was therefore a mixture of local worlds, in the sense of its social and geographical divisions, and the wider world, in respect of the connections with the centre of power enjoyed by many of its ruling élite.

---

[186] Saul, *Provincial Life*, 58; Haigh, *Lancashire*, 91.
[187] Thirsk, *Agrarian History*, 38–49.
[188] MacCulloch, *Suffolk*, 19 ff., 41–2.
[189] Ibid., 105–17, Ch. 6, *passim*.

3

THE TOWNSHENDS AND THE LAW

INTRODUCTION

The Townshends lived in an intensely litigious age, one reason why Roger I flourished as a lawyer. But what of them as litigants? Of course, one family's litigation cannot provide the basis for an extensive survey of the law in their period, ground which has in any case been well covered by scholars like Ives,[1] but it offers some worthwhile insights.

As experienced lawyers the Townshends were more able than most to avoid unwanted litigation, but they could not escape it altogether as landowners and they became involved in at least five major land disputes, discussed below. Not all of these were equally serious but they concerned manorial property, and in the case of the Brewes inheritance this was of not-inconsiderable value. By the later Middle Ages much land had passed through many hands, making ownership-rights convoluted, and there were few estate titles completely immune from challenge in a court of law.

But the Townshends' most serious land disputes did not usually concern lands they had purchased: litigation was not necessarily a corollary of extensive activity in the land market. Neither was violence necessarily a corollary of litigation; certainly, open violence is not easily discernible in any of the cases investigated below. In part, this must have been due to the safety-valve offered by the arbitration process, the prominence of which supports recent findings about arbitration, especially the argument that it was not inimical to the common law.

[1] Ives, *Kebell*.

(1) MAJOR PROPERTY DISPUTES

(i) Bale

The first of these disputes concerned the ownership of 'Nogeons', a manor in Bale, a township situated a few miles north-east of Raynham. It was not a straightforward affair, and Roger I himself found it complicated enough to seek the advice of two other lawyers, his friend John Sulyard and Thomas Rogers, before resorting to litigation in Chancery.[2]

The manor was formerly owned by William Hoppes, an obscure figure but probably of lesser-gentry status, who died heirless in late 1471. He had been a friend and trustee of Roger, who in turn had been one of his trustees for 'Nogeons'.[3] After he died, Hoppes's widow Agnes, the daughter of one Thomas Ditton, married William Wilby, a London pewterer of Norfolk origin who owned property in the Bale neighbourhood.[4]

The chronology of subsequent events is uncertain, but between mid-1474 and mid-1475 Roger presented a bill to the chancellor against Wilby and his wife, as well as Ditton in his capacity as a trustee of Hoppes. According to this and later bills, and further information that Roger provided the court, Hoppes had left him the manor and other lands in Bale in appreciation of his previous good friendship and advice and because he had agreed to satisfy Hoppes's creditors. At one stage during the proceedings Roger produced a copy of a will, dated 23 September 1470, declaring these intentions. This will, for which he was testamentary supervisor, also appointed Ditton as one of the executors. Roger's complaint was that the Wilbys and Ditton refused to allow him to take possession of the manor and that they detained all the deeds and evidences relating to it and the debts which Hoppes died owing.

Unfortunately for Roger, Wilby and Agnes disputed the validity of the will in favour of an earlier one in which Hoppes settled the manor on her for life, to be sold afterwards, the money raised to be put to charitable purposes for the good of his soul. The couple

---

[2] Unless otherwise indicated, what follows is based upon the surviving Chancery records relating to the dispute: PRO, C1/51/125–31; C1/54/383; C1/55/97–102; C1/55/124–8; C1/58/273.

[3] R49, Townshend cartulary, fos. 26ᵛ–27ᵛ.

[4] Died 26 Oct. 1502 seised of four manors in Bale and vicinity; he also had lands in Kent: *CIPM, Henry VII*, vol. iii, no. 606; PRO, PROB11/13, fos. 168–9.

themselves presented bills against Roger and Ditton at about the same time as Roger presented his—quite possibly it was they and not Roger who brought the dispute to Chancery in the first place—accusing them, as trustees of Hoppe's, of refusing to convey the manor to Agnes after Hoppes's death. Who was actually in possession of the manor at this or any other stage of the dispute is difficult to tell, but Roger's sheep-farming activities in the township suggest that it may have been in his hands from about 1475 until at least the second half of 1477.[5]

Rather unnecessarily, if he were truly confident about the validity of the later will, Roger responded to his opponents' bill by arguing that the earlier document had entitled Agnes to a life-interest in the manor only if she gave up her right to other lands in Norfolk which she had held jointly with her former husband. In return, she and Wilby replied that Hoppes should not have made such a provision, since when she and Hoppes married it was agreed that if they did not produce heirs the lands would revert to Hoppes's father (to whom they had originally belonged) and then to his father's heirs.

Ditton's participation in the dispute was a further complication. A landowner from Northwold in south-west Norfolk worth about £20 per annum, Ditton was perhaps a grazier since he was an associate of Simon Pigot of Lynn, a leading wool middleman. He probably knew Roger well, because he and Pigot bought both wool and malt from him during the 1470s.[6] He found himself at odds with both the main parties, who each took out bills against him for refusing to release his interest in the manor, which he claimed for himself. Ditton asserted that he was the rightful owner because he had lent Hoppes the 110 marks with which he bought it and the latter had never repaid this sum. Therefore, according to the conditions of the loan, he, Ditton, became the new owner. Needless to say, the other parties rejected his claim.

Sometime after mid-1478, but before Ditton died at the end of 1479, the dispute developed a new twist when Wilby took out another

---

[5] At Michaelmas 1475 he had a flock of 331 sheep at Bale, but, perhaps significantly, by Michaelmas 1477 it had dropped to 187 and he removed it altogether from the township during 1477/8, the sheep being sold or transferred to other flocks: NRO, B-L V, no. X. 31; R50, 1477/8 sheep accounts, fo. 14ᵛ.

[6] NRO, Townshend 56 MS 1,475 1F; K.J. Allison, 'The Wool Supply and the Worsted Cloth Industry in Norfolk in the Sixteenth and Seventeenth Centuries', Ph.D. thesis (Leeds, 1955), 199; NRO, B-L V, no. X. 45.

bill against Roger and Ditton for refusing, as his trustees, to re-enfeoff him of two other manors.[7] In earlier days both men must have been on good terms with Wilby for him to have appointed them his trustees. Possibly their refusal to comply with his wishes was an attempt to force him and his wife to surrender her claim to 'Nogeons'.

It is at this stage that our information concerning the dispute dries up, but Roger obviously won eventually, since he died possessed of the manor over a decade later.[8] There are two points worth noting about this dispute. The case came before the chancellor, first because it revolved around the settlement of land by will, not cognizable by common-law courts at this date; and secondly, because it also involved the detention of deeds. A court of common law had to see the relevant deeds or evidences before it could act to enforce them.[9]

(ii) Helhoughton

The problems that Roger I ran into concerning the former property of the Payn family appear considerably more complicated than the Bale affair, although this is partly due to the nature of the surviving evidence. Our main source of information is some legal notes in law French made for or by Roger at some stage after mid-1483 and, being composed for his own purposes, these are not always easy to interpret.[10]

In 1472 William Payn, rector of Denver in south-west Norfolk, sold (unfortunately the price is not known) to Roger his family's property, made up of a manor in Helhoughton, a township neighbouring Raynham, and various appurtenant lands.[11] This was a perfectly straightforward transaction, but the troubled recent history of the Payn lands meant that later Roger ran into difficulties over his title and found himself at odds with no less than Anthony Woodville, Earl Rivers, the king's brother-in-law.

[7] The bill refers to Roger as a serjeant at law and therefore post-dates his creation as such on 9 June 1478: *CCR* (1476–85), no. 177. Ditton died before 5 Dec. 1479: *CFR* (1471–85), no. 516. The properties concerned were Wilby's manors at Gunthorpe and Hindringham.

[8] *CIPM, Henry VII*, vol. i, no. 1,143.

[9] Spelman's *Reports*, ii. 192–203; J. H. Baker, *An Introduction to English Legal History*, 3rd edn. (London, 1990), 362–3.

[10] Two papers in R11, 'HELHOUGHTON. Temp. HEN VI (1441–1460)'. Unless otherwise indicated in the footnotes, what follows is based on these notes.

[11] Blomefield, viii. 319; R49, Townshend cartulary, fos. 40ᵛ–41ᵛ; NRO, B-L VIII b, no. 36 (ii); R50, 'Single deeds, Norfolk', deed of 2 Sept. 1472.

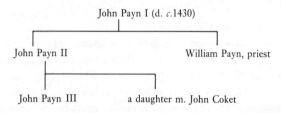

Fig. 3.1.   The Payn Family

Despite the name, the Payns appear to have had no connection with Sir John Fastolf's well-known servant.[12] A family of minor gentry who held their lands of the Townshends' manor at East Raynham, they also had mercantile interests in London.[13] In 1425 William Payn's father, John Payn (John Payn I), had settled his lands on feoffees to the use of his eldest son John (John Payn II) and his heirs, with contingent remainders to his younger sons, of whom William was one.[14] As it happened, it was William who eventually succeeded to the property as the last surviving member of his family.

The problems which later beset Roger had their origins in the days of John Payn II. During his lifetime the latter became short of money and resolved to sell some of his land. But, because this was held in trust, he was not its legal owner and the trustees refused to consent to his breaking his father's wishes by alienating any of it. Despite this, John sold several pieces of land to various neighbours at a reduced price (apparently because they were well aware that he could not pass good title), and in 1456 he granted a toft and some thirty acres to his son-in-law, John Coket.[15]

Shortly afterwards, Coket, a cloth-maker of Timworth, Suffolk,[16] obtained the remainder of John II's lands in return for a mortgage of £20. But because the later medieval mortgage involved the conveyance in fee simple of the land in question to the mortgagee, the mortgagor recovering his title if he repaid the money at an agreed

---

[12] *PL*, no. 692.

[13] *CIPM, Henry VII*, vol. i, no. 1,143; John Payn III was of Helhoughton and London gent., and was once in debt to a London mercer: deed of 2 Aug. 1466 and four bonds of 1468/9: R12, 'HELHOUGHTON Temp. EDW IV', and NRO, B-L V(1), nos. 188, 188a.

[14] R12, 'HELHOUGHTON Temp. EDW IV', deed of 2 Aug. 1466.

[15] NRO, B-L VIII b: copy of assize proceedings (see pp. 87–8 below).

[16] He was in some way connected to the Cokets of Ampton in the same county, but the relationship is unclear.

date,[17] this grant had no more legal validity than the earlier one. Roger's notes on the Helhoughton affair suggest that Coket exploited his father-in-law's poor financial and mental state to secure the mortgage, and, judging by later developments, there may have been some truth in the accusation.

How long Coket held the Payn lands is unclear, but John II later reasserted himself and ejected his son-in-law. However, he clearly never repaid the mortgage, and after he died (before the second half of 1466),[18] Coket re-entered and began to dispute possession with John's surviving son, John Payn III. An attempt was made to resolve the dispute informally, the parties seeking the opinion of Roger I, the nearest competent lawyer and the feudal lord of the Payn estate. He quite correctly judged Coket's title to be void in law. There is no reason to believe that this was not a disinterested opinion, because he himself did not buy the property until several years later.

Roger's opinion resolved nothing, however, because Coket sought for himself the protection of the most powerful magnate in west Norfolk, Anthony Woodville, Lord Scales. By means of two conveyances of October 1465, he had the Payn estate, which he claimed in fee simple, settled on himself and others, the most important of whom were Woodville, Sir William Yelverton the judge, and William Jenney, serjeant at law, while he continued to take the profits.[19] In an attempt to hamper any consequent legal action by John III these conveyances seem to have been made in secret, so that he would be ignorant of who exactly had seisin.[20] The arrangement was the work of one of Coket's trustees, Robert Wolvy. Wolvy, a 'wolman' from East Raynham, [21] was a customer for some of the finished woollen cloth that Coket produced, but, more importantly, he was also one of Woodville's bailiffs in north-west Norfolk.

John III nevertheless refused to be intimidated by Coket's powerful allies, and brought actions of forcible entry (by original writ of 3 January 1466)[22] and novel disseisin against Coket and Wolvy. After pleadings in King's Bench in January 1467, an assize jury sitting

---

[17] A. W. B. Simpson, *An Introduction to the History of the Land Law*, 2nd edn. (Oxford, 1986), 132–4.

[18] R12, 'HELHOUGHTON Temp. EDW IV', deed of 2 Aug. 1466.

[19] NRO, B-L V(1), nos. 201, 196.

[20] NRO, B-L VIII b: copy of assize proceedings (see below).

[21] *CCR* (1468–76), no. 643.

[22] NRO, B-L VIII b: copy of writ.

at Thetford the following September found that Coket had no title
to any of the Payn estate.[23] With regard to the toft and thirty acres
which he had acquired in 1456 (see above), this was because John
Payn II's grant had disseised the legal owner, John at Rydde, the
heir of the last survivor among the original trustees.[24]

John III, who probably died before the end of 1471, ran into
financial problems like his father, but the Payn estate nevertheless
passed to his uncle William.[25] Because William was the last of his
line it was bound ultimately to escheat to Roger I as feudal lord,
but, as we have seen, Roger chose to buy out the priest's reversionary
interest rather than wait for this to happen. Well versed as he must
have been in the property's past history, he probably felt he had
made a secure investment.

By his own reckoning Roger enjoyed a decade of trouble-free
possession after he bought it, but in the early 1480s this possession
was threatened. According to his notes, Robert Wolvy stirred up
trouble (*fist variannce*) between him and Anthony Woodville, now
Earl Rivers. Apparently Wolvy told the earl that he had a claim
to the Payn estate—perhaps through Coket's conveyances of 1465
(see above)—whereupon Woodville entered the land. Wolvy was
probably motivated by personal grievances against Roger as a local
landlord: in 1479 the latter had entered a suit against him in King's
Bench for trespass.[26] Moreover, he had at one time been Roger's
receiver, for in Hilary term 1480 Roger began a suit in Common
Pleas against him to make him render reasonable account for his time
in that office. Later, at the beginning of the sixteenth century, he
refused to pay certain rents to Roger II who responded by distraining
several of his livestock at East Raynham. In turn, he broke into
Roger's close and released them.[27]

In any case, Roger certainly did not enjoy good relations with
the earl in this period. As Lord Scales, Woodville was lord of 'Scales',
a manor in Raynham later acquired by the Townshends, and in
1481 he presented a bill in Chancery against James Lumbard, a

[23] NRO, B-L VIII b: copy of the assize proceedings.
[24] The trustees were joint tenants seised in survivorship. As each died the title
reposed in the survivors, eventually descending to the heirs of the last survivor after his
death. See Bean, *English Feudalism*, 153–4.
[25] See above, n. 13. John III was still alive on 30 Sept. 1471: NRO, B-L VIII b,
no. 36.
[26] PRO, KB27/872, rot. 2.
[27] PRO, CP40/871, rot. 56; CP40/956, rot. 257.

Townshend bailiff, for detaining a rental belonging to the manor and using it to Roger's profit.[28] Then, in March 1482, he claimed certain lands of Roger's in Helhoughton by suing him and Lumbard for a trespass which was supposed to have occurred some fourteen years earlier. Roger and Lumbard responded to the earl's plea by obtaining successive licences to imparl until Easter term 1483.[29]

This last case never came to judgement; memoranda written on a spare folio at the end of some of Roger's sheep accounts show that he and the earl met at Lynn on 20 March 1483, and then again at Walsingham five days later, to settle all their differences.[30] It seems they agreed that Woodville should have part of the former Payn lands, while their conflicting claims with regard to other lands in the Helhoughton neighbourhood should be put to the arbitration of the duke of Gloucester's council.[31]

It is unlikely that any of their agreement was implemented, however, because for reasons of high politics Woodville was arrested by Gloucester the following month and beheaded a few weeks later.[32] In July John Howard, the new duke of Norfolk, was granted Woodville's lands in west Norfolk.[33] At some stage after this, Coket and Wolvy re-entered the former Payn lands, claiming to be acting on Howard's behalf.[34] If they really were acting for Howard the latter must have been staking a claim as Woodville's successor, though the legal situation over the earl's estates after his execution is not clear.[35] Unfortunately it is at this point that Roger's notes end, after querying whether the duke could have any title to the Payn land.

Otherwise there appears to be no evidence that Howard, who was in any case killed at Bosworth two years later, pressed such a claim. Moreover, when Roger died in 1493 he was found to have been seised of the manor and lands which he had bought from William Payn over twenty years earlier.[36] His family's title to the property was

---

[28] Below, App. 6; PRO, C1/69/177.
[29] PRO, CP40/880, rot. 288, 378; CP40/881, rot. 302.
[30] R24, 1478/9 sheep accounts, fo. 15ᵛ. See Postscript at the end of this chapter.
[31] See Postscript at the end of this chapter.
[32] Lander, *Government and Community*, 313.
[33] At first 'during pleasure' but in tail male from Feb. 1485: *CPR* (1476-85), 365, 497.
[34] Roger's notes speak of the 'Duk de N' and this can only refer to Howard.
[35] Ives, 'Andrew Dymmock', 217 n.
[36] *CIPM, Henry VII*, vol. i, no. 1,143.

further secured in March 1495 when Coket, or perhaps by this date
his heir, made a formal release of any claim to it to the Townshends'
trustees.[37]

The nature of the evidence renders our knowledge of the difficulties
Roger I ran into with his lands in Helhoughton incomplete and in
many ways unsatisfactory, but the whole affair nevertheless raises
some interesting points.

In its origins the dispute demonstrates that the enfeoffment to
use could bring disadvantages along with its undoubted advantages
to the landowner. The settlement made by John Payn I was designed
to ensure the integrity of his family's property, but it also meant
that his son, John II, was not the legal owner of his own lands. When
the latter ignored this restriction and alienated part, and then all,
of his estate problems were bound to arise. It was not until 1484 that
statute law equated legal and beneficial ownership of real property
by making it possible for a *cestui que use* to dispose of land held for
him in trust as if it were held in fee at common law. After this date
any conveyance he made would hold good for him and his heirs
against his feoffees. As far as John II was concerned, however, any
grants he made had to be carried out through, and therefore with
the consent of, his trustees.[38]

The dispute, once under way, also highlights a major problem
for law enforcement in the later Middle Ages. Coket, as Roger told
him, had no legal title to the Payn estate, so he sought to overcome
this difficulty through the support of a great lord. Landholders with
shaky titles often chose powerful trustees who could be drawn into
any litigation which might occur.[39] It is unnecessary to go into the
well-known evils of maintenance here; what is worth noting is that
it was not always the occasion for great disorder. 'Good lordship'
did not inevitably mean the violent support of retainers against all
comers.[40] Woodville, the king's brother-in-law, was one of the most
powerful men in the country, and could well have supported the
claims of both Coket and himself with considerable force and
impunity. After all, in the same period Edward IV was prepared to

[37] R12, 'HELHOUGHTON, Temp. HEN VII', deed of 12 Mar. 1495.
[38] 1 Ric. III, c. 1 (*Statutes of the Realm*, ii. 477–8); Bean, *English Feudalism*, 177;
Simpson, *Land Law*, 215.
[39] M. A. Hicks, 'Restraint, Mediation and Private Justice: George, Duke of
Clarence as "Good Lord"', *Journal of Legal History*, 4 (1983), 59.
[40] Ibid., 61.

countenance the destruction that John Mowbray, duke of Norfolk, wrought on the Pastons' manor at Hellesdon.[41] But Woodville does not seem to have tried to prevent John Payn III from recovering his land, and he used the courts against Roger, and then negotiated with him, rather than resorting to such violence.

As we have seen, he and Roger intended to lay some of their differences before the duke of Gloucester's council. Baronial councils and their ancillary staffs—even those of the duke of Clarence, Edward IV's disreputable younger brother—often played a crucial role in determining many private disputes. Because most magnates retained legal specialists among their councillors, the baronial council was well-fitted for this role and played an important part in restricting the outbreaks of violence which are too-readily depicted as the norm in the later medieval period.[42]

(iii) East Beckham

The dispute over the ownership of the manor of East Beckham, one of the Townshends' more isolated Norfolk properties, situated near the north-east coast of the county, was one of the most prominent cases in which they were involved to be resolved by arbitration. It is perhaps not surprising that the Pastons, the property's former owners, should have claimed it from the Townshends, since they had parted with it reluctantly. Financial circumstance had forced them to mortgage it to Roger I for 100 marks in November 1469, and they were unable to redeem it within the year allowed them to repay him.[43] As the Townshends later asserted,[44] Roger's title does not seem to have been challenged during the rest of his life, although the Pastons still had hopes of recovering the manor in the early 1470s.[45]

Although it would be unwise to accept completely at face-value

---

[41] *PL*, no. 333.

[42] C. Rawcliffe, 'The Great Lord as Peacekeeper: Arbitration by English Noblemen and their Councils in the Later Middle Ages', in J. A. Guy and H. G. Beale (edd.), *Law and Social Change in British History* (London, 1984), 37; Hicks, 'Restraint, Mediation and Private Justice', *passim*.

[43] Ch. 4, 1 below; BL, Add. Ch. 14,526 (*PL*, no. 246). For the troubled and complicated ownership of the manor see C. Richmond, *The Paston Family in the Fifteenth Century: The First Phase* (Cambridge, 1990), Ch. 3.

[44] BL, Add. MS 41,139, fo. 8ᵛ.

[45] Hopes which seem to have been dashed by Nov. 1474 when Sir John Paston informed his mother, 'For Bekham, he [Roger I] spekyth no-thyng comfortably ther in; what he wyll doo, can I nott seye': *PL*, no. 286.

a claim made in the middle of the quarrel that later developed, the first sign of any trouble came several years after Roger I's death. Unfortunately it is unclear as to why matters should then have come to a head, but in 1499 Sir John Paston challenged the Townshends' title to East Beckham by suing Eleanor Townshend, her eldest son Roger II, and two family servants, Thomas Gygges and John Affordby, for forcible entry.[46] In the language of the plea rolls Paston was acting on behalf of the king as well as himself, because under the terms of the 1381 statute against forcible entries (5 Ric. II, c. 7) the king theoretically took a direct interest in charges brought against illegal entrants. Title to the land in such proceedings was immaterial, since the question of whether a forcible entry had occurred was what was being tried, but in practice a ruling on the issue of forcible entry could not fail to affect title.[47]

Paston pleaded that the defendants, in the company of half-a-dozen armed followers, entered the manor on 4 December 1498.[48] Eleanor responded with an action of detinue, first in the Duchy of Lancaster court at Frettenham, and then, because she claimed that the under-steward of that court received an annual retainer from Paston and she could not receive justice there, in the Common Pleas. The latter suit, entered in Michaelmas term 1499, charged that a day earlier (3 December 1498) Paston had unjustly seized and detained 500 sheep from her East Beckham flock.[49] Sure enough, the Townshends' sheep accounts show that at least one animal was killed by the 'dryvyng of the servantes' of Paston, that the sheep-reeve incurred various extraordinary expenses caused by 'the gret trobyll of Sir John Paston', that the flock decreased in size during the 1498/9 accounting-year from 716 to 216 sheep, and that no attempt was made to restock it.[50]

Neither party's action progressed beyond pleading; in each case successive licences to imparl until Hilary term 1500 were obtained by the defendants.[51] By then Eleanor was no longer alive, having died the previous September,[52] but in the meantime a considerable

---

[46] PRO, CP40/949, rot. 459.

[47] *Statutes of the Realm*, ii. 20; J. G. Bellamy, *Criminal Law and Society in Late Medieval and Tudor England* (Gloucester, 1984), 65.

[48] PRO, CP40/950, rot. 416.

[49] PRO, CP40/948, rot. 356; CP40/950, rot. 277; CP40/952, rot. 263.

[50] R50, 1498/9 sheep accounts, fos. 9^r, 15^r.

[51] PRO, CP40/952, rot. 263; CP40/950, rot. 416.

[52] *CIPM, Henry VII*, vol. ii, no. 493.

amount of negotiation between the two sides must have taken place, and in late 1500 or early 1501 they came together before the king's attorney James Hobart, one of the leading lawyers of East Anglia.[53] Associated with Roger II, now the leading representative for the Townshends, was Sir Robert Clere who, as executor of the recently deceased Eleanor Townshend, had an interest in the affairs of the Townshend estate. Under Hobart's direction the parties were able to reach an interim agreement or *compromissio* as a preliminary to the negotiations for a final settlement.[54] This appointed Hobart and serjeant John Yaxley, another prominent East Anglian lawyer, as arbitrators before whom they agreed to appear at Norwich a couple of days before the summer quarter sessions of 1501 were due to begin. In the meantime Clement Harward was appointed as a neutral receiver to collect the issues of the manor until an award was made, not an infrequent practice when the ownership of a property was being decided.[55]

The final award was dated 6 February 1503, so the lawyers may have had difficulty in working out a compromise acceptable to both parties. The delay may well have been largely the fault of the Townshends because, not long after Hobart became involved as a potential arbitrator, Roger II tried to strike a deal with Sir John Wyndham. He offered Wyndham possession of East Beckham for a term of up to seven years. During these seven years Wyndham would pay him an annuity of 10 marks from its issues until he could provide him with another manor (to be worth 10 marks per annum) in exchange; if Wyndham failed to provide such a manor, he was to buy East Beckham for 200 marks when the term was up.[56] East Beckham was worth annually about £10 rather than 10 marks, so Roger was prepared to lose out in order to rid himself of a problem.[57] But even if it were taken seriously, Wyndham's execution for treason in 1502 soon put paid to this rather dubious scheme.[58]

In their final award Hobart and Yaxley gave East Beckham to

---

[53] BL, Add. MS 41,139, fo. 6[r]; Wedgwood, 458-9.

[54] For the different stages of the arbitration process see E. Powell, 'Arbitration and the Law in England in the Late Middle Ages', *TRHS* 5th ser. 33 (1983), 53-6; id., 'Settlement of Disputes by Arbitration in Fifteenth Century England', *Law and History Review*, 2 (1984), 33-4.

[55] BL, Add. MS 41,139, fos. 6[r], 7[r], 8[r]; e.g. *PL*, no. 854.

[56] BL, Add. MS 41,139, fo. 9[r].

[57] R58, RT I memo-book, fo. 12[r].

[58] *DNB*, s.v. 'Thomas Wyndham (1510?-1553)'.

Sir John Paston, though the Townshends had title at common law. In doing so they may have been following a developing trend in equity with regard to the plight of defaulting mortgagors. In the case of East Beckham the indebted Pastons had certainly parted with the manor reluctantly, but they could expect little sympathy from the common law since it did not concern itself with why a mortgage was made in the first place, or whether it had been made in unfair circumstances. The chancellor therefore began to intervene in cases in the mid-fifteenth century, and by Elizabeth I's reign was allowing mortgagors to redeem the land upon payment, even though they had lost the land for ever at common law.[59]

Nevertheless, Paston was expected to pay Roger £100 in compensation, and if he refused the manor on these terms Roger was to have it and to pay Paston the same amount. Paston, given two days to decide, opted to take the manor and it passed permanently out of the Townshends' hands.[60] His title to it was reinforced by means of a fine in 1504.[61] An additional clause of the award required the party which ended up with the manor to pay the other side 10 marks—representing a share in the accumulated arrears of uncollected tenants' rent—over and above the £100.[62] The tenants at East Beckham had been lucky enough to escape paying either side during the dispute. Sometimes the tenants of a disputed property could find themselves in an almost impossible position, facing the prospect of paying rent to both parties or being distrained for non-payment by one after paying it to the other: the Paston Letters contain several examples of this sort of situation arising.[63]

Other aspects of the East Beckham dispute deserve comment. Norwich was chosen as a venue for bringing the parties together, since a town where the quarter sessions were about to commence offered a favourable setting for bringing a dispute to a satisfactory conclusion. Those gentry who had come to participate in the sessions could help to persuade the disputants to settle their differences, and they provided useful witnesses to the terms of any award should one of the parties later try to break them. Also noteworthy is that no discernible violence, except that suffered by the Townshends' unfortunate sheep, occurred. By this date much of the potential for violence

[59] Simpson, *Land Law*, 226-7.   [60] *PL*, no. 928.
[61] PRO, CP40/968, rot. 21.   [62] *PL*, no. 928.
[63] e.g. *PL*, nos. 338, 381, 875, 508.

arising out of entries into property had been defused by formalized ritual.[64]

But, above all, the Townshend–Paston dispute supports the view of Powell and others that the arbitration process was a complimentary adjunct to the common law rather than a sign of the common law's weakness.[65] Indeed, arbitration and law were intimately linked: Roger I presided over a case at the Horsham assizes in 1492 in which it was decided that the parties should put their dispute before a couple of arbitrators.[66] In this period arbitration rarely occurred in isolation from litigation,[67] and litigants commonly resorted to the tactic of using the lawcourts as a way of pressing an opponent to begin negotiating an out-of-court settlement. (This must have been the Pastons' intention in the case of East Beckham, because legally the Townshends were clearly the manor's owners.) Moreover, the East Beckham award was secured by the means of a fine, a common-law process. Collusive litigation provided essential confirmation of the terms of any award involving real property by making it enforceable in the common-law courts. Although there is no evidence that the Pastons or the Townshends did so, it was also normal for both sides to bind themselves by recognizances, again enforceable at common law, to abide by the decision of the arbitrators.[68] The close relationship between arbitration and the common law is further emphasized by the choice of Hobart and Yaxley as arbitrators. Arbitration was a routine part of the common lawyer's work, and Hobart was associated with Roger I in this role on at least one occasion.[69]

(iv) The Brewes Inheritance

The dispute over the Brewes inheritance had its roots in the second marriage of Sir Thomas Brewes of Fressingfield, Suffolk, the grandfather of Roger II's wife Amy, and the owner of substantial estates

---

[64] Bellamy, *Criminal Law and Society*, 68–9.

[65] Powell, 'Arbitration and the Law' and 'Settlement of Disputes'; Hicks, 'Restraint, Mediation and Private Justice', 63, 68; S. J. Payling, 'Law and Arbitration in Nottinghamshire 1399–1461', in J. Rosenthal and C. Richmond (edd.), *People, Politics and Community in the Later Middle Ages* (Gloucester, 1987), 151.

[66] R58, RT I memo-book, fo. 2ᵛ.

[67] Powell, 'Arbitration and the Law', 38; id., 'Settlement of Disputes', 57.

[68] Payling, 'Law and Arbitration', 151; Hicks, 'Restraint, Mediation and Private Justice', 63; Powell, 'Arbitration and the Law', 60.

[69] Id., 'Settlement of Disputes', 23; *CCR* (1476–85), no. 274; (1485–1500), no. 482.

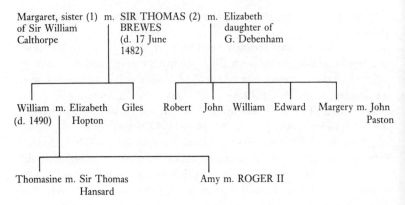

Fig. 3.2. The Brewes Family

in Suffolk, Norfolk, and Lincolnshire.[70] It began a decade after he died in 1482, but its seeds were sown in the mid-fifteenth century.

By his first wife, Margaret Calthorpe, Sir Thomas had several children, including his eldest son William, Amy's father. By 1440 he had married again, and he and his second wife, Elizabeth daughter of Gilbert Debenham esquire of Little Wenham, Suffolk,[71] had several more children.

When he married Elizabeth Sir Thomas settled the Suffolk manors of Akenham, Witnesham, and Hasketon on his wife and himself in tail male (that is, the estate was limited to their male heirs), and gave her a life-interest in Stinton Hall in Salle, Norfolk. This settlement was considerably to the detriment of William, his common-law heir, for these manors had been in the Brewes family for several generations and were a valuable part of their estate.[72] Sir Thomas reinforced it as late as 1455 when he had the three Suffolk manors, together with Hemmingstone in the same county, seised on himself and Elizabeth and their male heirs.[73] He probably made it in return for the

[70] Wedgwood, 108–9; *CIPM, Henry VII,* vol. i, nos. 645, 648, 1,025; R49, Townshend cartulary, fos. 32^v–34^v. Unless otherwise indicated, what follows is based upon the relevant Chancery proceedings (PRO, C1/96/22–6).

[71] Wedgwood, 108–9; Sayer, 'Norfolk Involvement', 323 n.; *CIPM, Henry VII,* vol. ii, no. 199. Wedgwood wrongly identifies Sir Thomas's first wife as the grand-daughter of Sir William Calthorpe.

[72] W. A. Copinger, *The Manors of Suffolk,* 7 vols. (Manchester, 1905–11), iii. 50–1, 122.

[73] PRO, CP25/1/225/119, no. 14.

generous marriage-portion given to Elizabeth by her father, and because Debenham, who had powerful local connections, was a man whose friendship was worth having.[74]

Sir Thomas nevertheless later overturned the settlement when William, his heir by his first marriage, married Elizabeth, daughter of John Hopton (by 1456).[75] He did so by resettling Akenham, Witnesham, and Hasketon on William and his wife and their heirs-general. He apparently used Elizabeth Hopton's marriage-portion to compensate his own wife by acquiring with it property of equal value which he thereupon settled upon themselves and his heirs by her. But this was not a satisfactory solution, for Elizabeth bitterly resented the barring of the earlier entail and began to trouble her stepson after Sir Thomas's death.[76] In 1484 she sued William for trespassing on Akenham and the other manors, and, after the latter died in 1490, she took possession and seized the evidences relating to them and Stinton Hall.[77]

Because she had seized the deeds, Thomasine and Amy, William's daughters and co-heirs, and their husbands, Sir Thomas Hansard[78] and Roger II, could not seek redress at common law and so they petitioned the chancellor in early 1491. In practice Roger I must have acted for his son and his wife, because although Roger II attained his majority before the dispute ended, he was only about 13 years old at this date. Elizabeth, pleading ill health, did not appear in person to answer their charge of illegal disseisin, and she was examined at home.[79] By this date the practice of taking written answers from the parties in a Chancery case made this possible.[80] Her defence was that the settlement made by Sir Thomas Brewes when she married him was still valid, and she presented a counter charge. She claimed that

---

[74] At least £1,000 in money, plate, and other goods according to Elizabeth: PRO, C1/96/25. For Debenham see W. I. Haward, 'Gilbert Debenham: A Medieval Rascal in Real Life', *History*, NS 13 (1928-9), 300-14; Wedgwood, 265.

[75] Richmond, *John Hopton*, 142.

[76] Ibid., 142-3.

[77] PRO, CP40/887, rot. 130. William died on 30 Oct.; a later inquisition mistakenly dated his death 20 May 1491: *CIPM, Henry VII*, vol. i, nos. 648, 1,025.

[78] Originally from Lincolnshire; younger son of Sir Richard Hansard of South Kelsey: *Lincolnshire Pedigrees*, ed. A. R. Maddison, 4 vols., Harleian Soc., 50-2, 53 (1902-6), ii. 455.

[79] PRO, C1/96/24. A notebook of Roger II shows she indeed suffered ill health in her later years: R58, RT II, memo-book, fo. 3ᵛ.

[80] *Select Cases in Chancery, 1364-1474*, ed. W. P. Baildon, Selden Soc., 10 (1896), pp. xxvi-xxvii.

her late husband had assigned her a year's revenues, to use towards
the performance of his will, from his manor of Whittingham Hall
in Fressingfield. But these revenues, she said, had been denied to
her by the senior branch of the family. (In 1487 she had temporarily
ejected William Brewes from the manor, perhaps in an attempt to
collect the money.)[81] She also asserted that the will assigned various
junior members of the Brewes family an interest in Whittingham Hall
in the form of annuities chargeable on its revenues, but raised doubts
as to whether they had been allowed to collect them.

The Townshend–Hansard bill, Elizabeth's reply, and a short
rejoinder by her opponents are the only evidence of proceedings in
Chancery, and the dispute was not settled there.[82] It widened in
scope before it ended, because its final resolution concerned the entire
Brewes estate. The reason why it took so long to resolve—it was not
until early 1500 that the parties agreed to submit to arbitration—is
unclear, but the delay was probably partly due to a separate quarrel
which had arisen in the meantime between the Townshends and
the Hansards.[83] The arbitrators were two leading gentlemen, Sir
Thomas Lovell and Sir Henry Heydon, and two lawyers, serjeant
Thomas Kebell and James Hobart, the king's attorney. Both parties
agreed to make out bonds obliging each to forfeit 500 marks to the
other side if they failed to comply with a future award. The bonds
were to be entrusted to Kebell,[84] who was not from Norfolk and
whose neutrality could be expected. Lovell, an important royal councillor and himself a lawyer, was also eminently suitable as an arbiter.
Indeed, the prestige of the panel as a whole makes it likely that
higher authority, perhaps the king, prompted the attempt to reach
a settlement.

One of the attractions of the arbitration process was that it offered
the chance to resolve a dispute more quickly than did the common
law, but the quarrel was not settled speedily: the final award was
recorded on a tripartite indenture made between the two parties
and Lovell dated 15 June 1502.[85] This was probably because a

---

[81] Richmond, *John Hopton*, 142–3.
[82] PRO, C1/96/22, 25–6.
[83] R58, RT II memo-book, fo. 3ᵛ; below, section v.
[84] R58, RT II memo-book, fo. 3ᵛ.
[85] Powell, 'Arbitration and Law', 56; R49, Townshend cartulary, fos. 32ᵛ.–34ᵛ.
Both sides kept a part of the indenture and Lovell retained the third part for reference
(cf. Powell, 'Settlement of Disputes', 34).

satisfactory compromise—the essence of a successful arbitration settlement—was difficult to achieve.[86] Lovell was the sole arbitrator named in the indenture, and it appears that he had adopted the role of an umpire who imposed a settlement because the original mediators were unable to reach a conclusion. An umpire had to be a person of authority like Lovell to ensure that the parties complied with the final decision.[87] His award was nevertheless a success, and by 1504 Robert Brewes, Elizabeth's eldest son and heir by Sir Thomas, was on good enough terms with the Townshends to act as a trustee for Roger II.[88]

Lovell's award divided the Brewes estate between the parties. It represented a true compromise, because both sides were obliged to make concessions. Of the manors at the centre of the dispute— Akenham, Witnesham, and Hasketon—Elizabeth and her heirs by Sir Thomas Brewes were allowed to keep Witnesham but received no more than a life-interest in the others. She and the junior branch of the family were, however, awarded another four manors in East Anglia,[89] and, with the exception of the Fressingfield and Lincolnshire properties, she was given a life-interest in almost the entire estate. The Hansards and the Townshends were, moreover, to pay £160 to Robert Brewes, her eldest son and heir by Sir Thomas. On the other hand, Thomasine and Amy were to succeed to all of William Brewes's inheritance—except Witnesham—after her death, and this made up the core of the estate. They did not have long to wait, as Elizabeth died in early 1503. Nevertheless, Roger II had by then already bought from her her life-interest in Amy's moiety of Hasketon.[90]

An interesting aspect of the affair was its possible political ramifications. Private disputes among the gentry could sometimes become entangled with politics.[91] While Richard III was king Sir Thomas Hansard was a 'malcontent', but the junior Brewes line identified

---

[86] Rawcliffe, 'Great Lord as Peacekeeper', 35–6; Payling, 'Law and Arbitration', 147; Powell, 'Settlement of Disputes', 37.

[87] Cf. Rawcliffe, 'Great Lord as Peacekeeper', 40.

[88] R49, Townshend cartulary, fos. 35ᵛ–36ᵛ.

[89] Topcroft and Denton in Norfolk, 'Stodhawe' in Suffolk, and 'Haukers' which straddled the Norfolk–Suffolk border.

[90] PRO, PROB11/13, fos. 151a–151b (will of 5 Dec. 1502; proved 9 Feb. 1503); R31, RT II estate book, fos. 15ᵛ, 27ᵛ.

[91] Cf. R. A. Griffiths, 'The Hazards of Civil War: The Mountford Family and the "Wars of the Roses"', *Midland History*, 5 (1979–80), 1–19.

with the regime. During Richard's reign no less than four commissions for Hansard's arrest were issued, although none achieved its purpose.[92] The first was addressed to the sheriff of Norfolk and Suffolk alone, but the others also appointed several gentlemen to apprehend him. These included Sir Gilbert Debenham, the brother of Elizabeth Brewes and one of Richard's household knights, and three of her sons by Sir Thomas Brewes, Robert, John, and William.[93] Also appointed were Sir John Paston, Elizabeth's son-in-law, and Ralph Willoughby. Not much can be made of Paston's Ricardian credentials, but Willoughby was an esquire of the body and a committed supporter of the last Yorkist king.[94]

Hansard's fortunes changed with the advent of Henry VII, and he earned a knighthood by fighting for Tudor at Stoke in 1487.[95] Debenham, on the other hand, lost permanently his place on the Norfolk bench and, although pardoned in 1486 for his adherence to Richard III, his loyalty was always suspect. He was eventually attainted in 1495 for supporting Perkin Warbeck.[96] Conceivably, the Townshends and the Hansards deliberately began their Chancery suit against Elizabeth in early 1491 because it was then that Sir Gilbert was ordered, perhaps banished, to Ireland, and she could not have expected many favours from the Crown.[97]

However, this long dispute is most interesting as an example of the problems that could arise from a second marriage. The growing sophistication of family settlements, made possible by the enfeoffment to use and the barring of entails, meant that a landowner could provide for his children by a second wife; but this was a frequent cause of strife when made at the expense of the offspring of his previous marriage.[98] By overturning the generous settlement he had made his second wife, Sir Thomas Brewes forestalled the very real possibility of serious discontent on the part of his common-law heirs. On the other hand, this gave the junior branch of the family legitimate cause for complaint and ensured that problems would arise in the future.

---

[92] Sayer, 'Norfolk Involvement', 318, 324 n.; *CPR* (1476–85), 493, 494, 543, 547.

[93] Debenham, Robert, and John were appointed to all three and William to two.

[94] *Harleian MS 433*, iii. 130; Sayer, 'Norfolk Involvement', 318.

[95] Ibid., 324 n.; *The Paston Letters*, vi. 187.

[96] Wedgwood, 266; *RP*, vi. 504. To reverse the attainder and recover the lands of her brother for her son Robert, Sir Gilbert's nearest male heir, Elizabeth was obliged to pay Henry VII £500: ibid., 549; *CPR* (1494–1509), 238–9, 351; BL, Add. MS 21,480, fo. 71ᵛ.

[97] Wedgwood, 266.

[98] Payling, 'Law and Arbitration', 151–4; Griffiths, 'Hazards of Civil War', 1–19.

(v) The Dispute with the Hansards

The dispute with Elizabeth Brewes perhaps dragged on for as long as it did because during it the Townshends and the Hansards quarrelled among themselves and, for a period, were not in any positon to come to terms with her. This separate quarrel arose over Whittingham Hall and 'Wakelyns', another manor at Fressingfield, and various appurtenant lands. Inherited by William Brewes, Elizabeth made no claims to ownership of them, although she had declared a limited interest in Whittingham Hall.[99] After William died at the end of October 1490, Sir Thomas Hansard took possession of the manors in his capacity as husband of one of the co-heirs. As far as 'Wakelyns' was concerned, however, the co-heirs possibly had no right to succeed. An inquisition later found that William had held it in tail male only, that the rightful heir was Giles, his younger brother, and that Hansard had disseised Giles when he entered the manor.[100] But this was a side-issue, and we hear no more of it.

The Townshend–Hansard quarrel began because, upon taking possession of the Fressingfield properties, the Hansards refused to acknowledge Amy's right to a moiety. In April 1495 matters came to a head, and a writ of novel disseisin was taken out against the Hansards on behalf of Roger and Amy. The case reached Common Pleas: in Trinity term 1496 the Hansards were licensed to imparl until the following Michaelmas, in which term they pleaded that Amy had no right to a moiety at Fressingfield and put themselves upon the country.[101] The case never reached *nisi prius*, however, because it was resolved by an out-of-court settlement.

The details of the final award do not survive, but a notebook of Eleanor Townshend records an undated preliminary agreement, mediated by the friends of both parties, which was made before her death in September 1499.[102] This agreement was between Hansard and his wife on the one part and Thomas Woodhouse esquire, representing his under-age brother-in-law, Roger II, and his wife on the other. It is an excellent example of compromise. The Hansards were to recognize Amy's right to a moiety of the Fressingfield property

---

[99] *CIPM, Henry VII*, vol. i, no. 654; R49, Townshend cartulary, fos. 32ᵛ–34ᵛ; PRO, C1/96/25.

[100] *CIPM, Henry VII*, vol. ii, no. 199. Giles also had a quarrel with Hansard concerning property at Mendham, Suffolk, and sued him for unlawful disseisin in early 1500: PRO, CP40/955, rot. 285; CP40/956, rot. 247.

[101] PRO, CP40/937, rot. 276; CP40/938, rot. 408.

[102] BL, Add. MS 41,305, fos. 28ᵗ–29ᵗ.

and to pay the Townshends all arrears of her share of its revenues. It was to be divided between the parties by Woodhouse, Sir Robert Clere, Thomas Hevingham esquire, serjeant John Yaxley, and James Hobart, the king's attorney. The Hansards would, however, in practice continue to occupy the whole of Fressingfield since Roger and Amy were to lease Amy's moiety to them. This lease was to last for twenty years, or until such time as Elizabeth Brewes's life-interest in Stinton Hall in Norfolk—which both parties acknowledged despite their quarrel with her—ended and it reverted to Thomasine and Amy as the co-heirs of the senior Brewes line. When it expired the Townshends were to surrender their moiety permanently to the Hansards in exchange for the Hansards' moiety of Stinton. This would leave each party an entire manor rather than a share in two, an arrangement which was administratively convenient and would help to prevent future disputes. Should Stinton be found to be worth less than Fressingfield, the Townshends were to receive the difference in the form of an annuity from the issues of the Suffolk properties.

If implemented, the agreement was to be ratified legally— presumably by means of a fine or recovery—under the supervision of Robert Rede, JKB.[103] An all-important proviso was that it required the assent of Eleanor Townshend before it became a final award. There is no evidence, however, that she objected to it. It must have resolved the dispute, because at the end of 1499 Roger II received £8 from Hansard, part of the rent owing for the farm of Amy's moiety of Fressingfield.[104] Relations between the Townshends and Hansards were amicable enough a few years later for Anthony Hansard, the son of Sir Thomas, to act as a trustee for Roger.[105]

Like the disputes previously discussed, the Townshend–Hansard quarrel demonstrates the connection between the common law and the arbitration process, not least because of the part played by common lawyers and common-law processes to resolve it. It shows also how the common-law system was often treated as a means to an end, such as an out-of-court settlement, rather than something which could bring about an end by itself. If the Townshends' resort to the Common Pleas was what encouraged the out-of-court settle-

---

[103] I have not discovered any signs of this on the plea rolls.

[104] R33, RT II receipt book, fo. 7ʳ.

[105] e.g. PRO, CP25/2/28/188, no. 10; R6, 'TOFTREES & SHEREFORD Temp. H VIII', deed of 2 Dec. 1511; R28, 'RAYNHAM HENRY VIII-PHILIP & MARY', deed of 12 Mar. 1514.

ment, then the common law had not failed but achieved its purpose. Litigation, negotiation, and arbitration could all occur simultaneously. A 'striking feature' of the English legal system was the popularity of arbitration as a means of settling quarrels out of court once mesne process had begun.[106] Powell has calculated that less than 10 per cent of private suits initiated in Common Pleas and King's Bench came to judgement in Henry VII's reign, and Rawcliffe found that only 6 out of 128 separate actions begun by the third duke of Buckingham ever reached a verdict.[107] There is no doubt that the use of arbitration explains why many cases did not.

The dispute with the Hansards also shows how the gentry could curb their own quarrels by self-regulation, because the Townshends and their opponents were encouraged to settle their differences by their peers.[108] This was not the only occasion on which Roger II and an opponent were persuaded to come to terms by their fellow gentry. In about 1510 he quarrelled with one of the Southwells over pasture-rights at Barmer, a township not far from Raynham. The two disputants were subsequently brought together at the house of Richard Norton, one of Roger's free tenants. It is not known what caused the quarrel or how it was resolved, but what is important to note is that several other gentlemen were present at Norton's house in order to see that a settlement was reached.[109] A few years later Roger had a dispute with John Eston, a minor gentleman from Syderstone, over various rents and farms which each claimed from the other.[110] Like the earlier quarrel it was resolved by arbitration. The mediators between the parties were Sir Thomas Wyndham, William Wotton, and Dr Geoffrey Knyght, and the final agreement was recorded in the presence of Sir William Paston.[111] Ultimately

[106] Wright, *Derbyshire Gentry*, 119–20; Powell, 'Arbitration and the Law', 57, 59; Rawcliffe, 'Great Lord as Peacekeeper', 34.

[107] Powell, 'Arbitration and the Law', 51; Rawcliffe, *Staffords*, 164–5.

[108] Cf. Wright, *Derbyshire Gentry*, 119; Bennett, 'A County Community', 25–7.

[109] NRO, B-L II e, 1501/2–1517/18 Townshend sheep accounts, fo. 161ᵛ. Norton is listed as one of Roger's tenants in a South Creake rental and firmal dated 2 Henry VII: R20.

[110] R19, 'N & S CREAKE Temp. HEN VII', deed of 12 May 1505. Eston may have been the John Eston of Wolsey's household: PRO, E179/69/9, 10.

[111] R(Attic), 'Legal and suit papers, 15th–19th cent.', indenture of 15 Jan. 1518. Knyght, a Cambridge theologian, held various Norfolk benefices. As a local landowner—he owned a manor in Pattesley which Roger II later acquired (see below, App. 6)—he made a suitable mediator. See Emden, *Biographical Register . . . Cambridge*, 340, for a summary of his career.

good order among the gentry often had little to do with the king and the central lawcourts. In these circumstances the gentry regulated themselves, though when those of East Anglia could not, the great magnates of the region were ready to impose settlements and to restrain the hot-headed.[112]

(2) THE TOWNSHENDS AS LITIGANTS

Beyond the five cases discussed above, the Townshends successfully avoided serious real property disputes during the lifetimes of Roger I and Roger II. Moreover, it is worth pointing out that two of these involved the inherited Brewes lands and so did not result from unwise speculation on the land market. A third, the Bale affair, concerned a manor which had been left to Roger I by will. We are therefore left with two disputes which arose over properties he had bought, and these do not seem to have been due to carelessness on his part. During his lifetime his title to East Beckham was secure and, as for Helhoughton, he had enjoyed some ten years of peaceful possession of the former Payn lands before any trouble started. Considering how complicated manorial titles had often become by the late Middle Ages, two major property disputes in a period of some one hundred years are not many for a new family which bought most of its estate.

Ruinous litigation did not invariably follow heavy investment in land in late medieval and early modern England; purchasers could avoid much trouble if they were careful in what they bought. As we might expect from a family of lawyers, the Townshends were meticulous in their record-keeping and catalogued all the deeds and evidences relating to the property which they acquired, and they stored them in various boxes (of which there were over sixty), bags, and baskets which, in turn, were kept in large chests in the 'vowte' (vault) at Raynham.[113] The great Tudor and early modern family archives, like that at Raynham, were created partly because the

---

[112] M. T. Clanchy, 'Law, Government and Society in Medieval England', *History*, 59 (1974), 78.

[113] NRO, Townshend 84 MS 1,503 1 D2 (1494/5 catalogue of books and evidences).

importance of record-keeping was engraved upon the legal mind.[114] Sir John Fastolf was equally careful in what he bought, and his long-suffering servant William Worcester made extensive tours around the country in search of evidences with which to prove his master's title to property. Taking into account the number of properties he obtained, and the size of the estate he built up, Fastolf was remarkably successful in avoiding challenges to title.[115]

Of course, gentlemen were not necessarily enthusiastic litigants. Saul's work on fourteenth-century Sussex shows that the head of one of the three families he studied was a far more regular plaintiff than the others. As for John Hopton, Richmond tells us that he avoided the lawcourts whenever he could, and argues that he may well have been more typical of his period than the Pastons and their interminable legal disputes.[116] Disputes may well appear more of the norm than they actually were, simply because they have left us a wealth of evidence.

The Townshends did not, however, shy away from the lawcourts; considering their legal backgrounds, and the ease of access to the central courts that Roger I in particular enjoyed, it would have been strange if they had. What follows on the family as litigants is based on the docket rolls for the periods when these are available, and searches through the actual plea rolls when they are not.

The docket rolls were contemporary indexes for the plea rolls of King's Bench and the Common Pleas; those for King's Bench begin at Michaelmas 1485 and those for the latter court at Michaelmas 1509.[117] They are not exhaustive indexes, but they are a satisfactory source for cases in advanced stages taking place in the two courts in a given year.[118] Of course, many more suits were begun than reached advanced stages and, therefore, entry on the docket rolls; the majority never got beyond mesne process.[119] But it is

---

[114] *Papers of Nathaniel Bacon*, vol. i, p. xviii.

[115] K. B. McFarlane, 'William Worcester: A Preliminary Survey, in id., *England*, 207; Smith, 'Litigation and Politics', 59–75.

[116] Saul, *Provincial Life*, 78; Richmond, *John Hopton*, 30.

[117] PRO, IND1/1325; IND1/1.

[118] C. W. Brooks, 'Litigants and Attorneys in the King's Bench and Common Pleas, 1560–1640', in J. H. Baker (ed.), *Legal Records and the Historian* (London, 1978), 41–2.

[119] D. J. Guth, 'The Age of Debt, the Reformation and English Law', in D. J. Guth and J. W. McKenna (edd.), *Tudor Rule and Revolution* (Cambridge, 1982), 76; M. Blatcher, *The Court of King's Bench, 1450–1550* (London, 1978), 59, 73.

nevertheless soon clear from the docket rolls, and from the plea rolls themselves, that the great majority of the legal actions initiated by the Townshends were actions of debt.[120] They therefore made far more extensive use of the Common Pleas (which enjoyed some 70 to 80 per cent of common-law business in this period)[121] than of King's Bench, since pleas of debt belonged to the former court.[122] During the first half of the 1480s, for example, Roger I seems to have been involved in only a single suit in King's Bench, the already-mentioned action of trespass he began against Robert Wolvy in late 1479.[123] As for Roger II, the King's Bench docket rolls record just one lawsuit in King's Bench which came to pleading in which he was a party, a trespass action which he took out in the early 1520s.[124]

Trespass and debt comprised the overwhelming bulk of pleas in the common-law courts in the Townshends' period.[125] Until the seventeenth century, debt on an obligation was the form of action which constituted the majority of cases entered on the plea rolls of the Common Pleas. The defendant was called upon to pay a monetary penalty to the plaintiff for failing to observe the terms of a written conditional bond into which he had entered with the latter. Technically speaking, the action was taken to enforce the bond—which the plaintiff or his attorney had to produce before the court—and the pleading did not concern itself with the details or circumstances of the agreement with which it was connected.[126]

Nevertheless, it is clear that those against whom the Townshends took out such actions were normally those who had provided bonds as security for sheep, wool, grain, or other agricultural produce sold on credit and who then failed to pay on time. It could be said that

---

[120] Between the beginning of 1480 to the end of Richard III's reign, for example, Roger I began at least twenty suits in the Common Pleas—eighteen actions of debt, one of account, one of trespass: PRO, CP40/871, rot. 44, 56, 195; 873, rot. 236; 874, rot. 236, 491, 495; 878, rot. 209, 356; 881, rot. 269; 882, rot. 82; 883, rot. 165; 888, rot. 234; 889, rot. 281, 284, 507.

[121] Ives, *Kebell*, 199; Blatcher, *King's Bench*, 24.

[122] Ibid., 7.

[123] Section 1(ii) above; PRO, KB27/872, rot. 2. Of course, after becoming a Common Pleas judge in September 1485, he had the privilege of suing all his actions there: M. Hastings, *The Court of Common Pleas in Fifteenth Century England* (Ithaca, NY, 1947), 17.

[124] PRO, KB27/1045, rot. 60.

[125] D. J. Guth, 'Enforcing Late-Medieval Law: Patterns in Litigation During Henry VIII's Reign', in Baker (ed.), *Legal Records and the Historian*, 86; Ives, *Kebell*, 199; Hastings, *Common Pleas*, 27.

[126] Baker, *Introduction*, 368-9.

they used the Common Pleas as a debt-collecting agency. In the early 1480s, for example, two yeomen, John Robyns of Hindolveston and William Newgate of Appleton, and a Fakenham butcher, John Prynce, were just three of those whom Roger I sued after they had fallen into arrears for sheep they had bought from him.[127] During her widowhood, Eleanor used the law on a regular basis against debtors (in the last year of her life she was chasing at least eighteen of them through the Common Pleas)[128], and she kept a record in her estate book of those bonds of defaulting obligees which she had sent to William Denne, her London attorney, so that he could commence suits on her behalf.[129] One of her debtors was Margaret Lumbard of Hadleigh in Suffolk, a customer for her wool in mid-1495. Nearly two years later, after Margaret had defaulted in her payment, Eleanor sent the relevant bond to Denne and the subsequent lawsuit eventually reached pleading.[130]

But many of the Townshends' actions never got beyond mesne process and disappear from the plea rolls after several terms, suggesting that they obtained satisfaction out of court. The point of initiating a suit in the first place was to put pressure on the debtor concerned; most claims for debt (and trespass) were never intended for judicial resolution.[131] In the majority of these cases it is unlikely that the defendants deliberately refused to pay. The general lack of ready money in this period meant that few had much cash to hand at any one time. In the mid-fifteenth century, for example, about one third of the bishop of Worcester's estate income was made up of arrears of payments that should have been made a year or two earlier.[132]

The Townshends were plaintiffs far more than they were defendants, but they were not necessarily more sinned against than sinning.[133] The gentry obviously had the greater wherewithal to sustain suits than did most of their social inferiors. On the eve of

[127] PRO, CP40/871, rot. 44; 873, rot. 236; NRO, B-L V, no. × . 45.
[128] PRO, CP40/946, rot. 226; 947, rot. 396; 948, rot. 356, 383; 949, rot. 136, 374; 950, rot. 187; 952, rot. 17, 58, 86, 405.
[129] BL, Add. MS 41,305, fos. 8ᵛ, 11ʳ, 12ʳ.
[130] Ibid., fo. 11ᵛ⁻ʳ; PRO, CP40/950, rot. 107.
[131] Guth, 'Enforcing Late-Medieval Law', 87.
[132] J. Youings, *Sixteenth Century England* (London, 1984), 155; C. Dyer, *Lords and Peasants in a Changing Society* (Cambridge, 1980), 180.
[133] For the first half of the 1480s, for example, I have found only two lawsuits in which Roger I was the defendant: PRO, CP40/876, rot. 244; 880, rot. 378.

the Civil War they constituted about 30 per cent of litigants in
Common Pleas and about 20 per cent in King's Bench, and were
therefore very much over-represented as a group in terms of the
general population.[134] Saul's work on fourteenth-century Sussex
suggests that the great majority of individuals against whom the
gentry brought suits were social inferiors, and this was certainly
true of the Townshends.[135] In only one of the thirteen suits Eleanor
pursued in the Common Pleas in the last year of her life was the
defendant her social equal.[136] As for Roger II, between 1509 and
his death all seven of the known cases in the same court which came
to pleading, in which he or his son Thomas was the plaintiff, were
against social inferiors.[137] One reason for not litigating against a
social equal may well have been that the stakes in many quarrels
with another gentleman were not sufficiently high to warrant the
time and expense needed, nor the enmity incurred: an opponent
of similar or greater resources was a tougher proposition than the
lesser man.[138]

Lesser men were certainly easier to pressurize, and there are signs
that the Townshends sometimes tried to intimidate their inferiors.
In 1494 William Yorke of London bound himself to Eleanor as a
surety for two London merchants who had purchased grain and
wool from her on credit. After they defaulted on their payments she
sued Yorke for just over £20 which she claimed he should forfeit by
virtue of his bond. Yorke, however, pleaded that she had extracted
the bond from him in the first place with threats to his person. Not
surprisingly she denied the charge, but it would be wrong to dismiss
it out of hand.[139] Later, in the early 1520s, Cecily, the widow
of William Capell of Stibbard (a troublesome tenant with whom
Eleanor had once had differences of opinion over grazing rights)[140]

[134] Brooks, 'Litigants and Attorneys', 44.

[135] Saul, *Provincial Life*, 80.

[136] PRO, CP40/947, rot. 396; 948, rot. 17, 184, 186, 356, 383; 949, rot. 136, 233,
318, 374, 396, 459; 950, rot. 107, 111, 202, 277, 416, 499; 951, rot. 17, 109, 391; 952,
rot. 17, 58, 86, 227, 263, 379, 403, 405; 953, rot. 73–5, 93, 202. The defendant was
Sir John Paston: CP40/950, rot. 277.

[137] PRO, CP40/1048A, rot. 522; 1052, rot. 429; 1051, rot. 121; 1123, rot. 131;
1143, rot. 112; 1145, rot. 515, 633. None of these defendants was above the rank of
lesser gentry.

[138] Cf. Fastolf's willingness to cut his losses and reach an accommodation with the
duke of Suffolk: Smith, 'Litigation and Politics', 67.

[139] BL, Add. MS 41,305, fo. 7; PRO, CP40/948, rot. 356; 949, rot. 318; 951,
rot. 109; 952, rot. 58.

[140] See Ch. 5, 4 below.

attempted, in association with another Townshend tenant, William Porter, to seek redress from Roger II for various unspecified wrongs he had done them.[141] Evidently resolved to appeal to one of the conciliar courts, they were forestalled by Sir James Boleyn 'labouring' on Roger's behalf, and were persuaded to put the matter to arbitration. Those who had a disagreement with a social superior were frequently obliged to agree that they would accept the latter's ruling in the affair, although this did not necessarily result in unfair awards.[142] But in this instance Roger did not attempt to settle the dispute himself and chose Boleyn to act as an arbitrator. Boleyn appears to have fulfilled the role fairly because, in an award of November 1523, he instructed Roger to pay Cecily 20 marks in compensation and to give up an unjust claim to some of William's land. Unfortunately for them, that was not the end of the matter: Porter's widow Margaret later presented a bill to the justices of assize in Norfolk, complaining that not only had Roger refused to abide by the terms of the award, but that he had continued to trouble William and Cecily for the rest of their lives and was now troubling her by, amongst other things, impounding her cattle.

Two other cases of grazing disputes with tenants which came to litigation occurred in the 1540s when agrarian tensions between landlords and tenants were high. John Calver began an action against Richard Townshend (Roger's grandson) and his mother Eleanor for seizing his livestock at Brampton, Suffolk, in July 1542. They claimed the beasts were spoiling their pasture; he, that the pasture in question was not theirs.[143] In the second dispute, which occurred on the eve of Ket's Rebellion, Reginald Porter of Stibbard, perhaps a son of the previously mentioned William, sued Thomas Townshend and Roger's steward, John Potter, for taking away the sheep he grazed on a local common. But, after hearing the plea, entered in Hilary 1549, Robert Coke, the Townshends' attorney, obtained leave from the court to imparl until the following term, and Porter subsequently failed to pursue it.[144] Possibly the interval had been used to intimidate him into submission. At the same time, however,

[141] Unless otherwise indicated, what follows on this dispute is taken from a 16th-cent. file of papers relating to grazing disputes at Stibbard and Ryburgh to be found in R36.

[142] Rawcliffe, 'Great Lord as Peacekeeper', 51.

[143] PRO, CP40/1130, rot. 137.

[144] PRO, CP40/1139, rot. 404; 1140, rot. 417.

these grazing disputes show that the common law was not a closed book for those with grievances against the gentry. What is perhaps surprising is that, except for a couple of cases in the Court of Requests involving Robert Townshend, Roger II's son, the Townshends were not sued by a social inferior in the conciliar courts. In one of these cases Robert Burbeck of Great Ryburgh sought remedy against Robert from the Requests in 1538 for unlawful disseisin, for withholding from him an earlier arbitration award of £8, and for procuring two men to lie in wait for him—a clear example of intimidation, if true. But whether he obtained justice is another matter, since one of the two local magistrates commissioned to investigate these charges was none other than Roger II.[145]

What of the Townshends as litigants in the other conciliar courts? If we can trust the surviving records, they never appeared in Star Chamber during our period, although it heard a considerable number of cases from East Anglia and was a court where the gentry, either as plaintiffs or defendants, made up the largest proportion of principals to litigation.[146] Chancery was a different matter: besides the Bale dispute and the quarrel with Elizabeth Brewes, the successive heads of the family (Roger I, Eleanor, and Roger II) were involved in five cases.

Roger I was the plaintiff in two. He sued the Lynn merchant Simon Pigot over a debt of £30 in the early 1460s and, in the late 1470s, a recalcitrant trustee.[147] Some years later Eleanor was sued by Simon White esquire for failing to convey an acre of land and advowson rights in Filby which Roger had sold to his father, Bartholomew White.[148] The remaining cases concerned Roger II. In association with Sir John Audley, he took action against the widow of Sir Robert Brandon and her second husband in 1528 in order to recover a sum which they had paid on Brandon's behalf. They resorted to the Chancery in this instance because they were without a remedy at common law, possessing no specialty (written evidence) obliging her to repay them.[149] Later, near the end of his life, the heirs of William Curteys troubled Roger II over some lands in central Norfolk

---

[145] PRO, REQ2/3/107; *LP*, vol. xiii, pt. i, no. 601. In the other case Robert Townshend was sued at some stage in the late 1530s, or 1540s, in his capacity as lessee of Bishop Rugge's palace in Norwich by the palace keeper: PRO, REQ2/3/45.

[146] J. A. Guy, *The Cardinal's Court: The Impact of Thomas Wolsey in Star Chamber* (Hassocks, 1977), 109–10.

[147] PRO, C1/29/181; C1/58/2.   [148] PRO, C1/233/85.   [149] PRO, C1/585/42.

which he had bought nearly half-a-century earlier.[150] However, none of these was a particularly serious affair and they do not alter our general picture of the Townshends as litigants. Indeed, conciliar litigation cannot be sharply differentiated from that of the common-law courts. Institutions like the Chancery were often better able than those courts to give many litigants what they wanted, and cases remediable at common law were feigned to bring them into the conciliar courts. Questions of real property lay behind at least 70 per cent of cases in the Chancery and royal council, and what were in effect civil disputes over property were often disguised as criminal trespasses and riots.[151]

(3) CONCLUSIONS

The Townshends lived in litigious times and were unable to avoid several major real-property disputes, but because they were careful buyers none of these was caused by unwise speculation in the land market.

Arbitration and out-of-court settlements played a central role in resolving these disputes. They occurred in a period in which the common-law courts suffered a serious decline in business,[152] but it is wrong to make the simple assumption that the law was therefore unable to cope with the needs of society and that the widespread use of arbitration was a sign of its failure. The idea of a 'defective' common law has been coloured by those historians, labelled 'King's Friends' by Clanchy, who would exaggerate the importance of the central common-law courts.[153] The roots of law and order ultimately lay in the localities and on the attitudes of the gentry and others towards their neighbours, and this is seen in the arbitration process. The use of arbitration was clearly not inimical to the common law, for which it was an invaluable support, and that is why it had such an important part to play in late medieval and early modern legal disputes, including those of the Townshends. Litigation was often

---

[150] PRO, C1/1277/49–51; R31, RT II estate book, fo. 27ʳ.
[151] Blatcher, *King's Bench*, 24–6; Guth, 'Enforcing Late-Medieval Law', 88, 94.
[152] Blatcher, *King's Bench*, 11 ff.
[153] Clanchy, 'Law, Government and Society', 75–8.

commenced in the common-law courts by the Townshends and other gentry to achieve out-of-court settlements rather than final resolutions within them. If we recognize these contemporary expectations, it is not so easy simply to dismiss the common-law system in their period as defective.

The use of arbitration helped to limit violence, and the frequency with which the gentry turned to it suggests that they preferred pacific means to force. Even in the 1450s feuds were exceptional: Bellamy's concentration on the colourful exploits of medieval criminal gangs and the like, therefore, gives his *Crime and Public Order* a massive imbalance.[154] There is no evidence that outright violence played a part in the Townshends' quarrels, although they may have tried occasionally to intimidate social inferiors. Violence was also absent from Sir John Fastolf's legal disputes, despite the value of some of the properties involved and the social status and political power of his opponents, and in the same period the leading men of Nottinghamshire did not normally engage in open disorder.[155] By the later Middle Ages potentially violent situations, particularly entries into disputed property, were defused by customized ritual: in the fifteenth century it was not even necessary for the claimant to enter physically the land in question. Force was used in a very circumscribed way, not least because it was rarely conclusive, and actual fights were exceptional.[156] Levels of violence are, in any case, extremely difficult to quantify. Spectacular crimes and lurid episodes found in sources like the Paston Letters are eye-catching but they were not day-to-day occurrences. The Pastons were plagued more than most by quarrels and litigation, but their letters are very largely concerned with ordinary matters of everyday life.

If history is written from the preambles to statutes, the denunciations of moralists and reformers, and the *ex parte* statements of those engaged in litigation, there is every chance that it will be a record of bloodshed and injustice. The reality was a good deal less sensational.[157]

---

[154] J. G. Bellamy, *Crime and Public Order in England in the Later Middle Ages* (London, 1973). Cf. Hicks, 'Restraint, Mediation and Private Justice', 69.

[155] Smith, 'Litigation and Politics', 70–1; Payling, thesis, 241.

[156] Smith, 'Litigation and Politics', 71; Wright, *Derbyshire Gentry*, 122; McFarlane, *Nobility*, 115. See also Bellamy's later work, *Criminal Law and Society*, 68–9.

[157] McFarlane, *Nobility*, 115.

POSTSCRIPT: THE HELHOUGHTON AFFAIR AND 1483[158]

Though not directly relevant to the Townshends, two points arising out of Roger I's meetings with Earl Rivers at Lynn and Walsingham in late March 1483 and their agreement to lay their dispute before Gloucester's council for arbitration deserve highlighting.

First, the meetings prove that Rivers, having spent Christmas 1482/3 in Norfolk before attending the parliament at Westminster which ended on 20 February, did, as Ives has speculated, return there before moving to Shropshire to be with the Prince of Wales.[159]

Secondly, Rivers is unlikely to have regarded Gloucester as an enemy, even at this date, if he was prepared to accept the arbitration of the latter's council. This remained the case after Edward IV's death, because he obviously did not suspect the violent outcome to his meeting with Gloucester at Northampton on 29–30 April.[160] Was there in fact a long-standing rivalry between Gloucester and the Woodvilles before 1483? The above evidence suggests not,[161] the logical corollary being that Gloucester made a ruthless pre-emptive strike at Northampton and Stony Stratford to ensure he would dominate a royal minority, even if he did not at this stage have the throne itself in sight.

---

[158] For an expanded version of this Postscript see my 'A Local Dispute and the Politics of 1483: Roger Townshend, Earl Rivers and the Duke of Gloucester', *The Ricardian*, 8 (1989), 305–7. Although this has been attacked (I. Wigram and M. Thone, 'A Local Dispute and the Politics of 1483: Two Reactions', ibid., 8 (1990), 414–16), I stand by my central point that there is no contemporary evidence of hostility between the Woodvilles and Gloucester before 1483.

[159] See Ives, 'Andrew Dymmock', 228.

[160] Ross, *Richard III*, 69–70.

[161] So supporting Horrox's recent stimulating interpretation of the events of 1483: *Richard III*, 89–128.

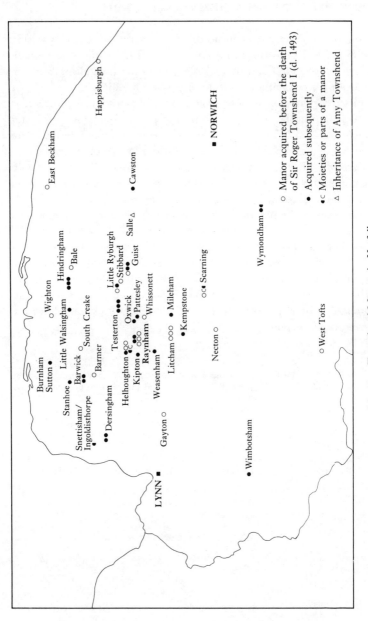

Map 1.   Townshend Manors in Norfolk

4

ESTATE, WEALTH, AND HOUSEHOLD

INTRODUCTION

The everyday life of gentry like the Pastons and Townshends was naturally centred upon their estates and the households these supported, because the most unambiguous, though by the later Middle Ages not the only, qualification for gentility was the ownership of land.[1] To keep his social status the landowner had to keep his land and, as McFarlane pointed out, this required more than a passing interest in its management and economic well-being.[2] Few gentlemen could afford to be disinterested *rentiers*, and even the greatest lords involved themselves in the day-to-day business of their estate and household.[3]

The Townshends were active landlords and seem to have run their estate and household efficiently. Their large scale sheep-farming motivated them to add to and rationalize this estate but, like other landowners, they also sought to augment their lands to provide for their younger children. Moreover, in the later Middle Ages falling rents sometimes made it necessary to accumulate more land simply to maintain the life-style of earlier, more favourable years.

The Townshend estate represented a considerable achievement since, as newcomers to the gentry, they built up most of it through purchase in a restricted land market, though one which became less so with the dissolution of the monasteries in Henry VIII's reign. Roger I owed much to his legal career for providing the opportunities and reserves of capital to buy land, though it is impossible to tell

---

[1] For gentry bureaucrats see R. L. Storey, 'Gentlemen-Bureaucrats', in Clough (ed.), *Profession, Vocation and Culture*, 90–129; for urban gentry see R. Horrox, 'The Urban Gentry in the Fifteenth Century', in J. A. F. Thomson (ed.), *Towns and Townspeople in the Fifteenth Century* (Gloucester, 1988), 22–44.

[2] McFarlane, *Nobility*, 49–53.

[3] e.g. *Household Books of John Duke of Norfolk and Thomas Earl of Surrey 1481–1490*, ed. J. Payne Collier, Roxburghe Club, 61 (1844), *passim*.

exactly how much these reserves would have come to at any one time. Roger II is known, however, to have had over £700 in ready cash to hand on one occasion in the mid-1530s.[4]

(1) ACQUISITION

In September 1452 John Townshend contracted to buy 'Haviles' and 'Rowses', two manors in Raynham, from Thomas Champeneys for £500. Within three years Champeneys, a clerk and the last surviving representative of his family, conveyed them to John and his trustees, and by January 1466 John had paid the last instalment of the purchase price to Champeney's executors.[5] But it was Roger I who was the true founder of the Townshend estate; an example of how a successful lawyer could invest the winnings gained from 'much travelling yn the law' in land.[6] We are lucky that his 1492/3 memorandum book has survived, for it lists the properties he bought during his lifetime and the prices paid for them. Fortunately his son continued this practice.[7]

Roger I made his first recorded purchase in 1468, shortly after his marriage (which brought him £300 in cash, if little land) and when he was becoming prominent as a lawyer.[8] He died the lord of a compact estate lying mainly in north-west Norfolk, but he also acquired manors in Suffolk and Bedfordshire.[9] Although he did buy property which was at a distance from Raynham, a compact group of lands suited his sheep-farming and was easier to manage. He often bought small plots of land in a piecemeal fashion to consolidate more substantial purchases.[10] Consolidation enabled the landlord to

[4] NRO, B-L VII (3), fos. 39ᵛ–42ᵛ.
[5] R27, 'RAYNHAM HEN. IV–HEN. VI', deed of 1 Apr. 1454; R32, loose deed of 1 Apr. 1455; R28, 'RAYNHAM EDW. IV to HENRY VII', deed of 7 Jan. 1466.
[6] Leland's *Itinerary*, ii. 12. Leland's comment refers specifically to Roger I.
[7] R58, RT I memo-book, fos. 7ʳ–8ᵛ; R31, RT II estate book, fos. 27ʳ–32ᵛ. These are not unique records. Another lawyer, Sir Robert Brudenell (d. 1531), recorded his 1494–1508 purchases in his 'Boke of the Covenantes of Purchases made by Robert Brudenell the Justyce': J. Wake, *The Brudenells of Deene*, 2nd edn. (London, 1954), 27.
[8] A holding called 'Scogans' in East Raynham, bought from the rector there: R58, RT I, memo-book, fo. 7ʳ.
[9] For the Norfolk manors, see map.
[10] e.g. R58, RT I memo-book, fos. 7ʳ, 8ʳ; R28, 'RAYNHAM EDW. IV to HENRY VII', deeds of 7 July 1475 and 8 Apr. 1485. See also the Raynham account rolls for

increase profits as it gave him the chance to enclose and bring lands into severalty.[11]

Roger intervened in the restricted late-medieval land market with considerable success. In this period manors normally descended by inheritance and marriage, and those with money to spend had to wait their chance. Purchasers usually did not buy from complete strangers, depending mainly upon local knowledge and the contacts of friends and associates, as well as the executors, trustees, and advisers of property owners, for news or rumour of prospective sales.[12] Roger enjoyed considerable advantages as a lawyer. Because members of his profession tended to have plentiful supplies of ready capital they were powerful competitors for land.[13] They were also well placed as counsellors of the landed to be the first to hear when land became available.

The best way of illustrating the nature of the land market is to take a series of examples of Roger I's activities in it. Personal contacts forged by his previous dealings with William Catesby, Richard III's henchman, may well have assisted him to acquire 'Bygottes', a manor at West Tofts in south-west Norfolk, in 1490. The former owner, Thomas Dayrell, had directed his executors to sell it after his death, and Roger subsequently paid one of these men, John Wake, £100 for the property.[14] The Wakes were related by marriage to the Catesbys, and John used to be on close terms with William Catesby.[15] Sometimes land almost fell Roger's way. Simon Blake of Swaffham, an ex-Woodville client for whom he had acted as a trustee, appointed him the supervisor of his will. No doubt in return for past services, as

---

relentless piecemeal consolidation, e.g. 1519/20 account: bailiff charged with the receipts for some meadows bought from a couple of tenants as well as various pieces of land bought from sixteen others or their executors: R(Attic), '*Norfolk manorial—Raynham Haviles*', 1519/20 Raynham accounts.

[11] Finch, *Northamptonshire Families*, 166.

[12] Hatcher, *Plague*, 36–7; McFarlane, *Nobility*, 55–6; A. R. Smith, 'Aspects of the Career of Sir John Fastolf (1380–1459)', D. Phil. thesis (Oxford, 1982), 28–31; *PL*, nos. 144, 489. The land market was not as 'tight', however, as McFarlane suggested: see Richmond, *Paston Family*, 42.

[13] Ives, *Kebell*, 336.

[14] Ch. 1, 3 above; *Bedfordshire Wills Proved in the Prerogative Court of Canterbury, 1353–1548*, ed. M. McGregor, Bedfordshire Historical Rec. Soc., 58 (1979), no. 22; R58, RT I memo-book, fo. 2ʳ.

[15] e.g. *CIPM, Henry VII*, vol. ii, nos. 847–9, 851; *CAD*, vol. iv, no. A.8,345; v, no. A.10,792; *CCR* (1485–1500), no. 149. Wake's elder brother married Catesby's sister: *VCH, Northamptonshire Families* (1906), 321–2.

well as for his future duties as supervisor, Blake directed in the will
that Roger should be given first option to buy his properties in Necton
and neighbouring townships. Roger took up the offer and, shortly
after Blake's death in 1489, he paid the executors the purchase-price
of 100 marks.[16]

Usually it was necessary to intervene more actively in the land
market to acquire property, and concessions had sometimes to be
made. Roger was therefore ready to sacrifice immediate returns
on his investments by buying reversions. Like his legal contemporary,
Thomas Kebell, he had the financial resources and the patience to
wait for the property concerned to come into his hands.[17] Of course,
many reversions brought no profit to those who bought them, but
the status of a landowner was just as important as economic considerations to the new man seeking land. In 1474 Roger paid John
Pagrave esquire and his associates 120 marks for the reversion of
a moiety of 'Skarnynges', a manor in Scarning, not long after buying
the reversion of 'Crispin's' in Happisburgh on the north-east Norfolk
coast from Isabel Cleymond. Some time later he paid £8 to a tenant,
James Petwyn, for the reversion of several tenements in South
Raynham.[18] Buying a reversion was a gamble, especially if it vested
only after the death of the occupier, since the purchaser might have
a long wait. Petwyn, for example, outlived Roger, if only just.[19]

Another gamble was the mortgage. In this period it amounted to
a conditional purchase by the mortgagee: the mortgagor redeemed
the property if he repaid the money by an agreed date. Unlike a reversion, a mortgage offered the mortgagee no more than the possibility
of a permanent title—although it gave him immediate possession
of the property—and Roger won the manor of East Beckham from
the Pastons (though not permanently as we have already seen)
because Sir John Paston, the mortgagor, defaulted.[20] In the same
period he also gained temporary possession of the Paston manor
at Sporle, in return for a loan of 400 marks. Paston had redeemed
Sporle by late 1474, but only after mortgaging other lands to another

---

[16] Ives, 'Andrew Dymmock', 228; Blomefield, vi. 202; NRO, NCC 20-2 Typpes;
R58, RT I memo-book, fo. 8[r]. The properties involved appear to have been two small
manors, 'Corbettes' and 'Byllettes'.

[17] Ives, *Kebell*, 340.

[18] R58, RT I, memo-book, fos. 7, 8[r], 10[v].

[19] Dead by Michaelmas 1494: R(Attic), '*Norfolk manorial*—Raynham Haviles',
1485/6–1508/9 Raynham accounts, m. 11.

[20] Simpson, *Land Law*, 32–4; Ch. 3, 1 (iii) above.

lawyer, his uncle William, hardly a satisfactory solution. He feared
the predatory instincts of both men: 'I am as moche a-ferde off thys
londe þat is in hys [William's] hande as I was off that þat was jn
Towneshendys hande.' Nevertheless, Sir John later mortgaged Sporle
to Roger a second time, although again he was able to recover it.[21]

In the late seventeenth century John Locke observed that the almost
universal cause of real-property sales was debt, and this is to some
extent applicable to the late fifteenth century.[22] The Pastons were
certainly not the only family whose financial difficulties Roger I
exploited. William Hoppes, one-time owner of 'Nogeons' in Bale,
may well have been a good friend, but the real reason for his grant
of the manor to Roger was the latter's promise to pay off his
creditors.[23] Perhaps the cost of equipping himself for Edward IV's
invasion of France led William Beaufoy, an esquire from Rutland,
to sell his Norfolk manor of 'Beaufoes' in South Creake to Roger
for £100 a few years later.[24] He did not take this step lightly, because
the manor had been part of his family's inheritance since the
thirteenth century. It also formed part of his wife's jointure, and
he had to compensate her with a life-interest in the family-seat in
Rutland.[25] The measures Roger took to hold him to the agreement
suggest that he was reluctant to sell. After the sale was completed
(by April 1475), Beaufoy agreed to convey to him and his assigns
part of his Rutland estate to hold in trust, promising that it would
forfeit to Roger permanently should an attempt be made to recover
South Creake. Furthermore, Roger took a bond for £100 from him
to ensure that he provided this security.[26]

The case of Sir William Tendale, from whom Roger bought the

---

[21] *PL*, nos. 355, 283, 286, 308. William Paston had, however, good reason to be
predatory since he had not received a fair share of the Pastons' estates: Richmond,
Paston Family, Ch. 6.
[22] H. J. Habakkuk, 'The Rise and Fall of English Landed Families, 1600–1800',
TRHS 5th ser. 29 (1979), 197. The most common cause of estates coming on to the
market in the 15th cent. was failure of heirs: Wright, *Derbyshire Gentry*, 27.
[23] See Ch. 3, 1 (i) above.
[24] PRO, C1/186/82; R18, 'N & S CREAKE, Temp. EDW. IV (1471–1481)', series of
deeds; R58, RT I memo-book, fo. 7ʳ.
[25] Blomefield, vii. 79; PRO, C1/186/82.
[26] R18, 'N & S CREAKE, Temp. EDW. IV (1471–1481)', indenture of 24 Apr. 1475;
R58, 'Raynham Deeds 1426–1480', bond, same date. Roger obtained a very favourable rate of return of 11 per cent for this purchase (nine years' purchase), suggesting
he was able to dictate terms to a man who needed to sell: R58, RT I memo-book,
fo. 11ʳ.

manors of Sharpenhoe in Bedfordshire (1485) and 'Scales' in Raynham (1490), is another good example of how lawyers could acquire real property from those with monetary difficulties. Tendale was either very unfortunate or financially profligate. As early as 1483 he had mortgaged the Northamptonshire manor of Deene, held by his family for five generations, and he sold it soon afterwards.[27] He had the good fortune to succeed to a share of the substantial Scales inheritance in west Norfolk and elsewhere not long after disposing of Sharpenhoe, but his problems continued and when he died in 1497 he was heavily in debt, both to the Crown and the lawyer Humphrey Coningsby. Before he died he had been obliged to enfeoff his estate on the latter's trustees (who included several of the foremost lawyers of the day) so that Coningsby could recover what he was owed from its issues. For good measure, Coningsby secured a permanent interest in the Tendale lands for his family by obtaining the wardship of John Tendale, Sir William's heir, and marrying John to his daughter, Amphelice Coningsby.[28]

John Hewer of Oxborough was a lesser man who fell into Roger's clutches.[29] On various occasions Roger gave him extensive credit for purchases of sheep but he was unable to pay the money when it was due. To provide a security for £80 out of a total of £105 which he owed, he agreed to mortgage to Roger lands in Oxborough and to hand over to him 600 or 700 sheep, as well as promising to repay the rest of the money on no less than a daily basis. This all took place before late 1492 when Roger sent his sheep-reeve and another servant to Oxborough to enforce the agreement.[30] On a different occasion (it is unclear when) he sent his men to take a distress from Hewer.[31] Although we cannot be sure, it seems unlikely that Hewer was able to redeem his lands and livestock since he also fell into debt to Thomas Thursby, the Lynn merchant. To raise the money to repay Thursby he sold a messuage and other lands in Oxborough to Hugh Coo in 1496. Coo later sold them to Eleanor Townshend, Roger's widow.[32] It is worth noting that, like Hewer, William Tendale was taken advantage of by a wealthy merchant as well as by

---

[27] Wake, *Brudenells*, 37.

[28] *CIPM, Henry VII*, vol. i, no. 33; vol. ii, nos. 11, 15, 16.

[29] A 'bocher' and 'yeoman': PRO, CP40/883, rot. 306.

[30] NRO, B-L V, no. ×. 13; R58, RT I memo-book, fo. 4ᵛ.

[31] R55, 1492/3–1497/8 sheep account, fo. 16ʳ.

[32] BL, Add. MS 41,305, fo. 33ʳ; R31, RT II estate book, fo. 30ᵛ.

a lawyer, for he mortgaged Deene to Sir Henry Colet of London.[33] The successful merchant's reserves of capital could make him as well placed as the lawyer to succeed in the land market.

This is also illustrated by the career of Geoffrey Boleyn, the great-grandfather of Queen Anne. Of a yeoman background, he left his native Norfolk and had a highly successful career as a London merchant. By his death in 1463 he owned a considerable, if somewhat scattered, estate spread over Norfolk, Sussex, and Kent, worth significantly more than the 100 marks of land with which John Leland credited him.[34] Possessing plentiful capital, like Roger I, Boleyn was prepared to sacrifice immediate returns on his investments since he bought the manor of Blickling from Sir John Fastolf on particularly stiff terms.[35] His connections, like Roger's, helped him to obtain land, and he acquired several properties from John Lewkenor, a relative of his wife's family.[36]

Roger I's widow and heir continued to expand and consolidate the Townshend estate.[37] Market conditions did not undergo any significant change between Roger I's death and the Dissolution: local knowledge and personal contacts were still all-important. In 1519, for example, Roger II bought a manor in Cawston from John Legge of Bedingham for whom he was a trustee.[38] Shortly afterwards, in 1522 or 1523, he bought 'Hindringhams' in Hindringham from an associate of one of his sons at Lincoln's Inn, the lawyer Gregory Davy of Gunthorpe.[39] Then in 1525 he bought the reversion of two small manors in Testerton from the executors of Robert Wolvy. As was the case in Roger I's day, executors (often those of deceased estate officials or tenants) were a useful source of real property.[40] About

---

[33] Wake, *Brudenells*, 37.

[34] W. L. E. Parsons, 'Some Notes on the Boleyn Family', *NA* 25 (1935), 386–96; *Calendarium Inquisitionum Post Mortem Sive Escaetarum*, iv, Record Commission (London, 1828), 321; NRO, MC 3/283 463 × 4; Leland's *Itinerary*, ii. 9–10.

[35] Parsons, 'Boleyn Family', 395; NRO, NRS 14,730 29 D 4; PRO, C1/18/67.

[36] Blomefield, ii. 333; vi. 386–7; vii. 249, 252; ix. 252–4; Wedgwood, 540–2.

[37] e.g. of consolidation by Roger II: 'Haviles' in East Raynham, the home manor, was worth *c.* £55 p.a. clear in 1507. By 1525 he had augmented it by buying various surrounding pieces of land and it was worth over £87: R55, RT II valors, fo. 1; R31, RT II estate book, fo. 33ʳ.

[38] PRO, E326/7259, 7261, 5728, 6867, 7266. For previous commercial dealings with Legge: R31, RT II estate book, fos. 5ᵛ, 7ʳ.

[39] Ibid., fo. 30ᵛ; LI *Admissions*, 35; LI *Black Books*, 188, 216. The younger Townshend (which one is not known) and Davy were fined for gambling in the inn in 1519: ibid., 188.

[40] e.g. R31, RT II estate book, fos. 14ʳ, 15ᵛ, 27ᵛ, 28ʳ, 30ʳ; NRO, Townshend 193 MS 1,612 1 C7, fo. 9ᵛ.

a year later he bought another manor in Testerton from Wolvy's widow and 'her second husband, William Pratt, a servant of the Townshends.[41] A better illustration of the importance of personal contacts in the pre-Dissolution land market would be difficult to find.

Roger II proved just as hard-headed as his father in adding to his estate, as no doubt Thomas Austyn, his bailiff at Raynham from 1509/10 to 1510/11,[42] would have agreed. A bill of acknowledgement shows that by about 1518 Roger was paying rent to Austyn, a small-scale landowner in the locality, for various pieces of land which he had bought from others around Raynham.[43] He must then have pressed Austyn to sell him land, perhaps that for which these rents were due, because the former bailiff wrote on the bill: 'I wyll yt ye shall notte haue my landys inne Bermere [Barmer] Nore xiij acres in Estrudham feld.'[44] Nevertheless, in 1520 he sold to Roger a copyhold garden in East Rudham as well as his freehold in Tattersett for £50.[45] The same predatory instinct is seen twenty years later when no less a gentleman than Nicholas Le Strange felt threatened. In a well-known letter to William Cecil in which he justified his conduct during Ket's Rebellion, Le Strange claimed that Roger and Sir Edmund Bedingfield, to whom he had refused to sell 'severall pecys of my londes whyche lythe nere them', were now conspiring to blame him as the 'begynnare of the commocions' of 1549.[46] What might not be achieved by fair means might be achieved by foul.

What Roger II could not buy he leased, like his father had before him. It could be profitable to farm lands from others. He calculated, for example, that those he leased at the end of 1516 were worth to him over £46 annually.[47] By the late Middle Ages the gentry were frequently farmers and were willing to farm copyholds as well as freeholds, as indeed were the Townshends.[48] The Townshends

---

[41] R31, RT II estate book, fo. 31[v]; Dashwood, 208; R12, 'HELHOUGHTON, Temp. HVIII', deed of 19 Mar. 1525; PRO, E179/150/221.

[42] NRO, Townshend 11 MS 1,430 1 A3.

[43] R59, 'BARMER Temp. HEN. VII', bill dated 11 Henry VIII.

[44] Ibid.

[45] R52, 'TATTERFORD, TATTERSETT Temp. HENRY VIII', indenture of 28 Apr. 1520.

[46] PRO, SP10/8/60.

[47] R31, RT II estate book, fos. 22[r], 42[v].

[48] F. R. H. Du Boulay, 'Who were Farming the English Demesnes at the End of the Middle Ages?', *EcHR* 2nd ser. 17 (1965), 450; J. N. Hare, 'The Demesne Lessees of Fifteenth-Century Wiltshire', *AHR* 29 (1981), 12–13; E. Kerridge, *Agrarian Problems in*

leased whole manors as well as numerous small pieces of land. By the late 1470s Roger I farmed 'Ingoldisthorpes', the Raynham manor which his son acquired for the family in 1543 from the widow of John Neville, Marquis Montague.[49] In the same period he leased a manor in Sculthorpe from Pontefract College and another in Fulmodestone from the Crown.[50] By the early 1480s he farmed 'Pekhalle' in Tittleshall from the marquis of Dorset, and during Richard III's reign the former De Vere manors at Toftrees and Shereford from the Crown.[51] He was the farmer of 'Scales' in South Raynham when William Tendale sold it to him in 1490.[52]

Roger II continued to farm 'Ingoldisthorpes' into the second decade of the sixteenth century.[53] In the same decade he farmed the Yelverton manor at Bayfield and another at Hoe, perhaps from the Ferrers family.[54] But his most important farms were probably in and around the townships of North and South Creake where he grazed one of his largest flocks. Here he leased at various stages during the first quarter of the sixteenth century a manor and sheepfold from the Howards and a manor which belonged to Creake Abbey and later to Christ's College, Cambridge.[55]

The Townshends also obtained lands on a temporary basis by buying wardships. There is no sign that Roger I ever had a minor in his charge, but Roger II acquired several wardships during his lifetime, and on various occasions he stood surety for other gentlemen

the Sixteenth Century and After (London, 1969), 74–6; R(Attic), '*Deeds*—Rudham . . . Toftrees', manor court estreat, *temp.* Edw. VI (refers to a copyhold of Roger I); R (Attic), 'Legal and suit papers, 15th–19th cent.', paper of *c.* 1514; R45, 1539 Toftrees and Shereford terrier.

[49] R58, Raynham account roll, mm. 11, 19.

[50] NRO, B-L V, no. X. 31; Blomefield, vii. 174–6, 89; 1474/5 receiver's account on a loose membrane from R58, Raynham account roll.

[51] R58, Raynham account roll, mm. 21, 25, 26; R(Attic), '*Norfolk manorial* T-W and mixed', 1484/5 Toftrees and Shereford account roll.

[52] NRO, Townshend 37 MS 1,456 1 B1, 1485/6–1508/9 Scales accounts, mm. 1–8.

[53] BL, Add. MS 41,139, fos. 9ᵛ, 10ʳ (1501 payment of £11 annual farm to receiver of Sir William Norris, second husband of Marchioness Montague). After 1512 the manor ceased to feature in the 'foreign receipts' section of the Raynham accounts, although this does not definitely prove that the lease was up.

[54] R31, RT II estate book, fos. 4ᵛ, 11ᵛ, 12ʳ; Blomefield, ix. 515; x. 50.

[55] NRO, B-L II e, 1501/2–1517/18 sheep accounts, fo. 15ʳ; R60, 1516/17 sheep accounts, fo. 11ᵛ; R55, RT II valors, fo. 4ʳ; R31, RT II estate book, fo. 13ʳ; BL, Add. MS 41,139, fo. 7ᵛ. Creake Abbey became defunct in 1507 and its estates were taken over by Christ's: J. Peile, *Christ's College* (London, 1900), 37–8.

who purchased them from the king.[56] In the case of only one of the five identifiable wards who came into his custody, William Wayte, is he known to have bought directly from the Crown. This is not unusual, for wardship rights could be a source of substantial income and were therefore often traded through several hands.[57]

The wardship and marriage of Wayte which Roger II and another lawyer, William Eyre, bought from the Crown in 1504 for £40, was not, however, very lucrative. Roger later reckoned that his income from the Wayte estate came to just under £16 per annum.[58] But the Waytes were small fry as gentry,[59] as were the Branches. In the same year, 1504, Roger paid Thomas Andrews of Great Ryburgh £68. 13s. 4d. for the wardship of John, grandson and heir of Robert Branche.[60]

Much more significant was the wardship of his nephew, John Castell, obtained in late 1511. Castell's inheritance was worth between £85 and £100 per annum.[61] He was only 4 years old when he succeeded his grandfather, Leonard Castell, so his family was faced with the prospect of a long minority.[62] Roger may well have acted on behalf of his relatives and not have taken the income from the Castell estate for himself. Relatives of an heir were often in the forefront of those who tried to secure the wardship, in order to keep the estate out of the hands of an exploiting stranger.[63] But it would be wrong to assume that they were always so altruistic: Roger also

[56] BL, Add. MS 21,480, fo. 47^v; BL, Add. MS 21,481, fos. 325^v, 327^v; PRO, E36/215/662, 666.
[57] J. Hurstfield, *The Queen's Wards* (London, 1958), 124.
[58] NRO, BRA 926/14 (*CPR* (1494–1509), 346), letters patent of 12 Feb. 1504; BL, Add. MS 21,480, fo. 91^v; R55, RT II valors, fos. 5^r, 18^v; R32, RT II estate book, fo. 4^v. For Eyre, a man connected to the Hoptons, see Richmond, *John Hopton*, 186, 194–5, 239. He acted as Roger I's attorney in several Common Pleas suits in the 1480s, e.g. PRO, CP40/879, rot. 270; 883, rot. 271; 890, rot. 284; 892, rot. 148.
[59] The Waytes were of Tittleshall. For their lands see *CIPM, Henry VII*, vol. ii, no. 56, though this valuation is a considerable under-assessment. Wayte's father, who died in 1497, served the Townshends as a secretary or scribe: R50, 1477/8 sheep accounts, fo. 19^v.
[60] NRO, B-L VII b(3), fo. 17^r. For the Branche family see *CIPM, Henry VII*, vol. ii, no. 706; Blomefield, ix. 440–1.
[61] Carthew, *Launditch*, i. 184; R(Attic), 'Norfolk manorial N & S Creake', 1509/10–1519/20 S. Creake accounts, m. 3 (bailiff allowed expenses for riding to Castell land at Boston, Lincs.); R31, RT II estate book, fos. 20^r, 38, 42^v.
[62] Carthew, *Launditch*, i. 184.
[63] H. E. Bell, *An Introduction to the History and Records of the Court of Wards and Liveries* (Cambridge, 1953), 115.

purchased the wardships of the children of his wife's nephew, Anthony Hansard, from the earl of Surrey in January 1519, only to resell them in October 1520 to a Lincolnshire esquire, Thomas Skipworth of Utterby, for £100.[64] Similarly, he did not allow his previous good relations with Sir John Audeley of Swaffham to obstruct personal profit, and he may well have exploited these associations to gain custody of Audeley's children.[65] Audeley died in 1531, and in the same year Roger sold the wardship of his grandson and heir, another John, to the countess of Oxford for £300 while keeping the wardship of Edmund, John's younger brother, for himself. He did, however, agree to surrender Edmund to the countess if John died before coming of age, thus denying her the chance to make the maximum profit on her investment.[66]

Roger II was primarily a Norfolk landowner like his father. His policy was to rationalize what he had inherited as well as what he himself acquired. He disposed of Roger I's property at Hadleigh, Layham, and Raydon on the Suffolk–Essex border in 1502,[67] and two years later exchanged his Oxborough lands for others in Setchley near Lynn.[68] The year before he died he sold Happisburgh to his servant Robert Coke.[69] Roger I had attempted to build up a block of lands in east Norfolk, but ever since the loss of East Beckham Happisburgh had remained isolated. Roger II did buy a manor in the Isle of Ely from Wolsey's servant Anthony Hansard in 1520, but this transaction was possibly connected with debts Hansard owed him.[70]

---

[64] R(Attic), 'Townshend family before 1552', indenture of 27 Oct. 1520. Anthony Hansard died on 5 Aug. 1517: *Lincolnshire Pedigrees*, ii. 455.

[65] Audeley was earlier one of his trustees: R19, 'N & S CREAKE. Temp. HEN VIII', deed of 20 Mar. 1512; R28, 'RAYNHAM, HENRY VIII-PHILIP & MARY', deed of 12 Mar. 1514, and they had acted together as sureties for Sir Robert Brandon: PRO, C1/585/42–7.

[66] PRO, C142/52/8; R58, 'Raynham Deeds 1492–1527', indenture of 12 May 1531.

[67] To William Barons, Master of the Rolls: R49, Townshend cartulary, fos. 34ᵛ–35ᵛ; PRO, CP25/1/224/123, no. 55.

[68] With John Grymstone: NRO, B-L VII b(3), fos. 17ʳ, 23ʳ; R31, RT II estate book, fo. 27ᵛ.

[69] PRO, CP25/2/61/481, no. 9.

[70] R(Attic), 'Cambridgeshire deeds & estate papers', indenture of 12 Nov. 1520; R38, loose deed of 20 Nov. 1520; R31, RT II estate book, fo. 28ᵛ. The manor was 'Hatchwood' in March. Hansard (d. 1534), Wolsey's servant (MacCulloch, *Suffolk*, 228; *LP*, vol. iii, pt. ii, no. 2,932 (2); PRO, E179/69/9–10; PRO, C142/53/43; PRO, PROB11/25, fos. 111b–112a), should not be confused with Amy Townshend's nephew, to whom he was not apparently related.

Alternatively, he might have bought it with a view to exchanging it in the future for land closer to home, not an infrequent ploy in a restricted property market.[71] He later conveyed it and Sharpenhoe in Bedfordshire to John Huddlestone, a Cambridgeshire esquire, in return for properties in west Norfolk.[72] In 1537 he bought a couple of manors in Teversham and Stow-Quy near Cambridge from Thomas Woodhouse of Waxham, only to exchange them in the following year for Pattesley, a manor neighbouring Raynham, with Gonville Hall, Cambridge. As an indenture stated, the exchange was agreed because Pattesley was 'very commodyous' for Roger, and the other manors equally so for the college.[73]

Roger II's activities in the land market were paralleled by other landlords in Norfolk and elsewhere. Sir Thomas Brudenell (d. 1549) of Deene, Northamptonshire, for example, rounded off what his father, Sir Robert Brudenell, a successful lawyer, had acquired.[74] He had far greater rationalizations to make than Roger, because Sir Robert's lands were scattered across several counties, but as the Spencers of Althorp prove, the Townshends were not exceptional in being able to build up a consolidated group of properties.[75] In Norfolk itself Sir James Hobart died in 1517 leaving a compact estate in the south-east, thereby fulfilling his ambition, declared forty years earlier, to become 'a Norfolk man'.[76] Another new family, the Fermors of East Barsham, were successful sheep-farmers because their lands were concentrated in the north-west of the county.[77] Carpenter's suggestion that the land market had begun to open up by the late fifteenth century seems reasonable, therefore, even though Youings argues that it was still very restricted.[78] There were nevertheless openings for families with ambition, ability, and capital like the Townshends to make bids for what became available.

---

[71] McFarlane, *Nobility*, 56.

[72] In 1543: R60, loose paper valuing the property to be exchanged; *LP*, vol. xviii, pt. i, no. 476 (3); PRO, C142/96/32. For Huddlestone, see *HP*, ii. 401–2.

[73] PRO, CP25/2/4/20, no. 49; NRO, Townshend 147 MS 1,566 1 C3. For Woodhouse, not to be confused with the Kimberley Woodhouses, see *HP*, iii. 652–3.

[74] Wake, *Brudenells*, 37.

[75] Youings, *Sixteenth Century England*, 154; Finch, *Northamptonshire Families*, 141, 38–44.

[76] PRO, PROB11/19, fos. 256 ff.; *PL*, no. 380. He was born in Suffolk: Richmond, *John Hopton*, 187.

[77] A. Simpson, *The Wealth of the Gentry* (Cambridge, 1961), 182 n.

[78] C. Carpenter, 'The Fifteenth Century English Gentry and their Estates', in Jones (ed.), *Gentry and Lesser Nobility*, 44; Youings, *Sixteenth Century England*, 154.

Much more land than hitherto became available after the Dissolution. By 1555 the gentry owned some 75 per cent of all the manors in Norfolk, whereas in 1535 they had owned about 64 per cent.[79] Roger II took the opportunity presented by the suppression of the monasteries to consolidate further.[80] His son Robert also entered the market, and in December 1539, before the Crown began to alienate former ecclesiastical property on a large scale, secured the lease of Binham Priory despite strong competition from Sir Christopher Jenney.[81]

Roger immediately alienated two of his ecclesiastical acquisitions, the rectories of Whitwell (obtained in 1543) and South Raynham (1549), but there is no evidence that he had obtained them in order to speculate.[82] One went to a servant and friend, Robert Coke, and another to a local man, Edward Eston,[83] so it is probable that he had applied to buy these properties on their behalf. It was not unusual and often convenient to use a third party to approach the Augmentations Office.[84]

Roger selected carefully the former church lands which he bought in order to augment his possessions in the Raynham vicinity. He probably knew better than most what he was applying to buy, for he had had unrivalled opportunities to learn much about Norfolk monastic estates through his experience as a Crown commissioner and as a steward or legal adviser for several religious houses.[85] Some of what he obtained he had recently farmed as a monastic lessee.[86] In all he spent over £1,000 on church lands worth about £65 per annum.[87] He did not, therefore, enjoy any special favours from the Crown which, during Henry VIII's reign at least, made few outright

[79] Swales, 'Redistribution', 43. Swales's figures demonstrate an increase in the gentry's share of the land, even if manors are a notoriously unsatisfactory unit of measurement.

[80] See App. 6.

[81] *LP*, vol. xiv, pt. i, nos. 1,355 (p. 603), 694; Addenda, pt. ii, no. 1,347.

[82] *LP*, vol. xviii, pt. ii, no. 529 (6); R55, loose deed of 14 June 1549.

[83] Of South Raynham, gent.; owned lands worth £5 p.a.: PRO, E179/150/310, 317; E179/151/334, 349.

[84] H.J. Habakkuk, 'The Market for Monastic Property, 1539–1603', *EcHR* 2nd ser. 10 (1958), 377–80. Joint applications naturally saved money on fees charged by the office.

[85] See Ch. 1, 4 (i) above.

[86] e.g. a manor and the rectory at Barwick (formerly Buckenham Priory) and West Acre Priory's foldcourse in Kipton and West Raynham: R41, Augmentations Office valor, 1543; *LP*, vol. xix, pt. ii, no. 527 (42).

[87] The rectories of Whitwell and South Raynham are excluded from this estimate.

free grants anywhere in the country. In Norfolk the duke of Norfolk received three-quarters of what was given away, and Sir Richard Southwell was the only major beneficiary among the established gentry.[88]

The Townshends realized that their best interests did not lie in widespread purchase of ecclesiastical property, and what they bought in the way of former church lands provides yet another example of their continuous efforts to consolidate. The rest of the county élite showed a similar concern. There were ten other leading families who are known to have bought and retained church lands.[89] Excluding the Augmentations officer Sir Richard Southwell, the size and circumstance of whose gains did not represent the norm, the average value of the lands which these families bought and retained was about £45 per annum.[90] Several newcomers did establish themselves among the county gentry by buying monastic estates but, as in the country generally, few new or appreciably enlarged estates were built up entirely or even principally out of monastic lands before 1558. The disposal of monastic lands by the Crown facilitated changes in land-ownership which were occurring anyway.[91]

Roger II was lucky to marry an heiress with an inheritance which was worth over £80 per annum by the mid-sixteenth century, but he himself had added substantially to the Townshends' lands when he died.[92] He must often have kept his younger sons as well as the integrity of his estate in mind when he purchased manors, because, with one exception, he did not settle on them any which he had inherited.[93] A desire to ensure his estate's integrity is also evident in the marriage settlements he bargained for his eldest son John and his grandson Richard. It is noteworthy that where these made immediate or near-immediate enfeoffments of family property on the betrothed couple, outlying or minor manors were involved.

---

[88] Swales, 'Redistribution', 20–2.

[89] Ibid., 22–6 (Bedingfield of Oxborough, Boleyn, Clere, Fermor, Heydon, Lovell, Shelton, Southwell, Le Strange, and Wyndham).

[90] Estimated from ibid. Sir Francis Lovell acquired as much as £100-worth; Sir John Clere as little as £3. 4s. 3d.

[91] Youings, *Sixteenth Century England*, 130; Swales, 'Redistribution', 26 ff. The most prominent new men were Sir Thomas Gresham (acquired estates worth over £350 p.a. by this date); the Woodhouses of Waxham (£210); Sir Thomas Paston (at least £150); John Corbet (c. £60); Nicholas Hare (£50).

[92] See App. 6.

[93] See App. 7. The exception was West Tofts, which he left to George.

Thus John and his wife received Brampton in Suffolk, Sharpenhoe in Bedfordshire, and Happisburgh in Norfolk, miles away from each other and the main part of the estate.[94]

What the Townshends owned in 1551 represented the fruits of over one hundred years of steady expenditure. John Townshend, Roger I's father, spent about £600 on land during his lifetime,[95] while Roger himself invested about £3,800 between 1468 and 1493, an average of over £150 per annum.[96] His widow spent at least £340 before her own death, a yearly average of about £50.[97] If we base our calculations on Roger II's own figures, he spent £4,551. 3s. 9¼d. between 1500 and 1551, an average of £90 per annum. However, his average expenditure during the first half of Henry VIII's reign, when he was most actively buying land, was about £137.[98] These sums do not compare with the £32,000 that another East Anglian, Lord Keeper Bacon, spent on land between 1540 and 1579, even allowing for the steep rise in prices after about 1540, but they demonstrate that the Townshends always had a steady flow of accessible capital.[99]

McFarlane believed that a rate of twenty years' purchase had become the norm in land transactions by the mid-fifteenth century, but this has since been challenged. Raban, for example, has suggested fifteen years for the late fifteenth and early sixteenth centuries, rising to twenty by the 1540s.[100] The rate of return the Townshends received for their investments supports these revisions. It is possible to calculate the rate obtained by Roger I in fourteen, and by Roger II in eighteen, manorial purchases. For the former the average was just over fourteen years and only once did he have to pay a price representing twenty years' purchase; but for Roger II the average was about nineteen-and-a-half.[101] These averages disguise, however,

<hr/>

[94] See App. 7.
[95] Possibly an underestimate since the prices John paid are known in only three instances: lands and tenements in the Raynhams and Helhoughton for 10 marks (1426); Caldewell close in Tittleshall for 40 marks (1444); 'Haviles' and 'Rowses' for £500: R35, 'South Raynham deeds 1409–78'; R54, 'GODWICK & TITTLESHALL Temp. HENRY VI'; R28, 'RAYNHAM EDW. IV to HENRY VII'.
[96] R58, RT I memo-book, fos. 7ʳ–8ᵛ.   [97] R31, RT II estate book, fo. 30ᵛ.
[98] Ibid., fos. 27ʳ–32ᵛ.   [99] Simpson, *Wealth of the Gentry*, 52.
[100] McFarlane, *Nobility*, 57; Smith, thesis, 31–2; S. Raban, *Mortmain Legislation and the English Church, 1279–1500* (Cambridge, 1982), 178–9.
[101] R58, RT I memo-book, fos. 10ᵛ–12ʳ; R31, RT II estate book, fos. 14ʳ, 27ᵛ–28ᵛ, 30ʳ, 31ᵛ–32ᵛ, 34ʳ, 35ʳ, 36; NRO, Townshend 193 MS 1,612 1 C7, fo. 18ʳ; R57, RT II 'declaration', fos. 14ʳ, 15ᵛ, 16ʳ; R41, Augmentations Office valor, 1543.

130 Estate, Wealth, and Household

the circumstances in which individual properties were bought. Roger I, for example, wrung a highly favourable six-and-three-quarter years from the Pastons for East Beckham, but then mortgagors were not in the position to demand normal rates.[102] His son, on the other hand, paid at a rate of nearly twenty-six years for Kipton in 1544, above the average for the 1540s.[103] This probably reflected the high social status of one of the vendors, the duchess of Richmond, as well as his desire to obtain the manor.

By 1551 the Townshends had created a substantial estate in an impressively short time, but what was it worth? Leland, the Tudor antiquary, thought he knew. He wrote that Roger I obtained lands to the value of about £100 per annum, that Roger II added another £100 worth, and that Amy, the latter's wife, brought property worth £200 to the family.[104] He was hopelessly wrong. Both Rogers acquired property worth considerably more than Leland realized, and he greatly exaggerated the value of Amy's inheritance. Just as untrustworthy are the relevant inquisitions post mortem.[105] Fortunately they can be supplemented with sixteenth-century subsidy assessments and various 'valors'.[106] Of course valors were statements of potential rather than actual income and are not always reliable.[107] The Townshends' valors are often little more than lists, sometimes written in their own hands, rather than the formal documents produced on great aristocratic estates.[108] Roger I, for example, valued his lands in his 1492/3 notebook, but since his 'valor' is simply a list of properties and corresponding sums one does not know on

[102] R58, RT I memo-book, fo. 12ʳ. Mortgagees did not usually lend as much as the mortgaged property was really worth.
[103] NRO, B-L VII b(5), deed of 26 Nov. 1544; R57, RT II 'declaration', fo. 14ʳ.
[104] Leland's *Itinerary*, ii. 12.
[105] *CIPM, Henry VII*, vol. i, nos. 1,028, 1,136, 1,143 (Roger I); PRO, C142/96/37; C142/98/70 (Amy); C142/96/32 (Roger II).
[106] PRO, E179/150/207, 259, 221, 251, 310; E179/151/317, 333; R58, RT I memo-book, fos. 10ᵛ–12ʳ; BL, Add. MS 41,139, fo. 11ᵛ; R55, RT II valors, fo. 16ʳ–18ᵛ; R31, RT II estate book, fos. 2ʳ–5ʳ, 14ʳ–22ʳ, 24ʳ–26ʳ; NRO, Townshend 193 MS 1,612 1 C7, fo. 18ᵛ; R57, RT II 'declaration', fos. 13ʳ–16ᵛ.
[107] Hatcher, *Plague*, 41; R. R. Davies, 'Baronial Accounts, Incomes, and Arrears in the Later Middle Ages', *EcHR* 2nd ser. 21 (1968), 217.
[108] Townshend 'valors': R58, RT I memo-book, fos. 10ᵛ–12ʳ (1492/3); BL, Add. MS 41,139, fo. 11ᵛ (c.1500); R55, RT II valors (1507, 1508); R31, RT II estate book, fos. 2–5, 17–21, 22, 24–6, 33–40, 42ᵛ (1509, 1515, 1516, 1518, 1525); NRO, Townshend 193 MS 1,612 1 C7, fos. 17–18 (1522).

what criteria his estimates were based.[109] These valors must, therefore, be treated with caution, but they are the best sources for assess-
ing the family's landed wealth since they were obviously intended
as statements of income.

Roger I inherited land worth about 50 marks per annum.[110] The
inquisitions post mortem held after his death valued his lands in
Norfolk at about £92 and those in Suffolk and Bedfordshire at £19
and £5 respectively.[111] These totals only underline the untrustworthi-
ness of such surveys, and more realistic figures are provided by
other sources. A family extent of 1551 estimated that Roger II
inherited an estate worth £294 per annum.[112] If we allow for the
lands worth £55 or more which Eleanor bought as a widow, Roger I's
estate was worth some £230–£240 per annum when he died.[113] In
other words, he acquired £200-worth of land during his lifetime.
This is quite impressive considering that none of the country's lawyers
of the rank of serjeant at law or above whose lands were assessed
for the 1524/5 subsidy was assessed for more than this amount.[114]

At the beginning of Henry VIII's reign the Townshend estate
was still worth about £290 clear per annum, but Roger II had not
yet made any major purchases.[115] Six years later it was worth just
over £353, of which the Norfolk lands made up about £260.[116] The
numerous purchases which he made between 1509 and 1515, many
involving very small amounts of land, account for this rise.[117] By
Michaelmas 1522 his Norfolk lands alone were worth just under
£390 (in the interval he had bought manors in Guist and Cawston
as well as lands in the south-west of the county) and in 1525 he valued
his whole estate at some £470, a sum which did not include the manors

---

[109] R58, RT I memo-book, fos. 10ᵛ–12ʳ.

[110] Ibid., fo. 10ᵛ.

[111] *CIPM, Henry VII*, vol. i, nos. 1,143, 1,136, 1,028.

[112] R57, RT II 'declaration', fo. 13ʳ.

[113] R31, RT II estate book, fo. 30ᵛ.

[114] *A Calendar of the Inner Temple Records*, ed. F. A. Inderwick and R. A. Roberts, 5
vols. (London, 1896–1936), i. 464–6. Those assessed on lands and fees were John
Hales, B.Exch. (£200); Humphrey Browne, serj. (£160); William Rudhale, serj.
(£160); Thomas Willoughby, serj. (£106); and John Spelman, serj. (£100). Spelman
died seised of lands worth at least 300 marks p.a.: PRO, E179/151/318.

[115] R31, RT II estate book, fos. 2ʳ–5ʳ; R55, RT II valors, fo. 3ᵛ. This figure
excludes income from fees and wardships, and lands he farmed.

[116] R31, RT II estate book, fos. 17ʳ–19ʳ. This total allows for the annual charge on
the estate of £22. 14s. 2½d. for the performance of Roger I's will.

[117] Ibid., fos. 14ʳ–15ʳ.

worth £40 per annum which he had settled on his heir John.[118] When he died the estate (including the lands which Amy brought him) was worth about £623 per annum.[119] His inquisition post mortem produced the woeful underestimate of £322.[120]

The tax assessments of Henry VIII's reign are not always trustworthy, but they are a better indicator of landed wealth than inquisitions post mortem, and those for the 1524/5 subsidy are fairly reliable.[121] Unfortunately there is nothing similar for Roger I's lifetime.[122] Roger II's lands were valued at £440 for the 1524/5 subsidy, a total not far off his own calculations of 1525. His son John was assessed particularly accurately at £40 per annum a year earlier.[123] Roger was assessed at only £320 in lands, fees, and annuities for the 1544/6 subsidy.[124] This drop is partly accounted for by several settlements which he had by then made for various members of his family,[125] but it also demonstrates how increasingly after the 1520s Tudor tax assessments deliberately underestimated landed wealth.[126]

The relatively dependable 1524/5 assessments are useful for comparing Roger II's landed wealth with that of seventeen other Norfolk knights of this date. For the purposes of comparison the figure for Roger II must obviously come from the subsidy rolls and not his own calculations. Appendix 8 confirms that they were of the county

[118] Ibid., fos. 28ᵛ, 31ʳ–32ʳ, 33ʳ–37ʳ; PRO, E326/7259; PRO, C142/96/32; App. 7 below.

[119] R57, RT II 'declaration', fos. 13ʳ–16ᵛ. The total using the figures supplied is actually £645. 1s. 9d., but the extent does not allow for the earlier sales of his manor in Cawston, and lands in Fordham and elsewhere worth about £22 p.a.

[120] PRO, C142/96/32.

[121] H. Miller, 'Subsidy Assessments of the Peerage in the Sixteenth Century', *BIHR* 28 (1955), 26, 30.

[122] There are two 15th-cent. books of returns covering two-thirds of Norfolk which Virgoe has proved to relate to the benevolence of 1481: PRO, E179/242/28; PRO, DL28/27/12; Virgoe, 'Benevolence', 25–45. Unfortunately, these do not record assessments of the wealth of each person listed, giving only the sums they had either already contributed or were expected to pay. Roger I features under East Raynham but his contribution is not recorded since he seems to have paid in London: PRO, E179/242/28; Virgoe, 'Benevolence', 41.

[123] PRO, E179/151/336; E179/150/221.

[124] PRO, E179/150/310; E179/151/317.

[125] Eleanor Townshend, John Townshend's widow, had a jointure interest in his £40-worth of lands and their son Richard was given lands worth over £26 p.a. George Townshend also had a share in the estate by this stage, two manors in Hindringham worth about £24 p.a., though Roger II reserved himself a life annuity of £14 from its issues (see below, App. 7).

[126] M.W. Beresford, *Lay Subsidies and Poll Taxes* (Canterbury, 1963), 12–13; Hoskins, *Age of Plunder*, 12; Miller, 'Subsidy Assessments', 19–23.

élite as landowners. However, the twenty-nine gentry assessed at £100 or more in lands in 1524/5 probably form a safer basis for placing the Townshends in a table of landowners, since knighthood was not always synonymous with landed wealth.[127] In fact the average scarcely changes, rising to only some £173 (indicating that knighthood was indeed largely contiguous with landed wealth in Norfolk by this date), and Roger II remains at the top of the list.[128] In neighbouring Suffolk, a wealthy county like Norfolk, no resident gentleman was assessed at more than £400 in lands.[129] The Townshends maintained this position during the rest of Roger's life, if the (albeit unsatisfactory) tax assessments of the later years of Henry VIII are anything to go by. The average landed wealth of the Norfolk knights assessed for the 1544/6 subsidy was £215; in that of 1546/7 it was £238. For landowners (including women) worth £100 or more the averages were respectively £158 and £163.[130] The knights were now considerably more substantial landowners, compared with the rest of the gentry, than they had been twenty years earlier. Significantly, the 1544/6 assessment of Roger II's landed wealth (£320) is well above these averages.[131]

As newcomers to the Norfolk gentry, the Townshends were the exception rather than the rule in terms of this wealth and the speed with which they accumulated it. The Hobarts and the Spelmans are examples of two other legal families which established themselves during this period, but neither was assessed at the same rates as Roger II during Henry VIII's reign.[132] Other newcomers, the Fermors of East Barsham, became impressively wealthy but their estates were far less substantial than the Townshends'.[133] The landed wealth the Townshends acquired, therefore, reveals a major success story.

[127] Cornwall, *Wealth and Society*, 146–7.

[128] See App. 4.

[129] *Suffolk in 1524, passim.*

[130] PRO, subsidy rolls (E179).

[131] PRO, E179/150/310; E179/151/317. He was not included in the 1546/7 assessments. This is puzzling because he was appointed one of the subsidy commissioners for the county, suggesting that he resided in Norfolk at this date: E179/151/336.

[132] The combined assessments of Walter Hobart and his younger brother Miles for 1524/5 come to £260: PRO, E179/150/251. Shortly before his death in 1546, the law reporter Sir John Spelman was assessed at 300 marks in lands and fees: E179/151/318.

[133] Swales, 'Redistribution', 25; PRO, E179/150/259, 251, 310; E179/151/334, 349. They were never assessed at more than £170 in lands during Henry VIII's reign.

(2) MOVEABLE WEALTH

Real property of course made up just part of what the Townshends owned, and something must also be said about their moveable wealth. Lack of evidence makes it extremely difficult to assess as far as Roger I is concerned, but it is known that he received as a serjeant at law at the end of Edward IV's reign an annual fee of £41. 6s. 11d. from the Crown, as did two other serjeants, Thomas Tremayle and Richard Pigot.[134] Later, as a judge, he could expect at the very least to earn something in the region of £250 per annum.[135] It is also worth noting that the account of his receiver, John Wagor, for the half-year beginning at Michaelmas 1490 shows that the officer was charged with collecting over £826. Unfortunately these receipts are not itemized, and it is impossible to know how much of this income came from land and how much from other sources.[136] The 1524/5 subsidy assessments of the country's leading lawyers also offer some idea of how much someone in Roger I's position might possess in the way of moveable goods. For this tax, the three chief justices, six of the puisne justices, five of the serjeants of law, and the king's attorney were assessed on their goods (the capital value of all their moveable possessions). At the top came Sir John Fyneux, CJKB (£666. 13s. 4d.), and at the bottom serjeant Thomas Fairfax (£100). The average was some £306.[137] One is tempted to place Roger I near the upper end of this scale.

For the sixteenth century we are far more fortunate, because Roger II included his moveable, as well as his landed, wealth in his valors. At the end of 1516 he valued his moveables at nearly £400, and for the 1524/5 subsidy he was assessed at a strikingly high £600 in goods, of which the Townshends owned more than the Heydons, Pastons, and other families of the Norfolk county élite.[138] Of the ninety-five identifiable gentlemen assessed on moveables for the subsidy, only one other, Henry Fermor, the newcomer of mercantile background, was given a higher rating than Roger II, 1,000 marks.[139] The average wealth in moveables of this sample was about

[134] *Harleian MS 433*, iii. 191.

[135] Ives, *Kebell*, 323.

[136] R(Attic), 'Norfolk manorial—Raynham Haviles', 1485/6–1508/9 Raynham accounts, m. 8.

[137] *Inner Temple Records*, i. 464–6.

[138] R31, RT II estate book, fo. 22ʳ; PRO, subsidy rolls (E179) for Norfolk.

[139] Source: PRO, subsidy rolls (E179) relating to Norfolk. For Fermor, see E179/150/259, 221.

£79, proving the point that a gentleman's personal estate was often small because it was more likely to represent a consumable surplus rather than the means of production necessary on a peasant holding.[140] Even among the Norwich oligarchy, who one would expect to possess large amounts of moveable wealth, only Robert Jamys was taxed on £600-worth.[141] Across the border in Suffolk, none of the resident gentry was assessed at more than £500 in goods, and only Sir Robert Drury was assessed for this much.[142]

Some notes Roger made in the 1530s are further evidence of his wealth. During this decade he held 100 marks'-worth of Sir Edmund Bedingfield's plate as security for a loan he had made to Bedingfield of the same amount in cash. This was a loan he could make with ease because at Michaelmas 1536 he had to hand £711 in ready cash.[143] One of the advantages of plate—an item on which the gentry spent lavishly—apart from its importance as an object of display, was that it could readily be used for pledges if the need arose.[144] Like many other families the Townshends possessed a substantial amount of it, though it is impossible to assess exactly how much they owned or what it all was worth.[145]

Further indications of the Townshends' wealth come from various accounts and documents. Roger I maintained other households apart from the one at Raynham. He and Eleanor spent the last quarter of 1478 at Whissonsett where Roger II was born, and by this date he also kept an establishment at Wissett in Suffolk.[146] By the 1480s he is known to have had a house at Norwich, as did other substantial

---

[140] Cornwall, *Wealth and Society*, 156.

[141] PRO, E179/150/254.

[142] *Suffolk in 1524, passim.*

[143] £700 in gold coins and £11 in silver: NRO, B-L VII (3), fos. 39^v–42^v. It is not especially surprising that he should have had so much available. Even when a landowner took great care to maintain and improve his estate, the central purpose of estate management was to ensure that he had the means to pursue a life-style commensurate with his status, rather than to plough back large sums into the estate. His most substantial investments, therefore, usually occurred when a large amount of land was being bought. Cf. Carpenter, 'Gentry and their Estates', 50.

[144] Ibid., 51. In 1475 Margaret Paston had to pledge her plate to help ensure that Roger I was repaid for the Sporle mortgage: *PL*, nos. 285, 291.

[145] A notebook of Roger II's indicates that he bought plate as an investment: NRO, B-L VII b(3), fo. 17^r. Various pieces owned by the family are listed in his and his mother's wills: BL, Add. MS 41,139, fos. 3^v, 10^r–11^r; NRO, NCC 31 Lyncolne. Among the more valuable items were a salter worth over £13 and a pair of candlesticks.

[146] R58, Raynham account roll, m. 19d; R50, 1477/8 sheep accounts, fos. 13^v, 12^v.

gentry families both during and after his lifetime,[147] and it was perhaps this house that was the object of his son's 'byldyng' in the city in the mid-1530s.[148] The Raynham household cost him about £100 to run in the accounting year 1476/7, and expenses would invariably have increased as his family grew.[149] At his death he had at least fifteen domestic servants.[150] In 1525 Roger II had at least twenty-two, five more than the undoubtedly wealthy Sir Robert Drury employed at the same date.[151] By the mid-sixteenth century Roger II's household cost him over £300 per annum in cash and kind.[152]

He and his father had not just their immediate family and domestic servants to provide for. Throughout Roger I's lifetime his widowed stepmother and her servants resided at Raynham.[153] A gentry household was, moreover, expected to exhibit a certain amount of largesse locally and could be sure of a constant stream of visitors. The Raynham stock and grain accounts always made allowance for feeding 'strangers'' horses.[154] These foddering expenses rose sharply during 1476/7 when Eleanor Townshend was ill and a large number of friends came to see her.[155] Unfortunately the accounts do not identify any of their guests, although they do show that troupes of travelling minstrels and players were accommodated.[156]

The family must have enjoyed a relatively high standard of living for the period. Lack of evidence means that it is not possible to explore their living-conditions and life-style to the extent that Ives has been

[147] R(Attic), 'Norfolk manorial—Raynham Haviles', 1483/4 account; *PL*, e.g. nos. 68, 113, 137, 405, 443, 681, and *passim*; Rye, *History of Norfolk*, 160. Gentry widows commonly took up residence in Norwich: e.g. PRO, E179/150/218, 251; E179/151/337, 372.

[148] R(Attic), 'Norfolk manorial—Raynham Haviles', 1483/4 Raynham account; NRO, B-L VII b(3), fo. 42r.

[149] R58, Raynham account roll, m. 10.

[150] PRO, PROB11/10, fo. 11.

[151] PRO, E179/150/221; *Suffolk in 1524*, 339. But these are probably not complete figures since even the households of minor gentry required about twenty household servants: K. Mertes, *The English Noble Household, 1250–1600* (Oxford, 1988), 103.

[152] R57, a later 16th-cent. copy of previously cited RT II 'declaration', fo. 43r.

[153] R58, Raynham account roll, mm. 8, 17; R58, RT I memo-book, fo. 12v.

[154] e.g. R58, Raynham account roll.

[155] Ibid., mm. 11d, 12d. Visitors' horses consumed six bushels of oats during this year but only three and one half in 1475/6.

[156] Ibid., m. 8. During Henry VIII's reign the Le Strange household was visited more than once by the king's players: 'Extracts', 489, 497–8. It is very likely that Raynham was also on their itinerary.

able to do for Thomas Kebell, but there is no reason to believe that they were not accustomed to a similar degree of comfort in an age when even rather minor figures lived in conditions of relative comfort and opulence.[157] When Robert Townshend's town-house at Norwich was plundered during Ket's Rebellion the looters appear to have made off with its entire contents. These were worth £40, and included no less than sixty pairs of linen sheets.[158] By the fifteenth century the days were past when a castle, let alone a lesser dwelling, was built primarily as a defensive structure.[159] Although there was a moat at Raynham, defence was hardly a consideration. Roger I added a tower made of bricks to the manor house there, not a construction best suited for resisting attackers. The house also had glass in its windows and Roger II—and no doubt his father before him—had the luxury of his own study.[160] The moat was probably most useful as a stretch of water for some of the swans which provided a delicacy for their table.[161]

The family could also afford spiritual as well as material comforts. Nearly all gentry households had at least one chaplain, and Roger I paid 4 marks annually to a resident priest, Robert Dapelyn, whose main duty appears to have been to sing for the soul of his father, John Townshend. He was obviously prepared to forgive clerical incontinence, because Dapelyn's son Godfrey at one stage also lived in the household.[162] After his death, Roger's widow Eleanor infringed ecclesiastical regulations by employing the rector of East Raynham, John Clyff, as a servant—and perhaps also as a private chaplain—instead of allowing him to reside in his rectory.[163]

---

[157] Ives, *Kebell*, 356–62; Carpenter, 'Gentry and their Estates', 50–1.

[158] PRO, CP40/1152, rot. 111. The looters, who were caught and brought to justice, did a pretty thorough job; they even took Robert's *sedes excrementorum*.

[159] Lander, *Government and Community*, 170.

[160] R58, Raynham account roll, m. 8; R58, RT II memo-book, fo. 3[r].

[161] R58, Raynham account roll, *passim*; R(Attic), 'Norfolk *manorial*—Raynham Haviles', 1485/6–1508/9 Raynham accounts, m. 13. Swans, always the most expensive type of poultry, were the preserve of the rich and eaten on special occasions: C. A. Wilson, *Food and Drink in Britain* (Harmondsworth, 1973), 109–11, 114–15.

[162] Mertes, *English Noble Household*, 46; R58, Raynham account roll, m. 17.

[163] C. Harper-Bill, 'A Late Medieval Visitation—The Diocese of Norwich in 1494', *Proceedings of the Suffolk Institute of Archaeology*, 34 (1980), 42.

(3) ESTATE MANAGEMENT AND THE RAYNHAM HOUSEHOLD

The late-medieval nobleman was a 'rent-enjoyer rather than a husbandman on a grand scale'[164] and, with the major exception of their sheep-farming, this was true of the Townshends during the late fifteenth and first half of the sixteenth centuries. Economic conditions generally did not suit direct exploitation of demesne lands. Although the slump for landlords was beginning to end by the 1520s, there seem to have been few changes on the Townshend estate.[165] This is reflected in its organization. The hallmarks of a gentry estate were a loosely organized and fluid structure and a lack of specialization among estate officers.[166] Although one man might occupy the role of a receiver-general (in Roger I's day men like William Fuller, Edmund Herberd, and John Wagor, and in Roger II's, John Skayman), his duties, which were not clearly demarcated, often overlapped with those of other officers. Herberd, for example, was both receiver and household steward at various stages in the late 1470s.[167] Except during Roger I's early years as a landowner, when his landed possessions did not amount to much, the shepherds and sheep-reeve accounted separately from the bailiffs. The latter were primarily rent-collectors and commonly responsible for several manors—not always making up coherent groups of land—at once.[168] By the 1540s nearly all the lands in the more-immediate vicinity of Raynham—most of the estate—were the charge of just two men, Hugh Rothwell and Thomas Bird. Other bailiffs were responsible

---

[164] McFarlane, *Nobility*, 153.

[165] Hatcher, *Plague*, 65. The most obvious change was the decline in the number of sheep they kept: see below, App. 9.

[166] Britnell, 'Pastons', *passim*, esp. 132, 144.

[167] 1475/6, ?1477/8, 1479/80: R58, Raynham account roll, mm. 8, 17, 20. Cf. Britnell, 'Pastons', 135.

[168] Thomas Gygges was bailiff at Raynham and Helhougton from 1477/8 to 1478/9: R58, Raynham account roll, mm. 18, 19. In 1490/1 he accounted for South Creake as well as Stibbard and Little Ryburgh, although South Creake was some distance from the other manors. Significantly, the accounts do not call him 'bailiff' of this second group of properties but rather 'collector of rents and farms': R41, 1484/5–1508/9 Stibbard and Little Ryburgh accounts, m. 8; R(Attic), '*Norfolk manorial* N & S Creake', 1485/6–1508/9 'Beaufoes' accounts, m. 2. From 1518/19 to 1526/7 John Blofeld was not only bailiff of the Raynham and Helhoughton manors but also of Stinton Hall in Salle, which did not neighbour these properties. The explanation for this perhaps lies in Roger II's desire to have his wife's valuable Norfolk inheritance administered with the centre of his own.

for the more-outlying Norfolk properties and those in Suffolk, and there was a single steward, John Potter.[169]

The bailiffs were often among the most prominent farmers on the estate.[170] Not surprisingly, the distant Bedfordshire manor of Sharpenhoe was farmed out whole.[171] Manors nearer home which were demised out whole in some years were not always treated as complete entities for farming purposes. East Beckham was farmed out to Simon Gunnore alone in 1476, but by the late 1490s it was in the hands of several farmers.[172] Different arrangements suited different times; a greater total farm might sometimes be realized through piecemeal leasing. This was an expedient considered in 1517 at Burnham, where one of Roger II's farmers threatened not to renew his lease unless it were lowered. John Skayman, Roger's estate officer, responded by telling the farmer that he could leave if he wished and he would let the land out in parcels instead.[173] Occasionally important reservations were made when properties were leased out: it was worth Roger II's while, for example, to retain in his own hands the rabbit warren at Cawston.[174]

Farms were a more important source of income to the Townshends than the rents paid by their manorial tenants, whether freeholders or copyholders. Where the total rent collected on a manor increased it was usually because they had added property to it and not because they had raised rents. There are no signs that they compensated for low assize rents by increasing fines. Sometimes they waived entry fines, so these cannot have been a lucrative source of income.[175] The situation regarding rents and fines on English estates before 1550 is far less clear than it is for a later date. But it is unusual to find evidence of general systematic increases, even in Norfolk where complaints about undue exactions were prominent among the grievances of the 1549 rebels. Apart from Wiltshire, where there was a strong and continuous upward tendency, conditions in most counties differed widely, but everywhere maximum pressure on rents was delayed until

---

[169] NRO, Townshend 163 MS 1,582 1 D4, fos. 2–29.
[170] e.g. R33, RT II receipt book, fo. 1^r; NRO, Townshend 47 MS 1,446 1 B4.
[171] BL, Add. MS 41,139, fo. 6^v; R33, RT II receipt book, fo. 7^v.
[172] NRO, WKC 1/45/1, 390 × 9; BL, Add. MS 41,305, fos. 41^r–42^v.
[173] NRO, B-L VII b(4) (estate memorandum book entitled 'Skaymans Book'), fo. 43^v.
[174] R50, 'Cawston', indenture, 31 May 1521.
[175] e.g. R61, 1526 court book, fo. 8^r.

at least 1540–50.[176] In East Anglia many fines were fixed or, when
arbitrary, kept 'reasonable' in practice by local custom.[177] On the
eve of the Dissolution two shillings per acre was the usual charge
on copyhold fines in East Anglia, and this was the case on the
Townshends' estate before and after this date.[178] There is no sign of
the four shillings per acre commonly demanded by the 1570s.[179]

In the early 1500s manorial lessees often enjoyed leases which
still had many years to run, since landlords had previously granted
out very long terms in order to attract tenants.[180] By the late fifteenth
century, however, the Townshends were granting out new leases
for periods of one to ten years, though five- or seven-year terms
were the norm.[181] The start of the sixteenth century presents a
similar picture. At midsummer 1501 Roger II demised sixteen farms.
The average term for fourteen of these was five-and-three-quarter
years.[182] Evidence from later in his lifetime is sparse, but there are
examples of his granting twenty-year terms.[183] This might seem odd
since one would not expect leases to have lengthened after the early
years of the sixteenth century. However, terms of twenty years cannot
be regarded as inordinately long, and these random examples may
well disguise an overall shortening of leases on the Townshend
estate. In sixteenth-century East Anglia the Crown and Church,
rather than the ordinary landlord, made long leases on a large
scale.[184]

Until about the second decade of the sixteenth century, the
Townshends' farmers normally bore the costs of all or at least part

[176] Cornwall, *Wealth and Society*, 162, 165.

[177] Kerridge, *Agrarian Problems*, 38–9.

[178] Simpson, *Wealth of the Gentry*, 79; court rolls and books in R13, R31, R49, and R61.

[179] Simpson, *Wealth of the Gentry*, 79–80.

[180] Youings, *Sixteenth Century England*, 56. Cf. Dyer, *Lords and Peasants*, 210, for the example of the bishop of Worcester's estates.

[181] Thirty-three leases, of Feb. 1487 to Nov. 1498, are recorded in Eleanor Townshend's estate book. The longest term was for 14 years and the shortest for 1; the average was 6.25: BL, Add. MS 41,305, fos. 21, 22ᵛ, 30–3, 35ʳ, 36ᵛ–38ᵛ, 39ᵛ–41ʳ, 42ʳ, 43ᵛ–45ʳ.

[182] R33, RT II receipt book, fos. 11ᵛ–12ʳ. There are no details for the other two.

[183] e.g. NRO, BRA 926/17 (372 × 8) (1516: 20 years); R31, RT II estate book, fo. 26ᵛ (1519: 20 years); R29, 'HORNINGTOFT Temp. HEN. VIII' (1540: 17 years); R6, 'TOFTREES & SHEREFORD Temp. EDW. VI', indenture of 20 Aug. 1552 (1547: 21 years). On the other hand, Cawston manor was leased out for 7 years in 1521: R50, 'Cawston', indenture of 31 May 1521.

[184] Simpson, *Wealth of the Gentry*, 214.

of the repairs of the demised holding. Some leases charged the farmer
with the expenses of fencing and ditching or with paying royal taxes;
others made them the lord's responsibility.[185] Clearly each case
involved a degree of negotiation between lessor and lessee. But a
list of demised holdings made by Roger II in his memorandum book
in 1519 suggests that the tables were now beginning to turn in his
favour.[186] The effect of renewed population-growth was to put land
at a greater premium than before, and landlords could be more
rigorous in their demands.[187] His list shows that in the case of no
less than twenty-three farms he had recently transferred the responsibility for repairs to the farmers, although admittedly he had to
allow two of them a reduction in rent in return. There is another list,
dated 1521, in the same book, and this details farm buildings for
which repairs were his responsibility. Significantly, some of the
entries are crossed out because the repairs had become the farmer's
business.[188]

Earlier, conditions were often much harder for landlords. The
Paston Letters are full of references to the difficulties of attracting
farmers and collecting rents in the mid-fifteenth century.[189] The
Pastons' farmer at Cowhaugh had to be warned in 1456 that he faced
distraint and eviction if he failed to pay his rent, and four years
later Richard Calle was obliged to inform his master that he could
not find a farmer for Mautby. Another letter Calle wrote in 1461
shows how dramatic cuts in rent had sometimes to be made before
any farmer would take up a property. No one would pay more
than 46s. 8d. per annum for a farm at Boyton formerly let at 76s.
8d.[190] In the same period Margaret Paston complained to her husband that 'as for gadryng of mony I sey nevyr a werse seson, for
Rychard Calle seyth he can get but lytyll in substans of that is
owyng'.[191]

Though the trough was reached in the mid-fifteenth century,

[185] BL, Add. MS 41,305, fos. 21ʳ–45ᵛ; R33, RT II receipt book, fos. 11ᵛ–12ᵛ. In
twelve of the twenty-one leases where the conditions are known, the farmers shared the
costs. There were only five definite cases of the farmer having to bear all charges.
[186] R31, RT II estate book, fo. 26ᵛ.
[187] Hatcher, *Plague*, 65; Youings, *Sixteenth Century England*, 136.
[188] R31, RT II estate book, fo. 26ᵛ.
[189] For the difficulties of Norfolk gentry landlords in the 1460s and 1470s, see
Britnell, 'Pastons'; Richmond, *Paston Family*, 23–30.
[190] *PL*, nos. 154, 551, 614, 653.
[191] Ibid., no. 168.

landlords' problems did not disappear.[192] The Pastons still had difficulties in attracting farmers and collecting rents in the 1470s.[193] Sir
William Calthorpe planned in the same period to reduce his household, because 'he can not be payd of his tenauntes as he hat before
this tyme'.[194] In 1476 Roger I began an attempt to rectify matters
at his new manor at Brampton in Suffolk. Like the Pastons, he was
prepared to adopt an aggressive approach to rent-collecting.[195] He
made a thorough inquiry into the state of the property, and started a
notebook containing an extent of the manor and various memoranda
on rents and farms there.[196] At their old level the farms totalled £12.
11s. 2d. Of the twelve farms, he almost immediately raised the rent
of one and calculated on being able to raise those of eight of the
others in order to bring in another £3 per annum.[197] He had not,
however, counted on the opposition of one of the farmers, William
Payn, who openly refused to pay any extra.[198] His fellows must
have followed his lead, because in 1479 Roger still seems to have
been receiving rents at their old levels.[199] The most dramatic increase
he had proposed was the addition of an extra 24s. 5d. to the
£7. 6s. 8d. paid annually by Geoffrey Sallowas who farmed the site
of the manor.[200] But an estreat roll of the early 1490s shows that
Roger was never able to wring more than an additional five shillings
per annum from him.[201] Sallowas was also none too prompt in
handing over what he was prepared to pay. By Michaelmas 1493
he owed a full year's rent for each of the previous three years, and
part of his farms for 1489 and 1490 remained unpaid.[202] He was still
settling his arrears after Roger died.[203]

Eleanor Townshend and Roger II also had problems during the
late 1490s and early 1500s. At the beginning of the 1490s the bailiff
of 'Scales' manor in South Raynham was charged with over £14

[192] Carpenter, 'Gentry and their Estates', 46; Hatcher, *Plague*, 35, 36–7; M. M.
Postan, 'The Fifteenth Century', *EcHR* 9 (1938–9), 162.
[193] e.g. *PL*, nos. 98, 207, 208.
[194] *PL*, no. 206.
[195] Britnell, 'Pastons', 140–1.
[196] In R45.
[197] Ibid., fo. 15ᵛ.
[198] Ibid., fo. 33ᵛ.
[199] Ibid., fo. 16.
[200] Ibid., fo. 15ʳ.
[201] NRO, B-L V, no. ×. 13.
[202] Ibid.
[203] BL, Add. MS 41,305, fo. 15ᵛ.

per annum in farms, but by the end of the decade these had sunk
to just over £10. At Michaelmas 1496 part of the rent of one farmer
had to be written off, 'or ellys he would not occupye it [his farm]'.
In 1499 150 acres formerly leased out remained in Eleanor's hands
for want of farmers. She had lowered the rent of one farm of thirty
acres from fifteen to eleven shillings, but no one had taken it up.
The water mill had previously brought in over £4 per annum but,
since the year before, was devastated (*devastatur*) and undemisable.
It still brought in no income a decade later.[204] The 'Scales' account
for 1505/6 shows that Roger II was also obliged to reduce farms.[205]
These problems were not unique to 'Scales': farms at the other
Raynham manors sank in the mid-1490s to the level of the late
1470s.[206] One should not exaggerate what may have been an
extremely localized situation, but it is worth pointing out that a
general down-swing in rents began around this time.[207] In any event,
the Townshends were in a position to weather it. A fall in the income
of individual properties was no disaster for the landlord with access
to other sources of wealth and the resources to increase overall landed
income by buying more land.

   Difficulties in sustaining the levels of rents and farms were certainly
not due to any lack of interest in estate-management on the part
of the Townshends. Not much can have escaped Roger I's eye.[208]
Particularly interesting are the notes he wrote concerning his husbandry, dated 13 August 1486, at the end of some sheep accounts.[209]
His shepherds were to beware the dangers of grazing on 'foule
mornynges' and of marauding dogs. He was also very critical of
his ploughmen, noting that they started work late and performed it
'so lecherly and untruely that it were better oftyn tymes undon
because of the gret losse'. Because they failed to till the arable properly
his corn suffered in quality. Like father, like son: Roger II's notebooks
contain the same careful attention to detail and the desire to improve,

[204] NRO, Townshend 37 MS 1,456 1 B 1. Eleanor was concerned enough about the
state of her rents and farms at Raynham to have new rentals and firmals drawn up in
1498: R47, 1 gathering; another copy is in R28.
[205] NRO, Townshend 37 MS 1,456 1 B 1.
[206] R(Attic), '*Norfolk manorial*—Raynham Haviles', 1484/5–1508/9 Raynham
account rolls.
[207] Blanchard, 'Population Change', 434–5.
[208] Cf. John Paston I's continued interest in the details of estate management when
he was away from home: Britnell, 'Pastons', 136.
[209] NRO, Townshend 56 MS 1,475 1F.

and Leland complimented him on his 'good husbandrie'.[210] The limited evidence relating to the Townshends' crop-yields in the late fifteenth century also suggests that they were good farmers by the standards of their day.[211] The care they showed was not unusual; other gentry like the Pastons concerned themselves with the minutiae of policy and administration on their estates.[212] McFarlane is just one of those who has pointed out that medieval landowners needed to take more than a perfunctory interest in managing their estates.[213] Moreover, in the sixteenth century Elizabeth I's lord keeper, Sir Nicholas Bacon, a substantial East Anglian landowner, gave the same careful consideration to digging ditches on his lands as he did to affairs of state.[214]

An active interest in estate-management was not confined to men. Richmond rightly suggests that Eleanor Townshend was a capable woman with a head for business.[215] She was a worthy contemporary of Margaret Paston, a lady sometimes 'exceptionally encumbered' with responsibility for the Pastons' estate.[216] There can be no doubt about who ran the family during Eleanor's widowhood. Accounts and other documents were written in English for her benefit, reverting back to conventional Latin after she died. As head of the family she enlarged the estate, built a mill at East Raynham, and kept a 'Boke off certeyn Bargeyns' in which she recorded her sales of agricultural produce and the leases she had made.[217]

Besides the manor house and its appurtenant buildings and outhouses, the Townshends kept in hand at Raynham several messuages and enclosures, pasture and meadow for grazing their cattle and horses and making hay, a few acres of 'Thakgrounde' (for thatch), several alder groves,[218] and over 200 acres of arable.[219] The manor at East Raynham was the focus of the Townshend estate and the centre of a small local economy. Barley was made into malt

[210] Leland's *Itinerary*, ii. 12.
[211] See pp. 156–58 below.
[212] Britnell, 'Pastons', 136.
[213] McFarlane, *Nobility*, 229–31.
[214] *Papers of Nathaniel Bacon*, vol. i, pp. xviii, 69.
[215] Richmond, *John Hopton*, 127.
[216] Britnell, 'Pastons', 136.
[217] R31, RT II estate book, fo. 30ᵛ; BL, Add. MS 41,305.
[218] The wood from these trees was occasionally sold: e.g. BL, Add. MS 41,139, fo. 15ᵛ.
[219] e.g. R(Attic), '*Norfolk manorial*—Raynham Haviles', account rolls for 1484/5, 1523/4, 1531/2, 1543/4.

there before being sold.[220] Another interesting household activity
was the preparation of harvested hemp. Hemp production was a
subsidiary enterprise in much of the sheep-corn region of East Anglia.
Usually a small farmer's crop, on the Townshend estate it seems
to have been grown by tenants rather than the family itself. There
was a 'hempe yerd' at Raynham which Eleanor leased to one of
her shepherds in the late fifteenth century.[221] The accounts of
Edmund Herberd, Roger I's household steward, from the mid-1470s
also reveal other household activities. Wool, for example, was spun
and woven and the resulting cloth fulled and dyed. Linen was another
cloth made on the manor, but the raw ingredient for this, flax, had
to be purchased.[222] The main recipients of this home-produced cloth
seem to have been the family's employees. Roger II's shepherds,
for example, were given a cloth livery as part of their wages.[223]

The same accounts show that Roger I undertook a substantial
amount of building work at this date. As Carpenter points out,
a family often signalled that it had entered the gentry class—or
risen further within it—by building or rebuilding their principal
residence.[224] This work must have provided considerable local
employment, for Roger bought bricks to construct a new tower, a
bay window inside the hall, and various outbuildings. During 1475/6
four stonemasons received over £4 for their work, and a Norwich
glazier was paid 11s. 6d. for glazing 'divers windows' throughout
the manor. Carpenters and roofers were also employed at various
times to work on new buildings and to carry out repairs.[225]

On the estate much of the Townshends' energy would have been
taken up with sheep-farming, a far larger concern than their other
enterprises.[226] They did, however, employ a messor to look after
their crops in the late fifteenth and early sixteenth centuries.[227]

[220] See pp. 149–51 below.
[221] BL, Add. MS 41,305, fo. 40ᵛ. For hemp-growing see Thirsk, *Agrarian History*,
43, 177, 426.
[222] R58, Raynham account roll, mm. 8, 10, 17.
[223] LSE, R(SR) 1,032, 88,918.
[224] Carpenter, 'Gentry and their Estates', 23. In 1519 Roger II planned to rebuild
the manor house at Raynham: R31, RT II estate book, fo. 26ᵛ. Whether he did or not
is unclear—the ruins near the present 17th-cent. Raynham Hall are not very infor-
mative to the untrained eye.
[225] R58, Raynham account roll, mm. 8, 10, 17.
[226] So deserving a chapter to itself: see below, Ch. 5.
[227] R58, Raynham account roll, mm. 7, 8; R41, 1471/2–1482/3 Stibbard and Little
Ryburgh account roll, m. 9d; BL, Add. MS 41,139, fo. 12ʳ.

Evidence concerning what they grew relates mainly to Raynham, although crops were also grown on a small scale at Stibbard and Little Ryburgh (during the first half of the 1480s at least), and elsewhere by their tenants.[228] Because they ceased to keep a stock and grain account on the dorse of the Raynham accounts after 1484/5, information on their arable farming is almost entirely restricted to the 1470s and early 1480s, and much of what follows relates to that period.[229] There is nothing to suggest, however, that Roger II did not continue to manage the demesne in a similar fashion.

At Raynham itself at the start and end of each accounting year tenants and others often held considerable amounts of the lord's grain.[230] One of these people in the mid-1470s was Thomas Barker, who acted as some kind of agent for Roger I at Lynn. The Townshends sent grain to Barker who stored it until he found a suitable purchaser. By Michaelmas 1475 he held forty-five quarters of wheat and forty quarters of maslin which, in the following year, he sold to another Lynn man on Roger I's behalf.[231] Such an arrangement must have been useful to Roger, since his busy career made it impossible for him always to make direct sales.

Tenants frequently held quantities of the family's grain through the practice of share-cropping. Roger I did not, for example, exploit his demesnes at Stibbard and Little Ryburgh directly but supplied his tenants there with the seed to plant on their holdings. In return for growing and tending the crop they took half of what was produced. In the early 1480s one man, John Steyne, share-cropped with the Townshends in these townships, growing barley, oats, wheat, and maslin on their behalf.[232] By the middle of the decade, however, at least four tenants were share-cropping, each growing a few acres of one or more of the same crops for Roger I.[233] Some tenants are distinguished in the Raynham accounts as holding quantities of the

---

[228] R41, 1471/2–1482/3 and 1483/4–1508/9 Stibbard and Little Ryburgh accounts; NRO, B-L V, nos. ✕. 31, 32.

[229] There is an account for the 'issues of the lord's barn' for 1485/6: R(Attic), 'Norfolk manorial—Raynham Haviles', bound with 1485/6–1508/9 account roll; but it is the only surviving one of its kind.

[230] e.g. R58, Raynham account roll, *passim*.

[231] Ibid., mm. 4d, 7d, 11d.

[232] R41, 1471/2–1482/3 Stibbard and Little Ryburgh accounts, mm. 2d, 9d, 10d.

[233] R41, 1484/5–1507/8 Stibbard and Little Ryburgh accounts, mm. 1d, 2d, 3d.

Townshends' grain as a 'loan' (*prestitum*).[234] Here share-cropping does not appear to have been taking place, and presumably the tenants concerned repaid the loan in grain. A small amount of rye, wheat, barley, peas, and oats was also grown for Roger at Dunton, where he had a barn.[235] Each year between the mid-1470s and early 1480s his sheep-reeve, John Stalworthy—or perhaps the latter's son, the Townshend shepherd in the parish—sowed these crops there on his behalf.[236] In the early 1500s Roger II had barns at Helhoughton and Oxborough,[237] but any crops stored in them were probably also grown by tenants or farmers. Other tenants in his father's day are recorded in the accounts as holding 'farm barley', that is grain which they owed as rent.[238] In fifteenth-century Norfolk it was common to lease out demesne land for grain rents which were usually paid in barley, and the Paston Letters show barley rents to have been a regular and important feature of the Pastons' income. It was, therefore, potentially serious when Richard Calle once found himself unable to obtain an offer of more than forty combs of barley as rent for one of their farms.[239] Another service performed for the Townshends was the threshing of harvested crops, a task given to various tenants. Some of them must have received part of the grain as payment for the job, since the Raynham stock accounts show that frequently the Townshends took a part only of what was threshed.[240]

Table 4.1 provides us with some idea of the scale of the Townshends' arable farming at Raynham during Roger I's lifetime. In medieval Norfolk the *warectum* was that part of the fallow arable being prepared for a return to cultivation in the following year, and it received special attention by way of extra ploughings and manurings. It was distinct from the *friscus*, another term used by contemporaries, which was fallow land left lying ley for several years.[241] The acreage the Townshends cultivated varied considerably

---

[234] e.g. R58, Raynham account roll, m. 18d; R(Attic), '*Norfolk manorial*—Raynham Haviles', 1483/4 and 1485/6 accounts.

[235] R58, Raynham account roll, m. 25d. He also had a water mill at Dunton. In 1476/7 he paid a carpenter to build two wheels for it: ibid., m. 10.

[236] Ibid., mm. 7d, 11d, 12d, 18d, 19d, 20d, 25d; R50, 1477/8 sheep accounts; R24, 1478/9 sheep accounts; NRO, Townshend 56 MS 1,475 1F.

[237] BL, Add. MS 41,139, fo. 6.

[238] e.g. R58, Raynham account roll, *passim*.

[239] *PL*, *passim*, no. 649.

[240] R58, Raynham account roll, *passim*.

[241] I am grateful to Dr B. M. S. Campbell for explaining these terms.

TABLE 4.1. *Raynham crop acreages, 1472/3–1485/6*

Year	Wheat	Rye	Maslin	Barley	Oats	Peas	Total acreage sown	Warectum*	Friscus†
1472/3	17.50(16)	0.00	15.00(13.7)	40.00(37.0)	28.00(26.0)	9.00(8.2)	109.50	?	?
1473/4	21.50(12.5)	2.50(1.5)	20.25(11.8)	79.00(46.0)	39.50(23.0)	9.00(5.2)	171.75	?	?
1474/5	41.75(18.6)	1.00(0.4)	24.00(10.7)	96.00(43.0)	49.25(22.0)	13.00(5.8)	225.00	60.50	?
1475/6	29.00(14.4)	2.50(1.2)	38.00(19.0)	86.00(42.6)	36.50(18.0)	10.00(5.0)	202.00	61.00	?
1476/7	39.25(20.0)	0.00	26.00(13.3)	98.75(50.6)	21.00(10.8)	10.00(5.1)	195.00	74.90	?
1477/8	36.40(18.0)	0.00	29.75(14.6)	97.25(48.0)	31.00(15.2)	10.00(4.9)	204.00	?	?
1478/9	40.00(21.0)	0.00	17.50 (9.1)	95.25(50.0)	28.50(14.8)	11.00(5.7)	192.25	?	?
1479/80	46.00	0.00	25.50	?	30.50	?	?	?	?
1480/1	40.25(20.4)	0.00	12.50 (6.3)	90.00(46.0)	47.00(24.0)	8.00(4.0)	197.75	?	?
1481/2	33.75(17.8)	3.25(1.7)	30.50(16.1)	69.50(36.7)	45.25(24.0)	7.00(3.7)	189.25	?	?
1482/3	40.75(20.4)	3.25(1.6)	22.75(11.4)	96.25(48.2)	28.00(14.0)	8.75(4.4)	199.75	49.75	116.75
1483/4	36.25(20.0)	0.00	12.50 (7.0)	62.00(35.0)	56.75(32.0)	10.00(5.6)	177.50	49.50	108.38(?)
1484/5	40.50(22.4)	0.00	18.00(10.0)	71.25(39.4)	43.75(24.2)	7.25(4.0)	180.75	47.50	135.75
1485/6	36.00(22.0)	0.00	16.75(10.2)	67.50(41.2)	35.75(21.8)	7.75(4.7)	163.75	56.75	144.75
Mean % of each crop sown, 1472/3–1485/6	18.73	0.49	11.78	43.40	20.75	5.10			

Note: Figures in brackets = % of total acreage sown; *warectum* = arable fallow being prepared for cultivation in the following year; †*friscus* = fallow land lying ley for several years.
Sources: R58, Raynham account roll; R(Attic), 'Norfolk manorial—Raynham Haviles', 1483/4 and 1484/5 accounts, 1485/6–1508/9 accounts, m. 1.

from year to year because they practised this system of long fallowing. The *warectum* thus represented only a part of the sum total of fallow land at any one time; the remainder was folded by their sheep to refertilize it and to allow it to recuperate, and it was returned to cultivation in a future year. In the first half of the 1480s, for which figures are available for the *friscus* as well as the *warectum*, the total arable at Raynham was some 365 acres, of which the Townshends sowed about 50 per cent each year. They were, therefore, far-less intensive cultivators than those of agriculturally advanced and well-populated east Norfolk between the late thirteenth and early fifteenth centuries.[242]

Barley was pre-eminent in north-west Norfolk's 'good sands' region of light and gravelly soils where the core of the Townshends' estate was situated, as it made fewer demands on the land than wheat and could grow in less-fertile areas.[243] It was easily their most important crop.[244] Some, the chaff barley, was used to fatten pigs or as feed for poultry and swans; as many as 26 quarters in 1480/1.[245] Small quantities were also regularly given away. Roger I normally allowed his ploughmen 2 bushels each year and donated 2 quarters in all to the four orders of friars, as represented by the local houses at Lynn, Burnham, and Walsingham. By 1484/5, however, one of these orders no longer received any such gift, but which order and why it was excluded is unfortunately a mystery.[246] Nevertheless, during this period, the Townshends malted most of their crop and sold little in the form of barley.[247] Malt was made both inside and outside the household. In Roger I's day household production was the responsibility of one of his wife's chamber-servants, Emma Rysby, who also

[242] Campbell, 'Agricultural Progress'. I am assuming that the anomalous figure of 108.38 acres of *friscus* given in the accounts for 1482/3 is due to scribal error—138.38 would make more sense.

[243] K. J. Allison, 'The Sheep-Corn Husbandry of Norfolk in the Sixteenth and Seventeenth Centuries', *AHR* 5 (1957), 13; E. Kerridge, *The Agricultural Revolution* (London, 1967), 74; Thirsk, *Agrarian History*, 170, 615.

[244] See Table 4.1 above. In the 16th cent. and beyond barley made up 50–75 per cent of the region's tillage crops: Kerridge, *Agricultural Revolution*, 74.

[245] R58, Raynham account roll, m. 21d.

[246] Ibid., mm. 11d, 12d, 18d, 19d, 20d, 21d, 25d, 26d; R(Attic), '*Norfolk manorial*—Raynham Haviles', 1484/5 account.

[247] In some years none was sold as barley: e.g. R58, Raynham account roll, mm. 4d, 7d, 18d, 19d, 20d, 25d, 26d. Roger I could well have malted his barley because he found it difficult to obtain a reasonable price for it. When barley prices were low the Pastons increased the amount they malted: Britnell, 'Pastons', 134.

supervised the kitchen and bakehouses and kept the poultry.[248] Outside the household tenants or farmers were often contracted to make it.[249] Some of the malt was brewed at Raynham (or at Whissonsett and Norwich when Roger I kept households there)[250] for home consumption—over 60 quarters per annum by the 1480s—but most was sold. For the period when data are available, a peak was reached in 1475/6 when almost 450 quarters of barley were allocated for malt-making.[251] Lynn merchants especially, but also buyers from townships along the north Norfolk coast—Cromer, Cley, and Thornham are three examples—were the main customers.[252] Carts bearing malt must have regularly left Raynham for Lynn. In 1473/4, 1 quarter of oats was expended as fodder for Roger I's horses which carted malt to Lynn and elsewhere on four separate occasions.[253] Much of the malt they sold was obviously destined for export or at least carried by ship to other parts of the country. Their 1476/7 receiver's account refers to the cost of transporting 60 quarters to a ship waiting at Wells.[254] The malt produced by the Norfolk gentry was often carried by sea rather than land. In the mid-fifteenth century Sir John Fastolf sent his by ship along the east coast to London.[255] At least some of the Townshends' malt also reached the capital. On at least two occasions in the early 1490s (when grain prices, especially those for wheat, sank) they found distant buyers, since they sold malt and wheat to a

---

[248] R58, Raynham account roll, mm. 7d, 8, 24d; R(Attic), 'Norfolk manorial— Raynham Haviles', 1483/4 account; R41, 1483/4–1508/9 Stibbard and Little Ryburgh accounts, m. 1d.

[249] e.g. R58, Raynham account roll, mm. 11d, 12d, 18d, 20d, 21d; NRO, B-L VII b(3).

[250] Ibid., m. 19d; R(Attic), 'Norfolk manorial—Raynham Haviles', 1483/4 Raynham account.

[251] R58, Raynham account roll, m. 21d.

[252] Ibid., mm. 3d, 11d, 12d, 18d, 19d. R(Attic), 'Norfolk manorial—Raynham Haviles', 1484/5 account, 1485/6–1508/9 accounts, m. 1. Cromer and Cley were secondary ports for this stretch of coastline: N. J. Williams, *The Maritime Trade of the East Anglian Ports* (Oxford, 1988), 52.

[253] R58, Raynham account roll, m. 4d. Lynn, 'the Liverpool of medieval times', was the chief corn-market of eastern England. It shipped corn to the Low Countries— the chief foreign market for Norfolk grain in the Townshends' period—and to the English ports of the north-east: Williams, *Maritime Trade*, 7, 70–2, 150–1.

[254] R58, Raynham account roll, m. 16. Wells possessed a considerable fleet of traders. Lying at the end of a principal road, the 'Pilgrims' Road', which passed near Raynham, it must have been the most convenient port for the Townshends: Williams, *Maritime Trade*, 5, 52.

[255] McFarlane, 'The Investment of Sir John Fastolf's Profits of War', in id., *England*, 197 n.

TABLE 4.2. *Malt sales, 1472/3–1485/6*

Year	Amount sold (quarters, bushels)	Retained (quarters, bushels)
1472/3	0, 4	44, 4
1473/4	0, 0	239, 2
1474/5	18, 4	359, 1
1475/6	300, 0	412, 3
1476/7	78, 0	627, 0
1477/8	664, 4	?
1478/9	161, 0	82, 6.5
1479/80	398, 0	8, 6.5
1480/1	20, 0	343, 3
1481/2	455, 0	50, 1
1482/3	267, 0	7, 2
1483/4	120, 0	31, 3
1484/5	120, 4	22, 2
1485/6	120, 0	44, 5

Sources: R58, Raynham account roll; R(Attic), '*Norfolk manorial*—Raynham Haviles', 1483/4, 1484/5–1508/9 accounts.

group of London merchants.[256] They also found customers for their malt in Suffolk. One of these was John Hopton—to whom they sold 10 quarters in 1477/8—but more important were two brewers from Walberswick on the east coast. In the same year Roger I sold to them a total of 140 quarters.[257]

The amount of malt Roger sold fluctuated widely from year to year. Table 4.2 indicates that he held over to a greater or lesser degree a quantity of the malt produced each year, and that therefore his sales would often be composed of malt from more than one year. It was to his advantage to accumulate grain and await a favourable moment to sell, an option not open to many men of smaller means. The smaller man was often obliged to sell his produce immediately, even if prices were low, because he would lack the capital resources of a wealthy gentleman like Roger I.

Wheat and oats were the Townshends' next most important crops,

[256] Thirsk, *Agrarian History*, 816; BL, Add. MS 41,305, fos. 7ʳ–8ᵛ, 11ʳ. Cf. Britnell, 'Pastons', 139. Norfolk and Essex were the capital's principal sources of wheat in the 16th cent.: Thirsk, *Agrarian History*, 507.
[257] NRO, B-L V, no. ×. 45; R58, Raynham account roll, mm. 16, 18d.

and on average each crop occupied about 20 per cent of their sown acreage between 1472/3 and 1485/6, but the quantity sown varied quite markedly from year to year.[258] Some of the wheat found its way to the kitchen each year. The main constituent of bread produced in the household was maslin, a mixture of wheat and rye, rather than pure wheat.[259] Probably the single most important occasion for which bread made solely of wheat-flour was baked was the annually observed anniversary of the death of John Townshend, the father of Roger I.[260] The bulk of the wheat they grew, however, was retained both for seed-corn and for immediate and future sale. The purchasers were usually Lynn merchants, although other sales were made to men from nearby towns and villages. One customer of the mid-1470s was Edmund Pety, a miller or baker from Walsingham, the famous pilgrimage centre.[261] Occasionally other gentry occurred among the purchasers. In the early sixteenth century, for example, the young Roger II sold wheat and other grain to his friend Robert Le Strange.[262] As was the case with malt, the amount the Townshends sold could vary greatly from year to year. It is probably no coincidence that Roger I sold very little in the early 1470s—a mere 2 bushels in 1472/3—when wheat prices were depressed.[263] As for oats, these were grown chiefly to feed horses and draught animals and to fatten pigs and poultry, and not as a cash crop.[264]

Like their oats, the maslin they grew was not primarily intended for the market. Most went to the household for baking, although a few bushels, as well as a few of barley, were given each year to the shepherds as part of their wages.[265] Peas and rye were also for internal household consumption. On average, just under ten acres of peas were grown annually during the 1470s and 1480s. Mainly a livestock

[258] See Table 4.1, above.

[259] Thus in 1472/3 10 bushels of wheat and 153 of maslin were baked but by 1484/5 the respective quantities were 78 and 284, an indication of how Roger I's household had grown: R58, Raynham account roll, m. 3d; R(Attic), 'Norfolk manorial—Raynham Haviles', 1484/5 account.

[260] e.g. R58, Raynham account roll, *passim*.

[261] Ibid.; NRO, B-L V, no. ×. 45.

[262] NRO, Townshend 193 MS 1,612 1 C7, fo. 12ʳ.

[263] R58, Raynham account roll, m. 3d; Thirsk, *Agrarian History*, 816.

[264] Roger I's sale of 60 quarters, *c.* 1476, to a Lynn man was pretty exceptional—between Michaelmas 1502 and Michaelmas 1505 Roger II sold none: NRO, B-L V, no. ×. 45; Townshend 193 MS 1,612 1 C7; B-L VII b(3).

[265] NRO, B-L V, nos. ×. 31, 45, 32; Townshend 193 MS 1,612 1 C7; B-L VII b(3); R55, 1493/4–1497/8 sheep accounts.

TABLE 4.3. *Thirteenth- and fourteenth-century Raynham seeding-rates* (bushels per acre)

Year	Wheat	Rye	Maslin	Barley	Oats	Peas
1284/5	2.5	2.4	2.4	4.0	4.0	2.1
1286/7	2.5	2.5	2.4	4.0	4.6	2.3
1287/8	2.5	2.5	—	4.0	4.5	2.4
1304/5	2.4	2.5	2.4	4.0	3.8	2.5
1315/16	2.5	2.4	2.4	3.9	4.0	2.4
1339/40	2.5	2.0	—	3.9	4.0	2.5
1342/3	2.5	2.4	—	4.0	4.0	2.5
1345/6	2.6	2.5	—	4.0	4.0	2.5
1348/9	2.4	—	2.6	4.1	4.0	2.5
Min.	2.4	2.0	2.4	3.9	3.8	2.1
Mean	2.5	2.4	2.4	4.0	4.1	2.4
Max.	2.6	2.5	2.6	4.1	4.6	2.5
1350/1	2.7	—	2.5	4.0	3.9	2.0
1372/3	2.5	—	2.5	4.0	3.7	2.0
1373/4	2.5	2.0	—	4.0	4.0	2.0
Min.	2.5	2.0	2.5	4.0	3.7	2.0
Mean	2.6	2.0	2.5	4.0	3.9	2.0
Max.	2.7	2.0	2.5	4.0	4.0	2.0

Sources: I am much obliged to Dr Campbell for the data for both this table and Table 4.6, which come from accounts for the manors of the Ingoldisthorpe family (now at Raynham Hall) and of the Scales lordship in Raynham (NRO, MS 1,455 1B1).

feed, a few bushels were sometimes sent to the kitchen.[266] Rye was the least important crop. When grown at all, a mere couple of acres or so were sown.[267] Since it was a constituent of maslin, it had to be bought when not grown.

Seeding-rates and the crop-yields achieved on a manorial demesne may provide us with some idea of the skill and efficiency—or otherwise—of the producer concerned.[268] For the Townshends, what

[266] Table 4.1; R58, Raynham account roll, *passim*.
[267] See Table 4.1.
[268] But some caution is needed here: Campbell has shown that where arable demesnes in later medieval east Norfolk were highly productive this had more to do with the practices of the farming region within which they lay, rather than with any supposed superior command over resources or commitment to agricultural progress on the part of the landlord: B. M. S. Campbell, 'Arable Productivity in Medieval England: Some Evidence from Norfolk', *Journal of Economic History*, 43 (1983), 397.

TABLE 4.4. *Roger I's Raynham seeding-rates* (bushels per acre)

Year	Wheat	Rye	Maslin	Barley	Oats	Peas
1472/3	2.8	—	3.1	3.7	3.5	2.1
1473/4	2.0	1.6	3.7	3.0	4.0	2.0
1474/5	2.2	?	2.0	3.3	4.1	2.0
1475/6	2.3	2.4	2.1	3.2	3.7	2.2
1476/7	2.4	—	2.0	3.5	4.0	2.4
1477/8	2.6	—	3.1	3.9	3.7	2.3
1478/9	2.6	—	2.5	3.6	3.9	2.0
1479/80	2.5	—	2.2	?	4.2	?
1480/1	2.5	—	2.6	4.0	?	2.3
1481/2	2.5	4.0	2.3	3.7	4.2	2.3
1482/3	2.5	4.0	2.5	3.8	4.0	2.7
1483/4	2.5	—	2.6	4.0	4.7	2.5
1484/5	3.0	—	3.1	4.0	?	2.2
1485/6	2.5	—	2.5	3.8	4.0	2.6
Min.	2.0	1.6	2.0	3.0	3.5	2.0
Mean	2.5	3.0	2.6	3.7	4.0	2.3
Max.	3.0	4.0	3.7	4.0	4.7	2.7

Sources: R58, Raynham account roll; R(Attic), '*Norfolk manorial*—Raynham Haviles', 1483/4 and 1484/5 accounts, 1485/6–1508/9 accounts, m. 1.

information there is relates to their demesnes at Raynham and at Stibbard/Little Ryburgh during a few years of the late fifteenth century. Although extremely limited, this evidence is worth attention since Norfolk productivity-data for this period are hard to come by.

In the thirteenth century Walter of Henley advocated sowing wheat at 2 to 2½ bushels per acre, and barley and oats at 4. A modern writer, Lord Ernle, concluded that in medieval England generally wheat, rye, and legumes were usually grown at 2 bushels per acre.[269] In fact, such figures are often not very helpful because medieval seeding-rates were much more variable than those of any subsequent period. On some estates seeding-rates could be higher than these averages as a result of physical problems of soil and terrain. Oats, for example, were sometimes sown densely to act as a smothering

[269] P. F. Brandon, 'Cereal Yields in the Sussex Estates of Battle Abbey during the Late Middle Ages', *EcHR* 2nd ser. 25 (1972), 408; Lord Ernle, *English Farming Past and Present*, 6th edn. (London, 1961), 10.

TABLE 4.5. *Roger I's seeding-rates, Stibbard/Little Ryburgh* (bushels per acre)

Year	Wheat	Maslin	Barley	Oats
1480/1	—	—	4.0	—
1481/2	—	—	—	4.0
1482/3	3.1	3.2	4.4	4.6
1483/4	2.7	3.5	4.0	4.2
1484/5	3.1	2.6	4.4	4.0
Min.	2.7	2.6	4.0	4.0
Mean.	3.0	3.1	4.2	4.2
Max.	3.1	3.5	4.4	4.6

Sources: R41, 1471/2–1482/3 and 1483/4–1508/9 Stibbard and Little Ryburgh accounts.

crop against weeds.[270] Tables 4.3 and 4.4, however, indicate that at Raynham in the late thirteenth and fourteenth centuries seeding-rates were close to those suggested by Walter of Henley and that little had changed by Roger I's lifetime. At Stibbard/Little Ryburgh, however, he was sowing more intensely (see Table 4.5).

Medieval crop-yields were far inferior to those of today and could vary tremendously from year to year, especially since the medieval farmer did not enjoy all the advantages of his modern counterpart. Lord Ernle calculated that wheat-yields rarely rose above 10 bushels per acre, whilst those for oats and barley ranged from about 12 to 16 bushels per acre.[271] Kerridge concurs as far as wheat-yields are concerned, stating that a normal yield was 1 quarter (8 bushels) per acre.[272]

Although soil-types and quality vary within Norfolk, as a county it lies in one of the most fertile regions of Britain and is capable of providing the farmer with higher-than-average yields. Its importance as a crop-growing county in the Townshends' period is underlined by the fact that nearly two-thirds of the corn supplied to the army in France in Henry VIII's reign was purchased in Norfolk, although at least some of it must have originally come from neighbouring Cambridgeshire and Huntingdonshire.[273] East Norfolk was particularly suited for arable farming. Campbell has shown how its rich soils

[270] Brandon, 'Cereal Yields', 407–9. [271] Ernle, *English Farming*, 10.
[272] *Agricultural Revolution*, 329. [273] Thirsk, *Agrarian History*, 520.

TABLE 4.6. *Thirteenth- and fourteenth-century Raynham yields* (bushels)

Year	Wheat	Rye	Maslin	Barley	Oats	Peas
*Yield per seed**						
1286/7	5.00	4.00	—	3.30	2.30	2.20
1338/9	—	—	—	6.40	3.20	6.20
1344/5	3.00	4.10	4.00	3.90	2.20	2.60
1347/8	3.60	—	—	3.00	1.90	2.00
1349/50	4.00	—	1.90	1.60	0.80	1.10
Min.	3.00	4.00	1.90	1.60	0.80	1.10
Mean	3.90	4.05	2.95	3.60	2.10	2.80
Max.	5.00	4.10	4.00	6.40	3.20	6.20
1371/2	1.70	—	—	3.30	3.40	2.30
1372/3	5.10	—	4.25	6.50	4.50	4.70
Mean	3.40	—	4.25	4.90	4.00	3.50
Yield per acre (bushels)						
1286/7	12.40	9.80	—	13.00	10.60	5.20
1338/9	—	—	—	25.00	12.80	15.50
1344/5	7.60	10.30	10.00	15.60	8.80	6.50
1347/8	8.60	—	—	12.20	7.60	5.00
1349/50	10.00	—	4.90	6.40	3.20	2.80
Min.	7.60	9.80	4.90	6.40	3.20	2.80
Mean	9.70	10.10	7.50	14.40	8.60	7.00
Max.	12.40	10.30	10.00	25.00	12.80	15.50

Note: *for each bushel planted.
Sources: I am most grateful to Dr Campbell for these data from his researches.

and the advanced methods employed by its medieval cultivators resulted in yields well above the country-wide average.[274] Well before the fifteenth century, yields of 15 bushels of wheat per acre were normal. The most productive demesnes averaged well over 20 bushels per acre, and in a good year 30 bushels per acre was possible. Broadly similar, if slightly lower, yields were achieved for barley.[275]

North-west Norfolk was a less fertile part of the county. Campbell has calculated that mean yields of 11.6 to 12.8 bushels per acre for wheat and 12.2 to 13.2 for barley were achieved there between 1375

[274] Campbell, 'Agricultural Progress', 26–46.   [275] Ibid., 21.

TABLE 4.7.   *Roger I's Raynham yields* (bushels per acre)

Year	Wheat	Rye	Maslin	Barley	Oats	Peas
*Yield per seed**						
1482/3	4.80	4.00	5.90	9.10	4.30	4.10
1484/5	7.40	—	5.10	5.00	?	?
Mean	6.10	4.00	5.50	7.05	4.30	4.10
Yield per acre (bushels)						
1482/3	12.00	16.20	14.70	34.10	17.40	12.25
1484/5	22.00	—	16.00	20.00	?	?
Mean	17.00	16.20	15.35	27.05	17.40	12.25

Note: *for each bushel planted.
Sources: R58, Raynham account roll, m. 26d; R(Attic), '*Norfolk manorial*—Raynham Haviles', 1484/5 account.

and 1425.[276] On the basis of this evidence, the Townshends' late fifteenth-century demesnes at Raynham and Stibbard/Little Ryburgh were performing at the upper end of the productivity range for the locality. Figures for two years in the 1480s only are obtainable for Raynham in the Townshends' day, and therefore must be treated with extreme caution, but it is worth comparing them with those relating to the same township in the late thirteenth and fourteenth centuries. If Roger I achieved similar yields in other years, he was doing considerably better than previous farmers (see Tables 4.6 and 4.7). Most striking is Roger I's barley yield for 1482/3. It would, however, be surprising if his 1484/5 yield for the same crop were not closer to the norm.

Owing to the lack of evidence, it is impossible to compare the yields the Townshends achieved at Stibbard/Little Ryburgh with data relating to those townships for an earlier period. Information is, however, available for Hindolveston, a neighbouring township, for the second half of the fourteenth and early fifteenth centuries. On the basis of this evidence Roger I also obtained good yields at Stibbard/ Little Ryburgh (see Tables 4.8 and 4.9). Roger I's superior yields are probably attributable to his use of a convertible husbandry system of long fallowing in conjunction with an integrated sheep-corn husbandry.

[276] My thanks to Dr Campbell for this information.

TABLE 4.8. *Hindolveston yields* (bushels per acre)

Year	Wheat	Barley	Oats	Legumes
1352/3	14.4	13.0	11.6	7.8
1360/61	18.2	8.3	8.6	7.1
1361/2	7.7	14.1	9.6	8.5
1362/3	—	18.3	18.0	12.0
1395/6	—	12.3	12.0	7.3
1396/7	11.0	10.3	9.8	5.2
1404/5	18.7	11.2	14.8	7.7
1405/6	10.1	12.6	11.1	7.2
1414/15	9.7	8.3	8.7	4.2
Min.	7.7	8.3	8.6	4.2
Mean	12.8	12.0	11.6	7.4
Max.	18.7	18.3	18.0	12.0

Sources: I am much obliged to Dr Campbell for these data, from the accounts for the prior of Norwich Cathedral's manor in the township (NRO, DCN 60/18/1–61; NRO, DCN 40/13; NRO, L'Estrange IB 4/4).

TABLE 4.9. *Roger I's Stibbard/Little Ryburgh yields* (bushels per acre)

Year	Wheat	Maslin	Barley	Oats
1479/80	16.6	19.3	—	—
1480/1	—	—	24.0	—
1481/2	—	—	—	?
1482/3	12.8	19.2	?	7.0
1483/4	16.8	20.3	15.4	13.8
Min.	12.8	19.2	15.4	7.0
Mean	15.4	19.6	19.7	10.4
Max.	16.8	20.3	24.0	13.8

Sources: R41, 1471/2–1482/3, 1483/4–1508/9 Stibbard and Little Ryburgh accounts.

Grain, as previously noted, was bought as well as grown by the Townshend family. During the late fifteenth and early sixteenth centuries at least, their needs were normally supplied locally. Frequently the vendors were their tenants, farmers, and estate officers.[277]

---

[277] e.g. BL, Add. MS 41,305, fos. 5ᵛ, 6ʳ, 19ʳ; R58, RT II memo-book, fo. 7ʳ; BL, Add. MS 41,139, fo. 21ᵛ; NRO, Townshend 193 MS 1,612 1 C7; B-L VII b(3). Between midsummer 1500 and spring 1501 Roger II spent £12. 13*s.* 4*d.* on grain, mainly barley and malt: BL, Add. MS 41,139, fo. 21ᵛ.

Private marketing in this period necessarily operated through a network of neighbours, friends, and relatives because of the general lack of credit facilities, and most East Anglian buyers and sellers of corn did not have to go far to find a market.[278] When the Townshends did range further afield, as when Roger I sold malt to John Hopton, the personal network continued to operate. The same must have been true in their commercial dealings with Londoners, since their legal careers gave them plenty of opportunity to familiarize themselves with the city and its inhabitants.

The Townshends resorted to the market for other produce besides grain, since the only foodstuff in which they were totally self-sufficient appears to have been mutton. Their household accounts of the mid-1470s show that they found it necessary to buy beef and cheese, although they did keep some cattle on the Raynham demesne.[279] The account for 1475/6, for example, records that Roger I's dairy at Raynham made 12½ stone of cheese for the household, but another 20 stone were bought in Suffolk, a county where cheese-production was a well-developed industry by the early sixteenth century.[280] Unlike north-west Norfolk, much of Suffolk was a traditional area for dairying and cattle-rearing, activities which provided the basis of its wealth. About three-quarters of the county was wood-pasture land while two-thirds of Norfolk was suited for a sheep-corn agricultural economy. Thus, although the Townshends may have looked to Suffolk for cheese, the Suffolk gentry in turn depended on the neighbouring counties of Norfolk and Cambridgeshire for corn.[281]

Fish, especially herring and ling, were another commodity which the Townshends had to purchase. Here again the importance of personal contacts came to the fore. Fish was landed at Norfolk ports: ships from Lynn fished in Icelandic waters—by the 1520s the town had a flourishing trade with the island—and Great Yarmouth was the home of England's herring fishery.[282] But despite this, Roger I bought a good deal of fish from John Hoo of Walberswick in Suffolk, John Hopton's bailiff.[283]

---

[278] Thirsk, *Agrarian History*, 557, 499.

[279] Roger II bought twenty 'sterys' (steers) at Newmarket in 1500: R58, RT II memo-book, fo. 7ʳ.

[280] R58, Raynham account roll, m. 8; MacCulloch, *Suffolk*, 18.

[281] Thirsk, *Agrarian History*, 46–7; MacCulloch, *Suffolk*, 16–18.

[282] Williams, *Maritime Trade*, 95, 7. For a Lynn mercantile dispute connected with the Icelandic trade, see PRO, C1/875/67–9.

[283] R58, Raynham account roll, mm. 8, 10. The ling acquired from John probably

A surprising omission from these household accounts is any mention of luxury foodstuffs: a great gentry household was used to a considerable variety of food and drink.[284] Perhaps this was because it
was not the business of the steward to acquire them. But it is likely
that there would have been a demand at Raynham for items like
spices, almonds, sugar, oranges, and dates, which the women in the
Paston Letters often requested their menfolk to buy.[285]

(4) CONCLUSIONS

The estate and wealth of the Townshends at the end of our period, the
mid-sixteenth century, represented a major success story and were a
result of their ambition and ability. A comparison of their landed and
moveable wealth with that of their fellow Norfolk gentry demonstrates
just how substantial they had become by Henry VIII's reign.

The gentry were not composed only of those privileged by birth,
and not all who entered their ranks had been fortunate enough to
marry an heiress: to a certain extent they were a meritocracy. The
Townshends show that men of ability, especially lawyers like Roger
I, who entered the land market in a sustained, determined and sometimes ruthless fashion, could acquire for themselves a large estate.
What makes Roger I's achievement in founding the family's fortunes
particularly impressive—though by no means exceptional—is the
compact nature of the estate he created.

Once they became landowners they were not content to rest on their
laurels, and Roger II consolidated and augmented considerably what
his father had left him. A landowner, moreover, had to take an
interest in his estate and its management if he were to keep it. In common with other gentry, the Townshends did have problems in collecting rents and attracting farmers when conditions were adverse
for the landlord. Yet they cannot be accused of bad management.
They were not innovators, but then neither was a successful East
Anglian landlord of the later sixteenth century, Lord Keeper Bacon,

came from Icelandic waters. At Aldeburgh, just down the coast from Walberswick,
merchants specialized in the fish trade with Iceland: Williams, *Maritime Trade*, 91–2.

[284] Carpenter, 'Gentry and their Estates', 50.
[285] *PL*, nos. 130, 209, 213, 215, 853.

who combined business acumen with conservative management.[286]
Like Bacon, they kept a careful eye on their lands and the limited
data relating to their crop-growing indicate that they were good
farmers.

[286] Simpson, *Wealth of the Gentry*, 7.

5

SHEEP

INTRODUCTION

Although part of the history of their estate, the Townshends' sheep-farming warrants a chapter to itself, for it was a major source of their wealth and they were among the greatest of the great gentry sheep-farmers of late medieval and early modern Norfolk. It is, however, of interest to more than just economic and agricultural historians, since gentry sheep-farming on such a scale could not fail to have a significant local impact. Inevitably it came to threaten the interests of the lesser man and played a major part in the political and social unrest of the period.

West Norfolk, where most of the Townshend estate lay, was an important sheep-farming region where a type of sheep-corn husbandry operated. This was suited to the physical geography of a region whose soils tended to be lighter and less fertile than those of intensively cultivated east Norfolk. To ensure the land's fertility it was tathed, or manured, by flocks of sheep after harvest and when it lay fallow. In west Norfolk sheep-rearing was at least as important as the grain production with which it was so closely linked.[1]

Here the unique foldcourse system operated.[2] The foldcourse was a defined area of grazing for sheep which included various kinds of pasture land—open-field arable, heathland, and sometimes arable and pasture closes—within its bounds. Ownership of the liberty of a foldcourse constituted a set of grazing-rights over the land concerned but did not necessarily entail ownership of the land itself.

---

[1] B. M. S. Campbell, 'The Regional Uniqueness of English Field Systems? Some Evidence from Eastern Norfolk', *AHR* 29 (1981), 16–28; id., 'Agricultural Progress', 26–46.

[2] For the foldcourse system see Allison, 'Sheep-Corn Husbandry'; Campbell, 'Regional Uniqueness', 17–18; and M. Bailey, 'Sand into Gold: The Evolution of the Foldcourse System in West Suffolk, 1200–1600', *AHR* 38 (1990), 40–57. Allison's is the pioneering work on an often baffling and complex subject, but he describes the foldcourse as it had evolved by the 17th cent. For the medieval period it is essential to consult Bailey.

When a tenant's land in the open fields fell within a foldcourse's bounds he was obliged to allow the foldcourse owner to graze his sheep upon it. Custom varied, but on the Townshend foldcourses tenants were compensated if a disproportionate amount of their land fell within that part of the foldcourse set aside as fallow ground for a particular year. Normally, compensation was either monetary or took the form of demesne land offered in exchange.[3] A memorandum book kept by one of Roger II's chief estate officers, John Skayman, in the mid-1510s records examples of this system operating.[4] In the company of the tenants of the township in question, Skayman would 'lay out'[5] the land to be taken up into the foldcourse that year and assign them an equivalent amount of demesne. He also paid tenants money in lieu of land, but this appears to have been a less-frequent practice.[6]

The gentry had come to monopolize sheep-farming in the fold-course areas of East Anglia by the seventeenth century, but before the later Middle Ages many foldcourses were in peasant hands, either temporarily under seigneurial licence or permanently as of customary right. After the Black Death, however, the gentry took a much keener interest in sheep-farming, probably because it was not labour-intensive and appeared the most viable option when economic and demographic conditions were generally unfavourable to landlords. Gentry sheep-farmers now sought to shape the existing foldcourse system and its cropping and pasturing arrangements to their own needs. Inevitably those gentlemen who became great flock-masters during the later fifteenth and the sixteenth centuries tried to restrict the rights of the peasantry to keep any sheep at all, since peasant sheep-farming hindered the expansion of their own flocks. The large numbers of peasant sheep which in earlier times had often been folded on the demesnes were now ousted by the lord's flocks and, to make

---

[3] Tenants with a 'cullet' right, the right to graze a few sheep with the lord's flock, could be compensated by being allowed to place extra sheep in the flock: Allison, 'Sheep-Corn Husbandry', 20.

[4] NRO, B-L VII b(4), 'Skaymans Book'. 'Estate officer' is rather an inadequate description for John. The Raynham bailiff in the mid-1510s, he also wrote the kitchen accounts and assisted Amy, Roger II's wife, with her household books. In the summer of 1515 he helped to 'make ready' for the 'comynge of the Frenche Quene', the royal duchess of Suffolk, when she and her husband were touring their East Anglian estates: NRO, Townshend 11 MS 1,430; 'Skaymans Book', fo. 19ᵛ; Gunn, *Brandon*, 39. Could they have visited the Townshends at Raynham?

[5] i.e. measure by pacing out.

[6] 'Skaymans Book', fos. 17, 25ʳ, 28ʳ, 39ʳ, 42ᵛ.

matters worse, these flocks were by the sixteenth century coming to
overwhelm communal pastures and heaths. The sheep-farming of the
Norfolk gentry therefore came to cause serious social discontent
among the lower orders.

(1) THE TOWNSHEND FLOCKS

Sheep-farming gave the Townshends a major incentive to expand and
consolidate their estate, and so prompted some of their incursions into
the land market. They concentrated on building up a compact estate
because successful large-scale sheep-farming depended on possessing
a coherent group of lands, and most of their flocks were pastured near
Raynham.[7] In some instances one can correlate their expanding
estate with their expanding flocks. At Michaelmas 1477, for example,
Roger I had 463 sheep at Stibbard. A year later he bought three
manors in the neighbourhood, allowing him to enlarge his flock there,
and by Michaelmas 1479 it contained over a thousand animals.[8]
Similarly, a decade later he began a new flock in Barmer where
recently he had bought a manor.[9]

   Surviving sheep accounts show that until the mid-sixteenth century
the general trend of the Townshends' sheep-farming was one of
growth.[10] These cover pretty fully the period between 1475 and
1518, although there are none for 1518/19–1543/4. Between the last
date and Roger II's death, however, there is a set of accounts for the
second half of the 1540s.[11]

   At Michaelmas 1475 Roger I had nearly 7,000 sheep in twelve
flocks. During the rest of his life numbers fluctuated, but in 1490 he
had over 12,000. His widow Eleanor never farmed less than 8,000
sheep, although there was a dramatic slump after she died, since
at Michaelmas 1501 Roger II owned a mere 4,000. However, he
increased his flocks substantially during the following decade- and-a-
half. By Michaelmas 1510 he owned over 17,000 sheep, and for a few

[7] The success of the contemporary sheep-farming Spencers of Northamptonshire
owed much to their compact estate: Finch, *Northamptonshire Families*, 38–44. For the
location of the Townshends' flocks at their height, see map 2.
[8] R50, 1477/8 sheep accounts, fos. 8[r], 11[v]; R49, Townshend cartulary, fos. 2[r]–5[r].
[9] Ibid., fo. 40; NRO, Townshend 56 MS 1,475 1F.
[10] See App. 9.
[11] See App. 9 for MS references.

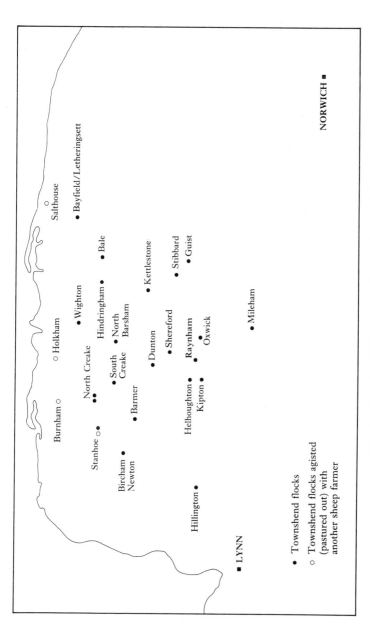

Map 2. Townshend Flocks at their Greatest Extent, 1516

years he kept a second set of flocks, under the charge of a second sheep-reeve, on hired pastures in south-west Norfolk. The high point was Michaelmas 1516, when he possessed 18,000 animals in twenty-six flocks (see map 2). The break in the series of accounts after 1518 is frustrating, but he is known to have had between 13,000 and 14,000 sheep in the early 1520s and about 10,000 at Michaelmas 1534.[12] The accounts for the second half of the 1540s show a considerably reduced enterprise, comprising no more than about 4,000 animals. By this stage Roger II's sheep, along with much other estate business, were in the care of his son Thomas.[13]

It is difficult to compare the scale of Roger I's sheep-farming with that of contemporaries, but the wills of other landlords indicate that many kept large numbers of sheep. Presumably the 1,500 that Sir William Calthorpe left to various people constituted no more than part of his flocks.[14] Calthorpe's son-in-law, William Gurney, another sheep-farmer, ordered that 700 of his stock were to remain at West Barsham after his death, but that his heir should have his other flocks.[15] There is also evidence of a more precise sort concerning Norwich Cathedral Priory, one of the few religious houses with an interest in sheep-farming comparable to that of the leading lay farmers. In 1475 it had just over 12,000 sheep, in 1485 4,000, and in 1495 over 7,000.[16] All in all, it is probably justifiable to place Roger I among the foremost Norfolk flock-masters of the late fifteenth century.

It is easier to make comparisons for Roger II. To his north-west, Sir Thomas Le Strange of Hunstanton farmed at least 1,000 sheep in 1520,[17] and there is good evidence for the enterprises of Henry Fermor and Richard Southwell, two of the largest Norfolk graziers

[12] Totals recorded in R31, RT II estate book, fo. 42[r], and R1, *Liber pro ovibus*, fo. 10[r]. For the *Liber* see section 1 below.

[13] Thomas's accounts, covering the accounting years 1544/5–1547/8 (misdated by Allison in 'Flock Management in the Sixteenth and Seventeenth Centuries', *EcHR* 2nd ser. 11 (1958), 103), state that they are for 'all' of his father's sheep: LSE, R(SR) 1,032, 88,918. However, Thomas also kept sheep on his own account since they mention animals being 'boute of' (bought off), as well as by, him to restock his father's flocks: e.g. fos. 3[v], 9[v], 18[v], 19[v]. In the 1540s he farmed Roger's foldcourse at Little Ryburgh and Stibbard, just as his younger brother Giles had done the previous decade: R41, 1547/8–1549/50 Stibbard and Little Ryburgh accounts; R41, 1509/10–1545/6 Stibbard and Little Ryburgh accounts, m. 27.

[14] PRO, PROB11/10, fos. 182–3. Calthorpe died in 1495.

[15] PRO, PROB11/15, fos. 283–4. He died in 1508.

[16] Allison, 'Flock Management', 99–100.

[17] 'Extracts', 438.

of the first half of the sixteenth century, since some of their sheep accounts have survived. Fermor's accounts cover a single year, 1521/2; he then owned between 16,000 and 17,000 sheep.[18] Southwell's accounts from the middle of the century show that he was a much more substantial farmer than was Roger II by that date, but he still operated on a smaller scale than did the Townshends in the 1510s: he had about 15,000 animals at Michaelmas 1544 and over 12,000 at Michaelmas 1551.[19] Evidence of this type led Allison to estimate that the greatest sixteenth-century Norfolk sheep-farmers owned upwards of 15,000 sheep.[20] During the second decade of the century at least, the Townshends were therefore clearly among the leaders, and it seems likely that sheep-farming in Norfolk had grown in scale since Roger I's day as it had elsewhere in the country. The flocks of the big sheep-farmers reached a peak under the early Tudors. In this period the greatest profits came from the greatest concerns.[21]

Flocks did not remain static in size: periodically they had to be restocked and surplus or old sheep removed, and some animals inevitably fell victim to marauding dogs or vermin each year.[22] But dramatic increases or decreases in numbers were often due to other reasons, and it is sometimes possible to explain why the Townshends' flocks shrunk or grew when they did. 'Murrain', an umbrella term applied to a variety of sheep diseases, often took a heavy toll.[23] Disease and bad weather were particularly devastating for Roger I's flocks in the early 1480s. In 1480/1 he lost over 2,000 sheep to murrain and the severe winter badly affected his lambing. The following summer, the fleece-weights he obtained were so low that his sheep-reeve called it 'an evell yere for wull'.[24] Murrain also partly explains the

[18] Allison, 'Flock Management', 100; Simpson, *Wealth of the Gentry*, 183.

[19] Ibid., 184; Allison, 'Flock Management', 100.

[20] Ibid., 99.

[21] P.J. Bowden, 'Movements in Wool Prices, 1490–1610', *Yorkshire Bulletin of Economic and Social Research*, 4 (1952), 118; id., *The Wool Trade in Tudor and Stuart England* (London, 1962), 2–3. Life was not, however, always rosy for the sheep-farmer at this date. Wool prices plunged at the end of the 15th cent.: T.H. Lloyd, *The Movement of Wool Prices in Medieval England*, EcHR supplement 6 (1973), 20; Thirsk, *Agrarian History*, 840–1.

[22] e.g. R24, 1478/9 sheep accounts, fo. 1ʳ; NRO, Townshend 56 MS 1,475 1F; R55, 1493/4–1497/8 accounts, fo. 97ʳ; NRO, B-L II e, 1501/2–1517/18 accounts, fo. 158ʳ.

[23] For murrain, see R. Trow-Smith, *A History of British Livestock Husbandry to 1700* (London, 1957), 155–9; M.J. Stephenson, 'Wool Yields in the Medieval Economy', *EcHR* 2nd ser. 41 (1988), 381–2.

[24] NRO, Townshend 56 MS 1,475 1F. The following year he lost another 1,700. In

hiatus in the growth of Roger II's flocks between 1510 and 1516.[25]

Market forces must also have affected flock-sizes, at least in the negative sense of dissuading expansion or reinvestment when numbers ran down. The relatively high wool-prices (by fifteenth-century standards) for much of the period between the early 1460s and mid-1480s probably encouraged Roger I to expand.[26] On the other hand, the dramatic decline in scale of the Townshends' sheep-farming at the end of the fifteenth and beginning of the sixteenth centuries occurred when wool-prices plunged. Their flocks grew again as prices recovered and rose; wool-prices were buoyant in the mid-1510s.[27]

Because of the lack of accounts one can only speculate as to why their flocks declined between 1534 and 1544. In 1534 'commonwealth'-minded legislators attempted to restrict by statute the numbers of sheep kept by landlords (no more than 2,400), and to prevent various abuses associated with sheep-farming.[28] Unfortunately we cannot tell for sure whether the Townshends reduced their flocks because of the act, or because they were already by this time beginning to specialize in meat- rather than wool-production. The act was in fact greatly undermined by several provisos introduced by its opponents in parliament which allowed most sheep-farmers to escape the 2,400 limit. Laymen, for example, could have the same numbers as they kept in the past, so long as these were confined to inherited lands.[29] But it did make Roger II anxious, and caused him to compile a volume which he entitled *Liber pro ovibus*.[30] In the *Liber* he

these years his ewes were lambing at well below the rate of 0.5–0.8 lambs per ewe which Allison describes as the normal range for 16th-cent. Norfolk ('Flock Management', 103). Lambing rates are not always possible to work out from the Townshends' sheep accounts, but in a good year Roger I's ewe flocks lambed at a rate easily near the top of this range. Allison affirms that a one-to-one ratio of lambs per ewe was never reached in this period (ibid. 103), but Eleanor Townshend's Litcham flock achieved it in 1498/9: R50, 1498/9 sheep accounts, fo. 2^r. Thomas Townshend achieved about 0.7 lambs per ewe in the mid-sixteenth century: LSE, R(SR), 1,032, 88,918.

[25] In 1511/12 he lost over 1,200 sheep: NRO, B-L II e, 1501/2–1517/18 sheep accounts, fo. 205^r.

[26] Thirsk, *Agrarian History*, 840–1; Lloyd, *Wool Prices*, 20.

[27] App. 9, below; Lloyd, *Wool Prices*, 20, 47; Bowden, 'Wool Prices', 113–14, 118; Thirsk, *Agrarian History*, 840–1, 858, 861.

[28] 25 Hen. VIII, c. 13 (*Statutes of the Realm*, iii. 451–4). For 'commonwealth' influence on government policy and legislation see Elton, *Reform and Reformation*, Chs. 7 and 9.

[29] The other major provisos excluded lambs under the age of one year from calculations of flock totals, allowed more than 2,400 sheep to be kept if they were for household consumption, and exempted spiritual persons from its terms.

[30] Contained in R1.

recorded his legal advisers' interpretations of its various clauses, as well as the depositions of tenants concerning the customary sizes of flocks in places where he kept sheep.

Even if the act did not in fact cause him to reduce numbers, it might well have encouraged him to reorganize his flocks considerably. The 10,000 sheep he had at Michaelmas 1534 were in thirteen flocks, only six of which were kept on inherited land. The rest were pastured on rented or bought land.[31] Significantly, the Townshends' sheep accounts for the late 1540s show, with possibly one exception, that each of their flocks was by then kept on inherited land.[32] The exception, if it was one, suggests that by the 1540s the strictures of the statute had receded in effect: 'it was virtually impossible to enforce over a long period a policy directly contrary to the interests of the landed classes.'[33] But Roger II's *Liber* is proof that 'commonwealth' legislation could not simply be ignored. He took the act seriously enough to send his sons, Robert and Thomas, and several estate officers to enquire from tenants and neighbours about the customary regulation of sheep-farming in his locality. Moreover, the lawyers he consulted were eminent men of their profession.[34] Even if much mid-Tudor commonwealth legislation attempted the impossible, Roger II's reaction to the act for sheep and farms shows there is some truth in Elton's argument that it was not always entirely futile.[35]

(2) PRODUCTION AND MARKETS

The Townshends were primarily wool-producers for much of our period. Until the mid-sixteenth century wool-prices very largely determined the size of a sheep-farmer's profit, mutton-production

---

[31] R1, *Liber pro ovibus*, fo. 10[r].

[32] LSE, R(SR) 1,032, 88,918. The possible exception was the Shereford flock, since at Michaelmas 1534 it was not kept on an inherited ground or foldcourse: R1, *Liber pro ovibus*, fo. 10[r]. The Shereford flock of the 1540s was, however, a new one and could well have been pastured on land which the Townshends had inherited in the township.

[33] P. Ramsey, *Tudor Economic Problems* (London, 1963), 40.

[34] R1, *Liber pro ovibus*, *passim*. For the lawyers, Christopher Jenney and Francis Monford, see *HP*, ii. 440-1, 611.

[35] Elton, *Reform and Reformation*, 220-7. Given the act's very real limitations in practice, it is somewhat surprising that Roger did take it so seriously. Are we perhaps witnessing the excessive reaction of a legal pedant?

being incidental.[36] The livestock they sold were either old or sick and not worth keeping alive[37] or, though fit, superfluous to their requirements. The purchasers came overwhelmingly from west Norfolk, though they sometimes included men from as far afield as Bedfordshire, Hertfordshire, and Northamptonshire and, on one occasion in the mid-1470s, one of their sheep-reeves, John Scony, drove some sheep to London.[38]

It is noticeable that market towns and fairs scarcely feature in the Townshends' sheep accounts and other memoranda. They made private deals and depended mainly on a network of personal contacts. A true 'market' in the formal sense appears not to have existed, and their tenants, farmers, and employees were prominent among those who bought their sheep.[39] They did sell to a few large-scale purchasers who might rely on them for stock over a period of years, but the majority of sales—often of just a few animals—were of a much more *ad hoc* nature. A striking number of people bought from them once and then apparently never again. Some of their more regular customers were local parish guilds, particularly during the early sixteenth century, testimony to the health of these institutions on the eve of the Reformation.[40] Other regular customers were 'butchers', often from Walsingham and its environs, a sign of the importance of this pilgrimage town before the Reformation.[41] Not all of these men were

---

[36] Bowden, *Wool Trade*, 6–8.

[37] e.g. crones and pockerells (old ewes and poor quality lambs) and sick animals described as 'desy' or 'dosey'. Their affliction may well have been a disease known as 'sturdy' or 'gid', now no longer a serious concern for the sheep-farmer. It is caused by the sheep ingesting a tapeworm larva—spread by dog excrement (it is again worth noting that dogs were a recurrent menace on the Townshends' pastures)—which forms a cyst on its brain. The animal then loses its co-ordination and it staggers about as if 'dizzy'. Sturdy is a separate disease from 'scrapie', the ovine form of BSE or 'mad cow disease': J. F. H. Thomas, *Sheep* (London, 1945), 87; H. B. Parry, *Scrapie Disease in Sheep* (London, 1983), 4. 'Desy' and 'dosey' are similar to the East Anglian 'dauzy', a dialect word for 'dizzy': W. Rye, *A Glossary of Words Used in East Anglia* (London, 1895), 57.

[38] BL, Add. MS 41,305, fo. 13^r; R55, 1492/3–1496/7 sheep accounts, fos. 63^r, 72^r; NRO, B-L II e, 1501/2–1517/18 sheep accounts, fos. 2, 4; NRO, B-L VII b(3), fo. 25^r; R58, Raynham account roll, m. 8. Scony's expenses—£20. 3s. 3d.—suggest he was driving quite a large number of animals. For the Townshends' customers, see App. 10.

[39] See App. 10.

[40] Ibid. The standard work on parish guilds is still H. F. Westlake, *The Parish Gilds of Medieval England* (London, 1919). Guilds were numerous in East Anglia, and nowhere more so than in the Townshends' locality: C. B. Firth, 'Village Gilds of Norfolk in the Fifteenth Century', *NA* 18 (1914), 167–8.

[41] See App. 10.

necessarily butchers in the modern sense, however; the term was also applied to graziers who acquired livestock for local markets.[42] One of the Townshends' tenants, Clement Anger of Weasenham—their most important customer during the second decade of the sixteenth century—was probably such a grazier.[43]

The Townshends themselves bought locally to replenish their flocks in this period. Again, many of the vendors were local men, tenants, or employees.[44] They not-infrequently acquired fresh stock from the executors of deceased sheep-farmers or of tenants who had kept some sheep during their lifetimes. It was obviously convenient to take over large parts of another man's concern rather than to make several smaller-scale purchases. On one occasion in the early 1500s Roger II bought nearly 500 sheep from the executors of a local sheep-farmer, William Sparke.[45]

During the late fifteenth century the Townshends were able to buy their stock from Raynham and its environs, but after 1500 they were obliged to range further afield.[46] This is directly attributable to the dramatic growth of Roger II's flocks at the time, since he could not expect to meet all his needs in his own immediate neighbourhood. Outside periods of substantial expansion, extensive purchasing was unnecessary as the flocks were largely self-sufficient. This required keeping a large number of ewes because of the poor lambing-rates of the late medieval and early modern period. During 1495/6, for example, nearly 50 per cent of their sheep were ewes, despite the fact that wethers (castrated males) produced the biggest and heaviest fleeces.[47]

[42] Land, *Kett's Rebellion*, 43. Sometimes the accounts refer to a *carnifex* rather than 'bocher'. The former was almost certainly a butcher in the modern sense.

[43] R58, Raynham account roll, mm. 21, 25; R(Attic), '*Norfolk manorial*—Raynham Haviles', 1483/4 and 1484/5 accounts; R28, Raynham rental; NRO, B-L II e, 1501/2–1517/18 sheep accounts, fos. 194ᵛ ff.; App. 10, below.

[44] App. 10. Also counted among them in the accounts were local clergy who accepted cash in lieu of tithe lambs, but since these were not genuine purchases I have excluded them from the Appendix.

[45] NRO, Townshend 193 MS 1,612 1 C7, fos. 2–4. For Sparke, a foldcourse owner at Fakenham posthumously charged with engrossing tenants' holdings, see PRO, STAC2/15/11–13.

[46] App. 10.

[47] R55, 1492/3–1496/7 sheep accounts, fo. 64ᵛ. The almost complete set of accounts for 1477/8–1517/18 show that on average 39 per cent of all their sheep were ewes but only 27 per cent wethers. In 16th- and 17th-cent. Norfolk 10–15 ewe fleeces usually provided a stone of wool. The same weight could be obtained from 7–10 wether fleeces: Allison, 'Flock Management', 105.

In the 1540s, however, Roger II's flocks were certainly not self-sufficient (see Appendix 12). As Allison points out, it was in his case profitable for them not to be, because his son Thomas was able to sell off superfluous animals for higher prices than he paid for his store lambs.[48] This constant restocking through purchase meant that the Townshends now had to look to recognized markets, and Thomas probably bought most of his wether hoggs (young wethers) from fairs.[49]

A significant reorientation had occurred. By now the Townshends were supplying the Norwich food market with prime-quality animals for meat. They must also have indirectly served the capital, since they found buyers for their sheep on the London road at Newmarket, quite possibly through the Cambridgeshire connections of two of their tenants and farmers, John Pepys of South Creake and his son-in-law John Norton.[50] The considerably reduced nature of Roger II's sheep-farming was probably mainly due to this change of emphasis. As large-scale wool-growers the Townshends had hitherto kept many more sheep because, until after the seventeenth century, the amount of wool a farmer produced depended almost solely upon the number of sheep he kept.[51] Fortunately for them, the Townshends had anticipated the slump in the wool trade which occurred in 1551, as well as the demand for prime-quality mutton in various parts of the country.[52]

Wool-production was nevertheless the main purpose of their sheep-farming for most of our period.[53] In contrast to their pre-1540s stock sales, they sold wool to a small number of customers and in some years to a single purchaser.[54] Using the limited evidence available to him, Allison concluded that Lynn merchants bought and exported much of

---

[48] Ibid., 102–3.

[49] LSE, R(SR) 1,032, 88,918.

[50] Bowden, *Wool Trade*, xvii, 8–9; Ramsey, *Tudor Economic Problems*, 24–5; LSE, R(SR) 1,032, 88,918; Allison, 'Flock Management', 108. Pepys originated from Cambridgeshire and, with an associate from that shire, bought sheep from Roger II on at least one occasion: R31, RT II estate book, fo. 12^r. Norton, also of South Creake earlier in the 16th cent., was probably John Norton of Newmarket who, with other Cambridgeshire men, bought sheep from the Townshends in the 1540s: LSE, R(SR) 1,032, 88,918.

[51] Allison, thesis, 318–19.

[52] Bowden, *Wool Trade*, 6–11.

[53] For more on the Townshends as wool producers see Allison's thesis and his 'Flock Management'.

[54] App. 11.

the wool grown by the Townshends and other wool-producers, that
some was sold to wool-broggers (middlemen), who in turn sold it to
the Norfolk worsted industry or to Essex and Suffolk clothiers, while
the wool-producers themselves sold the remainder directly to clothiers
from the latter two counties.[55] The sales to clothiers from outside the
county are a sure sign of the declining state of the once-thriving local
worsted industry by this date.[56]

Allison's analysis is basically correct. There were, for example,
several Lynn men among the Townshends' customers, although the
town had long since ceased to be an important centre for the wool-
export trade.[57] In 1495 Eleanor Townshend sold 120 stone of wool
to Margaret Lumbard of Hadleigh in Suffolk, part of the bargain
being that Margaret would provide Eleanor with household liveries
for a year.[58] She also sold another 360 stone in 1495 to a Norwich
mercer, Richard Peper, though the wool itself was delivered to a
Lavenham cloth-maker who was presumably working under contract
for Peper.[59] The Townshends nevertheless had a wider circle of
buyers than Allison thought, since in 1494 Eleanor sold nearly 1,000
stone to a couple of London merchants.[60] By the early 1500s they
had found a major customer on their doorstep, their tenant Robert
Wolvy. In 1504/5, for example, he bought all the wool then lying
in the Raynham wool-house.[61] Wolvy is an obscure figure, but was
possibly the son of the Robert Wolvy who features in a previous chapter.[62] It should come as no surprise that he could afford to buy so
much, because many Norfolk men besides the great flock-masters
grew rich through wool, to the benefit of the county's churches upon
which they bestowed some of their wealth.[63]

---

[55] 'Flock Management', 107.

[56] For the worsted industry, see K. J. Allison, 'The Norfolk Worsted Industry in
the Sixteenth and Seventeenth Centuries: 1. The Traditional Industry', *Yorkshire
Bulletin of Economic and Social Research*, 12 (1960), 73–83. Perhaps the fact that Roger I
ordered cloth from London for his servants' liveries at the end of the 1480s should be
treated as evidence of the industry's decline: NRO, B-L V11 b(3), note on inside of
front cover. Twenty years earlier John Paston had been proud to wear Norfolk worsted:
PL, no. 77.

[57] App. 11; *The Making of King's Lynn*, ed. D. M. Owen (London, 1984), 48.

[58] BL, Add. MS 41,305, fo. 11^v.

[59] Ibid., fos. 24^v–25^r, 26^r.

[60] Ibid., fos. 8, 20.

[61] R33, RT II receipt book, fo. 8^r; NRO, Townshend 193 MS 1,612 1 C7, fos. 15^v,
28^r; NRO, B-L VII b(3), fo. 15^r; R31, RT II estate book, fo. 12^r.

[62] See Ch. 3, 1(ii) above.

[63] D. H. Kennett, *Norfolk Villages* (London, 1980), 46–53.

The wool-house usually contained clips from more than one year, the oldest wool being sold first. At the beginning of 1477/8, for example, Roger I had some 875 stone of old wool and about 550 stone from that year's clip in the wool-house, and during the year he sold off all the old wool and 12 stone of the new.[64] Wool was often stored by the big producers with substantial reserves of capital so that they could select the most favourable opportunity to sell, an advantage not enjoyed by the man of lesser resources. The Townshends could also afford to sell wool on credit,[65] and creditors could demand higher prices than those who wanted an immediate payment in cash.[66] However, not all their wool was destined for the wool-house; each year a small quantity was sent to the household for cloth-making.[67] None of it would have been of a particularly high quality, as the Norfolk sheep—though physically well adapted to local conditions—grew a coarse, medium-light wool. Norfolk wool was best suited for the manufacture of worsted—as opposed to fine, short-fibred cloth—and was therefore combed rather than carded and afterwards rock-spun on a distaff rather than a wheel.[68] It usually required no fulling, though the Townshends' household accounts show that a small amount of fulling took place at Raynham.[69]

Wool was not the only commodity to come off a sheep's back. Important by-products were the fells and pelts of animals which had fallen victim to murrain or had been slaughtered in the kitchen.[70] These were stored in the wool-house and sold in much the same way as the wool-clip. The pelterers who bought them sometimes came from as far away as Norwich in Roger I's day, but in the early sixteenth century the Townshends did all their business with Andrew

---

[64] R50, 1477/8 sheep accounts, fo. 16[v].

[65] e.g. NRO, B-L V, nos. x . 31, 45, 32.

[66] Bowden, *Wool Trade*, 101. Bonds of obligation were taken as a matter of course when credit was given, e.g. NRO, B-L V, nos. x . 31, 45, 32. Some of the Townshends' legal actions of debt on an obligation (see Ch. 3, section 2) were against defaulting debtors who had been given credit for wool and sheep.

[67] From under 10 to 20 stone in the late 15th cent. and 20 stone by the 1540s: R58, Raynham account roll, m. 7d; NRO, Townshend 56 MS 1,475 1F; LSE, R(SR) 1,032, 88,918. For cloth-making at Raynham see Ch. 4, 3 above.

[68] Allison, 'Flock Management', 106; id., 'Worsted Industry', 73.

[69] M. Bailey, *A Marginal Economy? East Anglian Breckland in the Later Middle Ages* (Cambridge, 1989), 172; R58, Raynham account roll, mm. 8, 10.

[70] Wool fell = sheep skin with its wool; pelt = a shorn or plucked sheep skin. In 1480/1, when Roger I was particularly badly hit by murrain, 12 per cent of his sheep-reeve's charge was made up of receipts for sales of fells and pelts: NRO, Townshend 56 MS 1,475 1F.

Deane and, soon after Deane's death, with Henry Brinkley.[71] It is unclear where the latter came from, but Deane was from Mattishall, one of a group of villages in central Norfolk which lived off the wool trade. These were an important field of operation for wool-middlemen, and Mattishall was strategically situated between the wool-producing western and the worsted-weaving eastern halves of the county.[72] Deane is likely to have supplied the numerous small-scale spinners of east Norfolk with the wool from the fells he bought; the pelts probably went to the Norwich leather trade.[73]

(3) PROFITS

How profitable was sheep-farming to the Townshends? By the 1460s, when Roger I probably began sheep-farming on a large scale, wool-prices both locally and nationally had recovered from an earlier slump.[74] In 1460 Margaret Paston referred to wool fetching 20 pence per stone, and five years later the Pastons expected to sell their own at double this rate.[75] But prices dropped again in the 1470s, recovered in the 1480s, and then underwent another slump at the beginning of the sixteenth century.[76] The prices the Townshends received for their wool in the late fifteenth and early sixteenth centuries reflected these trends.[77] Sheep-farming was, therefore, certainly not the instant panacea to the economic problems of the landlord in Roger I's day, although it is worth noting that many in Norfolk found it worthwhile to farm sheep while leasing out everything else.[78] By the second decade of the sixteenth century, however, the Townshends shared in a period of 'remarkable prosperity' for sheep-farmers, the consequence of rising wool- and stock-prices.[79]

[71] NRO, B-L V, no. 45; NRO, B-L II e, 1501/2–1517/18 sheep accounts.
[72] Allison, 'Worsted Industry', 76.
[73] Thirsk, *Agrarian History*, 592.
[74] Lloyd, *Wool Prices*, 20; Thirsk, *Agrarian History*, 840–1, 861; Allison, thesis, app. 5.
[75] PL, nos. 154, 652.
[76] Thirsk, *Agrarian History*, 840–1, 861; Allison, thesis, app. 5.
[77] See App. 11.
[78] J. L. Bolton, *The Medieval English Economy, 1150–1500* (London, 1980), 228; Lloyd, *Wool Prices*, 24–9.
[79] Bowden, *Wool Trade*, p. xvii; Thirsk, *Agrarian History*, 841–2, 858, 861; App. 11, below.

The economics of the business were relatively straightforward. Income came mainly from the sale of wool, stock, and skins and various customary charges received from tenants. On the expenditure side was the outlay on hiring pasture where necessary, purchasing stock and various pieces of necessary equipment, and labour costs. Wool and stock which were surrendered as tithes or given away as gifts or alms have also to be taken into account.[80]

Most of the Townshends' sheep accounts present difficulties as far as calculating profits is concerned. The accounting official was normally the sheep-reeve, and he was rarely responsible for every item of income or expenditure. Sales of wool and most purchases and sales of stock, for example, do not necessarily feature in the accounts because they nearly always remained within the purview of the lord.[81] Moreover, it is usually impossible to calculate actual income from wool-sales made in a single year because the Townshends frequently gave lengthy credit.[82] The accounts for the years 1477/8–1480/1 nevertheless appear reasonably full, and they show a potential average net income of some £212 per annum. But these figures include receipts from credit sales which were due in the future rather than true receipts for the year in question. In reality, Roger I's sheep-reeve handed over an average of about £37 each year in actual cash during this period, with the prospect of large future takings from credit sales.[83] A more reliable indication of profits are Thomas Townshend's accounts of the 1540s.[84] They show profits ranging from £99 in 1544/5 to £143 in 1547/8; the average for the four years was £121. The cost of restocking caused the relatively low figure for the first year.[85]

Ten of Roger II's sheep valors dating from the first quarter of the sixteenth century, some of which were added to the end of the sheep accounts, have survived, and these show that his flocks made up a considerable proportion of his moveable wealth during this period (see

[80] Simpson, *Wealth of the Gentry*, 184–6.

[81] In his account for 1481/2 the sheep-reeve, William Howes, was charged with over £240, but this omitted the receipts from no less than 700 stones of wool sold by Roger I: NRO, Townshend 56 MS 1,475 1F. Also, shepherds' wages were not usually the sheep-reeve's concern and so did not always appear in the accounts: e.g. R55, 1492/3–1497/8, fo. 18ᵛ.

[82] Allison, thesis, 204.

[83] R50, 1477/8 sheep accounts; R24, 1478/9 sheep accounts; NRO, Townshend 56 MS 1,475 1F.

[84] Allison, 'Flock Management', 110.

[85] LSE, R(SR) 1,032, 88,918. These figures are rounded off.

Appendix 13). The £140 or so that his sheep were worth to him in 1524, therefore, constituted a significant proportion of the £600 in moveable wealth at which he was assessed for the 1524/5 subsidy.[86] Sheep were big business for the Townshends, and this meant that opponents of their sheep-farming activities, and those of other great Norfolk flock-masters, came up against substantial vested interests.

(4) SHEEP-FARMING AND SOCIAL UNREST

East Anglian sheep-farming during the lifetimes of the two Roger Townshends had wider implications than wool-prices or lambing-rates, as it provoked some of the popular disturbances which occurred in the region. Largely the preserve of the gentry, the abuses associated with sheep-farming caused conflict between landlord and tenant and helped to create the anti-gentry animus and disrespect for authority expressed by the lower orders.[87]

Mid-Tudor governments recognized that this was potentially dangerous and attempted to exercise some sort of control over sheep-farming. 'Commonwealth'-minded legislators sought to restrict it, and blamed it for problems with worrying social consequences, like rural depopulation and the decline in arable husbandry. The previously mentioned act of 1534 was just one of a series of measures. Three earlier acts (of 1489, 1514, and 1515) had prohibited unlicensed enclosing and ordered that land converted to pasture should be returned to tillage. These were followed by Wolsey's enclosure commissions of 1517 and by proclamations against enclosures in the late 1520s.[88]

As well as providing for prosecutions to be brought by a presenting jury, the 1534 legislation allowed private informations to be laid against those who broke it.[89] This process, which only assumed a clearly defined legal form under the common law during the late fifteenth century, had by the sixteenth become closely associated with

[86] PRO, E179/150/259.
[87] Moreton, 'Walsingham Conspiracy', 29–38. Cf. the West Country where sheep were likely to cause social tensions because flocks were generally not large and considerable numbers of smallholders kept sheep: J. Youings, 'The South-Western Rebellion of 1549', *Southern History*, 1 (1979), 106.
[88] Elton, *Reform and Reformation*, 67–8. See Ch. 7–9 for the 'commonwealth' men.
[89] *Statutes of the Realm*, iii. 452.

the so-called penal laws, of which the 1534 act was one. The informer, who need have no personal interest in the case, was permitted to lay his charge without putting his accusation into the proper juridical form. The penal laws set a pecuniary penalty to be paid by the committer of the statutory offence and, in the event of a successful prosecution, the informer shared part of the resulting proceeds with the Crown.[90] In the case of the 1534 act the offender was charged with 3*s*. 4*d*. for every sheep he possessed over the statutory limit, and the informer was awarded half the fine.[91]

Ultimately this legislation failed because the government could neither prevent nor control the economic and political forces which encouraged large-scale sheep-farming. Later, in 1550, it was forced to repeal the act for a poll tax on sheep granted in parliament in March 1549 because it ran into too many powerful vested interests.[92] A trickle of informations was nevertheless laid before the court of the Exchequer against those who broke the 1534 act by exceeding their quota of sheep. Allison discovered eight cases from the sixteenth and seventeenth centuries, but none of these occurred before Roger II's death.[93] A search using the repertory rolls and agenda books as indexes for the Exchequer memoranda rolls of the King's Remembrancer has, however, revealed two cases dating from his lifetime.[94]

The first took place on his doorstep. On 21 June 1537, William Porter, his yeoman tenant from Stibbard with whom he himself had clashed previously, appeared before the barons of the Exchequer to lay an information against John Pepys of South Creake.[95] Pepys, an ancestor of Samuel Pepys the diarist, was originally from Cambridge, the second son of a yeoman from Cottenham, William Pepys.[96] He nevertheless settled in South Creake—as did a sister who found herself

---

[90] Bellamy, *Criminal Law*, 90–5.

[91] *Statutes of the Realm*, iii. 452.

[92] M. W. Beresford, 'The Poll Tax and Census of Sheep, 1549', 2 parts, *AHR* 1 (1953), 9–15; 2 (1954), 15–29. Beresford acknowledged that the act (2 & 3 Edward VI, c. 36) was discussed solely as a revenue raiser whilst being drawn up, but asserted that Somerset's government hoped that it would deter sheep-farming: ibid., pt. 1, 11. More recently Bush argued that it was merely a financial expedient and no agrarian measure was intended: Bush, *Protector Somerset*, 52; but Beresford's analysis is more convincing.

[93] 'Flock Management', 101.

[94] PRO, IND1/7042–3, 17051. Informations of offences against penal statutes were recorded among the *communia* of the King's Remembrancer's rolls.

[95] See Ch. 3, 2 above; PRO, E159/316, Trin., rot. 18.

[96] PRO, PROB11/19, fos. 130–131^v, will of William Pepys (d. 1519); W. C. Pepys, *Genealogy of the Pepys Family, 1273–1887*, 2nd edn. (London, 1952).

a husband from the same parish—and married a local woman.[97] He was a prosperous man: in the 1520s he employed six servants and his moveable property, worth some £140 in 1523, was valued at £240 at the end of the decade.[98] By 1529 he rented two foldcourses and a close in the Burnham parishes from Sir Philip Calthorpe.[99] In 1536 he bought 'Roses', a manor in South Creake, from Edward Calthorpe, Sir Philip's uncle.[100] When he died in late 1541 or early 1542 he owned lands in north-west Norfolk, including another manor at Holkham, worth at least £25 per annum, and leased other lands in the same vicinity.[101] He was usually described as a 'merchant' (and sometimes 'yeoman') during his lifetime, but it is not entirely clear what his trade was.[102] Thomas, his son and heir, married into a minor gentry family and became a 'gentleman',[103] and one of his daughters eventually married another local man made good, William Whetley, chief prothonotary of the Common Pleas.[104]

Like Porter, John Pepys also had connections with the Townshends. He and his son-in-law John Norton were their tenants and farmers at South Creake but, more importantly, they were probably his principal suppliers of sheep in the second decade of the sixteenth century. During 1514/15, for instance, he bought over 700 wethers from Roger II. Two years later Roger sold him and Clement Anger nearly 2,000 sheep.[105] These business connections were

[97] Blomefield, vii. 81; Dashwood, 380–1.
[98] PRO, E179/150/207; 151/325; 150/223. His will shows he owned an impressive amount of silver plate and a well-furnished manor house with a private chapel at South Creake: PRO, PROB11/29, fos 11–13ᵛ.
[99] *CAD*, vol. v, no. A.13,557. In 1536 Calthorpe's successor extended the lease of one of the foldcourses for another ten years: ibid., no. A.13,518.
[100] PRO, E150/642/8; *Visitations*, 64–5.
[101] PRO, E150/642/8; PRO, PROB11/29, fos. 11–13ᵛ.
[102] When he died he had two apprentices. He used local shipping because he once had business dealings with a mariner from Beeston. Since he owned several 'mowlding troffys' he may well have been a lead producer. In 1540 he was again informed upon, this time for exporting lead and malt without paying customs: ibid.; PRO, C1/707/8; G. R. Elton, 'Informing for Profit: A Sidelight on Tudor Methods of Law-Enforcement', *Cambridge Historical Journal*, 11 (1954), 153.
[103] *CAD*, vol. v, no. A.13,557; Dashwood, 380–1; Blomefield, vii. 83. Thomas married a daughter of Giles Sefoull of Waterden. By Edward VI's reign a William Pepys, 'gent.'—probably John's younger son—resided at South Creake: PRO, E179/151/365; PRO, PROB11/29, fos. 11–13ᵛ.
[104] Dashwood, 380–1; Spelman's *Reports*, ii. 376.
[105] PRO, E150/642/8; PRO, PROB11/29, fos. 11–13ᵛ; R19, 'Beaufoes' rental and a South Creake terrier (both undated); R60, South Creake terrier, *temp*. Hen. VIII; NRO, B-L, II e, 1501/2–1517/18 sheep accounts, fos. 257ʳ, 259ʳ; R60, 1516/17 sheep

backed up by a more personal relationship; Pepys appointed Robert Townshend, Roger's second son, his testamentary supervisor.[106]

Pepys kept some of his sheep on his own land at South Creake, as well as three flocks on pastures in Holkham which he farmed from the earl of Wiltshire and John Gygges. Porter accused him of maintaining a total of 3,360 sheep in these parishes on top of a further 2,400 animals pastured on farmed lands in the Burnhams.[107] Pepys responded to the charge in the person of his attorney the following Michaelmas term (1537). Denying that he kept any sheep in the Burnhams, he further asserted that he kept no more than the permitted number—2,400—at South Creake and Holkham.[108] His story was largely vindicated by a jury at the Thetford assizes in mid-1540. They found that he kept no sheep in the Burnham parishes, but had 2,478 at South Creake and Holkham. He was therefore amerced £14 (3s. 4d. for each of the seventy-eight extra sheep), of which Porter as informer was to receive half.[109] But this was not the end of the matter; Pepys refused to accept the judgement and had the case removed to King's Bench by writ of error in the Michaelmas term of the same year.[110] There he challenged the information, the verdict, and the judgement on several technical points, mainly by pointing out apparent discrepancies on the face of the record. Porter was subsequently summoned to appear in King's Bench the following Hilary term, but failed to appear. The plea rolls eventually break off without his having done so, by which stage Pepys had died.[111]

Roger Houghton of Docking, the defendant in the second case which occurred during Roger II's lifetime, was also from north-west Norfolk. A sheep-farmer on a similar scale to John Pepys, Houghton

---

accounts, fo. 15ᵛ. In 1513/14 Pepys bought 619 wethers and in 1515/16 240, from Roger: NRO, B-L II e, fos. 238ᵛ, 245ʳ, 284ʳ, 289ʳ, 292ʳ. Unfortunately, lack of evidence makes it impossible to establish whether the Townshends were still such important suppliers when Pepys was prosecuted.

[106] PRO, PROB11/29, fos. 11–13ᵛ.

[107] PRO, E159/316, Trin., rot. 18, 3. The respective totals recorded are 2,800 and 2,000 but long hundreds of 120 were being used.

[108] PRO, E159/316, Trin., rot. 18. A puzzling claim since he had recently renewed his lease of a foldcourse in Burnham Overy from the Calthorpes: *CAD*, vol. v, no. A.13,518.

[109] PRO, E159/316, Trin., rot. 3.

[110] Ibid.; PRO, KB27/1117, rot. 67. He did so according to the terms of 14 & 15 Henry VIII, c. 15, which permitted cases involving error to be removed from the Exchequer to King's Bench: *Statutes of the Realm*, iii. 225–6.

[111] PRO, KB27/1117, rot. 67.

hovered between the yeomanry and lesser gentry.[112] At the age of 60 he succeeded to the lands of his elder brother, Thomas Houghton, rector of Anmer, in 1541.[113] Just as Pepys enjoyed good relations with the Townshends, the Houghtons looked to the Le Stranges of Hunstanton for patronage. Thomas farmed land from them and appointed Sir Thomas Le Strange and his son Nicholas supervisors of his will. In the will he asked his friends to pray for the soul of Sir Thomas's deceased uncle, John Le Strange.[114] Like his brother, Roger Houghton also leased land from the Le Stranges and he made Nicholas Le Strange his testamentary supervisor.[115]

Houghton's accuser, Thomas Sayer, a London haberdasher, laid his information before the Exchequer on 28 April 1545.[116] He claimed that Houghton kept 1,200 sheep at Anmer beyond the 2,400 he had at Docking and Flitcham.[117] The latter appeared in person the following Trinity term to answer the change. He said that he had no more than 1,800 sheep at Docking and Flitcham, whilst acknowledging that he had another 720 at Anmer. He nevertheless claimed that he was exempt from any statutory penalty because his brother Thomas had bequeathed the Anmer sheep to two 'cousins'—another Thomas Houghton and Thomas Warner—and so these flocks were only temporarily in his care while he acted as Thomas's executor.[118]

Houghton was clearly appealing to a proviso in the act of 1534 which exempted from any penalty those who broke it by virtue of their holding sheep on behalf of a minor.[119] A glance at his brother's will confirms that the priest bequeathed the sheep from his Anmer foldcourse to a couple of relatives who were to receive them at the end of a seven-year term. One of these was indeed Thomas Houghton, a minor, but the other was George Houghton, Roger's son, and not a

---

[112] 'Gentleman' when prosecuted but 'yeoman' in his will: PRO, E159/324, Easter, rot. 71; PRO, PROB11/31, fos. 76ᵛ–77.

[113] PRO, PROB11/29, fos. 40–1; PRO, C142/69/64; PRO, PROB11/31, fos. 76ᵛ–77.

[114] 'Extracts', 453; PRO, PROB11/29, fos. 40–1. Thomas Houghton was one of John Le Strange's executors: PRO, PROB11/18, fos. 282–3.

[115] PRO, PROB11/29, fos. 40–1; PRO, PROB11/31, fos. 76ᵛ–77.

[116] PRO, E159/324, Easter, rot. 71.

[117] Ibid. In 1538/9 Roger and an associate had secured from the crown a renewal of their lease of the manor of 'Snorynges' in Flitcham and Appleton which they had formerly farmed from Walsingham Priory: *LP*, vol. xiv, pt. i, nos. 1,355, 608, 610.

[118] PRO, E159/324, Easter, rot. 71.

[119] *Statutes of the Realm*, iii. 452.

Thomas Warner as claimed.[120] The most feasible explanation as to why Roger was less than honest with the court is that George was not a minor, and that taken together the sheep left to him and those belonging to his father exceeded the statutory limit. Dishonest though it was, this defence seems to have been accepted by the court because the memoranda rolls break off and do not record any further proceedings.[121]

Thomas Sayer is something of a mystery and, beyond his name and trade, he eludes positive identification. But since he also informed against Henry Castell, another sheep-farmer from the foldcourse region of north-west Norfolk, shortly after Roger II's death, he probably had connections with the county and may well have made informing something of a secondary occupation.[122] Castell himself appears to have had no obvious links with the Townshends' Castell relatives, but was perhaps a member of a cadet branch of the family. A minor gentleman from Egmere, he died in 1558.[123]

Sayer informed against Castell in October 1552, saying that the latter kept over 5,000 sheep in the parishes of Egmere, Barwick, and Witton. The following Trinity term Castell appeared in person before the Exchequer to claim that he should not be compelled to answer the charge because it was insufficient in law.[124] The court ordered him to reappear at Michaelmas while it sought advice on the case in the meantime. But a combination of the disruption to judicial business caused by the death of Edward VI and the delays inherent in common-law procedure ensured that Castell did not reappear until Trinity 1557, at which hearing the royal attorney-general said that the Crown did not wish to proceed any further because there was no case to answer.[125]

The above three cases indicate that even if the legislation of 1534 could not be ignored, it must usually have achieved little in practical

[120] PRO, PROB11/29, fos. 40–1.
[121] PRO, E159/324, Easter, rot. 75.
[122] Cf. Elton, 'Informing', 149–67, for another London haberdasher turned informer.
[123] PRO, PROB11/41, fo. 275. He was assessed at £40 in goods in the mid-1540s: PRO, E179/151/349. He married a woman from Lavenham who was related to the Springs, the famous clothier family: Dashwood, 263; B. McClenaghan, *The Springs of Lavenham and the Suffolk Cloth Trade in the Fifteenth and Sixteenth Centuries* (Ipswich, 1924), 85.
[124] PRO, E159/331, Mich., rot. 23. Unfortunately the basis of his claim is not recorded.
[125] PRO, E179/331, Mich., rot. 123.

terms. Informations tended to fail, particularly if the accused, like Pepys, Houghton, and Castell, was prepared to fight the charge against him.[126] It is worth noting that these men were not important individuals; the large-scale sheep-farmers like the Townshends were not so easy to tackle. The Pepys case in particular is interesting as an example of the animosities caused by the sheep-farming of a lesser man. It is improbable that William Porter informed on Pepys simply because he hoped for financial gain. A series of Porters had possessed lands in the Burnham parishes during the fifteenth and early sixteenth centuries, some of which passed into the hands of John Gygges, the gentleman from whom Pepys leased one of his sheep-pastures.[127] Quite possibly Porter was protesting against the activities of a parvenu who farmed his sheep on lands formerly held by the Porters and other tenants. Merchants and farmers who were outsiders were prone to agrarian opposition on the part of the commons because they did not understand or try to understand local agricultural customs, and they were less likely to be respected than longer-established landholders.[128] The lesser sheep-farmers—like William Wilby at Hindringham in the late fifteenth century, William Sparke at Fakenham in the early sixteenth, Martin Hastings at Hindringham in Edward VI's reign, and William Dey at Alethorpe in that of Elizabeth—provoked their fair share of complaints, which must have been especially bitter in cases where the offender had recently sprung from the lower orders and bettered himself partly at the expense of his former fellows.[129]

The abuses perpetrated by landlords in areas like west Norfolk were twofold. A great flockmaster might try to flout customary regulations by extending the bounds of his foldcourse or increasing the size of the flock he was entitled to keep on it. Otherwise he could simply ignore the rights of tenants who had holdings within the foldcourse.[130] In these areas enclosure was not usually an issue, though elsewhere in the

---

[126] Elton, 'Informing', 151, 166.

[127] *CAD*, vol. v, nos. A.10,749, 10,971-2, 11,189, 11,190, 11,192, 8,479, 13,342, 12,983, 13,343, 12,931; R(Attic), 'Deeds—Stanhoe & Barwick', deed of 10 July 1493; PRO, CP25/1/170/92, no. 50.

[128] R.B. Manning, *Village Revolts: Social Protest and Popular Disturbances in England, 1509-1640* (Oxford, 1988), 51.

[129] R1, *Liber pro ovibus*, fos. 15ᵛ-16ʳ; PRO, STAC 2/15/11-15; PRO, DL5/8/151-3; W.A. Day, 'Glimpses at Country Life in the Sixteenth Century', *NA* 10 (1888), 150-1.

[130] For these abuses see K.J. Allison, 'The Lost Villages of Norfolk', *NA* 31 (1957), 116-62.

county it caused conflict.[131] The foldcourse system required tenants
to keep their land open to the lord's sheep, so when enclosure did
occur it was often the work of a tenant reluctant to co-operate.[132]
As a result the landlord might sometimes encourage, or even lead,
an anti-enclosure riot. When John Rogers, a husbandman from
Broomstead, tried to hedge part of his holding in the 1540s, for example, the lord, Henry Dengayne, assembled a party of locals who
tore down his enclosures and assaulted him.[133] The most pressing
grievances of the common people were, however, engrossment and
the abuse of tenants' common rights, wrongs which occurred in all
parts of East Anglia.[134]

Sheep provoked open discord between the Townshends and their
tenants on more than one occasion. The disputes which Eleanor
Townshend had with Robert Gottes and William Capell in the 1490s
arose over grazing-rights and show how it was often the prosperous
freeholder, rather than the little man with few common rights, who
clashed with the sheep-farming gentry.[135] Their final outcomes are
unfortunately unknown. The clash with Gottes began after Eleanor's
servants removed his sheep from Ryburgh common where they were
overcharging the pasture. Gottes contested her right to make the
distraint, claiming she had no jurisdiction over the common.[136] Con-
flicts over feeding were frequent in foldcourse areas, because the
heaths and commons were expected to provide grazing for the animals
of both landlord and tenant.[137] Capell was the owner of a 'par right'
by virtue of his holding at Stibbard, a neighbouring township to
Ryburgh. This allowed him to fold sheep, in his case 180, within
Eleanor's foldcourse at Stibbard.[138] Other tenants complained that

---

[131] East Anglia as a whole was responsible for most of the enclosure cases in Star
Chamber under Wolsey: Guy, *Cardinal's Court*, 110.
[132] Allison, 'Lost Villages', 131–4; MacCulloch, 'Kett's Rebellion', 51.
[133] PRO, STAC2/29/100. PRO, STAC2/29/13, 65 for a similar instance at Great
Carbrooke.
[134] The term 'enclosure' can have a wider application than in the sense used here.
Contemporaries also used it for practices like engrossment and encroachment upon the
commons.
[135] A. Simpson, 'The East Anglian Foldcourse: Some Queries', *AHR* 6 (1958), 93.
The would-be rebels at Walsingham in 1537 were not 'beggars', as first assumed, and
most fell within the prosperous-freeholder category: Moreton, 'Walsingham Conspiracy', 32.
[136] R36, 16th-cent. file of papers relating to grazing disputes at Stibbard and
Ryburgh.
[137] Allison, 'Lost Villages', 135.
[138] R36, file of papers (see n. 136 above); R1, *Liber pro ovibus*, fo. 15[r]. The 'par

Capell overcharged the common and damaged their crops, but her grievance against him was that daily he drove his sheep in front of her flock and took the best grazing.[139] Eventually she distrained the animals, prompting Capell, in the company of his wife and daughter, to confront her servants. Capell claimed that his livelihood was undone, and his daughter heightened the drama of the occasion: she 'cryed and schryked as achylde out of mend [mind]'.[140]

Disputes could, however, end amicably, like a quarrel between Roger II and some of his tenants at Helhoughton. When Wolsey's enclosure commissioners reached the township in November 1517, four of the inhabitants accused Roger of converting arable to pasture, though they do not seem to have convinced the commissioners. But differences were settled, since by the time the latter departed he and the men of Helhoughton had reached a compromise over common rights.[141]

These problems did not arise out of any lack of rules; Norfolk husbandry was beset with customary regulations.[142] When the Townshends broke them it was in a gradual rather than a flagrant manner. Engrossment was their particular sin, the inevitable consequence of an expanding estate and flocks. By the end of 1514, for instance, they no longer collected any assize rents at Barmer because the land in question was now totally in their hands.[143] In connection with their sheep-farming, engrossment appears at its most obvious in the case of cullet rights and tathing.

Like the par right, the cullet right was a privilege attached to certain tenant-holdings and was peculiar to the foldcourse system. It allowed the tenant to place a certain number of sheep (determined by the size of his holding) with the lord's flock, often in return for a fee calculated

---

right' is one of the more enigmatic features of the foldcourse system. To par (or parr) is to enclose or confine; to shut up in an enclosure; to fold, pen, etc. (*OED*).

[139] No doubt Eleanor strongly encouraged the suits which two of her tenants and estate officers, John Scony and Edmund Herberd, took out against Capell in the Common Pleas in Michaelmas term 1499: PRO, CP40/950, rot. 309, 310.

[140] R36, file of papers (see n. 135 above).

[141] NRO, B-L VII b(4), 'Skayman's Book', fo. 38. For the Norfolk commissioners' returns see Leadam, 'Inquisition', 134–218. The commissioners did not uncover much evidence of large-scale enclosure, which is no surprise as far as the foldcourse areas are concerned. Roger II was, however, charged with converting arable into pasture at Stanhoe (280 acres) and Bayfield (60 acres): ibid., 169, 170, 164.

[142] Allison, thesis, 308.

[143] R(Attic), '*Norfolk manorial* A-M . . . ', 1509/10–1549/50 Barmer accounts, m. 5.

on a per capita basis.[144] The 1534 statute for sheep and farms not only tried to limit flock-sizes. It also provided for the foldcourse regions of East Anglia by directing landlords to respect cullet rights and forbidding them to engross cullets (holdings possessing that right) by taking them into farm.[145] The concern shown about cullets by Roger II in his *Liber pro ovibus* suggests an uneasy conscience. Among its contents is a copy of a list of instructions which he gave his son Thomas and his servant William Salmon in early 1535. These included the order to return to their owners any cullets that he might have in his hands and to ensure that their rights were respected.[146] After the mid-1540s, however, the Townshends had ceased to collect any cullet fees because there were no longer any tenants' sheep in their flocks: as Thomas Townshend's accounts state, 'the sheepe be all nowe my Fathers'. They had, in other words, accumulated into their own hands all those holdings possessing cullet rights.[147] Two decades earlier their neighbour, Henry Fermor of East Barsham, was less subtle in his approach and was reported to the Star Chamber. It emerged that when Fermor did recognize the cullet rights of tenants within his foldcourse at Fakenham he demanded more than the customary fee. He would also accept cullet sheep into his flock and then later deny all knowledge of their existence; a plain case of downright theft.[148]

By the mid-1540s the Townshends also no longer took tathing fees, again because all the land manured by their sheep was now in their hands.[149] If there were any tenants left they were being denied the benefit of dunging.[150] The absence of cullet and tathing fees suggests that the Townshends were engrossing land in order to create perma-

---

[144] Allison, thesis, 98–9; id., 'Sheep-Corn Husbandry', 21. It appears from Roger II's *Liber pro ovibus*, however, that cullet sheep could in some cases be kept separate from the lord's flock (fo. 15).

[145] 25 Henry VIII, c. 13 (*Statutes of the Realm*, iii. 453).

[146] R1, *Liber pro ovibus*, fo. 25ᵛ. Roger also consulted his lawyers Jenney and Monford on the question of cullets: ibid., fo. 11ʳ.

[147] LSE, R(SR) 1,032, 88,918, fo. 2ᵛ. Alternatively, it is conceivable that they were simply denying cullet rights to those entitled to them.

[148] PRO, STAC2/15/11–13.

[149] LSE, R(SR) 1,032, 88,918. Tenants whose land was grazed by the foldcourse owner's flock had to pay for the privilege of receiving the animals' dung: Allison, thesis, 53; id., 'Sheep-Corn Husbandry', 20.

[150] One abuse committed by landlords was to fold all the sheep, including tenants' cullet sheep where they existed, on their own land, thus taking all the manure for themselves: Campbell, 'Regional Uniqueness', 18.

nent sheep-walks. Significantly, the would-be rebels at Walsingham
in 1537 charged the gentry with taking up all the farms and 'cattle'
into their own hands so that poor men could have no living.[151]
The dispute with Robert Gottes shows that the Townshends contributed to the other great grievance of the common people, the denial
or abuse of what they perceived to be their common rights by the
gentry. Common rights had frequently caused conflict in the past as
well as in the sixteenth century,[152] and those who broke customary
by-laws concerning them were often not gentry, but the gentry were
likely to do far greater harm with their sheep than the wilful peasant
with a handful of pigs. The interests of tenants suffered when their
cattle had to share grazing-land with a landlord's sheep, because
sheep crop grass closely, leaving little for other animals to bite.[153] It
was, therefore, a common farming custom that no one was to enter
stubble ground with his sheep before it had been pastured by other
livestock, but this was no solace to the tenant where the landlord
flouted custom.[154]

In the foldcourse areas the landlord not only had the right to pasture
his sheep on tenants' arable but also on common land, which he could
be tempted to overstock. At Kipton, near Raynham, the Southwells
owned a manor and the right to graze 720 sheep on Helhoughton common. In the early sixteenth century they bought a foldcourse liberty
in the neighbourhood and began to graze an additional 480 foldcourse
sheep on the common.[155] Hindringham near Walsingham was a
township especially troubled by landlord–tenant commons disputes.
In the late fifteenth century there was 'groge [grudge] and besynes'
there between William Wilby and local tenants, according to a depo-
nent of 1535, who also declared that more sheep grazed the common
than ever before.[156] Trouble continued at Hindringham into Edward
VI's reign.[157]

---

[151] PRO, SP1/119/37–8 (*LP*, vol. xii, pt. i, no. 1,056 (2)).
[152] e.g. numerous manorial court rolls and books in the Raynham archive. Roger
I's father John was a nuisance to neighbours with his sheep: e.g. R57, 'Scales' in
Raynham court and leet roll, 1430–61, m. 10; R32, 'Ingoldisthorpes' in Raynham
court and leet roll, 1434–56, m. 18. Nearly half of the thirty-six entries on the
Townshends' court roll of 1548-9 for the same manors relate to grazing offences (R31).
[153] W. O. Ault, *Open-Field Farming in Medieval England* (London, 1972), 46–7.
[154] Ibid.
[155] 'Skayman's Book', fo. 16^v.
[156] R1, *Liber pro ovibus*, fos. 15^v–16^r.
[157] PRO, DL5/8/151–3.

As we have seen in the case of Henry Fermor, some of the most serious disputes over common rights between tenants and landlords who farmed sheep on a large scale like the Townshends (although not apparently any of those in which the Townshends were involved) ended up in the Star Chamber.[158] In 1539 the tenants of the township of Hingham clashed with Sir Henry Parker, the son of the local landlord, Lord Morley. In a bill of complaint addressed to the Star Chamber, Sir Henry accused several of them of forcibly entering onto 'Stollonde', a local common under the jurisdiction of the Parker manor at Hingham, and illegally pasturing some sheep there. When his bailiff impounded the sheep, the defendants broke into the pound to recover them, making it clear that neither he nor any other was going to prevent them. They then, he claimed, confederated with others from Hingham and neighbouring townships in order to menace the farmers of his foldcourse, threatening to kill any sheep the farmers placed on the common. The tenants, needless to say, disputed Parker's version of events and denied any misdemeanour or threatening behaviour on their part. They acknowledged that the common belonged to the manor but denied that Parker had the right of free warren or to pasture 500 sheep there as he claimed. Parker asserted that the tenants were permitted to pasture a certain number of their great cattle according to their tenures on the common, but they claimed the customary right to graze all their livestock—including sheep—without any restriction.[159] In a bill of their own the 'whole commonalty and inhabitants of the town of Hingham' accused Parker of attempting to exclude them from the common altogether by leasing it out to his farmers, 'covetous persons' who overcharged it with so many sheep and other livestock that they were prevented from grazing their own animals. To add weight to their case, they warned that they would soon fall into such poverty that they would be unable either to pay the king's taxes or to support him in his wars.[160] Their animosity towards the farmers was especially venomous because the latter were also Hingham men but had broken ranks with their fellow commons, having regard only to their own 'private lucre and peculyere commodyte . . . to the decay and utter dystruccone of the Comon welthe of the seid Towne'.[161] One of the

[158] See p. 186 above.
[159] PRO, STAC2/29/140; STAC2/27/55.
[160] Ibid.
[161] Ibid. Cf. the above examples of Pepys and others.

farmers, John Portman, was the son of an opponent of Parker among the tenantry.[162]

Various inhabitants of Hingham and other townships were examined in October 1540 in an attempt to establish the respective common rights of lord and tenant at Hingham.[163] The main problem seems to have been that the sheep-farming requirements of Parker and his lessees led him to claim grazing-rights over the common which he had not previously exercised: the soil of a common might fall under the jurisdiction of a manorial lord, but his possession was qualified by the recognition in common law of use-rights attaching to copyholds and freeholds within the manor.[164] This dispute, a perfect example of the serious social tensions which sheep-farming could engender, was not satisfactorily resolved and dangerous animosities continued between Parker and his tenants at Hingham and elsewhere. (He later embroiled himself in another dispute—concerned with boundaries and the right to cut wood—with some tenants on the Parker manor at Foulsham, in which his injudicious and probably illegal use of the stocks and their intemperate language against him did not bode well for the future.)[165] Grazing rights at Hingham remained a live issue at the time of Ket. Ket's men established a camp for a time in the township, and Parker was a member of the unsuccessful army led by the marquis of Northampton against the rebels.[166] The East Anglian rebels of 1549 were particularly concerned about the erosion of commons and common rights, one of their most clearly emphasized grievances. After the revolt, several men from Great Ellingham were accused of planning to present a bill to Ket on Mousehold Heath, condemning one of their landlords, Leonard Chamberlain, for illegally demanding the right to take a fine from those who wished to use their local common.[167] It was tenants like these who made the drastic demand in the third article of Ket's manifesto that landlords should no longer graze the commons.[168]

[162] PRO, STAC2/10/118d.
[163] PRO, STAC2/10/113–18, 338, 338a–f.
[164] Manning, *Village Revolts*, 19.
[165] PRO, STAC3/6/30.
[166] *HP*, iii. 58–9; Land, *Kett's Rebellion*, 100, 86.
[167] PRO, C1/1206/15, 16.
[168] Allison, thesis, 153; MacCulloch, 'Kett's Rebellion', 51; Beer, *Rebellion and Riot*, 110. The articles are listed in ibid., 105–7.

(5) CONCLUSIONS

The Townshends' flocks illustrate the considerable size of some of the sheep-farming enterprises of the East Anglian gentry during the late medieval and early modern periods. The fluctuations in the number of animals they had are not always readily explicable, but the expansion of their flocks in the early sixteenth-century coincided with favourable economic trends, and Roger II owed an important part of his wealth to his sheep. In common with other flock-masters, the Townshends were largely wool-producers for most of our period, though they anticipated the growing importance of the meat market.

The often limited and undeveloped nature of their markets (before the 1540s at least) shows that, as in other spheres, theirs was a local world, but this should not conjure up pictures of rural cosiness. Large-scale sheep-farming as practised by the Townshends had the potential to cause much trouble. Norfolk sheep-farmers must share some of the blame for the social unrest which afflicted East Anglia in the Tudor period. In his pioneering work, Allison was perhaps too anxious to emphasize the 'oppressions' of sheep-owning landlords: as a later writer has pointed out, he was unable to measure the true extent of abuses.[169] The animus displayed against the Townshends and their fellow gentry by the lower orders could not, however, have existed if serious abuses, in both foldcourse and non-foldcourse areas, had occurred only on a limited scale. Engrossment—the overriding agrarian grievance of the Walsingham conspirators[170]—was a major cause of complaint, and the vexed question of common rights was at the forefront of the demands of the 1549 rebels. Ket's Rebellion was one of a series of revolts which brought about Protector Somerset's downfall.[171] Norfolk sheep, therefore, contributed to that downfall, illustrating how economic and social issues were inextricably bound up with the political history of the Townshends' England.

---

[169] Allison, thesis, 153 ff.; id., 'Lost Villages'; Simpson, 'East Anglian Foldcourse', 92.

[170] It does not feature as such in the demands of Ket and his followers, though it is hinted at in article 21 of his manifesto: Beer, *Rebellion and Riot*, 106.

[171] Ibid., 128, 178, 211–12; Bush, *Protector Somerset*, 98–9.

6

CONCLUSIONS

J. H. Hexter once fiercely condemned what he termed 'tunnel history', the work of historians predisposed to split the past

into a series of tunnels, each continuous from the remote past to the present, but practically self-contained at every point and sealed off from contact with or contamination by anything that was going on in any of the other tunnels. At their entrance these tunnels bore signs saying diplomatic history, political history . . . ecclesiastical history . . . economic history, legal history, agricultural history . . .[1]

A study of the Townshends which failed to consider the political and economic as well as the social aspects of their time would be incomplete, for during the one hundred years or so covered by this book each aspect played an interrelated part in their affairs. Too often our knowledge of the English gentry in this period is hampered by lack of evidence, but the relatively abundant source material associated with the Townshends makes possible a discussion of several of these aspects, making them too important to ignore.

The last chapter examined the Townshends as great flock-masters. Their sheep were obviously important to them economically: sheep, it might be said, were to them what turnips were to one of their better-known descendants. But sheep-farming cannot be discussed solely in economic terms; it was also inseparable from the political and social issues of their day, and helped to provoke the grievances expressed in outbreaks of popular discontent, including a major rising, Ket's Rebellion. Sheep-farming—albeit on a far smaller scale than that of his successors—was probably largely responsible for John Townshend's prosperity.

This book is about a substantial gentry family. However, the prosperous lesser men—sometimes 'gentlemen' but in most cases 'yeomen'—have recurred throughout. John Townshend, trusted by a magnate and commissioned by a bishop, a man with the ambition

---

[1] *Reappraisals in History*, 2nd edn. (London, 1979), 194.

and means to send his son to an inn of court, was one of them. So were the leaders of popular disturbances, like those encountered in Chapter 2 (though in some cases—for example, John Pepys and Sir Henry Parker's farmers at Hingham—they were themselves the targets of popular discontent). It was men like these who were the most prominent customers for the produce of the Townshends' estate—and the main target of their litigation. Clearly, a full understanding of East Anglian—indeed, national history—is not possible until this large and amorphous group receives the attention it deserves.[2]

John Townshend was fortunate to have a son able to exploit fully the opportunities of a legal education. The Townshends would surely have reached gentry status if Roger I had not had a legal career, but it is unlikely that they would have climbed above the level of parish gentry before the mid-sixteenth century. Roger's career, like those of James Hobart, Thomas Kebell, and other able contemporaries, shows that professional ability could secure rapid social advance, culminating with entry into the gentry. As Ives has pointed out, the law offered the socially ambitious the best chances of an acceptable level of success.[3] Social ambition and a legal career went hand in hand: an 'age of ambition',[4] the later Middle Ages was inevitably an 'age of the lawyer'. Yet it was also a conservative age. Social mobility was not a new phenomenon and did not threaten the established order, whatever the claims of contemporary moralists.[5] Individuals sought to join their social superiors, not to supplant them. The Townshends and countless others were simply absorbed by the established order; the parvenu was 'the captive, not the conqueror, of the countryside'.[6]

The rewards of his profession enabled Roger I to acquire a substantial estate, and to become a sheep-farmer on a really large scale. As a result, he and Roger II were accepted as members of the upper gentry and of the governing élite of their county. Not forgetting the importance of land-ownership as a symbol of social status and an investment of wealth, sheep-farming gave both of them an added incentive to acquire more land and to create a consolidated

---

[2] MacCulloch has indicated what can be done in his *Suffolk and the Tudors*, 285–337.
[3] *Kebell*, 328.
[4] F. R. H. Du Boulay, *An Age of Ambition* (London, 1970).
[5] J. H. Hexter, 'The Myth of the Middle Class in Tudor England', in *Reappraisals*, 71–116, esp. 76–81.
[6] Ibid., 195.

estate.[7] This in turn played its part in provoking serious social tension and ensured that Roger II was kept busy as a justice of the peace.

These social tensions, exacerbated by the government's fiscal and religious innovations, had important political consequences, in that they ensured the loyalty of the East Anglian gentry to the Crown. Since the Yorkist period, the Crown, concerned about the disorder of the great, sought to strengthen its links with the ruling élites of the shires. In Norfolk it achieved this by associating its gentry more closely with the royal household and by promoting those who were most amenable to government control as candidates for parliamentary representation and the magistrates' bench. It was also helped by responsible behaviour on the part of the magnates; in Henry VIII's reign the duke of Norfolk in particular played an important role in overseeing local government. The Norfolk gentry's contacts with the central authorities are one reason why they remained loyal to Henry VIII and demonstrated their loyalty by helping to force through, rather than oppose, his innovations.

The government relied on the support of men like Roger II. He repaid its trust, rendering his greatest service by helping to crush the Walsingham Conspiracy in 1537. Conspicuously loyal as an administrator, he was consequently something of a time-server with regard to intermediate masters like the duke of Norfolk. But he and his father before him (both as a lawyer and a gentleman) and many other gentry had more sense than to become exclusively attached to any one magnate, because those who did sometimes shared a master's downfall.[8] In essence, the sixteenth-century bastard-feudal relationship was no different from that of the previous century. *Circumspecte agatis*, the motto of a fifteenth-century Norfolk man, James Gresham, remained a useful maxim.[9]

Since the Townshends had much to lose, this sort of reasoning would have made much sense to them. They had built up an estate extensive enough to place them among the ruling élite of their county in a remarkably short time. By the standards of their day they seem

---

[7] Perhaps to some extent the acquisition of land encouraged more extensive sheep-farming: or are we in danger of playing conceptual games here?

[8] Presuming they became attached to any magnate at all. Richmond's findings concerning the Townshends' relative, John Hopton, changed his assumptions about 15th-cent. society; though Carpenter has questioned whether John did in fact lead such a quiet and uninvolved life: Richmond, *John Hopton*, pp. xv–xvi; Carpenter, 'Biographies', 730.

[9] *PL*, no. 454.

to have managed it efficiently, if in a conservative fashion. They were certainly thrusting sheep-farmers, but the foldcourse was not a progressive farming method since the tenant had to conform with a communal cultivation system enforced by the landlord. He could not improve his land independently, because he was obliged to leave it open for the latter's sheep. The persistence of the foldcourse custom was to impede later agricultural developments like the introduction of convertible husbandry.[10] Should we, in any case, always expect to find the 'progressive' estate manager in every new landlord? What the parvenu most desired was acceptance of his newly won status, not something which he would easily achieve if he launched a full-scale attack on customary practices observed by his established gentry neighbours.

The care the Townshends took in acquiring their estate partly explains why, although they were regular litigants, they were relatively successful in avoiding serious legal disputes concerning land. When these did occur, out-of-court settlements brought about by arbitration were a striking feature. This might at first suggest great shortcomings in the common-law system. In fact the arbitration process was closely linked to that system. Working outside the common-law courts, but not in opposition to the common law, it successfully resolved many gentry disputes and was a useful curb on violence. Despite the reputation of their period, violence had no recognizable part in the Townshends' disputes and this was probably the rule rather than the exception for most gentry. The essence of the arbitration process was compromise, often encouraged by the disputants' fellow gentry. In the final analysis good order in the localities depended on the self-regulation of the gentry.

The ruling élites of the localities, including Norfolk, underwent a crucial transition from unruly local factionalism in the mid-fifteenth century to closer ties with the Crown in the sixteenth. In some areas these links were severely strained and sometimes broken during the crises of Henry VIII's reign; yet in Norfolk the Walsingham Conspiracy and similar episodes show how the need to control the restless lower orders made it essential to co-operate with the Crown in governing the shire. The anti-gentry animus of the lower orders made the gentry's participation in any rebellion unlikely and gave them good reason to remain loyal to the Crown. It is unwise to dwell

---

[10] Manning, *Village Revolts*, 37.

upon might-have-beens, but the political history of England would surely have been very different had the region's rulers allowed East Anglia to join the Pilgrimage of Grace.[11] It is only with an understanding of Norfolk's peculiar socio-economic circumstances that we can explain why it differed from other parts of the country.

Norfolk was distinct, but it would be wrong to assume that this distinctiveness took the shape of a gentry 'county community'. In the case of Norfolk this concept, applied by historians to the seventeenth century and adopted by those working on earlier periods,[12] breaks down. In East Anglia sheer physical geography—and therefore farming practices and their social and economic consequences—transcended county boundaries. Landowners and farmers from the sheep-farming area of west Norfolk shared more in common with their fellows in similar areas of Suffolk than they did with those from other parts of their own county. The classic county community, as posited by Everitt for seventeenth-century Kent, presupposes a wonderful degree of co-operation, unity, and mutual goodwill among the gentry.[13] In Norfolk this was an impossible ideal: by controlling the gentry powerful local magnates could create the illusion of a county community, but this superficial unity did not survive their absence. MacCulloch's attempt to present the gentry of Tudor Suffolk as a county community in contrast to their unruly counterparts in Norfolk fails to convince, and the best part of his book is the section on East Anglia's politically aware, independently minded, and sometimes rebellious lower orders.[14] Yet this in turn begs the question: could the gentry of either Norfolk or Suffolk have been a 'county community' when such a politically and socially significant part of the population of each county did not share—and often opposed—their interests?[15]

The 'county community' idea has been pressed too far and has been presented at a level of conceptual purity that can only lead to artificial, and therefore pointless, for-and-against debates. Beneath it all, however, elements of reality lurk, for it underlines the local nature of

[11] It has been suggested that if the duke of Norfolk had joined the Pilgrims he might well have brought East Anglia with him: Davies, 'Pilgrimage of Grace', 38.

[12] e.g. Bennett, 'County Community'; Saul, *Knights and Esquires*, 258; J.R. Maddicott, 'The County Community and the Making of Public Opinion in Fourteenth-Century England', *TRHS* 5th ser. 28 (1978), 27–43.

[13] Everitt, *Community of Kent*; Holmes, 'County Community', 68.

[14] *Suffolk*, 285–337.

[15] Cf. ibid., 72.

English society and, as concrete examples like the Townshends show, England was still very much a collection of localities. The Townshends were no backwoodsmen—their careers and social status ensured that they (and other gentry) had contact with London and the wider world—but their everyday horizons were local. This is nowhere more evident than in their nexus of friends and trustees and in the networks through which they bought and sold livestock and other agricultural produce. In terms of social relationships this was no doubt a matter of choice: they knew the outside world but chose to limit their contact with it. This might appear a prosaic note on which to end; but reality is often prosaic. Not every gentry family was afflicted with trials and tribulations as great as those of the fifteenth-century Pastons. By reminding us of this, the Townshends serve us well.

APPENDIX 1. TOWNSHEND TRUSTEES

(a) Roger I's Trustees

L = Contemporary at Lincoln's Inn
R = Relative
S = Servant or dependant
T = Tenant

Trustee	From
Sir Edmund Bedingfield	SW Norfolk
Edward Blake, gent.	SW Norfolk
Simon Blake, gent.	SW Norfolk
John Blakeney, esq. (R)	E Norfolk
Thomas Blakeney, esq. (R)	E Norfolk
John Bonerour, clerk	? NW Norfolk
John Bougeour, clerk (?S)	NW Norfolk
Robert Brandon, esq.	Suffolk
Philip Calthorpe, esq.	NW Norfolk
Sir William Calthorpe	NW Norfolk
William Candeler, chaplain (S)	NW Norfolk
Sir Robert Clere	E Norfolk
John Clyff, clerk (S)	NW Norfolk
John Clyfton (T)	NW Norfolk
William Clopton, esq.	Suffolk
William Cobbe, gent.	NW Norfolk
William Dengayne, gent.	NE Norfolk
Thomas Dighton	SW Norfolk
Laurence Drake	NW Norfolk
John Eyre, clerk	? NW Norfolk
Thomas Eyre[1]	London
William Farehurst (S)	NW Norfolk
Henry Fermor, gent.	NW Norfolk
Walter Fernfeld[2]	? Norwich
Edmund Fincham, gent.	NW Norfolk
John Fincham, gent.	W Norfolk

---

[1] Merchant; associate of the Hoptons; brother of William Eyre of Great Cressingham: Richmond, *John Hopton*, 194.

[2] Possibly a Norwich mercer and alderman: PRO, C1/66/227.

William Fuller (S)	NW Norfolk
William Gurney, esq. (L)	Central Norfolk
John Gygges, gent. (R)	NW Norfolk
Thomas Gygges, gent. (R, S)[3]	NW Norfolk
Edmund Herberd, clerk (S)	NW Norfolk
Sir Henry Heydon	NE Norfolk
John Hoo[4]	Suffolk
William Hoppes	NW Norfolk
Edmund Jenney, esq.	Suffolk
Edward Knyvet (R)[5]	Essex
Henry Le Strange, esq.	NW Norfolk
James Lumbard (S)	NW Norfolk
William Pickenham (R)[6]	Suffolk
John Pigeon (S)	Norwich
John Pykard, chaplain (?S)[7]	? NW Norfolk
Roger Sambroke, esq.	NW Norfolk
Thomas Sefoull, gent. (S)	NW Norfolk
Thomas Shouldham, esq.	W Norfolk
Nicholas Sidney, esq. (R)	Suffolk
Henry Spelman, gent.	South Norfolk
John Stalworthy (S)	NW Norfolk
John Sulyard, esq. (L, R)[8]	Suffolk
William Tendering, esq. (R)	Suffolk
John Wagor (S)	NW Norfolk
William Wayte (S)	NW Norfolk
Sir Robert Wingfield	SE Norfolk
Thomas Woodhouse, esq. (R)	SE Norfolk

(b) Roger II's Trustees

C = Contemporary at court
H = Howard follower or connection
R = Relative
S = Servant or dependant

---

[3] Problems of identification mean that more than one Thomas Gygges could be conflated here.

[4] A Hopton servant.

[5] Relative of Eleanor Townshend: Richmond, *John Hopton*, 49, 124 n., 125.

[6] Relative of Eleanor Townshend: ibid., 153, 215.

[7] He was possibly presented to the vicarage of Castle Acre in 1492: Blomefield, viii. 364.

[8] Relative of Eleanor Townshend: Richmond, *John Hopton*, 241.

Trustee	From
John Affordby (S)	NE Norfolk
Giles Alington, esq. (C)	Cambridgeshire
Nicholas Appleyard, esq. (H)	SE Norfolk
Sir John Audeley	SW Norfolk
Sir Edmund Bedingfield (R)	SW Norfolk
Sir Thomas Bedingfield (R)	SW Norfolk
John Blakeney, esq. (R)	E Norfolk
George Bokenham, esq.	NW Norfolk
James Boleyn, esq. (H)	NE Norfolk
John Bosom, esq. (R)[9]	NW Norfolk
Richard Bosom (R)[9]	NW Norfolk
Robert Bradshaw, clerk (S)	NW Norfolk
Sir Charles Brandon (C)	Royal Court
John Brewes, esq. (R)	Norfolk/Suffolk
Robert Brewes, esq. (R)	Suffolk
John Broughton, esq. (H)	Suffolk
John Broun (S)	NW Norfolk
Christopher Calthorpe, esq. (R)[10]	NW Norfolk
Sir Philip Calthorpe	NW Norfolk
Ralph Castell, esq. (H, R)	SE Norfolk
Sir Robert Clere (C, H)	E Norfolk
Stephen Cleydon (S)	NW Norfolk
Sir William Clopton	Suffolk
Henry Clyfton (S)	NW Norfolk
Robert Coke, gent. (S)	NW Norfolk
William Coningsby, esq.	W Norfolk
Sir John Cressener (R)	S Norfolk/Suffolk/Essex
Thomas Cressener, esq. (R)	NW Norfolk/Essex
William Denys (S)	NW Norfolk/Suffolk
Robert Godfrey, clerk (S)	NW Norfolk
Thomas Grandon, clerk (S)	NW Norfolk
Anthony Gurney, esq.	SW Norfolk
Anthony Hansard, esq. (R)	Suffolk
John Heveningham, esq.	SE Norfolk
Sir Christopher Heydon	NW Norfolk
Henry Heydon, esq.	NE Norfolk
Sir John Heydon (R)	NE Norfolk
Richard Heydon, esq.	Norfolk/London
Miles Hobart, esq.	SE Norfolk

[9] The Bosoms were connected to the Woodhouses and Cresseners: *HP*, i. 479-80.

[10] Married the widow of William Brewes, Amy Townshend's father: Bulwer, 441.

Robert Holdich, esq. (H)	SE Norfolk
Arthur Hopton, esq. (C, R)	Suffolk
Edmund Howard, esq. (C, H)	Royal Court
Sir Edward Howard (C, H)	Royal Court
Henry Hunston, esq.	NW Norfolk
Christopher Jenney, esq.	SW Norfolk
John Le Strange, esq.	NW Norfolk
Robert Le Strange, esq.	NW Norfolk
Sir Thomas Le Strange	NW Norfolk
Francis Monford, esq.	SW Norfolk
David Moresby, clerk (S)	NW Norfolk
Robert Nicols, clerk (S)	NW Norfolk
Sir William Paston (C)	E Norfolk
John Pigeon (S)	Norwich
John Potter (S)	NW Norfolk
Oliver Reymes, gent.	NW Norfolk
William Salmon (S)	NW Norfolk
Richard Sefoull, gent. (S)	NW Norfolk
William Shaw (S)	NW Norfolk
Sir John Shelton (C)	SE Norfolk
Thomas Shorte (S)	NW Norfolk
Nicholas Sidney, esq. (R)	Suffolk
Thomas Sidney, gent.	NW Norfolk
Sir William Sidney (C, R)	Suffolk
John Skayman (S)	NW Norfolk
John Spelman, esq.	SW Norfolk
Thomas Thursby, esq.	NW Norfolk
Sir Philip Tilney (H)	Suffolk
Sir John Vere (C)	Essex
Thomas Walpole (S)	NW Norfolk
William Warryson, chaplain (S)[11]	NW Norfolk
Edward White, esq. (H)	SE Norfolk
Humphrey Wilson, clerk (S)[12]	NW Norfolk
Anthony Wingfield, esq. (C)	Suffolk
Thomas Wingfield, gent. (R)[13]	NW Norfolk
Henry Winter, esq.	N Norfolk
Roger Woodhouse, esq. (H, R)	SE Norfolk
Sir Thomas Woodhouse (C, R)	SE Norfolk
William Wotton, esq.	Central Norfolk

[11] Presented to Salle by Roger II, 1538: Blomefield, viii. 274.

[12] Townshend auditor by the late 1540s: NRO, Townshend 163 MS 1,582 1 D4, fo. 42^r.

[13] Married a daughter of Sir Thomas Woodhouse: Wingfield, *Wingfield Family*, 36.

Edmund Wyndham, esq. (H, R)	NE Norfolk
Sir Thomas Wyndham (H, R)	NE Norfolk
William Yelverton, esq.	NW Norfolk

APPENDIX 2. ROGER II's BOOK OF ASSESSMENTS FOR THE LOAN OF 1522/3

This booklet of forty paper folios bound in parchment contains assessments for the hundreds of Gallow, Brothercross, Smithdon, North and South Greenhoe, Launditch, Clackclose, Freebridge Lynn and Marshland, and the town of Lynn. It should be added to the list of surviving records of Wolsey's proscription: see J. Cornwall, 'A Tudor Domesday: The Musters of 1522', *Journal of the Society of Archivists*, 3 (1965-9), 21-3; Goring, 'General Proscription', 687 n., 688 n.

Although undated, there can be no doubt that it relates to the proscription:
(i) Folios 37^r-9^r are concerned with the muster side of the survey and include a copy of instructions to the commissioners regarding the liabilities of those who should keep military harness;
(ii) The rest of the booklet, concerned with its fiscal side, accords with the circumstances of the intended loan. For the first instalment, the commissioners were instructed to ask for a contribution of 10 per cent on all incomes and personal estate from those assessed at £20-£300 p.a., and 13.5 per cent from those assessed at £300-£1000: *The County Community under Henry VIII*, ed. J. Cornwall, Rutland Rec. Soc., 1 (1980), 4. In the booklet the prospective contributors fall within the terms of this first instalment, all being worth at least £20 per annum. On folios 2^r-26^r they are listed under their townships, together with an assessment of their wealth. Underneath each name is entered the sum they had agreed to lend and, in many cases, the signature of the lender. On folios 26^v-34^v the contributors are again listed, in a neater fashion: their township, followed by their name, an assessment of their wealth, and the sum they were to lend are entered in columns across the page. This second list was obviously a final check-list for receipt of payments and above each name *sol* has later been written. The contributors paid at either one of the two rates, according to their personal circumstances. Thus William King of West Rudham was expected to lend 40s., 10 per cent of the £20 at which he was assessed; but the wealthy Thomas Thursby of Gayton, assessed at £500, was expected to lend £66. 13s. 4d. at the higher rate of 13.5 per cent (fos. 4^r, 20^v). It is worth noting that there is a blank space opposite the name of William Coningsby the lawyer, who is listed under Lynn but was probably assessed in London (fo. 18^r). Also interesting is a note in the first list under the name of William Skipwith, a gentleman from Fordham, to the effect that Roger II had promised to lend him the £6 he was expected to pay (fo. 25^r).

APPENDIX 3. RESIDENT NORFOLK GENTRY IN THE MID-1520s[1]

m = marks
< = less than[2]
L = Lawyer

(a) Esquires and above

Gentleman	Township	Lands	Offices[3]
Roger Appleyard	Bracon Ash	£80	
Thomas Asteley	Melton Constable	£50	
Sir John Audeley	Swaffham	£100	J
Sir Edmund Bedingfield[4]	Great Bircham	£100	J/S
Peter Bedingfield[4]	Quidenham	£40	
Sir Thomas Bedingfield[4]	Oxborough	£300	J/MP
John Berney[5]	Reedham	£120	
Ralph Berney (L)[5]	Gunton/Cromer	£50	J
Thomas Billingford	Stoke Holy Cross	£40	
Sir Thomas Blennerhasset	Frenze	£100	
Richard Blyant	Intwood	£100	
Sir Edward Boleyn[6]	Shelton	£40	
Sir James Boleyn	Blickling	£40	J/MP
John Brampton (L)	Brampton	£80	
Sir Robert Brandon	Crostwight	£200	J/MP/S

[1] Source: PRO, subsidy rolls (E179).

[2] The figures following this symbol are for gentlemen with no assessment for landed income in the subsidy rolls. In these cases the individuals concerned were taxed on their moveable wealth, which must, therefore, have been greater than their annual landed incomes.

[3] Norfolk offices held before, during, or after this date. E = escheator; J = justice of the peace; MP = member of parliament; S = sheriff.

[4] The three Bedingfields were all sons of Sir Edmund Bedingfield (d. 1497). Peter was the youngest. Edmund succeeded his issueless elder brother Thomas in 1538: K. Bedingfeld, *The Bedingfelds of Oxburgh* (privately published, 1912), 11; PRO, C142/61/5, 9.

[5] Ralph of Gunton was John of Reedham's uncle: Rye, *Norfolk Families*, 820; *Visitations*, 16; *CIPM, Henry VII*, vol. iii, no. 239.

[6] Younger brother of Sir James: Blomefield, vi. 388.

Christopher Calthorpe[7]	Cockthorpe	<£50	
Edward Calthorpe[7]	Ludham	10m	J
William Calthorpe[7]	Crostwick	<40m	
Edward Chamberlain	Barnham Broom	£90	
Edmund Clere	Stokesby	£20	E
Sir Robert Clere (L)	Ormesby	£180	J/MP/S
Thomas Clere[8]	Acle	<£40	J
Christopher Coo	Saham Toney	£50[9]	
Sir John Cressener	Attleborough	£80	
John Curson	Bylaugh	£100	J
Thomas Dereham	Crimplesham	100m	
William Ellis (L)	Attlebridge	100m[10]	J
John Fincham	Fincham	100m	
Richard Gawsell	Watlington	£50	
Thomas Godsalve (L)	City of Norwich	100m[11]	
John Groos	Crostwight	<£50	
Anthony Gurney	West Barsham	£100	
Sir Christopher Heydon[12]	Thursford	£40	J
Henry Heydon[12]	Thwaite	£50	
Sir John Heydon[12]	Baconsthorpe	£100	J/S
Miles Hobart (L)	Little Plumstead	£80	
Walter Hobart (L)[13]	Loddon	£180	J/S
Robert Holdich	Ranworth	£70	J
John Inglose	Crostwight	£120	
Christopher Jenney (L)	Great Cressingham	£40	J
John Jermy	Sprowston	£120	J/S
Robert Kempe[14]	Flordon	<£50	
Sir Edward Knyvet	Wymondham	£180	

[7] Edward Calthorpe was the eldest son of Sir William Calthorpe (d. 1495) by his second wife. Christopher was the son and heir of John Calthorpe of Cockthorpe, the third son of Sir William's second marriage. William of Crostwick must have been the William Calthorpe who died in 1527, a younger son of Sir William Calthorpe's first marriage: Bulwer, 441; *Visitations*, 66-7; Blomefield, viii. 77; PRO, C142/51/64; NRO, NCC 282 Attmere.

[8] Thomas and his elder brother Edmund were of the Stokesby branch of the family and were cousins of Sir Robert: Bulwer, 265-6, 270-1.

[9] Including fees.

[10] Including fees.

[11] Including fees.

[12] Henry was Sir John's younger brother and Sir Christopher his heir: Wedgwood, 451; *HP*, ii. 352.

[13] Elder brother of Miles: Bulwer, 60-2.

[14] Robert Kempe of Gissing (d. 1526), father of Bartholomew: PRO, C142/46/3; see following list. The Kempes succeeded to a manor in Flordon in the 15th cent.: Rye, *Norfolk Families*, 426; *Visitations*, 175-6; Blomefield, v. 72.

Sir Thomas Lovell[15]	Barton Bendish	100m	J
Francis Monford (L)	Feltwell	100m	J/MP
Henry Noon	Shelfhanger	£40	J
Andrew Ogard	Emneth	£60	
Sir William Paston	Paston	£300	J/S
Sir William Pennington	Roudham	£120	J
Thomas Sharington	Craneworth	50m	
Sir John Shelton	Shelton	£200	
Ralph Shelton[16]	Broome	<£40	E
William Skipwith	Fordham	£40	
Andrew Sulyard (L)	City of Norwich	£100	J
John Tendale	Hockwold	£140	J
John Townshend	East Raynham	£40	
Sir Roger Townshend (L)	East Raynham	£440[17]	J/MP/S
Edward White (L)	Shotesham	£60[18]	J
Henry Winter	Town Barningham	£40	
Roger Woodhouse[19]	Kimberley	£20	J
Sir Thomas Woodhouse	Kimberley	£150	J/E
William Wotton (L)	North Tuddenham	£120	J
William Yelverton	Rougham	£50	J

Total of sample = 63
Escheators = 2
Justices of the peace = 30
Members of parliament = 6
Sheriffs = 7
Average landed income = £96 p.a.[20]

(b) Gentlemen

Gentleman	Township	Lands	Offices
Robert Aldyrton	Salle	<£30	
William Andrew	Great Ryburgh	<£10	E
Thomas Appleyard	Dunston	<£60	
William Arnold	Cromer	£6	
William Aslake	City of Norwich	£32	

[15] Nephew of his namesake, the Tudor councillor: Sayer, 'Norfolk Involvement', 317; *HP*, ii. 548–9.
[16] Sir John's younger brother: Bulwer, 345.
[17] Including fees.
[18] Including fees.
[19] Eldest son and heir of Sir Thomas: Dashwood, 104.
[20] Based on the fifty-six assessments on land for which an exact figure is available.

Henry Bagott[21]	City of Norwich	<£10	
John Baker	Hillington	?	
John Bastard	Watlington	20m	
John Bettes I[22]	Heydon	<£8	
John Bettes II[22]	Irmingland	20m	
William Bishop	Marsham	<£40	
Thomas Bolton[23]	Ashill	?	
William Bolton[23]	Garboldisham	£16	
William Brampton	Attleborough	£20	J
Thomas Brette	Gimingham	?	
Thomas Briggis	Heacham	40m	
George Brown	Bawsey	£10	
John Calibut (L)	Castle Acre	<£100	J
Richard Calle	City of Norwich	<£40	
Richard Calthorpe[24]	Overstrand	£60	
Humphrey Carville[25]	Wiggenhall	£100	
Thomas Carville[25]	Watlington	<£20	
Adelard Castell (? L)	City of Norwich	?	
Henry Chancey (? L)	City of Norwich	< £20	
Geoffrey Cobbe	Sandringham	100m	E
William Cobbe[26]	Gayton	<£50	
William Coningsby (L)	Lynn town	200m	J/MP
Hugh Coo[27]	Saham Toney	?	
Christopher Coote	Blo Norton	£17	
John Corbet (L)	Sprowston	<£50	J/MP
Thomas Crampton	Lynn town	?	
John Curatt	? Cotton	£10	
John Cushyn (L)	Hingham	40m	E
Richard Dade	Witton	£18	
Ralph Daniel	Swaffham	<10m	
Gregory Davy (L)	Gunthorpe	£16	J

[21] 'Doctor of Physic'; studied at the University of Bologna: PRO, C1/117/38.
[22] John II was the eldest son of Thomas Bettes of Irmingland: Blomefield, vi. 324.
[23] Sons of Edward Bolton of Brisingham; William was Thomas's elder brother: Blomefield, i. 60; PRO, C142/56/52.
[24] Younger brother of Christopher Calthorpe of Cockthorpe in the preceding list; he died in 1554: *Visitations*, 66–7; Blomefield, viii. 77.
[25] Humphrey of Wiggenhall died in late 1526 or early 1527: PRO, PROB11/22, fos. 126ᵛ–127; Thomas of Watlington was of another branch of the family.
[26] Geoffrey's younger half-brother: *CIPM, Henry VII*, vol. i, no. 872; Dashwood, 317–18.
[27] Possibly the father of the Christopher in the preceding list. The Coos of Saham Toney had no apparent links with the Coos of Essex and Suffolk. They held the manor of Saham Toney in this period: J. G. Bartlett, *Robert Coe, Puritan, his Ancestors and Descendants, 1340–1910* (Boston, Mass., 1911), 7–8.

John Dedick	Beechamwell	< £50	
Henry Dengayne	Broomstead	£8	
Baldwin Dereham	Crimplesham	< £30	
Edmund Dogett	Honingham	£10	
John Drury[28]	Besthorpe	24s. 4d.	
William Drury I[28]	Besthorpe	£40	
William Drury II[28]	East Harling	£10	
James Elme	Rackheath	£40	
Laurence Fayeclay	Metton	< £2	
Henry Fermor	East Barsham	£167	J/S
Thomas Flyte (?L)[29]	Waterden	< 200m	
Robert Gavell	Claxton	?	
William Gawcell	Billoughby	£8	
Fulk Grey[30]	Larling	< £15	
John Grey[30]	Horsham St Faiths	£10[31]	
John Grympton	Oxborough	£5	
Anthony Grysse[32]	Tivetshall	£8	
William Grysse[32]	Brockdish	< £50	E
Richard Gunnor	East Beckham	10m	
Thomas Gurney	Hempstead	?	
Thomas Guybon	Lynn town	£100	J/S/MP
John Gygges	Burnham Overy	8m	
Robert Gygges[33]	Sparham	< £30	
Walter Gylloure	Ryston	< £50	
John Hacon (L)	Wheatacre	£20	
William Hale	? Heverland	< £50	
Hugh Hastings	Elsing	£20	
John Herward[34]	South Reppes	£10	
Robert Herward I[34]	Booton	< £60	
Robert Herward II[34]	Aldborough	20m	E

[28] John and William I were sons of Roger Drury of Hawstead, Suffolk (d. 1496). Their brother Sir Robert Drury was a Tudor privy councillor. William II was William I's second son: Blomefield, i. 277; *HP*, ii. 57–8; A. Campling, *The History of the Family of Drury* (London, 1937), 100–5.

[29] Legal training suggested by his being an arbiter in a minor dispute between Roger II and the Prior of Coxford: R(Attic), 'Legal and suit papers, 15th–19th cent.'

[30] The relationship, if any, between Fulk and John is unknown. Fulk, the second son of William Grey of Merton, died in 1560: *Visitations*, 137–8; NRO, NCC 139–42 Cowlles.

[31] Including fees.

[32] Anthony was the eldest son and heir of William: *Visitations*, 187–8.

[33] Uncle of John: *CAD*, vol. iv, no. A.8,471; vol. v, nos. A.13,487, 13,542, 13,492; NRO, NCC 289–93 Ryxe.

[34] Robert of Booton was the uncle of Robert of Aldborough. John was perhaps the latter's younger brother: Dashwood, 300, 302.

208   *Appendix 3*

Philip Hill	City of Norwich	<100m	
Thomas Holdich	Breccles	<£50	
Henry Hunston (L)	Walpole	£100	J
James Jernegan[35]	Oxborough	?	
Bartholomew Kempe[36]	Gissing	£8	
John Kempe[36]	Fundenhall	£2	
William Knightley (L)	City of Norwich	<£100	
Thomas Lombe	Wymondham	£10	
Edmund Lumnour	Mannington	£20	
William Methwold	Langford	<£48	E
James Moore	Wolterton	£5	
John Mortofte	Itteringham	<£40	
John Mownteney	?	<£6	
Henry Palmer	Monkton	<£160	
Edmund Playter	Oby	£30	
Robert Poppy	Bintree	<£20	
John Power	Lynn town	<£200	
John Pronze	Houghton	<£6	
John Redelles	Salhouse	£40	
Thomas Redelles[37]	Salhouse	10m	
Oliver Reymes	Little Walsingham	<£20	
Henry Richers	Swannington	<100m	E
Thomas Robyns	Cromer	<£80	
Roger Rokewood[38]	Oxborough	?	
Henry Russell	Sedgeford	<£40	E
Robert Salter	North Wotton	<£50	
William Seyve	Mundford	<£60	
John Shouldham	Marham	20m	
Thomas Sidney	Little Walsingham	?	
Richard Smith	City of Norwich	<£10	
Christopher Spelman[39]	Stowe Bedon	?	
Henry Spelman I[39]	Wymondham	10m	

[35] Obviously resident in the Bedingfield household at Oxborough. Margaret, daughter of Sir Edmund Bedingfield, married Edward Jernegan of Somerleyton, Suffolk: Blomefield, ii. 414–15.

[36] Bartholomew was the son and heir of Robert Kempe in the preceding list. John was probably his uncle, the younger brother of Robert: PRO, C142/46/3; Blomefield, i. 177–8; Rye, *Norfolk Families*, 426; *Visitations*, 175–6; NRO, NCC 27–8 Jerves.

[37] Possibly John's son.

[38] Resident in the Bedingfield household. Sir Thomas Bedingfield of Oxborough's second wife was Alice, widow of Edmund Rokewood of Euston: Blomefield, vi, pedigree between 178–9.

[39] Henry II was the eldest son and Christopher a nephew of Thomas Spelman of Great Ellingham. Henry I was probably Thomas's younger brother: Dashwood, 251–2.

Henry Spelman II[39]	Great Ellingham	£46	
Leonard Spencer (L)	Blofield	80m	E/J
John Stede[40]	Little Walsingham	£20	E
Thomas Storme	Horstead with Stanninghall	£4	
John Stubbe	Scottow	<£40	
Lewes Thomas	City of Norwich	<£100	
Thomas Thursby I[41]	Ashwicken	£17	
Thomas Thursby II[41]	Gayton	<£400	E
John Tutfeld	Swaffham	<£40	
Edward Walpole	Houghton	20m	
Henry Walpole[42]	Harpley	<£50	
William Walsh	Colby	£15	
Henry Warde (L)	Paston	£3	J/MP
John Whitwell	Felmingham	<£20	
John Willeby	Tilney	<£30	
John Willoughby	Paston	?	
Richard Winter	Tuttington	<£2	
Richard Yaxley	City of Norwich	<£2	

Total of sample = 116
Escheators = 11
Justices of the peace = 9
Members of parliament = 4
Sheriffs = 2
Average landed income = £27 p.a.[43]

---

[40] Stede was not assessed on lands for the subsidy but Roger II identified him in 1521 as a £20 landowner: PRO, SP1/233/56 (*LP*, Addenda, no. 319).

[41] Cousins: Thomas of Gayton was the eldest son of Thomas Thursby of Lynn (d. 1510). Thomas of Ashwicken was the grandson of Robert Thursby of Lynn, Thomas of Lynn's elder brother: *Visitations*, 141, 200; Wedgwood, 847; *CIPM, Henry VII*, vol. ii, no. 367; vol. iii, no. 413; Blomefield, viii. 422.

[42] Younger brother of Edward: A. Jessopp, *One Generation of a Norfolk House* (Norwich, 1878), 19–20.

[43] Based on the fifty-four assessments on land for which an exact figure is available.

APPENDIX 4. NORFOLK LANDOWNERS ASSESSED AT £100 OR MORE FOR THE 1524/5 SUBSIDY

Assessment	Landowner
£440	Sir Roger Townshend
£400	Sir John Heydon
£366. 13s. 4d.	Francis Lovell
£300	Sir William Paston
£300	Sir Thomas Bedingfield
£200	Sir John Shelton
£200	Sir Robert Brandon
£200	Sir Philip Calthorpe
£180	Sir Edward Knyvet
£180	Sir Robert Clere
£180	Walter Hobart
£166. 13s. 4d.	Henry Fermor
£150	Sir Thomas Woodhouse
£140	John Tendale
£120	William Coningsby
£120	John Inglose
£120	John Berney
£120	John Jermy
£120	Thomas Thursby
£120	William Wotton
£100	Sir John Audeley
£100	Sir Thomas Blennerhasset
£100	Anthony Gurney
£100	Sir Edmund Bedingfield
£100	Andrew Sulyard
£100	Henry Hunston
£100	Humphrey Carville
£100	Thomas Guybon
£100	Edmund Wyndham

Source: PRO, subsidy rolls (E179).

APPENDIX 5. GENTRY MEMBERS OF THE 11 FEBRUARY 1526 COMMISSION OF THE PEACE, IN ORDER OF PRECEDENCE

L = Lawyer
* = Listed in Appendix 4
Sir Philip Calthorpe*
Sir Philip Tilney
Sir Robert Clere*
Sir William Paston*
Sir John Shelton*
Sir Roger Townshend*
Sir Thomas Woodhouse*
Sir Edmund Bedingfield*
Sir James Boleyn
William Ellis (L)
William Wotton (L)*
John Spelman (L)
Robert Holdich
Edmund Wyndham*
Thomas Le Strange[1]
John Tendale*
Thomas Wingfield
William Coningsby (L)*
Francis Monford (L)
Christopher Jenney
Edward White (L)
Robert Townshend (L)
Source: *LP*, vol. iv, pt. i, no. 2,002.

---

[1] Le Strange ought to feature in App. 4 but his assessment is lost because of damage to the subsidy returns.

APPENDIX 6. TOWNSHEND MANORS

(a) Properties acquired by John Townshend, Roger I, Eleanor Townshend, and Roger II

The dates refer to date of acquisition or purchase. (A) = purchase price; (B) = approximate value (per annum) at date of acquisition; (C) = approximate rate of purchase (in years); m = marks.

[1] *'Haviles' and 'Rowses' in East Raynham* (1452/5) from Thomas Champeneys, clerk.
(A) £500
(B) *c.* £35
(C) 14.3

[2] *East Beckham* (1469) from Sir John Paston.
(A) 100 m
(B) £10
(C) 6.7
A foreclosed mortgage; regained by the Pastons in 1503.

[3] *'Paynes' in Helhoughton* (1472) from William Payn, clerk.
(A) ?
(B) *c.* £7
(C) ?
Bought as a reversion.

[4] *'Crispin's' in Happisburgh* (*c.*1472/3) from Isabella Cleymond.
(A) £80
(B) £8
(C) 10.0
Bought as a reversion; sold to Robert Coke in 1550.

[5] *'Beaufoes' in South Creake* (1473/5) from William Beaufoy, esquire.
(A) £100

[1] R28, 'RAYNHAM EDW. IV to HENRY VII', deed of 7 Jan. 1466; R49, Townshend cartulary, fos. 18-19, 21-2; R58, Raynham account roll, mm. 4, 7.

[2] *PL*, no. 246; R58, RT I memo-book, fo. 11^r; PRO, CP25/1/170/196, no. 84.

[3] R49, Townshend cartulary, fos. 40-1; R13, 1472/3-1483/4 Helhoughton accounts, mm. 4, 6, 8; R58, Raynham account roll, mm. 4, 7.

[4] R58, RT I memo-book, fos. 7^r, 12^r; PRO, CP25/2/61/481, no. 9.

[5] R58, RT I memo-book, fos. 7^v, 9^v, 11^v; R18, 'N & S CREAKE, Temp. EDW. IV (1471-1481)', deeds of 20 Nov. 1473, 8 Mar., and 24 Apr. 1475.

(B) £11

(C) 9.1

6   *Scarning: (i) moiety of 'Skarnyngs'* from John Pagrave, esquire, and associates; *(ii) purparty of Scarning Hall* from Thomas Sharington, esquire (both 1474/6).

(A) 120 m (i); 100s. (ii)

(B) 10 m (i and ii)

(C) 12.8 (i and ii)

7   *'Nogeons' in Bale* (*c.* 1474) from William Hoppes.

(A) Not acquired by purchase

(B) *c.* £2

(C) Not acquired by purchase

See above, Ch. 3.

8   *Brampton, Suffolk* (1475) from Thomas Duke, esquire.

(A) 400 m

(B) £17

(C) 15.7

9   *'Esthall', 'Stannowall', and 'Feltons' in Litcham* (1475) from Sir Edward Woodhouse.

(A) £400

(B) £22

(C) 18.2

Possibly bought as part of the agreement for the marriage of Thomas Woodhouse and Thomasine Townshend, since Roger I settled the reversion on the couple in 1488.

10   *'Lyngs' in Whissonsett* (pre-1478) from Joan Lyng, widow.

(A) £38 (?)

(B) ?

(C) ?

11   *'Halles' in Helhoughton* (1478) from the daughters and co-heirs of Thomas Halle, esquire.

(A) £104

(B) £6

(C) 17.3

---

6 R58, RT I memo-book, fos. 7, 12ʳ.

7 Ibid., fo. 7ʳ; PRO, C1/51/127, 131.

8 R58, RT I memo-book, fos. 7ʳ, 10ʳ.

9 Ibid., fos. 7ʳ, 12ʳ; *CCR* (1468-76), no. 1,485; (1476-85), no. 154; R49, Townshend cartulary, fos. 41-2.

10 R58, RT I memo-book, fos. 7ʳ, 10ᵛ; NRO, Townshend MS 11,991 35 B3; *CCR* (1476-85), no. 297; R12, 'HELHOUGHTON Temp. EDW. IV', file of 4 docs., 1477-9; R49, Townshend cartulary, fo. 40ʳ; R28, 'RAYNHAM EDW. IV to HENRY VII', indenture of 5 Apr. 1480; R13, 1472/3-1483/4 Helhoughton accounts, m. 10d.

11 R49, Townshend cartulary, fos. 2, 4-5, 7-8; R58, RT I memo-book, fos. 7ʳ, 12ʳ.

Halle's daughters and co-heirs were: Cecily, wife of Henry Argentenn of Hemingford Abbot, Hunts.; Elizabeth, wife of Richard Olyver of London, 'sherman'; and Margaret, apparently unmarried. £12 of the purchase-price went to Reginald Ashfield of Hunston, Suffolk, a former trustee of Thomas Halle with an interest in an attached messuage called 'Morehous'. Roger was also obliged to pay Halle's widow an annuity of 40s. from the issues of the manor.

[12] *'Reppes' in Little Ryburgh; 'Paveleys' in Stibbard; a manor in Guist* (1478/80) from George Neville, Lord Burgavenny, and his wife Margaret.

(A) 400 m

(B) £17

(C) 15.7

[13] *'George of Wightones' in Wighton* (c. 1480) from John Gygges of Wighton.

(A) 100 m

(B) 5 m

(C) 20.0

[14] *Sharpenhoe, Bedfordshire* (1485) from William Tendale, esquire.

(A) £300

(B) £16

(C) 18.8

Later exchanged with John Huddlestone (see nos. 25, 42).

[15] *Moiety of 'Staples' in Helhoughton* (1487/8) from William Dynne, esquire.

(A) 80 m

(B) £3. 18s. 2d.

(C) 13.6

Roger II acquired the other moiety in 1541 (see no. 38).

[16] *Barmer* (1489) from Thomas Gygges of Heacham.

(A) £200

(B) £12

(C) 16.7

[17] *'Corbettes' in Necton and 'Byllettes' in Gayton* (1489) from the executors of Simon Blake.

(A) 100 m

(B) £6. 6s. 8d.

(C) 10.5

---

[12] R58, RT I memo-book, fos. 8ʳ, 11ʳ.
[13] Ibid., fos. 8ʳ, 12ʳ.
[14] Ibid., fos. 8ʳ, 12ʳ; R60, paper valuing properties to be exchanged; *HP*, ii. 401-2.
[15] R58, RT I memo-book, fos. 8ʳ, 10ᵛ; R49, Townshend cartulary, fos. 44-5; R12, 'HELHOUGHTON Temp. HEN. VII', deed of 6 Feb. 1488.
[16] R49, Townshend cartulary, fo. 40; R58, RT I memo-book, fo. 10ᵛ.
[17] Ibid., fos. 8ʳ, 11ʳ; NRO, NCC 20-2 Typpes.

Blake directed his executors to give Roger I first option of purchase.
[18] *'Scales'* in South Raynham (1490) from Sir William Tendale.
(A) ?
(B) *c.* £18
(C) ?
[19] *'Bygottes'* in West Tofts (1490) from John Wake, esquire, executor of Thomas Dayrell.
(A) £100
(B) £8
(C) 12.5
[20] *'Fynchams'* in Weasenham (1496) from William and Robert Fyncham.
(A) 100 m
(B) £3. 6s. 8d.
(C) 20.0
William and Robert were sons of Edmund Fyncham of Rougham by his second marriage. 'Fynchams' was a very minor property which William Curteys of Necton, a local public notary, bought on Eleanor Townshend's behalf.
[21] *'Shernburnes'* in Raynham (1510) from Henry Shernburne, esquire.
(A) £20
(B) 20s.
(C) 20.0
[22] *'Shernburnes'* in Stanhoe (1510) from Henry Shernburne, esquire.
(A) £24
(B) 31s. 8d.
(C) 15.2
[23] *'Southall'* in Guist (1518) from Robert Drury, gent.
(A) £94
(B) £7. 10s. 3d.
(C) 12.5
Robert was a member of a lesser branch of a prominent East Anglian family. Later, in 1533, Roger II had to pay William, Robert's brother, £53. 6s. 8d. to secure his title to the manor.

---

[18] R49, Townshend cartulary, fos. 42–3; R58, RT I memo-book, fo. 10ᵛ.
[19] Ibid., fos. 8ʳ, 11ʳ.
[20] Carthew, *Launditch,* i. 227; NRO, NCC 228 Jekkys; R58, 'Raynham Deeds 1496-1599', deed of 28 Oct. 1496; R31, RT II estate book, fo. 30ᵛ. For Curteys, who seems to have served the Townshends, see G. A. Carthew, *A History of the Parishes of West and East Bradenham, with those of Necton and Holme Hale* (Norwich, 1883), 173-4; R58, RT II memo-book, fos. 3ʳ, 4ᵛ.
[21] R31, RT II estate book, fos. 14ᵛ, 27ᵛ; PRO, CP25/2/28/188, no. 10.
[22] As for n. 21.
[23] R31, RT II estate book, fos. 28ʳ, 32ʳ, 35ʳ; PRO, WARD7/6/68.

[24] *'Leches' in Cawston* (1519) from John Legge.

(A) £200

(B) £16. 13*s*. 4*d*.

(C) 12.0

Roger II originally settled the reversion of this manor on his younger son Thomas, but it was sold in 1548 to Sir James Boleyn.

[25] *'Hatchwood' in March, Cambridgeshire* (1520) from Anthony Hansard, esquire.

(A) £460

(B) £23

(C) 20.0

Later exchanged with John Huddlestone (see nos. 14, 42).

[26] *'Hindringhams' in Hindringham* (1522/3) from Gregory Davy, gent.

(A) £150

(B) £7. 10*s*.

(C) 20.0

[27] *'Cursons' in Barwick* (1524) from Thomas Thursby, esquire.

(A) £100

(B) £5

(C) 20.0

[28] *'Pakenhams' and 'Snoryng Hall' in Dersingham* (1524/5) from Thomas Thursby, esquire.

(A) £200

(B) £10

(C) 20.0

[29] *'Scottes' and 'Paveleys' in Testerton* (1525) from the executors of Robert Wolvy.

(A) £113. 6*s*. 8*d*.

(B) ?

(C) ?

A reversion which was to vest ten years after Wolvy's death in 1525.

[30] *'Dunnels' in Burnham Sutton* (1526) from Sir Henry Sacheverell.

(A) 100 m

(B) *c*. £3

[24] PRO, E326/7259, 7261, 7064, 7262; NRO, Townshend 193 MS 1,612 1 C7, fo. 18[r]; PRO, E326/7263, 6455, 7265.

[25] R(Attic), 'Cambridgeshire deeds & estate papers', indenture of 12 Nov. 1520; R31, RT II estate book, fo. 28[v]; R60, paper cited in n. 14, above.

[26] R31, RT II estate book, fo. 30[r].

[27] R(Attic), 'Deeds—Stanhoe & Barwick', indenture of 25 Sept. 1524; R31, RT II estate book, fo. 30[r].

[28] Ibid., fos. 30[r], 36[v].

[29] Ibid., fo. 30[r]; PRO, PROB11/21, fo. 240.

[30] R31, RT II estate book, fo. 31[v]; *CIPM, Henry VII*, vol. i, no. 423; *LP*, vol. i,

(C) 22.2

A reversion. Sacheverell, a Derbyshire gentleman and follower of the Talbot earls of Shrewsbury, succeeded to the manor through his mother, Joan, daughter and heir of Henry Statham.

[31] *'Wrightes'* in *Testerton* (*c.* 1526) from William Pratt and his wife Beatrice.

(A) £53. 6s. 8d.

(B) ?

(C) ?

[32] *'Sigars' in Oxwick* (? 1526/7) from Sir John Heydon.

(A) £250

(B) ?

(C) ?

[33] *'Dengaynes' in Teversham and Stow-Quy, Cambridgeshire* (1537) from Thomas Woodhouse of Waxham.

(A) ?

(B) ?

(C) ?

These two manors were exchanged in 1538 with Gonville Hall, Cambridge, for Pattesley.

[34] *Pattesley* (1538) from the Master and Fellows of Gonville Hall.

(A) Not acquired by purchase

(B) ?

(C) Not acquired by purchase

As Pattesley was worth less than the Cambridgeshire manors he exchanged for it, Roger II also received £176 in cash.

[35] *'Nowers' in Hindringham* (1538/9) from Thomas Asteley, esquire.

(A) £90

(B) £4. 6s.

(C) 21.0

[36] *'Nothes' and a third part of 'Burfeld Hall' in Wymondham* (1538/9) from Thomas Blake and his wife Margaret.

no. 1,948 (40); xi, no. 562; A. Cameron, 'Complaint and Reform in Henry VII's Reign: The Origins of the Statute of 3 Henry VII, c. 2?', *BIHR* 51 (1978), 83; Blomefield, x. 419; *The Visitation of Nottinghamshire*, ed. G. D. Squibb, Harleian Soc., NS 5 (1986), 11–13.

[31] R31, RT II estate book, fo. 31[r].

[32] Ibid., fo. 31[v].

[33] PRO, CP25/2/4/20, no. 49; NRO, Townshend 147 MS 1,566 1 C3; Gonville and Caius College MS XVIII. 4.

[34] R31, RT II estate book, fo. 32[r]; R57, RT II 'declaration', fo. 14[v]; NRO, Townshend 147 MS 1,566 1 C3; Gonville and Caius MS XVIII. 4.

[35] R31, RT II estate book, fo. 32[r]; R57, RT II 'declaration', fo. 16[r].

[36] R31, RT II estate book, fo. 32[r]; NRO, Townshend 163 MS 1,582 1 D4, fos. 12[v], 13[r], 58[r]; R57, RT II 'declaration', fo. 9[v].

(A) 100 m

(B) ?

(C) ?

[37] *'Coldham Hall' in Hindringham* (1541) from Sir William Fermor.

(A) £247

(B) £14. 6s.

(C) 17.3

Fermor had no children of his own and was succeeded by his nephew Thomas. He sold a moiety of 'Staples' in Helhoughton to Roger II at the same time.

[38] *Moiety of 'Staples' in Helhoughton* (1541) from Sir William Fermor.

(A) 100 m

(B) £3. 6s. 8d.

(C) 20.0

Fermor had acquired this moiety earlier in the same year for 100 marks from William Gaskyn of St Albans, yeoman, who held it in the right of his wife.

[39] *Purparty of Scarning Hall in Scarning* (1541/2) from William Sharington, esquire.

(A) £120

(B) £6. 3s. 8d.

(C) 19.4

Sharington probably sold this outlying piece of his property because he invested heavily in land in his native Wiltshire and the West Country in the 1540s. A decade earlier he had sold his Norfolk manor of Craneworth to Sir Richard Southwell.

[40] *Manor and rectory in Helhoughton; a manor in Little Ryburgh; a manor and rectory in Guist; a manor and rectory in Barwick; a rectory in Whitwell* (1543) from the Crown.

(A) £436. 10s. $\frac{1}{4}d$.

(B) £20. 15s. $3\frac{1}{4}d$.

(C) 21.0

The property in Helhoughton and Little Ryburgh formerly belonged to the priory of Horsham St Faith; that in Guist to the abbey of Waltham Holy Cross, Essex; that in Barwick to Buckenham Priory; and Whitwell to Pentney Priory. The price was the annual value, at 21 years' purchase, with 13s. 4d.

---

[37] R31, RT II estate book, fo. 32^r; R57, RT II 'declaration', fo. 16^r; PRO, WARD7/6/68; PRO, CP25/2/30/208, no. 47a; Blomefield, vii. 56; R(Attic), 'Miscellaneous, unidentified & fragmentary', copy of will of Sir William Fermor, 4 Aug. 1557.

[38] R31, RT II estate book, fo. 32^v; R57, RT II 'declaration', fo. 14^v; PRO, CP25/2/30/208, no. 47a; R12, 'HELHOUGHTON Temp. HEN. VIII', indenture of 16 June 1541.

[39] R31, RT II estate book, fo. 32^r; R57, RT II 'declaration', fo. 15^v; *HP*, iii. 302–3; PRO, CP25/2/29/195, no. 31.

[40] R41, Augmentations Office valor, 1543; *LP*, vol. xviii, pt. ii, no. 529 (3, 6).

added for woods. Whitwell rectory was acquired on behalf of Robert Coke and was not retained.

[41] *Kempstone* (1543) from the duke of Norfolk.

(A) £381

(B) £19

(C) 20.0

Formerly the property of Castleacre Priory.

[42] *(i) 'Ingoldisthorpes' in East Raynham; (ii) 'Ingoldisthorpes' in Wimbotsham; (iii) purparty of 'Ingoldisthorpes' in Snettisham and Ingoldisthorpe* (1543) from John Huddlestone, esquire.

(A) Not acquired by purchase

(B) *c.* £13 (i); £9 (ii); £10 (iii)

(C) Not acquired by purchase

Received in exchange from John Huddlestone of Sawston, Cambridgeshire, esquire, in return for 'Hatchwood' and Sharpenhoe (see nos. 14, 25).

[43] *Kipton* (1544) from the duchess of Richmond, John Williams, and Thomas Broke.

(A) £46. 11*s.*

(B) 36*s.*

(C) 25.9

Formerly owned by West Acre Priory, it was granted to the duchess for life on 15 March 1539. Roger II had farmed the manor's foldcourse since pre-Dissolution days. Broke and Williams were two Londoners who had paid the Crown for the reversion of the manor after the duchess died.

[44] *Friars' House in Walsingham* (1545/6) from John Eyre.

(A) £80

(B) £3

(C) 26.7

By 1541 Roger II was farming the site of the former Franciscan friary from the Crown for 42*s.* p.a. Eyre, a local receiver of the Augmentations, bought it in early 1545.

[45] *'Burghwood' in Mileham* (1547) from Sir Henry Capel.

(A) £220

---

[41] R31, RT II estate book, fo. 32ᵛ; PRO, WARD7/6/68.

[42] R60, paper (see nn. 14 and 25, above); R28, 'RAYNHAM HENRY VIII-P & M', letters patent of 24 Apr. 1543 (*LP*, vol. xix, pt. i, no. 476 (3)).

[43] R31, RT II estate book, fo. 32ᵛ; R57, RT II 'declaration', fo. 14ʳ; AO valor (see above, n. 40); *LP*, vol. xix, pt. ii, no. 527 (42); NRO, B-L VII b(5) (*LP*, vol. xix, pt. ii, no. 690).

[44] R31, RT II estate book, fo. 32ᵛ; *Valor Ecclesiasticus*, iii. 388; A. R. Martin, 'The Greyfriars of Walsingham', *NA* 25 (1935), 235–6, 267–8; *LP*, vol. xx, pt. i, no. 282 (37).

[45] R31, RT II estate book, fo. 32ᵛ; R57, RT II 'declaration', fo. 16ʳ; PRO, CP25/2/61/478, no. 31, CP25/2/75/635, no. 52.

(B) £11. 3s.
(C) 19.7
Subsequently sold by George Townshend to Robert Coke in 1555.

(b) Amy Townshend's Inheritance

[46] *Akenham, Suffolk* (worth *c.* £33 p.a.).
[47] *Moiety of Hasketon, Suffolk* (£8).
[48] *Salle, Norfolk* (*c.* £35).
By the mid-sixteenth century these properties were valued at £80. 13s. 2d. p.a.

(c) Robert Townshend's Manors

[49] *Guist Regis or Luton Fee in Guist*: worth *c.* £5 p.a., this manor was formerly owned by Sir Richard Southwell. Southwell sold it to the Crown and Robert bought it from the king in 1544.

[50] *'Foxleys' in Guist, and 'Swantons' in Fouldsham and Twyford*: seised on Robert and his wife Alice as part of her marriage portion by her father, Robert Poppy, *c.* 1516. Worth at least £18 p.a.

[51] *Binham Priory* (lease): Robert acquired the lease from the Crown on 5 March 1539 for twenty-one years, despite strong competition from Sir Christopher Jenney.

[52] *Ludlow Priory, Shropshire* (lease): dissolved in 1538, the priory was leased to Robert by the Crown for twenty-one years on 12 December 1547.

---

[46] R55, RT II valors, fos. 2ᵛ, 16ᵛ; R31, RT II estate book, fos. 2ᵛ, 3ʳ, 18, 25, 26ᵛ, 35; R57, RT II 'declaration', fo. 13ᵛ.
[47] As for n. 46.
[48] Ibid.
[49] PRO, C142/108/69; *LP*, vol. xix, pt. ii, nos. 20, 586.
[50] PRO, C142/108/69.
[51] *LP*, vol. xiv, pt. i, nos. 1,355 (p. 603), 694; vol. xiv, pt. ii, no. 264 (18); Addenda, no. 1,347.
[52] *LP*, vol. xiii, pt. ii, no. 67; PRO, E150/873/4.

APPENDIX 7. SETTLEMENTS OF ROGER II

(a) Heirs

(1) John Townshend II (d. 1540)

By an indenture of 31 October 1511[1] Roger II agreed to enfeoff his trustees of:

(i) Sharpenhoe (worth £16) and 'Crispin's' in Happisburgh (£8), from which they were to provide John and his wife Eleanor (Heydon) £20 p.a. until John reached the age of 20. Thereafter the trustees were to hold the same, together with Brampton, Suffolk (£17), to the use of the couple for life in survivorship, remainder to John's male heirs;

(ii) 'Beaufoes' in South Creake (£11), 'Nogeons' in Bale (£2), 'Paveleys' and 'Reppes' in Stibbard and Little Ryburgh (£17), and 'Shernburnes' in Stanhoe (31s. 8d.), to hold to the use of Roger II for life, remainder to John and Eleanor for life in survivorship, remainder to John's male heirs;

(iii) All the remaining Townshend properties, to hold to the use of Roger II and his wife for life in survivorship, remainder to John and his heirs general. Eleanor's jointure, both immediate and future, was therefore worth c. £70 p.a. and represented about one-quarter of the Townshend estate. When Sharpenhoe and Happisburgh were alienated (in 1543 and 1550) Eleanor was compensated with a life interest in a moiety of Scarning Hall and various lands in Whissonsett, Barwick, Stanhoe, and North Creake (for Sharpenhoe), and a life annuity of £7. 6s. $8\frac{1}{2}d$. from the issues of the other moiety of Scarning Hall (for Happisburgh).[2]

(2) Richard Townshend (d. 1551)

By an indenture of 3 July 1537[3] Roger II and Richard's father John agreed to enfeoff their trustees of:

(i) 'Corbettes' in Necton, 'Byllettes' in Gayton, and lands in surrounding townships (£10. 0s. $10\frac{3}{4}d$), to hold to the use of Richard and his wife Katherine (Browne) for life in survivorship, remainder to Richard's male heirs;

(ii) 'Pakenhams' and 'Snorynghall' in Dersingham, 'George of Wightones'

---

[1] R(Attic), 'MARRIAGE SETTLEMENTS, PAPERS, etc.', packet: 'Marriage Settlement re John Townshend & Eleanor Heydon 1511/1516'.

[2] PRO, WARD7/6/68; R57, RT II 'declaration', fos. 7^v, 18^r.

[3] R(Attic), 'MARRIAGE SETTLEMENTS, PAPERS, etc.', indenture of 3 July 1537.

in Wighton, and lands in surrounding parishes (£16. 4s. 7¾ d.), to hold to
the use of Roger II until Richard reached the age of 21 (and until Richard
returned a gift of 560 sheep which he had earlier received from Roger), and
thereafter to the use of Richard and Katherine for life in survivorship,
remainder to Richard's heirs male.[4] Richard and his wife were also given a
future interest in other Townshend properties in Norfolk and Suffolk worth
£75 p.a., but this was to vest only after the death of Roger II. Katherine's jointure, both immediate and future, was therefore worth some £100 p.a.

The above settlements demonstrate Roger II's concern for the integrity of his
estate. John and Eleanor were provided with only three isolated properties
during his lifetime, while the manors in Dersingham, Gayton, Necton, and
Wighton given to Richard and his wife were minor properties situated on the
fringes of the estate in Norfolk (see map in Ch. 4).

(b) Younger Sons

(1) Robert Townshend[5]
To receive after Roger II's death:
The manors of 'Southall' in Guist (worth £7. 15s. 6d. yearly),[6] 'Coldham
Hall' in Hindringham (£14. 6s.), and a manor and rectory in Guist formerly
of the abbey of Waltham Holy Cross, Essex (£5. 16s. 6d.) Total: £27. 18s.

(2) George Townshend[7]
His father settled on him and his wife, Alice Thurston, the manors of 'Hindringhams' (£20) and 'Nowers' (£4. 6s.) in Hindringham in about 1536, when
they married. Roger however reserved himself a life annuity of £14 p.a. from
these properties. George was also to receive, after his father's death, the
manors of 'Burghwood' in Mileham (£11. 3s.), and 'Bygottes' in West Tofts
(£8). His wife was not given a jointure interest in these latter two manors.
Total: £43. 9s.

(3) Thomas Townshend[8]
To receive after Roger II's death:
The manors of Kempstone (£29), 'Wrightes', 'Scottes', and 'Paveleys' in
Testerton (£10. 16s. 9d.), and lands in Hardwick[9] (£19. 13s.) Total: £59. 9s.
9d.

---

[4] Richard farmed sheep at Akenham: NRO, NCC 30 Lyncolne.
[5] R57, RT II 'declaration', fo. 16ʳ.
[6] This and the following bracketed sums in section (b) are all mid-16th-cent. values.
[7] R57, RT II 'declaration', fos. 10ʳ, 16ʳ.
[8] Ibid., fo. 16ʳ.
[9] Assigned to Thomas's younger brother Giles for life, remainder to Thomas in fee
simple.

(4) *Giles Townshend*[10]
To receive after Roger II's death:
The former house of the Franciscans in Walsingham (66s. 8d.), lands in Hardwick[11] (£19. 13s.), and an annuity of 20 marks from the issues of 'Ingoldisthorpes' in Raynham and other lands in Norfolk (£13. 6s. 8d.) Total: £36. 6s. 4d.

(5) *John Townshend (grandson)*[12]
To receive after Roger II's death:
A purparty of the manor of 'Burfeld Hall' in Wymondham (74s. 8d.)

Roger II therefore alienated from the main line of the family lands worth £170. 17s. 9d. from an estate worth over £600 p.a. But 'Bygottes' in West Tofts was the only inherited manor which he alienated to a younger son and all the others were purchased. He was more generous than some sixteenth-century landowners in providing for his younger sons,[13] but then he could afford to be. Robert and Giles might at first sight appear not to have been very well provided for, but Robert was a self-made man in his father's lifetime and the latter, who had no dependants, must have enjoyed a reasonable income from his relatively successful legal career. Giles's will shows no sign of penury: he owed no debts and left at least £130 in cash or goods by way of bequests, excluding several gifts which it is impossible to value.[14] Lack of means prevented some younger sons from marrying, but Giles's reason for not doing so cannot have been because he was a penniless cadet.[15]

[10] Ibid., fos. 10^r, 16^v.
[11] See n. 9 above.
[12] Ibid., fo. 16^v. He was the younger son of John Townshend, Roger II's eldest son.
[13] e.g. Euseby Isham of Lamport, Northamptonshire, made no permanent alienations of real property to his younger sons: Finch, *Northamptonshire Families*, 23-4.
[14] NRO, B-L, VII b(1).
[15] Cf. J. Thirsk, 'Younger Sons in the Seventeenth Century', in ead., *Rural Economy of England* (London, 1984), 340-1.

APPENDIX 8. NORFOLK LANDOWNERS, MID-1520s

Knight	Value of lands (p.a.)
Roger Townshend	£440[1]
John Heydon	£400
William Paston	£300
Thomas Bedingfield	£300
Philip Calthorpe[2]	£200
John Shelton	£200
Robert Brandon	£200
Edward Knyvet	£180
Thomas Woodhouse	£150
William Pennington	£120
John Audeley	£100
Thomas Blennerhasset	£100
Edmund Bedingfield	£100
John Cressener	£80
Thomas Lovell	£66. 13s. 4d.
Christopher Heydon	£40
James Boleyn	£40
Edward Boleyn	£40
Source: PRO, subsidy rolls (E179).	(Average = £170)

[1] Probably nearer £400 in lands alone because this assessment included his fees.
[2] As Princess Mary's chamberlain the only non-resident (E179/69/3a, 3).

APPENDIX 9. THE TOWNSHEND FLOCKS[1]

Date (Michaelmas)	Number of sheep[2]	Number of flocks
1474	?	8
1475	6,477	10
1476	?	?
1477	6,033	13
1478	7,236	11
1479	7,911	11
1480	8,374	11
1481	7,039 (7,375)	10
1482	6,477	10
1483	6,025	11
1484	?	?
1485	6,678	10
1486	6,475 (6,349)	7
1487	7,286	?
1488	?	?
1489	9,035 (9,335)	9
1490	12,091 (11,627)	14
1491	?	?
1492	10,168	11
1493	?	?
1494	11,224	15
1495	10,342	14
1496	9,168	10
1497	9,366	10
1498	9,447	11
1499	8,680	10
1500	?	?
1501	4,062	4

[1] Sources: R58, Raynham account roll, m. 4d (1473/4); NRO, B-L V, no. ×. 32 (1474/5); R50 (1477/8, 1498/9); R24 (1478/9); NRO, Townshend 56 MS 1,475 1F (1479/80–1482/3, 1485/6, 1489/90); R55 (1493/4–1497/8); NRO, B-L II e (1501/2–1517/18 (excluding 1516/17)); R60 (1516/17); R31, RT II estate book, fo. 42ʳ (1523/4); R1, *Liber pro ovibus*, fo. 10ʳ (1534); LSE, R(SR) 1,032, 88,918 (1544/5–1547/8).

[2] The figures in brackets are corrected totals; the accounts have their fair share of discrepancies.

1502	4,515	6
1503	5,238 (5,260)	6
1504	6,206 (*c.* 6,140)	10
1505	?	?
1506	?	?
1507	8,418	9
1508	10,626 (10,617)	13
1509	17,105 (17,104)	20
1510	17,674 (17,647)	20
1511	16,338	18
1512	15,704	16
1513	15,519	20
1514	16,962	20
1515	16,735	20
1516	18,468	26
1517	16,795	22
1518	16,967	20

[1518/19–1543/4: no accounts survive]

1523	13,564	?
1524	14,572	?
1534	10,443	13
1544	3,120	4
1545	3,960	4
1546	3,960	4
1547	3,960	4
1548	4,200	5

APPENDIX 10. TOWNSHEND SHEEP SALES AND PURCHASES[1]

E = Bailiff or other estate officer
H = Household servant or dependant
P = Townshend presentee
R = Relative
S = Sheep-reeve or shepherd
T = Tenant or farmer
1 = single purchase
< 5 = more than 1 but under 5 known purchases
< 10 = more than 5 but under 10, etc.

(a) Sales

(i) LATE FIFTEENTH CENTURY

Purchaser	*Origin*	*Approx. frequency of purchase*
Abbot of Wymondham	Wymondham	1
Thomas Alpe	Reepham	< 5
Clement Anger (T)	Weasenham	< 15
Robert Baker	Bilney	1
John Bakone	?	1
William Barsham	? Toftrees	1
William Becham	Ringland	1
Thomas Becke	Hoddesdon, Herts.	1
Thomas Beverle	?	1
Stephen Bilney (?T)	? West Tofts	1
Robert Blogge	?	1
Reginald Blome	Middleton	< 5
Gilbert 'Bocher'	Walsingham	< 5
John 'Bocher'	Oxborough	1
John 'Bocher'	Walsingham	< 5
Robert Bolton (T)	Middleton	< 5

[1] The number of tenants, employees, and other connections of the Townshends identified in these lists is based on the evidence that is available and should therefore be regarded as a minimum.

Purchaser	*Origin*	*Approx. frequency of purchase*
John Brake	Fulmodestone	1
John Brandon	Foulsham	1
John Brecham	Sharrington	< 10
John Broun[2]	Norwich	1
Thomas Bullok	Dersingham	< 5
'Master' Castell (R)[3]	Raveningham	< 5
John Clyff, rector (H)	Raynham	1
Thomas Cobbe	?	1
Stephen Cobbes	? Brisley	1
Richard Codlyng	Yaxham	1
Robert Colles (?T)	Foulsham	1
Robert Cosener	Field Dalling	1
John Colte	?	1
Richard Couper	Marham	< 5
John Cressenell	?	1
William Curteys	Necton	< 5
John Davy, *carnifex*	Walsingham	< 5
Andrew Deane[4]	Mattishall	< 10
John Est	Brisley	< 5
John Everard (?T)	Gateley	1
Thomas Everard (?T)	Gateley	1
William Everard (?T)	Gateley	1
Richard Faldyate (E, T)	Bale	1
Richard Farewell (T)	Raynham	1
John Fisher (T)	Scarning	< 10
Richard Fisher (E, T)	Litcham	1
Thomas Galle	Snetterton	< 10
Edmund Gayton, gent. (T)	Gayton	1
Robert Godfrey, 'bocher'	Walsingham	1
John Gronte (T)	Raynham	1
Guild of Dunton	Dunton	< 5
Guild of St John Baptist	South Raynham	1
Symond Harlestone[5]	Mattishall	< 15
John Harpor	Thorpland	1
Thomas Herward (T)	South Creake	< 10
John Hewer, 'bocher'	Oxborough	< 10
John Hewer jnr.	? Oxborough	< 10

[2] A Norwich draper: BL, Add. MS 41,139, fo. 19[r].
[3] Probably Leonard Castell, esquire.
[4] Pelterer: see Ch. 5, 2 above.
[5] 'Wollechapman'; sued for debt by Eleanor Townshend: PRO, CP40/952, rot. 86.

Purchaser	Origin	Approx. frequency of purchase
William Hoker	?	1
William Holle	Burnham Norton	< 5
John atte Hoo, 'bocher' (T)	Brisley	1
William Hykkes	?	< 10
Robert Hynton (T)	Silsoe, Beds.	< 10
Hugh Jagge	Norwich	1
John, household cook (H)	Raynham	1
John Kenstone	Congham	< 5
Thomas Kerre (S)	Wood Norton	1
John Kykkes	?	1
John Kyppyng	Gooderstone	1
Robert Lely (T)	Helhoughton	< 5
Thomas Lessor	Watton	< 10
John Leveryche	Thuxton	1
Robert Mannyng, 'bocher'	Lynn	1
William Mannyng	?	< 5
William Marham (S)	? Raynham	1
Thomas Mathew	Edgefield	1
Symond atte Mere	Swaffham	< 5
Richard Myott (T)	Hardwick	< 5
John Newgate	Appleton	1
William Newgate	Appleton	1
Robert Newporte (E, T)	Hardwick	1
John Parson (S)	Stibbard	1
Robert Pery[6]	Breccles	< 25
Prior of Coxford	Coxford	< 5
Richard Prowberd	Congham	1
John Prynce, 'bocher'	Fakenham	< 10
John Purveys (H)	Raynham	1
John Robynson	Hindolveston	1
John Rowse	Lexham	1
John Scony (S)	Cawston	< 5
John Sheryngham	Guestwick	< 5
John Shymyng, rector (T)	Burnham Norton	1
Robert Smith (T)	Raynham	1
Thomas Smith (T)	Raynham	1
John Snellyng, 'bocher'	East Dereham	< 10
John Stalworthy jnr. (S, T)	Dunton	< 5
Stephen atte Style	Bintree	1
John Swyfte	Oxborough	1

[6] 'Wolman': PRO, CP40/950, rot. 499.

Purchaser	Origin	Approx. frequency of purchase
—— Tomstone	Thetford	1
George Watson	Ashill	< 5
John West	Brisley	< 5
Thomas Whitlak (T)	Raynham	1
Ralph Wite (T)	Stibbard	1
John Withe and associates	?	1
Richard Wright	Gooderstone	1
Robert Wright	East Rudham	< 5
Thomas Yar[. . .]	?	1

(ii) FIRST TWO DECADES OF THE SIXTEENTH CENTURY

Purchaser	Origin	Approx. frequency of purchase
Peter Adams (H)	Raynham	1
John Aggs (T)	Cawston	1
Edmund Amyson	? Burnham Westgate	< 5
John Amyson, 'bocher'	Burnham Westgate	< 15
Clement Anger (T)	Weasenham	over 50
Laurence Avery	?	< 5
John Baker	Hillington	1
Edmund Barker	? Tatterford	1
William Barker (T)	South Creake	< 5
Robert Baxster (?T)	Stanhoe	1
Robert Benehale	?	1
John Blakeney, esq. (R)	Honingham	< 10
'Bocher' of Creake	Creake	< 5
'Bocher' of Ryburgh	Ryburgh	1
'Bocher' of Yarmouth	Great Yarmouth	1
James 'Bocher'	South Creake	< 5
John 'Bocher'	Cley next the Sea	1
Reginald 'Bocher'	?	1
Thomas 'Bocher'	?	1
William Boole (T)	Raynham	1
Robert Boston	Burnham	1
John Brandon	Foulsham	1
Henry Brinkley[7]	?	< 40
John Broun (?H)	? Raynham	1
Robert Broun	?	< 5
Andrew Brygges	Wells next the Sea	1

---

[7] Pelterer: see ref., note 4 above.

Purchaser	Origin	Approx. frequency of purchase
Henry Bryghteve	? Forncet	< 15
Robert Bryghteve	Forncet	< 5
John Burgeys (T)	Raynham	< 5
A *carnifex*	Bedfordshire	< 5
Edward Chamberlain, esq.	Barnham Broom	1
William Chylderhouse	?	< 5
John Clerk	'Wikelsbery'	1
Sir William Clopton	Long Melford, Suffolk	1
Robert Cobolde	?	1
Edmund Colles (T)	Stibbard	< 5
Robert Colles (?T)	Foulsham	< 5
William Colles	Bintree	1
Richard Constabylle	Great Cressingham	< 5
Thomas Couper (S, T)	Stanhoe	1
John Davy, *carnifex*	Walsingham	< 5
Andrew Deane[8]	Mattishall	< 5
—— Denys	Denver	1
Gregory Denys (S)	North Creake	1
John Denys	? Sheringham	1
William Denys (E)	Akenham, Suffolk	< 20
Robert Dey	East Rudham	1
John Doo (?T)	? Raynham/ South Creake	1
Thomas Dowe	Saham Toney	< 5
Robert Downyng	? Scoulton	< 5
John Dykman	?	1
Thomas Ely (S)	Hempton	< 5
Thomas Everard (?T)	Gateley	1
Farmers at Egmere (T)	Egmere	1
John Faukener (T)	Helhoughton	1
Edmund Ferror	Gressenhall	1
John Fisher (T)	Scarning	< 10
Reginald Fraunceys, 'bocher'	?	< 5
John Funteyn	Cawston	< 5
William Funteyn	Cawston	< 5
'Geyton's wife'	? Gayton	1
William Gladdyn, 'bocher'	South Creake	1
Robert Godfrey, rector (P)	Salle	1

---

[8] Pelterer: see ref. note 4 above.

Purchaser	Origin	Approx. frequency of purchase
Thomas Grandon, rector (P)	Stibbard	< 5
Nicholas Grene (T)	Foulsham	< 5
Richard Grene	Walsingham	< 25
Thomas Grene (T)	South Creake	1
William Grene	? Stiffkey	1
Robert Grewe, 'bocher'[9]	Norwich	< 5
Guild of All Saints	Stanhoe	< 5
Guild of B. V. Mary	East Raynham	< 10
Guild of B. V. Mary	South Creake	< 5
Guild of Corpus Christi	South Raynham	< 5
Guild of the Crucifixion	South Creake	1
Guild of the Holy Cross	South Creake	< 5
Guild of the Holy Trinity	Beeston next Mileham	1
Guild of the Holy Trinity	Helhoughton	< 5
Guild at Oxwick	Oxwick	1
Guild of the Resurrection	West Raynham	1
Guild of St John	East Raynham	1
Guild of St John the Baptist	South Raynham	1
Guild of St Martin	South Raynham	1
Guild of St Thomas	Toftrees	< 5
Thomas Gygges (E, R)	? Heacham	1
Symond Harlestone	Mattishall	1
John Haryson	?	< 5
Thomas Herward (T)	Barmer/South Creake	1
Robert Heygrene (?T)	? Shereford	1
John Hoker, *carnifex*	Walsingham	< 5
William Hoker, 'bocher'	Walsingham	< 5
Richard Hooke (E)	? Raynham	1
Christopher Howes	?	< 10
John Howes, 'bocher'	Brisley	< 5
Robert Hynton (T)	Silsoe, Beds.	1
Christopher Jenney, gent.[10]	Great Cressingham	1
John Jonson, 'bocher'	Lynn	1
John Ladill	?	1

---

[9] Agisted sheep with the Townshend flock at North Elmham: NRO, B-L II e, 1501/2–1517/18 sheep accounts, fo. 120ᵛ.

[10] Bought the whole of the Townshends' Great Cressingham flock of 660 sheep in 1514/15: ibid., fo. 268ᵛ.

Purchaser	Origin	Approx. frequency of purchase
Geoffrey Lammyng (S)	Kettlestone	1
John Lawse (?T)	Stibbard	< 5
Stacy Lawse	?	< 5
Thomas Lawse	Newton[11]	< 5
John Lebe	?	1
John Lecke	? Tittleshall	1
John Lemman (T)	Weasenham	1
Thomas Lewman, 'bocher'	Lynn	1
John Lord (?T)	Whissonsett	1
Robert Maddy (?T)	? Raynham	1
'Man of Beeston'	Beeston next Mileham	1
'Man of Helhoughton'	Helhoughton	1
'Man of Thornham'	Thornham	1
'Dr Manfelde'[12]	Norwich	< 10
John Manser (T)	North Creake	< 5
Richard Manser (T)	North Creake	1
John Markaunt (?T)	Wighton	1
Nicholas Markaunt	? Wighton	1
William Mayde (T)	Raynham	1
'Merchant' of Northants.	Northamptonshire	1
Two 'men of Netesyerd'	Neatishead	1
John Myller	Thornham	1
Thomas Myller	?	1
Thomas Nicolson	Docking	1
William Oxwick	?	< 10
John Pedder	Syderstone	1
John Pepys (T)	South Creake	< 30
Thomas Perse (T)	Stibbard	< 5
James Pery	? Breccles	< 20
Thomas Plane	Field Dalling	< 5
John Plum (E)[13]	? Hilborough	1
Thomas Poynter	?	1
John Purveys (H)	Raynham	< 5
—— Pye	?	< 5

[11] Newton by Castle Acre.

[12] Andrew Manfelde, physician of Norwich and Hainford, gent., graduate of Cambridge and sheep-farmer at Helhoughton and North Creake by the late 1530s: *LP*, vol. v, no. 186; PRO, E179/151/337; NRO, NCC 263 Wilkins; Emden, *Biographical Register . . . Cambridge*, 387; R12, 'HELHOUGHTON Temp. HEN VIII', deed of 6 Sept. 1537.

[13] Townshend auditor at the turn of the century: NRO, B-L II e, 1501/2–1517/18 sheep accounts, fo. 11^r.

Purchaser	Origin	Approx. frequency of purchase
John Rawlyns (S, T)	East Beckham	1
Thomas Reve (S)	Stibbard/Guist	1
Oliver Reymes, gent.	Little Walsingham	< 10
John Richer	Hempton	1
William Roper	?	1
Richard Ryplyngham, gent.	Cawston	1
Robert Sabyn	Barwick	1
George Sakker	?	1
Thomas Salter	? Wotton	1
—— Sande	Lynn	1
John Selle (?T)	Toftrees	1
John Sheryngham	Guestwick	< 5
Thomas Sidney, gent.	Little Walsingham	< 5
John Skutte	Whissonsett	1
Walter Skygges, rector (P)	Brampton, Suffolk	< 10
Andrew Skylcorne	?	1
Thomas Skypponer (E)	Weasenham	< 10
John Smith (E)	Stanhoe/Wighton	< 10
Robert Smith (T)	Raynham	1
John Snellyng, 'bocher'	East Dereham	< 20
John Sooham (E)	Bale	< 5
'Mr Spelman'[14]	? Stowe Bedon	< 5
William Spelman, gent.	Stowe Bedon	< 5
Edmund Sterlyng, 'bocher'	Fakenham	1
Thomas Sybley (?T)	? South Creake	1
John Syre, *carnifex*	Walsingham	< 10
Thomas Themylthorpe	Swannington	< 5
John Thornham	?	1
Paul Trumpe (T)	Raynham	1
John Tuddenham	?	1
Richard Tylney (E)	'Bircham'[15]	< 5
Thomas Virley (T)	Raynham	< 5
George Walpole	? Walsingham	1
Thomas Walpole (E)	Walsingham	1
Thomas Warner (?T)	Raynham	1
Reginald Webster	? Weasenham	1

[14] William Spelman?
[15] Either Bircham Newton or one of the neighbouring parishes of Great Bircham and Bircham Tofts.

Purchaser	Origin	Approx. frequency of purchase
John Wode	?	< 5
Thomas Woderoffe (H)	Raynham	1
John Worcoppe (T)	Raynham	< 5
Mr Vincent Worcoppe (T)[16]	Raynham	1
William Wotton, esq.	North Tuddenham	< 5
'Mr Yelverton'[17]	Rougham	< 5

(iii) THE 1540s

Purchaser	Origin	Approx. frequency of purchase
Robert Baxster (?T)	Stanhoe	< 5
Robert Coke (S)	Mileham	1
Thomas Howse, 'bocher'	Norwich	< 10
John Fulburne	Mattishall	< 5
John Norton (?T) and associates	Newmarket, Cambridgeshire	< 5
—— Taylor	Cambridgeshire	1
?	Cambridgeshire	1

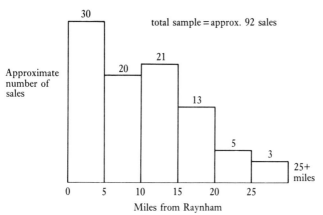

Appendix Fig. 1.   Sheep sales, late fifteenth century

---

[16] A local chaplain.
[17] William Yelverton, esquire.

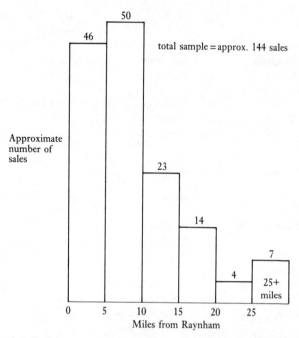

Appendix Fig. 2.   Sheep sales, first two decades of the sixteenth century

(b) Purchases[18]

(i) LATE FIFTEENTH CENTURY

Vendor	Origin	Approx. frequency of purchase
John Amyson, 'bocher'	Burnham Westgate	< 5
William 'Bocher'	?	1
Nicholas Clifton (T)	Toftrees	< 5
William Deryng (S)	Stibbard	1
John Dowse (S)	Bircham Newton	1
Robert Erle (S)	Stibbard	1
Thomas Faukener (E)	Helhoughton	< 5
Henry Fermor, gent.	East Barsham	< 5
Edmund Herberd (H)	Raynham	< 5
Richard Hooke (E)	? Raynham	1
Alan Lawse	Newton[19]	1

[18] Note: the 1540s accounts are not used because they do not name the vendors, apart from Thomas Townshend.
[19] Newton by Castle Acre.

Vendor	Origin	Approx. frequency of purchase
Thomas Maddy (E, S, T)	Raynham	1
Robert Mannyng (S)	Raynham	1
Prior of Coxford	Coxford	< 5
Prior of Norwich	Norwich	< 5
Rector of Dunton	Dunton	1
John Stalworthy snr. (S, T)	Dunton	< 5
Stalworthy's executors	Dunton	< 5
John Stalworthy jnr. (S, T)	Dunton	< 5
Robert Stampe (S, T)	Helhoughton	1
William Ulffe (S, T)	South Creake	1
Robert Warner	Docking	1
William Warner	Docking	1
Robert Wright (S)	Raynham	1
Nicholas Yelverton, gent.	Rougham	1
Bought at[20]:	Fakenham	1
	Tattersett	1

(ii) FIRST TWO DECADES OF THE SIXTEENTH CENTURY

Vendor	Origin	Approx. frequency of purchase
John Amyson, 'bocher'	Burnham Westgate	< 5
Geoffrey Appleyard	Blickling/Aylsham	< 10
William Barbur	Walsingham	1
Robert Baxster	Stanhoe	1
Thomas Baxster	Stanhoe	< 5
John Becham	Creake	< 5
—— Bernwell	?	< 5
Peter Bethe	?	1
John Betson (T)	Oxborough	1
William Blake	Northwold	< 5
Executors of Thomas Blakeney, esq. (R)	Honingham	1
Richard Bolter (T)	South Creake	< 5
Executors of John Broun	?	1
Executors of Andrew Brygges	Wells next the Sea	< 10
John Buk	?	1
William Buk	?	< 5
John Bulman (T)	Stibbard	1

[20] Vendors not named in the accounts.

Vendor	*Origin*	*Approx. frequency of purchase*
John Byllet (S, T)	Stanhoe/Barmer	1
Thomas Candeler (T)	Raynham	1
Thomas Candeler's wife	Raynham	1
Simon Carter	?	1
William Chamberlain	?	1
William Choket (S)	Raynham	1
Nicholas Clyfton (T)	Toftrees	< 10
William Coke (T)	Weasenham	1
Richard Constabylle	Great Cressingham	1
'Master Coo'[21]	Saham Toney	1
Thomas Couper (S, T)	Stanhoe/Barwick	1
Thomas Crakeheld (?T)	? South Creake	< 5
Robert Croft	?	1
Thomas Culcy (S)	North Creake	1
John Curson	Letheringsett	1
Henry Denys	?	1
John Denys	? Sheringham	< 5
John Deryng (S)	Dunton	< 10
John Docking	?	1
John Dowdy	Hindringham	1
John Downyng (?T)	? Stibbard	1
John Dowse (S)	Bircham Newton	1
John Dreme	?	1
John Drewye	?	1
Sir Robert Drury	Suffolk	1
John Dykman	?	< 5
Robert Erle (S)	Stibbard	< 10
John Eston, gent. (T)	Raynham	< 10
John Everard	Gateley	1
William Eyvery	?	1
Robert Farewell (T)	Raynham	< 5
Thomas Faukener (E)	Helhoughton	1
Faukener's executors	Helhoughton	< 10
Faukener's widow	Helhoughton	< 5
John Fermor	?	< 10
John Fleming	?	< 10
Giles Flode'(S, T)	Raynham	< 10
John Foket (S)	Raynham	1
Robert Fraunceys	? Pulham	1

[21] Probably Hugh Coo, gent.

Vendor	Origin	Approx. frequency of purchase
John Fuller	?	1
Robert Fysske (E, T)	South Creake	< 5
Thomas Gayton, gent. (T)	Gayton	< 5
James Gebone (S)	Hindringham	1
Robert Goldyng (S)	North Barsham	< 5
Richard Gottes (T)	Stibbard	1
Thomas Gowce	?	1
Thomas Grandon, rector (P)	Stibbard	< 5
____ Grey, 'bocher'	?	1
Thomas Grey (T)	North Creake	1
Thomas Gygges (R)	Burnham St Clement	< 5
Gygges's widow and executrix	Burnham St Clement	< 5
Richard Gyrlyng	?	< 5
Geoffrey Hammond	?	1
William Harryson	?	1
John Hawkyn (S)	? Sporle	< 5
Robert Hendry	Diss	1
Richard Hervy (T)	Raynham	< 5
Thomas Hewer (T)	Oxborough	< 5
John Heygrene (S)	Congham/Sporle	1
Richard Heygrene (?)	Shereford	< 5
Robert Heygrene (?)	? Shereford	< 5
Richard Hooke (E)	? Raynham	< 5
John Horn (T)	Stibbard	1
Henry Howman (T)	Stanhoe	< 5
William Howse	? Tittleshall	< 5
John Jekelyn	?	< 5
John Jonson[22]	? Lynn	1
Executors of Nicholas Kerre (S)	Wood Norton	1
Geoffrey Lammyng (S)	Kettlestone	1
John Lane[23]	Coxford	1
'Laurence'	Wood Norton	1
Henry Lychefeld (H)	Raynham	< 5

[22] Probably the same man in the list of purchasers above.
[23] Shepherd of the prior of Coxford and responsible for one of the flocks the Townshends agisted with the prior in the 1490s: R55, 1493/4–1497/8 sheep accounts, fo. 7^r.

Vendor	Origin	Approx. frequency of purchase
William Malby	?	1
'Man of Brancaster'	Brancaster	1
'Man of Docking'	Docking	1
'Man of Little Snoring'	Little Snoring	1
'Man of Snettisham'	Snettisham	1
'Man of Stiffkey'	Stiffkey	1
'Man of Watton'	Watton	1
John Manser (T)	North Creake	< 10
Richard Manser (T)	North Creake	< 5
Robert Manser (T)	North Creake	< 5
Robert Mayne	?	1
John Molle	? Weasenham	< 5
Richard Mower	Cranworth	1
Richard Neston	?	1
John Nicolson	? Walsingham	1
Thomas Nicolson	Docking	< 10
Richard Norton (T)	South Creake	1
Thomas Okke	West Newton	1
Thomas Peryman	?	1
William Pollard	Northwold	< 5
Prior of Coxford	Coxford	< 10
Richard Pynnys	?	1
Rector of 'Bircham'	? Bircham Newton	1
Rector of Cranworth	Cranworth	1
Rector of North Creake	North Creake	1
Executors of the same	North Creake	< 5
John Roberde	Oxborough/ Foulden	1
Henry Russell, gent.	West Rudham	< 10
Henry Russell jnr.	West Rudham	1
John Ryplyngham (?T)	? Dunton	1
Richard Ryplyngham, gent.	Cawston	< 5
Osburne Say	Gayton	< 5
John Scony (E, S)	Cawston	1
Henry Sergeaunt (T)	Stanhoe	< 5
John Skayman (E, T)	South Creake	< 5
John Skutte's executors	Whissonsett	1
John Skutte's widow	Whissonsett	< 5
William Skutte	? Whissonsett	1
John Smith (E)	Wighton/Stanhoe	1
John Snellyng, 'bocher'	East Dereham	1
John Sooham (E)	Bale	< 5

Vendor	Origin	Approx. frequency of purchase
Executors of Robert Southwell	Wood Rising	1
William Sparke	Fakenham	1
Sparke's executors	Fakenham	< 5
Robert Stampe (S, T)	Helhoughton	< 10
Executors of Thomas Stywarde	Swaffham	1
Richard Suffolk (?T)	? South Creake	1
Robert Sylvester (T)	Little Ryburgh	1
John Syre, *carnifex*	Walsingham	1
—— Tomson	Stanhoe	1
Richard Tylney (E)	'Bircham'[24]	< 10
John Ulffe (S, T)	South Creake	< 10
William Ulffe (S, T)	South Creake	< 5
Vicar of Toftrees	Toftrees	1
John Wace (T)	Sculthorpe	1
Thomas Walpole (E)	Walsingham	< 5
'Lord Walter'[25]	? Attleborough	< 5
John Webster	?	< 5
Reginald Webster	? Weasenham	1
Sir Thomas Woodhouse (R)	Kimberley	1
John Wright (S, T)	Raynham	1
Robert Wright (S)	Raynham	1
—— Wylly	Docking	1
John Yemanson	?	1
Bought at[26]:	Briston	1
	Colkirk	1
	Docking	1
	Gatesend	1
	Hempton	1
	Hindringham	< 5
	Testerton	1
	Thetford	< 5

[24] Bircham Newton, Great Bircham, or Bircham Tofts.
[25] Robert Radcliffe, Lord Fitzwalter?
[26] Vendors not named in the accounts.

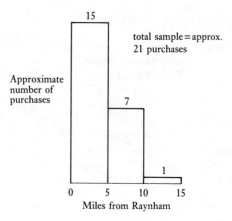

Appendix Fig. 3.   Sheep purchases, late fifteenth century

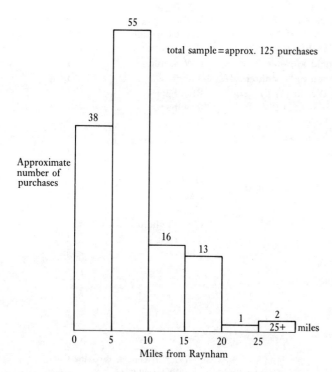

Appendix Fig. 4.   Sheep purchases, first two decades of the sixteenth century

APPENDIX 11. WOOL SALES[1]

(1) Prices

Accounting year	Amount sold (stones)	Prices per stone
1474/5	500 st.	1*s.* 8*d.*; 2*s.*
1475/6	720 st.	2*s.* 4*d.*
1476/7	120 st.	?
1477/8	887 st.[2]	2*s.* 4*d.*
1478/9	1,032 st. 7 lb	2*s.* 2*d.*; 2*s.* 7*d.*
1479/80	416 st. 7 lb[3]	2*s.* 2*d.*
1480/1	221 st.[4]	2*s.* 2*d.*
1481/2	886 st.	?
1482/3	937 st.[5]	3*s.* 3*d.*
1483/4	810 st.	?
1485/6	?[6]	2*s.* 10*d.*
1486/7	?[6]	2*s.* 9*d.*
1487/8	?[6]	2*s.* 9*d.*
1488/9	630 st.[6]	3*s.* 4*d.*
1489/90	877 st. 9 lb	2*s.* 8*d.*
1493/4	1,080 st.	2*s.* 8*d.*
1494/5	480 st.	2*s.* 2*d.*; 2*s.* 4*d.*
1496/7	?[6]	2*s.* 2*d.*
1497/8	?[7]	1*s.* 8*d.*; 1*s.* 10*d.*
1502/3	?[8]	1*s.* 8*d.*
1504/5	?[8]	1*s.* 11*d.*

[1] Sources: Allison, 'Flock Management'; R58, Raynham account roll, loose membrane (1474/5 receiver's account), m. 11; NRO, B-L.V, nos. ×. 31, 45; R24, 1478/9 sheep accounts, fos. 15ʳ, 16ʳ; BL, Add. MS 41,305, fos. 7ᵛ, 8, 11ᵛ, 20, 22ʳ, 24ᵛ-5ʳ, 26ʳ, 46; NRO, Townshend 193 MS 1,612 1 C 7, fo. 15ᵛ; NRO, B-L VII b(3), fo. 15ʳ; R55, RT II valors, fo. 14ʳ; NRO, B-L II e, 1501/2-1517/18 sheep accounts, fos. 66ᵛ, 101ʳ, 146ᵛ, 188ʳ, 205ʳ, 228ʳ, 250ᵛ, 274ʳ, 297ᵛ, 319ᵛ; R60, 1516/17 sheep accounts, fo. 16ᵛ; LSE, R(SR) 1,032, 88,819.

[2] All of the wool from previous years' clips; some of the current clip.

[3] All of the two-year old; some of the year old; none of the current clip.

[4] All of the two-year old.

[5] All of the two-year old; all of the year old; none of the current.

[6] All of the current clip.

[7] All the remaining clips from previous years; 50 stone of the new wool; sold at 1*s.* 8*d.* per stone for the old and 1*s.* 10*d.* for the new.

[8] All of the current clip.

Accounting year	Amount sold (stones)	Prices per stone
1505/6	551 st.	1s. 8d.
1507/8	663 st. 4 lb	2s.
1508/9	803 st.	2s. 4d.
1509/10	1,111 st.	2s. 4d.; 2s. 8d.
1510/11	887 st.	2s. 10d.
1511/12	1,074 st.	2s. 8d.
1512/13	989 st.	2s. 6d.
1513/14	1,138 st.	3s.
1514/15	1,024 st.	3s. 6d.
1515/16	1,254 st.	3s. 6d.
1516/17	1,217 st.	3s. 6d.
1517/18	1,142 st.	3s. 8d.
1544/5	220 st.	3s. 4d.
1545/6	282 st.	3s. 4d.
1547/8	341 st.	6s. 8d.

(2) Purchasers (where known)

Accounting year	Purchaser	Origin
pre-1474/5	Nicholas Candeler	Walsingham
	William Congham	Walsingham
	John Haliday	Lynn
	William Palle	Walsingham
1474/5	Nicholas Candeler	Walsingham
	John Cheny	South Creake
	William Cheny	South Creake
	William Congham	Walsingham
	John Haliday	Lynn
	John Jonson[9]	Norwich
	William Palle	Walsingham
	Simon Pigot	Lynn
1475/6	John Clerk	Tunstead
	William Congham	Walsingham
1476/7	William Cheny	South Creake
1477/8	Thomas Ditton	Northwold
	Simon Pigot	Lynn

[9] Possibly the mason who worked on the manor house at East Raynham in the mid-1470s: R58, Raynham account roll, m. 8; he bought only 20 stone.

Accounting year	Purchaser	Origin
1478/9	John Blaunche	Lynn
	Thomas Ditton	Northwold
	John Grene	Lynn
	John Heyward	?
	Thomas Knyght	?
	William Mowteney[10]	Wilby
	William Payn	Timworth, Suffolk
	John Prynchet	Kenninghall
	Simon Pigot	Lynn
1482/3	Calibut & Broun	Sporle
	Palmage	Bacton, Suffolk
1492/3	John Bradman &	
	Richard Heberden	London
1493/4	Nicholas Candeler	Pickenham
	Symond atte Mere[11]	Swaffham
1494/5	Margaret Lumbard	Hadleigh, Suffolk
1495/6	Richard Peper[12]	Norwich
1496/7	Symond atte Mere	Swaffham
1497/8	William Coo	Swaffham
1504/5	Robert Wolvy	East Raynham
c.1515	Robert Wolvy	East Raynham

[10] William Mowteney of Wilby, gent.; with his associate Prynchet, a husbandman, he was sued for debt by Roger I in 1480: PRO, CP40/571, rot. 195.

[11] 'Husbandman': BL, Add. MS 41,305, fo. 22[r].

[12] Mercer: see Ch. 5, 2 above.

APPENDIX 12. TOWNSHEND SHEEP PURCHASES IN THE 1540s[1]

Year ending, Michaelmas	Number of sheep owned	Number of these bought that year
1545	3,960	2,039
1546	3,960	1,019
1547	3,960	918
1548	4,200	1,089

[1] LSE, R(SR) 1,032, 88,918.

APPENDIX 13. TOWNSHEND SHEEP VALORS[1]

Accounting year	Value
Lent 1506/7	£93 9s. 3d.
Lent 1507/8	£115 6s. 11d.
Lent 1508/9	£112 6s. 10½d.
Mich. 1512/13	£141 4s. 5d.
Mich. 1513/14	£276 8s. 0d.
Mich. 1514/15	£321 0s. 17d.
Mich. 1515/16	£353 8s. 5½d.
Mich. 1516/17	£317 0s. 8½d.
Mich. 1517/18	£257 16s. 11d.
Mich. 1523/4	£139 5s. 3½d.

[1] Figures are corrected where there are discrepancies in the original calculations. Sources: R55, RT II valors, fos. 10^r–14^v, 23^r–24^v; R31, RT II estate book, fos. 10^r–11^v, 42^r; NRO, B-L II e, 1501/2–1517/18 sheep accounts, fos. 233^v, 254^v, 277^v, 300^v, 322^v; R60, 1516/17 sheep accounts, fo. 19^v.

BIBLIOGRAPHY

1. Manuscript Sources

Cambridge

Gonville and Caius College, MSS XVIII. 2, 4, 5 (indentures relating to Roger II's 1538 purchase of Pattesley).
University Library, Pembroke MS 300 (1526/7 'Booke of Emptions' of the Howard household at Stoke-by-Nayland).

East Raynham, Raynham Hall

Deeds, accounts, and other estate and personal papers in the library, in drawers numbered: Raynham Box 1 (R1), R5–14, R18–20, R22–9, R31–3, R35–42, R44–5, R47–50, R52–61, R126.

Deeds, accounts, and other estate and personal papers in the attic:
(a) *unsorted*: contained in several large chests and tin trunks; for example, a large black tin trunk (approximately 3 feet high, 4 feet long, and 2 feet wide) with 'Deeds, leases. Misc. unexamined, C14–18th cents' chalked on the lid.
(b) *roughly sorted*, in boxes labelled:
'*Barsham/Smyth estate papers (Colkirk and Oxwick)*'
'Bundle marked "Comes Oxoniae"'
'Cambridgeshire deeds & estate papers'
'Coxford Priory'
'Deeds—Barsham, Burnhams, Colkirk, Creake (loose in box), Dunton, Foulsham, Gaywood'
'*Deeds*—E. Harling, Honingham, Horningtoft, Langhale, Marham, Marston, Necton, Norwich, Pattesley, Raynhams (loose in box)'
'*Deeds*—Rudham, Salle . . . Toftrees'
'*Deeds*—Stanford (loose in box), Warham . . . Wiggenhall'
'Deeds various counties (*not* Norfolk)'
'*Essex deeds*'
'Legal and suit papers, 15th–19th cent.'
'*Manor of Akenham*, Suffolk accounts 1283/4–1548/9 (part)'
'Manor of Akenham, Suffolk . . . (part)'
'MARRIAGE SETTLEMENTS, PAPERS, ETC'
'Miscellaneous, unidentified & fragmentary'

'*Norfolk manorial* A-M . . . '
'*Norfolk manorial* N & S Creake'
'*Norfolk manorial* R-S (not Raynham, Stanford)'
'*Norfolk manorial*—Raynhams'
'*Norfolk manorial*—Raynham Haviles'
'*Norfolk manorial* T-W and mixed'
'Suffolk deeds'
'Townshend family before 1552'

London

British Library

Additional Charters:
14,526 (Townshend-Paston indenture, 1469)
19,085 (1537/8–1549/50 Hindringham accounts)
Additional MSS:
21,480, 21,481, 35,182 (royal household books, 1499–1505, 1509–18, 1531/2)
27,447 (letter from Sir Roger Townshend II to Sir William Paston, 1546)
27,451 (accounts of the keeper of Framlingham deer park, 1508–13)
41,139 (memorandum book of Roger Townshend II, 1500/1)
41,305 (estate memorandum book of Eleanor Townshend, 1493–9 with added
   sixteenth-century draft estate accounts and notes)
41,655, fo. 51 (valuation of the lands of Sir John Townshend after his death
   in 1603)
Additional Rolls:
16,554, 17,745 (accounts of the keeper of Framlingham deer park, 1515/16)
Cotton MSS:
Cleopatra EIV (state papers, Henry VIII)
Nero EVII (Walsingham Priory cartulary)
Othello EXI (papers relating to levies, musters, and defence of ports, Henry
   VIII and Elizabeth I)
Egerton MS 2,604 (book of wages, royal household, 1525/6)
Harleian MSS:
4,756, fo. 36 (Townshend pedigree)
5,177, fo. 102 (list of knights made, Henry VI–1582)
Lansdowne MSS:
12 (57), fos. 124–5 (Burghley Papers, list of councillors appointed to sit in the
   Court of Requests, 1528/9)
639 (lists of royal councillors, *temp.* Henry VIII)
Royal MS 7F. XIV 100 (list of royal household officers, *c.* 1533)
Stowe MS 571 (lists of ministers and officers of the royal household, Edward
   VI and Elizabeth I)

City of London Record Office

Hustings Roll 231

Rep. 10 (Repertory Books)

London School of Economics

MS R(SR) 1,032, 88,918 (1544/5–1547/8 Townshend sheep accounts)

Public Record Office, Chancery Lane

Classes consulted:

C1	Early Chancery Proceedings
C67	Patent Rolls, Supplementary
C142	Inquisitions Post Mortem
C219	Writs and Returns of Members to Parliament
CP25	Feet of Fines
CP40	Common Pleas, Plea Rolls
DL5	Duchy of Lancaster, Equity Proceedings, Entry Books of Decrees and Orders
E36	Treasury of Receipt, Miscellaneous Books
E101	Accounts, Various
E150	Inquisitions Post Mortem
E159	Memoranda Rolls
E179	Lay Subsidy Rolls
E198	Returns of Knights' Fees
E315	Augmentations Office, Miscellaneous Books
E326	Augmentations Office, Ancient Deeds
E403	Issue Rolls
IND1	Index Volumes and Rolls
KB9	King's Bench, Ancient Indictments
KB27	King's Bench, De Banco Rolls
PROB11	Prerogative Court of Canterbury, Registered Copy Wills
REQ2	Court of Requests Proceedings
SC8	Ancient Petitions
SP1	State Papers, Henry VIII
SP5	Suppression Papers
SP10	State Papers Domestic, Edward VI
STAC2	Star Chamber Proceedings, Henry VIII
STAC3	Star Chamber Proceedings, Edward VI
WARD7	Inquisitions Post Mortem

Norfolk Record Office, Norwich

Bradfer-Lawrence Collection (deeds, accounts, and estate documents, Townshend and other)

BRA (Papers, Townshend and other, on permanent loan from the British Records Association)

MC 3/283 (463 × 4) (seventeenth-century copy of will of Sir Geoffrey Boleyn, d. 1463)

NCC (wills, Norwich Consistory Court Registers)

NRS MSS:

14,730 29 D4 (memorandum of agreement between Geoffrey Boleyn and Sir John Fastolf, 1453)

24,745 (134 × 5), 24,755 (134 × 5) (miscellaneous deeds)

Phi MS 405 (deed of 1504 from the Phillips collection)

Le Strange MSS AE 2, 4; EM 21, 22 (wills and deeds)

Townshend MSS (deeds, accounts, and estate documents):

MS 1,968 2 C6

MS 11,991 35 B3

2 MS 1,421 1 A1

11 MS 1,430 1 A3

12 MS 1,431 1 A3

13 MS 1,432 1 A3

16 MS 1,435 1 A4

17 MS 1,436 1 A4

24 MS 1,443 1 A6

26 MS 1,445 1 A7

36 MS 1,445 1 B1

37 MS 1,456 1 B1

44 MS 1,463 1 B2

51 MS 1,470 1 B5

56 MS 1,475 1 F

84 MS 1,503 1 D2

147 MS 1,566 1 C3

155 MS 1,574 1 C5

159 MS 1,578 1 D8

163 MS 1,582 1 D4

169 MS 1,588 1 C6

193 MS 1,612 1 C7

WKC MSS (deeds from the William Ketton-Cremer collection)

Oxford

All Souls College MS 155, fos. 365–67ᵛ, a seventeenth-century copy of a manuscript list of Norfolk gentry, *c.*1500, now in the Huntington Library, San Marino, Calif. (MS HM 19,959)

2. Printed Sources

PRIMARY SOURCES

Bedfordshire Wills Proved in the Prerogative Court of Canterbury, 1353–1548, ed. M. McGregor, Bedfordshire Historical Rec. Soc., 58 (1979).
British Library Harleian Manuscript 433, ed. R. Horrox and P. W. Hammond, 4 vols., Richard III Soc. (1979–83).
A Calendar of the Feet of Fines for Suffolk, ed. W. Rye (Ipswich, 1900).
A Calendar of the Inner Temple Records, ed. F. A. Inderwick and R. A. Roberts, 5 vols. (London, 1896–1936).
Calendarium Inquisitionum Post Mortem Sive Escaetarum, iv, Record Commission (London, 1828).
Calendars of the Proceedings in Chancery in the Reign of Queen Elizabeth, ed. J. Bailey, 3 vols. (London, 1827–32).
Christ Church Letters, ed. J. B. Sheppard, Camden Soc., NS 19 (1877).
The Chronicle of Jocelin of Brakelond, ed. H. E. Butler (London, 1949).
' "The Commosyon in Norfolk, 1549": A Narrative of Popular Rebellion in Sixteenth Century England', ed. B. L. Beer, *Journal of Medieval and Renaissance Studies*, 6 (1976), 73–99.
The Coronation of Richard III: The Extant Documents, ed. A. F. Sutton and P. W. Hammond (Gloucester, 1983).
The County Community Under Henry VIII, ed. J. Cornwall, Rutland Rec. Soc., 1 (1980).
'Extracts from the Household and Privy Purse Expenditure of Le Strange of Hunstanton, 1519–78', ed. D. Gurney, *Archaeologia*, 25 (1834), 411–569.
Faculty Office Registers, 1534–1549, ed. D. S. Chambers (Oxford, 1966).
Grace Book B, ed. M. Bateson, 2 vols. (Cambridge, 1903–5).
Household Books of John Duke of Norfolk and Thomas Earl of Surrey 1481–1490, ed. J. Payne Collier, Roxburghe Club, 61 (1844).
An Index of Persons Named in Early Chancery Proceedings, Richard II (1385) to Edward IV (1467), Preserved in the Public Record Office, London, ed. C. A. Walmisley, 2 vols., Harleian Soc., 78–9 (1927–8).
Itineraries (of William Worcester), ed. J. H. Harvey (Oxford, 1969).
The Itinerary of John Leland, ed. L. Toulmin Smith, 5 vols. (London, 1906–10).
The Knyvet Letters, 1620–1644, ed. B. Schofield, Norfolk Rec. Soc., 20 (1949).
'The Last Testament and Inventory of John de Veer, Thirteenth Earl of Oxford', ed. W. H. St John Hope, *Archaeologia*, 66 (1914–15).
De Laudibus Legum Angliae (of Sir John Fortescue), ed. S. B. Chrimes (Cambridge, 1942).
Lay Subsidy Rolls, 1524–5, ed J. Cornwall, Sussex Rec. Soc., 56 (1956).

Lincolnshire Pedigrees, ed. A. R. Maddison, 4 vols., Harleian Soc., 50-2, 55 (1902-6).

Lists of Sheriffs for England and Wales, PRO Lists and Indexes, 9 (1898).

Lists of Escheators for England, PRO Lists and Indexes, 72 (1932).

The Making of King's Lynn, ed. D. M. Owen (London, 1984).

Manners and Household Expenses of England in the Thirteenth and Fifteenth Centuries, ed. T. H. Turner, Roxburghe Club, 57 (1841).

Memorials of the Holles Family, 1493-1656, ed. A. C. Wood, Camden Soc., 3rd ser. 55 (1937).

The Military Survey of 1522 for Babergh Hundred, ed. J. Pound, Suffolk Rec. Soc., 28 (1986).

Ministers' Accounts of the Warwickshire Estates of the Duke of Clarence, 1479-80, ed. R. H. Hilton, Dugdale Soc., 21 (1944).

'Muster Roll for the Hundred of North Greenhoe (*circa* 1523)', ed. M. Dale, Norfolk Rec. Soc., 1 (1931), 41-68.

'Norfolk Subsidy Roll, 15 Hen. VIII', ed. W. Rye, *Norfolk Antiquarian Miscellany*, 2 (1883), 399-410.

Original Letters Illustrative of English History, ed. H. Ellis, 3 series, 11 vols. (London, 1824-46).

The Papers of Nathaniel Bacon of Stiffkey, ed. A. Hassell Smith *et al.*, 2 vols., Norfolk Rec. Soc., 46, 49 (1979-83).

The Paston Letters, ed. J. Gairdner, repr. of 1904 edn. (Gloucester, 1986).

Pedes Finium: or, Fines Relating to the County of Cambridge . . ., ed. W. Rye, Cambridge Antiquarian Soc., 26 (1891).

Proceedings and Ordinances of the Privy Council, ed. N. H. Nicolas, 7 vols. (London, 1834-7).

Proceedings before the Justices of the Peace in the Fourteenth and Fifteenth Centuries, ed. B. H. Putnam (London, 1938).

Records of the City of Norwich, ed. W. Hudson and J. C. Tingey, 2 vols. (Norwich, 1906-10).

The Reports of Sir John Spelman, ed. J. H. Baker, 2 vols., Selden Soc., 93-4 (1977-8).

Select Cases in Chancery, 1364-1474, ed. W. P. Baildon, Selden Soc., 10 (1896).

Select Cases in the Council of Henry VII, ed. C. G. Bayne and W. H. Dunham, Selden Soc., 75 (1956).

Select Cases in the Court of Requests, A. D. 1497-1569, ed. I. S. Leadam, Selden Soc., 12 (1898).

A Short Calendar of the Feet of Fines for Norfolk, ii, ed. W. Rye (Norwich, 1886).

The Stonor Letters and Papers, 1290-1483, ed. C. L. Kingsford, Camden Soc., 3rd ser. 29-30 (1919).

Suffolk in 1524: Being the Return for a Subsidy Granted in 1523, ed. S. H. A. H[ervey], Suffolk Green Books, 10 (1910).

Testamenta Vetusta, ed. N. H. Nicolas, 2 vols. (London, 1826).

Valor Ecclesiasticus, ed. J. Caley and J. Hunter, 6 vols. (London, 1810-34).

The Visitation of Nottinghamshire, ed. G. D. Squibb, Harleian Soc., NS 5 (1986).
Woods, R., *Norfolke Furies, and their Foyle* (London, 1623), a translation of Alexander Neville's *De Furoribus Norfolciensium Ketto Duce* (1575).

SECONDARY SOURCES

ALLISON, K. J., 'The Wool Supply and the Worsted Cloth Industry in Norfolk in the Sixteenth and Seventeenth Centuries', Ph.D. thesis (Leeds, 1955).
—— 'The Lost Villages of Norfolk', *NA* 31 (1957), 116-62.
—— 'The Sheep-Corn Husbandry of Norfolk in the Sixteenth and Seventeenth Centuries', *AHR* 5 (1957), 12-30.
—— 'Flock Management in the Sixteenth and Seventeenth Centuries', *EcHR* 2nd ser. 11 (1958), 98-112.
—— 'The Norfolk Worsted Industry in the Sixteenth and Seventeenth Centuries: 1. The Traditional Industry', *Yorkshire Bulletin of Economic and Social Research*, 12 (1960), 73-83.
ALLMAND, C. T., 'The Civil Lawyers', in C. H. Clough (ed.), *Profession, Vocation and Culture in Later Medieval England* (Liverpool, 1982), 155-80.
AULT, W. O., *Open-Field Farming in Medieval England* (London, 1972).
AVERY, M. E., 'The History of the Equitable Jurisdiction of Chancery before 1460', *BIHR* 42 (1969), 129-44.
BAILEY, M., *A Marginal Economy? East Anglian Breckland in the Later Middle Ages* (Cambridge, 1989).
—— 'Sand into Gold: The Evolution of the Foldcourse System in West Suffolk, 1200-1600', *AHR* 38 (1990), 40-57.
BAKER, J. H., 'Criminal Courts and Procedure at Common Law, 1500-1800', in J. S. Cockburn (ed.), *Crime in England 1550-1800* (London, 1977), 15-48.
—— *An Introduction to English Legal History*, 3rd edn. (London, 1990).
BARNES, T. G., *Somerset 1625-1640: A County's Government During the 'Personal Rule'* (London, 1961).
BARNES, T. G., and SMITH, A. HASSELL, 'Justices of the Peace from 1558 to 1688—A Revised List of Sources', *BIHR* 32 (1959), 221-42.
BARTLETT, J. G., *Robert Coe, Puritan, his Ancestors and Descendants, 1340-1910* (Boston, Mass., 1911).
BASKERVILLE, G., 'Married Clergy and Pensioned Religious in Norwich Diocese, 1555', *EHR* 48 (1933), 43-64, 199-228.
BATTEN, B., 'The Heyday of the Heydons of Baconsthorpe, Norfolk and West Wickham, Kent', unpublished thesis (Coloma College of Education, Kent, c. 1960).

BEAN, J. M. W., *The Decline of English Feudalism, 1215-1540* (Manchester, 1968).

BEAVEN, A. W., *Aldermen of the City of London*, 2 vols. (London, 1908-13).

BEDINGFELD, K., *The Bedingfelds of Oxburgh* (privately published, 1912).

BEER, B. L., *Rebellion and Riot* (Kent, Ohio, 1982).

BELL, H. E., *An Introduction to the History and Records of the Courts of Wards and Liveries* (Cambridge, 1953).

BELLAMY, J. G., *Crime and Public Order in England in the Later Middle Ages* (London, 1973).

—— *Criminal Law and Society in Late Medieval and Tudor England* (Gloucester, 1984).

BENNETT, H. S., *The Pastons and their England*, 2nd edn. (Cambridge, 1932), 24-44.

—— *Chaucer and the Fifteenth Century* (Oxford, 1947).

BENNETT, M. J., 'A County Community: Social Cohesion Amongst the Cheshire Gentry, 1400-1425', *Northern History*, 8 (1973), 24-44.

BERESFORD, M. W., 'The Poll Tax and Census of Sheep, 1549', 2 Parts, *AHR* 1 (1953), 9-15; 2 (1954), 15-29.

—— 'The Common Informer, the Penal Statutes and Economic Regulation', *EcHR* 2nd ser. 10 (1957-8).

—— *Lay Subsidies and Poll Taxes* (Canterbury, 1963).

BERNARD, G. W., *The Power of the Early Tudor Nobility* (Brighton, 1985).

—— *War, Taxation and Rebellion in Early Tudor England: Henry VIII, Wolsey and the Amicable Grant of 1525* (Brighton, 1986).

BINDOFF, S. T., 'Ket's Rebellion', in J. Hurstfield (ed.), *The Tudors* (London, 1973), 72-102.

BLAKE, W. J., 'Fuller's List of Norfolk Gentry', *NA* 32 (1961), 261-91.

BLANCHARD, I., 'Population Change, Enclosure, and the Early Tudor Economy', *EcHR* 2nd ser. 23 (1970), 427-45.

BLATCHER, M., *The Court of King's Bench, 1450-1550* (London, 1978).

BOLTON, J. L., *The Medieval English Economy, 1150-1500* (London, 1980).

BOWDEN, P. J., 'Movements in Wool Prices, 1490-1610', *Yorkshire Bulletin of Economic and Social Research*, 4 (1952), 109-124.

—— 'Wool Supply and the Woollen Industry', *EcHR* 2nd ser. 9 (1956-7), 44-58.

—— *The Wool Trade in Tudor and Stuart England* (London, 1962).

BRANDON, P. F., 'Cereal Yields in the Sussex Estates of Battle Abbey during the Late Middle Ages', *EcHR* 2nd ser. 25 (1972), 403-30.

BRENAN, G., and STATHAM, E. P., *The House of Howard*, 2 vols. (London, 1907).

BRITNELL, R. H., 'The Pastons and their Norfolk', *AHR* 36 (1988), 132-44.

BROOKS, C. W., 'Litigants and Attorneys in the King's Bench and Common Pleas, 1560-1640', in J. H. Baker (ed.), *Legal Records and the Historian* (London, 1978), 41-59.

256   *Bibliography*

BURSTALL, E. B., 'The Pastons and their Manor of Binham', *NA* 30 (1952), 101-29.

BUSH, M. L., *The Government Policy of Protector Somerset* (London, 1975).

CAMERON, A., 'Complaint and Reform in Henry VII's Reign: The Origins of the Statute of 3 Henry VII, c. 2?', *BIHR* 51 (1978), 83-9.

CAMPBELL, B. M. S., 'The Regional Uniqueness of English Field Systems? Some Evidence from Eastern Norfolk', *AHR* 29 (1981), 16-28.

—— 'Arable Productivity in Medieval England: Some Evidence from Norfolk', *Journal of Economic History*, 43 (1983), 379-404.

—— 'Agricultural Progress in Medieval England: Some Evidence from Eastern Norfolk', *EcHR* 2nd ser. 36 (1983), 26-46.

CAMPBELL, M. L., *The English Yeoman under Elizabeth and the Early Stuarts*, 2nd edn. (London, 1960).

CAMPLING, A., *The History of the Family of Drury* (London, 1937).

—— *East Anglian Pedigrees*, Norfolk Rec. Soc., 13 (1940).

CARPENTER, C., 'The Beauchamp Affinity: A Study of Bastard Feudalism at Work', *EHR* 95 (1980), 514-32.

—— 'Fifteenth Century Biographies', *Historical Journal*, 25 (1982), 729-34.

—— 'The Fifteenth Century English Gentry and their Estates', in Jones (ed.), *Gentry and Lesser Nobility in Late Medieval Europe*, 36-60.

CARTHEW, G. A., *The Hundred of Launditch and Deanery of Brisley in the County of Norfolk*, 3 vols. (Norwich, 1877-9).

—— *A History of the Parishes of West and East Bradenham, with those of Necton and Holme Hale* (Norwich, 1883).

CHAMBERS, R. W., *Thomas More* (London, 1938).

CHARLESWORTH, A. (ed.), *An Atlas of Rural Protest in Britain, 1548-1900* (London, 1983).

CHRIMES, S. B., *Henry VII* (London, 1972).

CLANCHY, M. T., 'Law, Government and Society in Medieval England', *History*, 59 (1974), 73-8.

CLARK, P., *English Provincial Society from the Reformation to the Revolution: Religion, Politics and Society in Kent, 1500-1640* (Hassocks, 1977).

CLIFFE, J. T., *The Yorkshire Gentry from the Reformation to the Civil War* (London, 1969).

COCKBURN, J. S., *A History of the English Assizes, 1558-1714* (Cambridge, 1972).

COLEMAN, D. C., *The Economy of England, 1450-1750* (Oxford, 1977).

COLLINS, A., *Peerage of England*, rev. edn., 9 vols. (London, 1812).

COOPER, C. H., and T., *Athenae Cantabrigiensis*, 3 vols. (Cambridge, 1858-1913).

COOPER, J. P., 'Patterns of Inheritance and Settlement by Great Landowners from the Fifteenth to the Eighteenth Centuries', in J. Goody, J. Thirsk, and E. P. Thompson (edd.), *Family and Inheritance: Rural Society in Western Europe, 1200-1800* (Cambridge, 1976), 192-327.

—— *Land, Men and Beliefs* (Oxford, 1983).

COPINGER, W. A., *The Manors of Suffolk*, 7 vols. (Manchester, 1905-11).

CORNWALL, J., 'The People of Rutland in 1522', *Transactions of the Leicestershire Archaeological and Historical Society*, 37 (1961-2), 7-28.

—— 'The Early Tudor Gentry', *EcHR* 2nd ser. 17 (1964), 456-71.

—— 'A Tudor Domesday: The Musters of 1522', *Journal of the Society of Archivists*, 3 (1965-9), 21-3.

—— 'Sussex Wealth and Society in the Reign of Henry VIII', *Sussex Archaeological Collections*, 114 (1976), 1-26.

—— 'Kett's Rebellion in Context', *PP* 93 (1981), 160-4.

—— *Wealth and Society in Early Sixteenth Century England* (London, 1988).

COZENS-HARDY, B., 'Norfolk Lawyers', *NA* 33 (1965), 266-97.

CRAWFORD, A., 'The Career of John Howard, Duke of Norfolk, 1420-85', M. Phil. thesis (London, 1975).

DARROCH, E., and TAYLOR, B. (edd.), *A Bibliography of Norfolk History* (Norwich, 1975).

DAVIES, C. S. L., 'The Pilgrimage of Grace Reconsidered', in P. Slack (ed.), *Rebellion, Popular Protest and the Social Order in Early Modern England* (Cambridge, 1984), 16-38.

—— 'Popular Religion and the Pilgrimage of Grace', in Fletcher and Stevenson (edd.), *Order and Disorder in Early Modern England* (Cambridge, 1985), 58-91.

DAVIES, J. CONWAY (ed.), *Catalogue of Manuscripts in the Library of the Honourable Society of the Inner Temple*, 3 vols. (Oxford, 1972).

DAVIES, R. R., 'Baronial Accounts, Incomes, and Arrears in the Later Middle Ages', *EcHR* 2nd ser. 21 (1968), 211-29.

DAY, W. A., 'Glimpses at Country Life in the Sixteenth Century', *NA* 10 (1888), 143-65.

DENHOLM-YOUNG, N., *Seigneurial Administration in England* (Oxford, 1937).

—— *The Country Gentry in the Fourteenth Century* (Oxford, 1969).

DICKENS, A. G., *The English Reformation* (London, 1964).

—— 'Secular and Religious Motivation in the Pilgrimage of Grace', in G. J. Cuming (ed.), *Studies in Church History*, iv (Leiden, 1967), 39-64.

DODDS, M. H., and DODDS, R., *The Pilgrimage of Grace, 1536-1537, and the Exeter Conspiracy, 1538*, 2 vols. (Cambridge, 1915).

DOUGLAS, D. C., *The Social Structure of Medieval East Anglia* (Oxford, 1927).

DU BOULAY, F. R. H., 'Who were Farming the English Demesnes at the End of the Middle Ages?', *EcHR* 2nd ser. 17 (1965), 443-55.

—— *An Age of Ambition* (London, 1970).

DURHAM, J., *The Townshends of Raynham* (Cambridge, 1922).

DYER, C., 'A Small Landowner in the Fifteenth Century', *Midland History*, 1 (1971-2), 1-14.

—— *Lords and Peasants in a Changing Society* (Cambridge, 1980)

EDWARDS, J. G., 'The Emergence of Majority Rule in English Parliamentary Elections', *TRHS* 5th ser. 14 (1964), 175–96.

—— 'The Huntingdonshire Parliamentary Elections of 1450', in T. A. Sandquist and M. Powicke (edd.), *Essays in Medieval History Presented to Bertie Wilkinson* (Toronto, 1969), 383–95.

ELTON, G. R., 'Informing for Profit: A Sidelight on Tudor Methods of Law-Enforcement', *Cambridge Historical Journal*, 11 (1954), 149–67.

—— *Policy and Police: The Enforcement of the Reformation in the Age of Thomas Cromwell* (Cambridge, 1972).

—— 'Tudor Government: The Points of Contact I. Parliament', *TRHS* 5th ser. 24 (1974), 183–200; 'II. The Council', *TRHS* 5th ser., 25 (1975), 195–212; 'III. The Court', *TRHS* 5th ser., 26 (1976), 211–28.

—— *Reform and Reformation* (London, 1977).

—— 'Politics and the Pilgrimage of Grace', in id., *Studies in Tudor Politics and Government*, iii (Cambridge, 1983), 183–215.

EMDEN, A. B., *Biographical Register of the University of Oxford to AD 1500*, 3 vols. (Oxford, 1957–9).

—— *Biographical Register of the University of Cambridge to 1500* (Cambridge, 1963).

ERNLE, LORD, *English Farming Past and Present*, 6th edn. (London, 1961).

EVERITT, A., *The Community of Kent and the Great Rebellion 1640–1660* (Leicester, 1966).

—— 'The County Community', in E. W. Ives (ed.), *The English Revolution, 1600–1660* (London, 1968), 48–63.

FARROW, M. A., *Index of Wills Proved at Norwich, 1370–1550*, 3 vols., Norfolk Rec. Soc., 16 (1943–5).

FINCH, M. E., *Five Northamptonshire Families, 1540–1640*, Northamptonshire Rec. Soc., 19 (1956).

FIRTH, C. B., 'Village Gilds of Norfolk in the Fifteenth Century', *NA* 18 (1914), 161–203.

FLEMING, P. W., 'Charity, Faith and the Gentry of Kent', in Pollard, (ed.), *Property and Politics*, 36–58.

FLETCHER, A., *A County Community in Peace and War: Sussex 1600–1660* (London, 1975).

—— *Tudor Rebellions*, 3rd edn. (London, 1983).

—— and STEVENSON, J. (edd.), *Order and Disorder in Early Modern England* (Cambridge, 1985).

FORD, F., *Mary Tudor: A Retrospective Sketch* (Bury St Edmunds, 1882).

FOSS, E., *Biographical Dictionary of the Judges of England* (London, 1870).

GIBBS, V., *et al.* (edd.), *The Complete Peerage*, 13 vols. (London, 1910–40).

GIVEN-WILSON, C., *The English Nobility in the Late Middle Ages: The Fourteenth-Century Political Community* (London, 1987).

GORING, J. J., 'The General Proscription of 1522', *EHR* 86 (1971), 681–705.

GOWER, G. L., 'Notices of the Family of Uvedale', *Surrey Archaeological Collections*, 3 (1865), 63–192.

GRACE, F. R., 'The Life and Career of Thomas Howard, Third Duke of Norfolk (1473-1554)', MA thesis (Nottingham, 1961).

GRAY, H. L., *English Field Systems* (Cambridge, 1915).

GRIFFITHS, R. A., 'The Hazards of Civil War: The Mountford Family and the "Wars of the Roses"', *Midland History*, 5 (1979-80), 1-19.

—— *The Reign of King Henry VI* (London, 1981).

GUNN, S. J., *Charles Brandon, Duke of Suffolk, c. 1484-1545* (Oxford, 1988).

GUTH, D. J., 'Enforcing Late-Medieval Law: Patterns in Litigation During Henry VIII's Reign', in J. H. Baker (ed.), *Legal Records and the Historian* (London, 1978), 80-96.

—— 'The Age of Debt, the Reformation and English Law', in D. J. Guth and J. W. McKenna (edd.), *Tudor Rule and Revolution* (Cambridge, 1982), 69-86.

GUY, J. A., *The Cardinal's Court: The Impact of Thomas Wolsey in Star Chamber* (Hassocks, 1977).

HABAKKUK, H. J., 'Marriage Settlements in the Eighteenth Century', *TRHS* 4th ser. 32 (1950), 15-30.

—— 'The Market for Monastic Property, 1539-1603', *EcHR* 2nd ser. 10 (1958), 362-80.

—— 'The Rise and Fall of English Landed Families, 1600-1800', *TRHS* 5th ser. 29 (1979), 187-208.

HABON, E. A., *Edward Coke* (Cleveland, Ohio, 1949).

HAIGH, C., *Reformation and Resistance in Tudor Lancashire* (Cambridge, 1975).

—— (ed.), *The English Reformation Revised* (Cambridge, 1987).

HARDING, A., *The Law Courts of Medieval England* (London, 1973).

HARE, J. N., 'The Demesne Lessees of Fifteenth-Century Wiltshire', *AHR* 29 (1981), 1-15.

HARPER-BILL, C., 'A Late Medieval Visitation—The Diocese of Norwich in 1494', *Proceedings of the Suffolk Institute of Archaeology*, 34 (1980), 35-47.

HARRIS, B. J., *Edward Stafford, Third Duke of Buckingham, 1478-1521* (Stanford, Calif., 1986).

HASLER, P. W. (ed.), *The History of Parliament, 1558-1603*, 3 vols. (London, 1981).

HASTINGS, M., *The Court of Common Pleas in Fifteenth Century England* (Ithaca, NY, 1947).

HATCHER, J., *Plague, Population and the English Economy, 1348-1530* (London, 1977).

HAWARD, W. I., 'Economic Aspects of the Wars of the Roses in East Anglia', *EHR* 41 (1926), 170-89.

—— 'Gilbert Debenham: A Medieval Rascal in Real Life', *History*, NS 13 (1928-9), 300-14.

HENNING, B. (ed.), *The History of Parliament, 1660-1690*, 3 vols. (London, 1983).

HEXTER, J. H., *Reappraisals in History*, 2nd edn. (London, 1979).

HICKS, M.A., 'Restraint, Mediation and Private Justice: George, Duke of Clarence as "Good Lord" ', *Journal of Legal History*, 4 (1983), 56–71.

—— 'The Last Days of Elizabeth Countess of Oxford', *EHR* 103 (1988), 76–95.

HIGHFIELD, J.R.L., and JEFFS, R. (edd.), *The Crown and Local Communities in England and France in the Fifteenth Century* (Gloucester, 1981).

HILTON, R.H., 'The Content and Sources of English Agrarian History Before 1500', *AHR* 3 (1955), 3–19.

HOLMES, C., 'The County Community in Stuart Historiography', *Journal of British Studies*, 19 (1980), 54–73.

HORN, J.M., *Fasti Ecclesiae Anglicanae 1300–1541*, iii (London, 1962).

HORROX, R., 'The Urban Gentry in the Fifteenth Century', in J.A.F. Thomson (ed.), *Towns and Townspeople in the Fifteenth Century* (Gloucester, 1988), 22–44.

—— *Richard III: A Study of Service* (Cambridge, 1989).

HOSKINS, W.G., 'Harvest Fluctuations and English Economic History, 1480–1619', *AHR* 12 (1964), 28–46.

—— *The Age of Plunder* (London, 1976).

HOUGHTON, N.K., 'Theory and Practice in Borough Elections to Parliament in the Later Fifteenth Century', *BIHR* 39 (1966), 130–40.

HOULBROOKE, R.A., *Church Courts and the People During the English Reformation, 1520–1570* (Oxford, 1979).

—— *The English Family, 1450–1700* (London, 1984).

HUNTER, J., *An Introduction to the 'Valor Ecclesiasticus'* (London, 1834).

HURSTFIELD, J., *The Queen's Wards* (London, 1958).

IVES, E.W., 'Promotion in the Legal Profession of Yorkist and Early Tudor England', *LQR* 75 (1959), 348–63.

—— 'The Reputation of the Common Lawyers in English Society, 1450–1550', *Univ. of Birmingham Historical Journal*, 7 (1960), 130–61.

—— 'Andrew Dymmock and the Papers of Antony Woodville, Earl Rivers, 1482–83', *BIHR* 41 (1968), 216–28.

—— 'The Common Lawyers in Pre-Reformation England', *TRHS* 5th ser. 18 (1968), 145–73.

—— 'Court and County Palatine in the Reign of Henry VIII: The Career of William Brereton of Malpas', *Transactions of the Historic Society of Lancashire and Cheshire*, 123 (1972), 1–38.

—— 'The Common Lawyers', in C.H. Clough (ed.), *Profession, Vocation and Culture in Later Medieval England* (Liverpool, 1982), 181–217.

—— *The Common Lawyers of Pre-Reformation England: Thomas Kebell: A Case Study* (Cambridge, 1983).

JACOB, E.F., 'Thomas Brouns, Bishop of Norwich, 1436–45', in H.R. Trevor-Roper (ed.), *Essays in British History Presented to Sir Keith Feiling* (London, 1964), 61–83.

JALLAND, P., 'The Influence of the Aristocracy on Shire Elections in the

North of England, 1450-70', *Speculum*, 47 (1972), 483-507.

—— 'The "Revolution" in Northern Borough Representation in Mid-Fifteenth Century England', *Northern History*, 11 (1976 for 1975), 27-51.

JAMES, M. E., 'Obedience and Dissent in Henrician England: The Lincolnshire Rebellion 1536', *PP* 48 (1970), 3-78.

JESSOP, A., *One Generation of a Norfolk House* (Norwich, 1878).

JONES, M. (ed.), *Gentry and Lesser Nobility in Later Medieval Europe* (Gloucester, 1986).

KEEN, M. H., *England in the Later Middle Ages* (London, 1973).

KENNETT, D. H., *Norfolk Villages* (London, 1980).

KERRIDGE, E., *The Agricultural Revolution* (London, 1967).

—— *Agrarian Problems of the Sixteenth Century and After* (London, 1969).

KNOWLES, M. D., *The Religious Orders in England*, vol. iii (Cambridge, 1959).

—— and HADCOCK, R. N., *Medieval Religious Houses, England and Wales*, 2nd edn. (London, 1971).

LAND, S. K., *Kett's Rebellion* (Ipswich, 1977).

LANDER, J. R., *Government and Community: England 1450-1509* (London, 1980).

LEADAM, I. S., 'The Inquisition of 1517. Inclosures and Evictions. II', *TRHS* NS 7 (1893),127-292.

LEHMBERG, S. E., *The Reformation Parliament, 1529-1536* (Cambridge, 1970).

—— *The Later Parliaments of Henry VIII, 1536-1547* (Cambridge, 1977).

LE STRANGE, H., *Norfolk Official Lists* (Norwich, 1890).

LEWIS, P. S., 'Sir John Fastolf's Lawsuit over Titchwell, 1448-1455', *Historical Journal*, 1 (1958), 1-20.

LLOYD, T. H., *The Movement of Wool Prices in Medieval England, EcHR* supplement 6 (1973).

LOADES, D. M., *The Tudor Court* (London, 1980).

MCCLENAGHAN, B., *The Springs of Lavenham and the Suffolk Cloth Trade in the Fifteenth and Sixteenth Centuries* (Ipswich, 1924).

MACCULLOCH, D. N. J., 'Kett's Rebellion in Context', *PP* 84 (1979), 36-59.

—— 'Kett's Rebellion in Context. A Rejoinder', *PP* 93 (1981), 165-73.

—— *Suffolk and the Tudors* (Oxford, 1986).

MACFARLANE, A., *Marriage and Love in England: Modes of Reproduction, 1300-1840* (Oxford, 1986).

MCFARLANE, K. B., *The Nobility of Later Medieval England* (Oxford, 1973).

—— *England in the Fifteenth Century* (London, 1981).

MADDERN, P. C., 'Violence, Crime and Public Disorder in East Anglia, 1422-1442', D.Phil. thesis (Oxford, 1984).

MADDICOTT, J. R., 'The County Community and the Making of Public Opinion in Fourteenth-Century England', *TRHS* 5th ser. 28 (1978), 27-43.

MAITLAND, F. W., *English Law and the Renaissance* (Cambridge, 1901).

MANNING, R. B., 'Violence and Social Conflict in Mid-Tudor Rebellions',

Journal of British Studies, 16 (1977), 18–40.

—— *Village Revolts: Social Protest and Popular Disturbances in England, 1509–1640* (Oxford, 1988).

MARTIN, A. R., 'The Greyfriars of Walsingham', *NA* 25 (1935), 227–71.

MASON, R. H., *A History of Norfolk* (London, 1882).

MERTES, K., *The English Noble Household, 1250–1600* (Oxford, 1988).

MILLER, H., 'Subsidy Assessments of the Peerage in the Sixteenth Century', *BIHR* 28 (1955), 15–34.

—— 'London and Parliament in the Reign of Henry VIII', *BIHR* 35 (1962), 128–49.

—— 'Lords and Commons: Relations Between the Two Houses of Parliament, 1509–1558', *Parliamentary History*, 1 (1982), 13–24.

—— *Henry VIII and the English Nobility* (Oxford, 1986).

MILSOM, S. F. C., *Historical Foundations of the Common Law*, 2nd edn. (London, 1981).

MINGAY, G. E., *The Gentry: The Rise and Fall of a Ruling Class* (London, 1976).

MORETON, C. E., 'The Townshend Family, *c.* 1450–1551', D. Phil. thesis (Oxford, 1989).

—— 'A Local Dispute and the Politics of 1483: Roger Townshend, Earl Rivers and the Duke of Gloucester', *The Ricardian*, 8 (1989), 305–7.

—— 'The Walsingham Conspiracy of 1537', *Historical Research*, 63 (1990), 29–43.

—— 'A "best betrustyd frende"?: A Late Medieval Lawyer and His Clients', *Journal of Legal History*, 11 (1990), 183–90.

—— 'A Social Gulf? The Upper and Lesser Gentry of Later Medieval England', *The Journal of Medieval History*, 17 (1991), 255–62.

—— 'The "Library" of a Late Fifteenth-Century Lawyer', *The Library*, 6th ser. 13 (1991), 338–46.

MORGAN, D. A. L., 'The Individual Style of the English Gentleman', in Jones (ed.), *Gentry and Lesser Nobility*, 15–35.

—— 'The House of Policy: The Political Role of the Late Plantaganet Household, 1422–1485', in Starkey (ed.), *The English Court from the Wars of the Roses to the Civil War*, 25–70.

MORRILL, J. S., *Cheshire 1630–1660: County Government and Society during the English Revolution* (Oxford, 1974).

NAMIER, L. B., and BROOKE, J. (edd.), *The History of Parliament, 1754–1790*, 3 vols. (London, 1964).

OTWAY-RUTHVEN, A. J., *The King's Secretary and the Signet Office in the Fifteenth Century* (Cambridge, 1939).

PALLISER, D. M., 'Popular Reactions to the Reformation During the Years of Uncertainty, 1530–70', in Haigh (ed.), *The English Reformation Revised*, 94–113.

PARRY, H. B., *Scrapie Disease in Sheep* (London, 1983).

PARSONS, W. L. E., 'Some Notes on the Boleyn Family', *NA* 25 (1935), 386–407.

PATCH, H. R., *The Goddess Fortuna in Mediaeval Literature* (Cambridge, Mass., 1927).

PAYLING, S. J., 'Political Society in Lancastrian Nottinghamshire', D. Phil. thesis (Oxford, 1987).

—— 'Law and Arbitration in Nottinghamshire, 1399–1461', in J. Rosenthal and C. Richmond (edd.), *People, Politics and Community in the Later Middle Ages* (Gloucester, 1987), 140–60.

PEILE, J., *Christ's College* (London, 1900).

PEPYS, W. C., *Genealogy of the Pepys Family, 1273–1887*, 2nd edn. (London, 1952).

PETTEGREE, A., *Foreign Protestant Communities in Sixteenth-Century London* (Oxford, 1986).

POLLARD, A. J. (ed.), *Property and Politics, Essays in Later Medieval English History* (Gloucester, 1984).

POST, J. B., 'Equitable Resorts Before 1450', in E. W. Ives and A. H. Manchester (edd.), *Law, Litigants and the Legal Profession* (London, 1983), 68–79.

POSTAN, M. M., 'The Fifteenth Century', *EcHR* 9 (1938–9), 160–7.

POWELL, E., 'Arbitration and the Law in England in the Late Middle Ages', *TRHS* 5th ser. 33 (1983), 49–67.

—— 'The Settlement of Disputes by Arbitration in Fifteenth Century England', *Law and History Review*, 2 (1984), 21–43.

PREST, W. R., *The Inns of Court under Elizabeth I and the Early Stuarts, 1590–1640* (London, 1972).

RABAN, S., *Mortmain Legislation and the English Church, 1279–1500* (Cambridge, 1982).

RAMSEY, P., *Tudor Economic Problems* (London, 1963).

RAWCLIFFE, C., *The Staffords, Earls of Stafford and Dukes of Buckingham, 1394–1521* (Cambridge, 1978).

—— 'The Great Lord as Peacekeeper: Arbitration by English Noblemen and their Councils in the Later Middle Ages', in J. A. Guy and H. G. Beale (edd.), *Law and Social Change in British History* (London, 1984), 34–54.

RICHARDSON, W. C., *A History of the Court of Augmentations* (Baton Rouge, La., 1961).

RICHMOND, C., *John Hopton: A Fifteenth-Century Suffolk Gentleman* (Cambridge, 1981).

—— 'The Expenses of Thomas Playter of Sottesley, 1459–60', *Proceedings of the Suffolk Institute of Archaeology*, 35 (1981), 41–52.

—— 'The Sulyard Papers: The Rewards of a Small Family Archive', in D. Williams (ed.), *England in the Fifteenth Century* (Woodbridge, 1987), 199–228.

—— *The Paston Family in the Fifteenth Century: The First Phase* (Cambridge, 1990).

ROBBINS, E. C., 'The Cursed Norfolk Justice', *NA* 26 (1938), 1–51.

ROSKELL, J. S., 'William Catesby, Counsellor to Richard III', *Bulletin of the John Rylands Library*, 42 (1959), 145–74.

ROSS, C., *The Estates and Finances of Richard Beauchamp, Earl of Warwick*, Dugdale Soc., Occasional Papers, 12 (1956).

—— *Edward IV* (London, 1974).

—— *Richard III* (London, 1981).

ROWNEY, I., 'Arbitration in Gentry Disputes of the Later Middle Ages', *History*, 67 (1982), 367–76.

RUSSELL, F. W., *Kett's Rebellion in Norfolk* (London, 1859).

RYE, W., *A History of Norfolk* (London, 1885).

—— *A Glossary of Words Used in East Anglia* (London, 1895).

—— *Norfolk Families*, 2 vols. (Norwich, 1913).

SAUL, N., *Knights and Esquires: The Gloucestershire Gentry in the Fourteenth Century* (Oxford, 1981).

—— *Scenes from Provincial Life: Knightly Families in Sussex, 1280–1400* (Oxford, 1986).

SAUNDERS, H. W., 'A History of Coxford Priory', *NA* 17 (1900), 284–370.

SAYER, M., 'Norfolk Involvement in Dynastic Conflict, 1469–71 and 1483–1487', *NA* 36 (1977), 305–26.

SCARISBRICK, J. J., *The Reformation and the English People* (Oxford, 1984).

SHAW, W. A., *The Knights of England*, 2 vols. (London, 1906).

SHEEHAN, M., *The Will in Medieval England* (Toronto, 1963).

SHIRLEY, T. F., *Thomas Thirlby, Tudor Bishop* (London, 1964).

SIMPSON, A., 'The East Anglian Foldcourse: Some Queries', *AHR* 6 (1958), 87–96.

—— *The Wealth of the Gentry* (Cambridge, 1961).

SIMPSON, A. W. B., 'The Circulation of Year Books in the Fifteenth Century', *LQR* 73 (1957), 492–505.

—— *An Introduction to the History of the Land Law*, 2nd edn. (Oxford, 1986).

—— 'The Source and Function of the Later Year Books', *LQR* 87 (1971), 94–118.

SMITH, A. HASSELL, 'Justices at Work in Elizabethan Norfolk', *NA* 34 (1969), 93–110.

—— *County and Court: Government and Politics in Norfolk, 1558–1603* (Oxford, 1974).

SMITH, A. R., 'Aspects of the Career of Sir John Fastolf (1380–1459)', D. Phil. thesis (Oxford, 1982).

—— 'Litigation and Politics: Sir John Fastolf's Defence of his English Property', in Pollard (ed.), *Property and Politics*, 59–75.

SOMERVILLE, R., 'Henry VII's "Council Learned in the Law"', *EHR* 54 (1939), 427–42.

SQUIBB, G. D., *Doctors' Commons: A History of the College of Advocates and Doctors of Law* (Oxford, 1977).

STARKEY, D., *The English Court from the Wars of the Roses to the Civil War* (London, 1987).

STEPHEN, L., and LEE, S., *The Dictionary of National Biography*, 2nd edn., 22 vols. (London, 1908-9).

STEPHENSON, M. J., 'Wool Yields in the Medieval Economy', *EcHR* 2nd ser. 41 (1988), 368-91.

STONE, L., 'The Anatomy of the Elizabethan Aristocracy', *EcHR* 18 (1948), 1-53.

——, and FAWTIER STONE, J. C., *An Open Elite? England 1540-1880* (Oxford, 1984).

STOREY, R. L., *The Reign of Henry VII* (London, 1968).

—— 'Gentleman Bureaucrats', in C. H. Clough (ed.), *Profession, Vocation and Culture in Later Medieval England: Essays Devoted to the Memory of A. R. Myers* (Liverpool, 1982), 90-129.

SWALES, R. J., 'The Howard Interest in Sussex Elections', *Sussex Archaeological Collections*, 114 (1976), 49-60.

SWALES, T. H., 'Opposition to the Suppression of Norfolk Monasteries', *NA* 33 (1965), 254-65.

—— 'The Sequestration of Religious Property in Norfolk at the Dissolution', Ph.D. thesis (Sheffield, 1965).

—— 'The Redistribution of the Monastic Lands in Norfolk at the Dissolution', *NA* 34 (1966), 4-44.

TAWNEY, R. H., 'The Rise of the Gentry 1558-1640', *EcHR* 11 (1941), 1-38.

THIRSK, J., *The Rural Economy of England* (London, 1984).

—— (ed.), *The Agrarian History of England and Wales*, iv (Cambridge, 1967).

THOMAS, J. F. H., *Sheep* (London, 1945).

THORNE, R. G. (ed.), *The History of Parliament, 1790-1820*, 5 vols. (London, 1986).

TITTLER, R., and BATTELEY, S., 'The Local Community and the Crown in 1553: The Accession of Mary Tudor Revisited', *BIHR* 57 (1984), 131-9.

TOWNSEND, C., *The Direct Ancestry and Posterity of Judge Charles Townsend, a Pioneer of Buffalo, New York* (Orange, NJ, 1897).

TOWNSHEND, C. H., *The Townshend Family of Lynn, in Old and New England* (New Haven, Conn., 1875).

TREVOR-ROPER, H. R., 'The Elizabethan Aristocracy: An Anatomy Re-anatomised', *EcHR* 2nd ser. 3 (1951), 279-98.

—— *The Gentry 1540-1640, EcHR* supplement 1 (1953).

TROW-SMITH, R., *A History of British Livestock Husbandry to 1700* (London, 1957).

TUCKER, M , *The Life of Thomas Howard, Earl of Surrey and Second Duke of Norfolk, 1443-1523* (The Hague, 1964).

VIRGOE, R., 'Three Suffolk Parliamentary Elections of the Mid-Fifteenth Century', *BIHR* 39 (1966), 185–96.

—— 'The Murder of James Andrew: Suffolk Faction in the 1430s', *Proceedings of the Suffolk Institute of Archaeology*, 34 (1980), 263–8.

—— 'The Recovery of the Howards in East Anglia, 1485–1529', in E. W. Ives, J.J. Scarisbrick, and R.J. Knecht (edd.), *Wealth and Power in Tudor England* (London, 1978), 1–20.

—— 'The Crown, Magnates and Local Government in East Anglia', in Highfield and Jeffs (edd.), *The Crown and Local Communities*, 72–87.

—— 'An Election Dispute of 1483', *Historical Research*, 60 (1987), 24–44.

—— 'The Benevolence of 1481', *EHR* 104 (1989), 25–45.

WAKE, J., *The Brudenells of Deene*, 2nd edn. (London, 1954).

WEDGWOOD, J. C., *History of Parliament, Register of the Ministers and Members of Both Houses, 1439–1509* (London, 1938).

WESTLAKE, H. F., *The Parish Gilds of Medieval England* (London, 1919).

WIGRAM, I., and THONE, M., 'A Local Dispute and the Politics of 1483: Two Reactions', *The Ricardian*, 8 (1990), 414–16.

WILLIAMS, C. H., 'A Norfolk Parliamentary Election, 1461', *EHR* 40 (1925), 79–86.

WILLIAMS, N., *Thomas Howard, Fourth Duke of Norfolk* (London, 1964).

WILLIAMS, N. J., *The Maritime Trade of the East Anglian Ports* (Oxford, 1988).

WILLIAMS, P., *The Tudor Regime* (Oxford, 1979).

WILSON, C. A., *Food and Drink in Britain* (Harmondsworth, 1973).

WINGFIELD, J. M., *Some Records of the Wingfield Family* (London, 1925).

WRIGHT, S. M., *The Derbyshire Gentry in the Fifteenth Century*, Derbyshire Rec. Soc., 8 (1983).

WYNDHAM, H. A., *A Family History, 1410–1688: The Wyndhams of Norfolk and Somerset* (London, 1939).

YOUINGS, J., 'The Terms of the Disposal of the Devon Monastic Lands, 1536–58', *EHR* 69 (1954), 18–38.

—— *The Dissolution of the Monasteries* (London, 1971).

—— 'The South-Western Rebellion of 1549', *Southern History*, 1 (1979), 99–122.

—— *Sixteenth-Century England* (London, 1984).

ZELL, M. L., 'Early Tudor Justices of the Peace at Work', *Archaeologia Cantiana*, 93 (1977), 125–43.

INDEX

abp = archbishop; bp = bishop; c. =
    countess; d. = duke or duchess;
    e. = earl; JP = justice of the
    peace; kt = knight; m. =
    marquis; p. = prior

Affordby, John, Townshend
    servant 92, 199
Aideburgh (Suff.) 160 n.
Alethorpe (Norf.) 183
Alington, Giles 46, 49 n., 199
Allison, K.J. 167, 172-3, 178, 190
'amicable grant', see taxation
Andrews, Thomas 124
Anger, Clement, Townshend tenant
    171, 179, 227, 230
Anmer (Norf.) 181
Anne of Cleves 36
Appleton (Norf.), manor 181 n.
Appleyard, Nicholas 31, 46, 199
Appulby, Robert 8
arbitration 18, 82, 89, 91, 93-4, 95,
    98-9, 101-4, 109, 111-12, 113,
    194
Arblaster, James 62 n.
Arundel, e. of 8 n., 28 n.
Ashburnham, Helena 29
Aske, Robert 73
assizes and assize circuits 11-13, 22,
    23, 66
Audeley, Edmund 125
Audeley, John 125
Audeley, John, kt (d. 1531) 49 n.,
    65 n., 110, 125, 199, 203, 210, 224
Augmentations Office 127, 219
Austyn, Thomas, Townshend
    bailiff 122

Bacon, Nathaniel 26 n.
Bacon, Nicholas, Lord Keeper 129,
    144, 160-1
Barker, Thomas, Townshend factor
    146
Barking Abbey 22
barley, see crops and crop yields

Barmer (Norf.) 103, 122, 164, 185
Berwick (Norf.) 182, 221
Baskerville, James 61-2
bastard feudalism 14, 51-6, 80, 90-1,
    193
Bayfield (Norf.) 185 n.
    manor 47, 123
Beaufoy, William 119, 212
Bedfordshire 170
Bedingfield, family 40, 46, 128 n.
Bedingfield, Edmund, kt 40, 199, 203,
    210, 211, 224
Bedingfield, Henry 39-40
Bedingfield, Thomas, kt 40, 49 n., 64,
    65 n., 199, 203, 208 n., 210, 224
Bedingham (Norf.), manor 22
Beeston (Norf.) 179 n.
Bellamy, J.G. 112
benevolences (1474/5, 1481), see
    taxation
Berney, family 18
Berney, John 57 n.
Berney, John, of Reedham 64, 203,
    210
Binham (Norf.) 77
    priory 28 n., 127, 220
Bird, Thomas, Townshend bailiff 138
Bishop, Richard, would-be rebel from
    Bungay 71, 77
Blackfriars, Norwich, p. of 32, 74
Blake, Simon 117-18, 197, 214-15
Blakeney, family 9-10, 46
Blakeney, John 9-10, 23, 197
Blakeney, Thomas 10, 197, 237
Blennerhasset, Thomas, kt 65 n., 203,
    210, 224
Blickling (Norf.), manor 121
Blofeld, John, Townshend bailiff 138 n.
Boleyn, family 58, 128 n.
Boleyn, Anne, queen of England 121
Boleyn, Edward, kt 65 n., 67, 203, 224
Boleyn, Geoffrey 121
Boleyn, James, kt 58, 63, 64-5, 109,
    199, 203, 211, 216, 224
Boleyn, Thomas, e. of Wiltshire 180

Fuller, William, antiquary 10
Fuller, William, Townshend receiver
    25, 138, 198
Fulmodestone (Norf.), manor 123
Fyneux, John, kt, chief justice 134

Gayton (Norf.) 69
'general proscription' (1522/3), *see*
    taxation
gentry:
    historiography of 1–4
    income and living standards 132–7,
      160
    as landlords 138–44, 160–1, 194; *see*
      also sheep-farming
    lesser or parish gentry 181, 192
    as litigants 105, 107–8
    narrow horizons of 22, 26–7, 49,
      195–6
    piety 18
    social relationships 26, 48–9, 196
Gloucester, Richard, d. of, later
    Richard III 11, 15, 79 n., 89, 91,
    100, 113
Gonville Hall, Cambridge 126, 217
Goodrich, John 68
Goodrich, Thomas, bp of Ely 75–6
Gottes, Robert, Townshend tenant 184,
    187
Grafton, Richard, king's printer 75, 76
Gray, William, bp of Ely 61 n.
Great Carbrooke (Norf.) 184 n.
Great Ellingham (Norf.) 189
Great Massingham (Norf.) 38
Great Yarmouth (Norf.) 34, 159
Gresham, James 193
Gresham, Thomas, kt 128 n.
Grevill, William, justice 12 n.
Grey, Thomas, m. of Dorset 14, 123
Guildford (Surrey) 12
guilds 170
Guisborough, George, Walsingham
    conspirator 33
Gunnore, Simon, Townshend
    farmer 139
Gunthorpe (Norf.), manor 85 n.
Gurney, Anthony 64, 199, 204, 210
Gurney, William 17, 25, 166, 198
Gygges, family 25
Gygges, John 48, 180, 183, 207
Gygges, John of Burnham 26
Gygges, John of Wighton 8, 9, 214
Gygges, Susan 48

Gygges, Thomas, Townshend bailiff
    25, 26, 92, 138 n., 198
Gygges, Thomas of Burnham 48, 239
Gygges, William 9

Hadleigh (Suff.) 125
Hales, John, baron of the
    Exchequer 131 n.
Hansard, family 98, 100, 101, 102,
    103
Hansard, Anthony 46, 102, 125, 199
Hansard, Anthony, Wolsey's servant
    125, 216
Hansard, Richard, kt 97 n.
Hansard, Thomas, kt 46, 96, 97,
    99–100, 101, 102
Hansard, Thomasine 96, 97, 99, 102
Harcourt, Richard, kt 57 n., 58
Hare, Nicholas 128 n.
Harward, Clement 93
Hastings, Edward, Lord Hastings 18
Hastings, Martin 183
Hastings, William, Lord Hastings 14,
    52, 56
'Hankers', manor (Norf. and Suff.)
    99 n.
Helhoughton (Norf.) 129 n., 147, 185
Hellesdon (Norf.), manor 91
Hemmingstone (Suff.), manor 96
hemp, *see* crops and crop yields
Henry VI 15
Henry VII 24, 62–3, 100
Henry VIII 29, 69, 75
Herberd, Edmund, Townshend servant
    25, 138, 145, 185 n., 198, 236
Herbert, William, Lord 52
Hertfordshire 12, 170
Heveningham, John 49 n.
Heveningham, John, kt 18 n.
Hevingham, Thomas 102
Hewer, John 120, 228
Hexter, J. H. 191
Heydon (Norf.), rectory 42, 43 n.
Heydon, family 128 n., 134
Heydon, Christopher, kt
    (d. 1541) 46 n., 65 n., 199, 204,
    224
Heydon, Christopher, kt
    (d. 1579) 58 n.
Heydon, Henry, kt 98, 198
Heydon, John 78
Heydon, John, kt 34, 38, 64, 65 n.,
    69, 199, 204, 210, 217, 224